Real Estate Law

Second Edition

Charles J. Jacobus

Prentice Hall
Upper Saddle River, New Jersey 07458

Library of Congress Cataloging-in-Publication Data

Jacobus, Charles J.
  Real estate law / Charles J. Jacobus.
      p.   cm.
  Includes index.
  ISBN 0-13-631813-4
  1. Vendors and purchasers—United States. 2. Real property—
United States. 3. Real estate business—Law and legislation—
United States. I. Title.
346.7304'3—dc21   97-2369
                                                                   CIP

Acquisitions Editor: Elizabeth Sugg
Director of Production and Manufacturing: Bruce Johnson
Managing Editor: Mary Carnis
Editorial/Production Supervision: Inkwell Publishing Services
Manufacturing Buyer: Marc Bove

 © 1998 by Prentice-Hall, Inc.
Simon & Schuster / A Viacom Company
Upper Saddle River, New Jersey 07458

Printed in the United States of America

10 9 8 7 6 5 4 3 2 1

ISBN 0-13-631813-4

Prentice-Hall International (UK) Limited, *London*
Prentice-Hall of Australia, Pty. Limited, *Sydney*
Prentice-Hall Canada Inc., *Toronto*
Prentice-Hall Hispanoamericana, S.A., *Mexico*
Prentice-Hall of India Private Limited, *New Delhi*
Prentice-Hall of Japan, Inc., *Tokyo*
Simon & Schuster Asia Pte. Ltd., *Singapore*
Editora Prentice-Hall do Brasil, Ltda., *Rio de Janeiro*

Contents

3
How Ownership Is Held, 37

4
Fixtures and Easements, 67

7

Contracts for the Sale of Real Estate, 143

Preface

The primary purpose of any instructional text is to be both easy to understand and authoritative. This is not a simple matter when discussing real estate law. When made simple to understand, concepts often become so nebulous, and so many details and exceptions are overlooked, that an "easy-to-understand" text may tend to be misleading, vague, and subject to overgeneralization. It has been my experience, in teaching the basic principles of real estate, to find licensed salespeople and brokers misconstruing a basic implication of property law because of overbroad statements they have heard or read through "easy-to-understand" instruction.

On the other hand, most people find it too frustrating and time-consuming to search through *Powell on Real Property*⸰ to understand the basics of a standard mortgage form. It has often been a criticism of attorneys that they are so detail conscious that they "can't see the forest for the trees," and that they tend to hinder a real estate transaction rather than seek to expedite the closing process.

This book is intended to make some headway in bridging the gap between these two extremes. I have attempted to cover most pertinent topics in real estate law as it exists today. An in-depth study of dower and curtesy and fee tail estates and the long history of seizin and feoffments have been minimized to narrow the broker's scope of instruction to more up-to-date applicable prob-

---

⸰ Richard R. Powell, *Powell on Real Property*, Patrick J. Rohan, Ed. (New York: Matthew Bender & Company, Inc.). This constantly updated set of books is considered to be one of the most authoritative works on real property law.

lems and solutions. In this same vein, the more complex areas of securities law, federal regulations, sophisticated zoning theories, and other more complicated collateral sources of law and their effect on real estate have been omitted to avoid confusion. These areas will be left to the never-ending accumulation of litigation, legislation, and articles published for the benefit of the legal profession.

A special effort has been made, however, to utilize a certain amount of detail in those areas of real estate law prompting the bulk of questions that occur during the day-to-day operation in the broker's office and relating to the real estate basics that lawyers who are engaged in the business of general practice of law will encounter. Legal periodicals, statutes, and cases are used freely in an effort to facilitate the steps toward more intensive research to aid the more advanced student of the law. To aid in understanding, uniform state laws have been referred to where applicable both to emphasize the similarities and to clarify the differences existing among the states.

Forms have been inserted for illustrative purposes only. No standard form can be used for all purposes, and competent legal counsel should be employed to draft and interpret all legal documents. To prevent monotony, there has even been an attempt to inject humor into some of these magnificently interesting topics.

New To This Edition   This edition has been updated to include new RESPA rules, lead-based paint disclosure, new theories involving agency concepts, new forms of ownership, revised federal tax laws, and new environmental issues.

I welcome constructive criticism of this textbook and would appreciate hearing comments.

Charles J. Jacobus

Introduction to the Basic Processes of Real Estate Law

Brokers and lawyers will surely agree on one thing—that the real estate business is becoming more and more complex. The common-law doctrines that have controlled real estate law for centuries are eroding away as a result of innumerable statutes, at both the federal and the state levels, which often seem to create more problems than they solve. However, this erosion is yielding some benefits in that it requires both brokers and lawyers to become more proficient and more sophisticated in keeping up with these areas of the law, and this requirement could well force both brokers and lawyers to be more conscientious in representing their clients' interests. It has also drawn much more attention to the fact that real estate is a constantly changing subject and one that is rapidly becoming a field for true professionals.

THE ROLE OF REAL ESTATE LAW

The real estate laws have become so diversified that one can no longer think of real estate law as only one subject. Real estate law used to consist basically of brokerage negotiation, drawing legal instruments, and establishing and litigating various property rights. Only a few years ago, real estate law was just a small segment of every lawyer's practice. Today, real estate involves a much broader scope of law as a result of constantly changing aspects of mortgage law, new developments in usury, changing definitions of "interest," and modifications of agency theory. There have also been new developments in contract law, securities law, and land use planning law. In addition, there are frequent changes and supplements to landlord and tenant laws, mechanics' and materialmen's liens, and the probate, estate, and community property laws that are unique to each state. To this list one must add the never-ending plethora of federal regulations.

A good example of this problem of diversity is a situation that arose as a result of a marketing suggestion from a real estate agent who represented a builder. The agent had a good idea of marketing his client's townhouses by selling them as real estate investment "packages" to investors across the country. It was a very elaborate and well done scheme, and would have probably been very successful. However, imagine the look on this man's face—very enthusiastic about marketing this real estate (and anticipating his commission money rolling in!)—when he was told that such a marketing plan, although involving the sale of real estate, violated the Securities and Exchange Acts of 1933 and 1934 and was unquestionably illegal. His particular marketing plan changed the character of these real estate parcels into "securities," as defined by the Securities and Exchange Commission. Such startling discoveries are now becoming quite commonplace in a field where the interaction of various laws can further complicate the transactions of real estate agents and businesspeople.

As we accept this premise, yet a deeper problem is much more intrinsic to the real estate business; that is, a client often has two representatives, his real estate agent and his attorney. Couple this with the fact that there are at least two clients in most transactions (making a total of at least six interested parties—*all* of whom are striving to "protect" someone). The result is that the problems, stories, and third-hand information (and misinformation) contribute mistrust and confusion to what is already the overregulated field of real estate law. This results in brokers versus lawyers, brokers versus brokers, lawyers versus lawyers, clients versus clients, and every other combination that can logically result from the proverbial "can of worms."

THE VARIOUS LAWS

It is interesting to note the various priorities of the laws and how they have come to interact with each other over their years of development. There are two basic sources of statutory law: state and federal. In the area of real estate, state law has generally been considered controlling because of the peculiarities of the backgrounds and doctrines that various states have evolved over the years. However, we are finding in more recent times that the federal government is now taking a vital interest in protecting people from themselves and in passing voluminous amounts of federal legislation to regulate the real estate business.

Constitutions

Our basic sources of law are found in our state and federal constitutions. The U.S. Constitution is the primary source and vests in all citizens of the United States certain inalienable rights that are considered inviolate—so basic to our system of government that no statute, ordinance, or any contractual right can waive the obligations or privileges therein contained. It is from this document that our individual freedoms and prohibition from abridging these individual freedoms are derived. For instance, discrimination on the grounds of race, color, or creed is considered patently unconstitutional, as is the denial of one's property rights without "due process of law." No statute, contract, or restriction upholding them will ever be enforced. Constitutional rights are, of course, the most important legal rights that one can have, and these rights can be altered only by constitutional amendment.

It must also be remembered that this same Constitution also gives the federal government extraordinary powers of enforcement when it comes to federal laws or federal issues that are considered within the parameters and scope of the Constitution. In the field of real estate, one of the more important areas comes under the interstate commerce clause. For example, Congress is finding more and more ways to regulate *intrastate* real estate activities because of the far-reaching effects these have on other states by virtue of the use of the U.S. mail, telephone, or other means of *interstate* commerce. This will be discussed in greater detail in a later chapter.

Each state also has a constitution, and in this constitution are certain inalienable rights that apply to the citizens of that state. These rights basically come from the codification and derivation of the heritage of the state and embrace a myriad of subjects, including the homestead laws, certain mechanics' and materialmen's lien laws, and the community property rights or other marital property rights that may exist. One must remember that when these rights are constitutional, they cannot be waived by private contract or by subsequent statute or ordinance. The individual rights embraced by the state constitution are usually far-reaching and much more detailed than those of the U.S. Constitution. However, if there is a conflict between the U.S. Constitution and the state constitution, one can generally consider that the U.S. Constitution would control if the issues involve a federal issue (i.e., an issue over which power has been delegated to the federal government by the Constitution) rather than a substantive state question. If the issues involved are purely state issues and do not involve powers granted to the federal government or rights reserved to individuals, the U.S. Constitution would not be involved because of the Tenth Amendment, which reserves all powers not so granted to the states respectively. If the courts determine that a federal issue exists, the U.S. Constitution would control over the state constitution.

Statutes   The sources of law that affect property rights in greater detail (than what is favored in the federal or state constitutions) are those created by our legislatures, both state and federal, in their infinite wisdom. Of course, a law or a statute can be declared unconstitutional and its enforcement prohibited, which, of course, was what happened to laws on racial discrimination in the South for many years. The conflict between statutes and constitutions is often a very technical and complicated legal problem and need not be delved into at this point. However, it is clearly understood that all statutes have the force of law until declared unconstitutional by the courts. In case of a conflict between federal and state laws, federal law would control if there was a federal question involved. However, as in constitutional matters, if the issue is a particularly unique state matter of substantive law, the state statute would control. The theory is that, under the Tenth Amendment to the U.S. Constitution and the derivation of local laws, the local statute is probably more pertinent to conditions as they exist in that state. In more current times, however, federal statutes seem to be getting more favoritism because of the more liberal interpretation of the federal powers given by the courts.

Ordinances and   Beyond the statutes at the state level, we generally encounter the
Regulations   various categories of municipal and county ordinances, as well as the rulings and regulations of the various state agencies. Those decisions made by state agencies that have quasijudicial power (the agency can make binding decisions pursuant to the scope and powers under which that agency was created) are generally considered to have the force of law unless there is a clear abuse of discretion on the part of that state agency. City and county ordinances must, of course, undergo the same constitutional scrutiny that state statutes are subject to. The local ordinances are inferior to state statutes when there is a conflict between the two laws.

Beyond the statutes at the federal or state level, one encounters the far more extensive rulings and regulations of state and federal agencies. The large numbers of regulations are a result of the fact that the various laws are often very broad, often vague, and always confusing. The particular agency whose duty it is to enforce the law, therefore, passes its own regulations that serve as guidelines on how that agency is going to interpret and enforce the law passed by the legislature. These regulations can be changed at the whim of the regulatory agency. For instance, the Internal Revenue Service can change its position on particular tax exemptions or how it will interpret a certain portion of the Internal Revenue Code. This same type of change in position can occur in all agencies, and each agency regularly publishes rules and regulations that can even expand that agency's scope of jurisdiction; a rule or regulation can be issued to clarify a stand that the agency may have taken previously, even though the effect on the taxpayer may be entirely different. These rules and regulations issued by the agencies have, of course, the effect of law, subject to review by the courts. It is in this area that the federal government is gaining more and more power, which may or may not have been the purpose of the original Congressional acts enacting the legislation.

Too often the interplay of people's emotions and interpretations of laws result in decisions being made by the final arbiter, the court system. Although sometimes unpredictable, this system is probably the best in the world. It is the basis from which precedents are set and priorities are maintained, and the courts often expose additional questions and interpretations that then become the foundation for new laws and statutes.

Judicial Interpretation

Our present court system arose from a centuries-old system of an objective third party making a fair and just decision to solve a problem between two adversaries. As our structure of the law developed through basic legal principles and doctrines of equity, the written aspects of a transaction were carefully and rigorously adhered to, as being important for an orderly society. Since the principles of law were fairly well settled back in the seventeenth century, when one might consider disorder as being a little more commonplace, this rigorous interpretation of law was probably a logical approach to setting up a civilized and ordered society. As a result, we fell into the situation in which, if a man breached his agreement by being a day late for his mortgage payment, the mortgagee thereunder could foreclose, having the agreement strictly upheld in the courts of law. The mortgagor (who is generally the purchaser), could then lose his property because he was a day late in making his mortgage payment, or for some other minor breach of the contract between the parties, even though the circumstances surrounding this breach may have been beyond his control.

HISTORICAL BACKGROUND OF THE COURTS

Courts of Law

As our system of justice evolved, however, courts of equity were established to soften the impact of these strict legal principles. These equity courts had particular significance in the area of real estate, since real estate is considered unique and money damages could not compensate for its loss. The equity courts had concurrent

Courts of Equity

jurisdiction with the courts of law, which were still in existence and would impose their jurisdiction when fairness or equity dictated that the rules in some circumstances were too strict, sometimes changing the result. For instance, if a farmer could not make his mortgage payment on the day it was due because of matters beyond his control, the court of equity could impose its jurisdiction to do what was fair and would allow him to make his payment a day late, a month late, or whatever was "reasonable" to see that equity and justice were done.

The courts of equity also imposed precedent by establishing certain equitable principles. These principles, such as "unjust enrichment," "unconscionability," and "irreparable harm," were used as reasons to find an equitable conclusion. They were created and construed ad infinitum (or ad nauseum, depending on your point of view) and resulted in literally hundreds of cliches, often called *equitable maxims,* which were ultimately used as precedents to control later decisions. Although having no true legal effect, these maxims could always be used as grounds for the defendant and were easy to roll off the lips, so that silver-tongued orators could constantly remind the court that "he who seeks equity must do equity," "equity does that which ought to be done," and, the all-time favorite, "he who seeks equity must have clean hands."

It was in these courts that equitable remedies such as specific performance, rescission and restitution, quantum meruit, and quasicontractual recovery (to name a few) were imposed. These remedies, of course, differ from damages and actions in tort or contract, which arise under the law (and for which the damaged party can get money damages or recovery of his property). *Specific performance,* for instance, is generally granted where damages are not shown to be adequate and just remedy and can only be enforced when there is not an adequate remedy at law. *Rescission and restitution* generally arise when the breach of the contract constitutes a failure of the consideration bargained for and the nonbreaching party prefers to rescind the contract and sue for complete restitution of whatever benefits have accrued to date. *Rescission* is the voiding of the contract or agreement. *Restitution* is the restoration of the parties' original rights. In this particular equitable remedy, the parties are put back in the same condition that they were in prior to execution of the contract. *Quasicontractual* principles generally arise when there has been something material omitted in the original contract and the court imposes its own contractual principles as if these had been bargained for and written in the contract itself. This is also the principle behind *quantum meruit,* where one party performs his part of the obligation and the breaching party refuses to pay (or perform). In this situation, the court can impose quasicontractual remedies in order that the party performing the duties be paid the reasonable value of the performance rendered.

It is interesting to note that these remedies, which are not by any means all of the equitable remedies available, are not conferred by statute or by any other type of codified jurisprudential consideration. They are remedies that have evolved over the years through the courts seeking fair and just results, and are particularly applicable to real estate. Real estate has always been considered to be unique and valuable. Courts have therefore tended to use these equitable principles to prohibit loss of title, foreclosures, or restrictions on use when there is only a minor breach of obligations.

THE CURRENT CIVIL COURTS SYSTEM

The court systems, as they exist today, have both legal and equitable jurisdiction merged into the same court. The distinction between the different state courts, although their legal and equitable jurisdictions are similar, is not always simple. The jurisdictions of these courts are statutory and are maintained separate and distinct for the purposes of expediting the judicial process and facilitating access to the court system. To help simplify this explanation, we will discuss only the civil (and not the criminal) court systems. These civil court systems, for the purposes of this discussion, will be divided into two distinct and separate systems. The first is the state court system, which, in order of ascending importance, includes the small claims, trial courts, courts of civil appeals, and the state supreme court. The second system is the federal system, which, in order of ascending importance, includes the federal district courts, circuit courts of appeals, and the United States Supreme Court.

State Courts

Small Claims Court. At the lowest level there generally exists a court of small claims (which may go by various names, depending on the state). These courts function to provide a forum for claims involving relatively small amounts of money (often less than $500), and their dockets (schedule of cases to be decided) are usually such as to permit rapid decisions on the claim. The respective parties often operate as their own counsel, since the services of a licensed attorney are usually not required or perhaps not affordable.

Characteristically, only nominal filing fees and court costs are associated with these courts, although a trial by jury is usually available if requested by one of the parties. Courts of small claims are generally not "courts of record," meaning that no transcript is compiled of case proceedings.

Partially because of this fact, a *de novo* appeal is often available to the next higher court. A *de novo* appeal simply means that either party has an absolute right to appeal the decision of this court to the next higher court in the state court system. Since no transcript was kept in the court of small claims, a complete new full-scale trial on the merits of the case will be held in the court to which the case is appealed. As we shall see later, this differs from most "appeals" from other courts, as such appeals characteristically involve only a review of whether one of the parties was prejudicially affected during the trial because of some erroneous procedure or ruling.

Consequently, it can be said that the purpose of courts of small claims is to provide a rapid but fair disposition of lawsuits involving relatively small amounts of money. Since the amount of money at stake is relatively small, these cases are not generally appealed to the next higher court because of the expense associated with the appeal and subsequent new trial. However, the right to appeal is present.

Basic Trial Courts. The second level within the state court system generally contains the basic trial court. Although it may also be called by different names (e.g., district, county, or circuit court), this court is readily recognizable as one in which most civil lawsuits are initiated (all except those initiated in the small claims courts). The basic trial court has a territorial and/or monetary jurisdictional limit with the boundaries of its authority often being coextensive with county lines or some other political subdivision.

In the basic trial court, if the losing party believes that the judge has prejudicially affected his rights by an erroneous ruling or procedure, he may *appeal* the decision to a higher level court within the state system, i.e., to a court of appeals (see next section). It is often said that the losing party must "attack" the adverse trial court judgment directly rather than collaterally. This means that in order to assail the correctness of the trial court decision, the party must ask a higher court to review the rulings and procedure occurring in the trial court. He cannot complain about the correctness of the decision by bringing a new suit on the same issue at a different court at the same level. Such "collateral" attacks on the validity of a judgment are prohibited since they would make it impossible to determine when a dispute was finally litigated. Consequently, it can be said that a system of direct appeal to a higher court is essential to the orderly and proper administration of justice. Either party in a civil suit has the right to appeal the trial court's decision.

Courts of Appeal. Although again the name may vary, most

states have one or more courts of appeal which lie between the basic trial court and the state supreme court. These courts rule on appeals, with their jurisdictional boundaries usually being set by either *subject matter* or the *amount of money* in controversy. They do not review the facts as determined by the jury, but only issues of law. If they believe that the appellant's (appealing party's) rights were prejudicially affected as he claims, they will reverse the trial court decision and will often *remand* it (send it back) to the trial court for a new trial or simply *reverse* the lower court and avoid another trial. If they find the appellant's rights were not prejudicially affected by erroneous rulings, they will *affirm* (declare correct) the decision of the trial court.

In ruling on appeals, the courts of appeal primarily review the trial court's transcript, findings of fact, and the briefs filed by attorneys for the respective parties. In some cases, a party not involved in the case but who is interested in its outcome, called *amicus curiae* (friend of the court), may also file a brief to give the court further information about the applicable law.

State Supreme Court.   Although once more there are exceptions, the highest court in a state is usually referred to as *the state supreme court*. It handles some cases appealed directly from the basic trial courts, but most cases are now being appealed to the state supreme court from the courts of appeal.

The state supreme court is the court charged with the ultimate responsibility for interpreting state law (although on relatively rare occasions, cases may be taken from it to the United States Supreme Court). As such, a decision rendered by it may be cited as "case precedent" should a similar case arise in the future. *Precedent* means that this case is the first and/or leading judicial decision on a particular point of law, and this precedent is likely to be followed by other courts in the future. Judicial precedents help attorneys make precise and up-to-date determinations of legal interpretations of law. Thus, case precedent (also called the principle of *stare decisis*) helps lawyers plan their clients' legal affairs.

Federal Courts

The federal court system consists of the district courts, the circuit courts of appeal, and the United States Supreme Court. The federal courts differ from state courts primarily in jurisdiction. They primarily handle only those cases involving (1) interpretation of federal law and (2) citizens of different states where there is a substantial sum of money in controversy.

The federal district courts are the basic trial courts of the federal system. The federal circuit courts of appeal serve essentially the same function in the federal system as the courts of appeal in the state system. And, of course, the United States Supreme Court is the final interpreter of law.

Court Procedure   Cases can bounce from the state system to the federal system and sometimes back, depending on jurisdictional problems, amounts in controversy, and what are termed *federal questions.* It is at this point that you may very often find the demarcation between an attorney who deals primarily in real estate law and one who deals primarily in trial practice. An attorney may have a particular expertise in the area of real estate law, but may want a "trial attorney" or an attorney who specializes in trial practice, whether it is in federal jurisdictions or state jurisdictions, to handle the case because of the technicalities involved in trial and appellate procedure. In this age of specialization for attorneys, an increased specialization in the field of real estate law or trial practice is to be expected.

Interesting points about the trial procedure itself can give you some insight as to why these complexities exist and why the details of the law are often elusive to an individual reading the statutes, a text, or reported case law. First, there are two deciding bodies, the judge and the jury. In state courts, judges are usually elected to their positions, must be members of the bar (except perhaps in low-level courts), and are paid a salary according to state statute. In federal courts, the judges are appointed by the President of the United States, with advice and consent of the Senate, and must pass very strict scrutiny prior to their appointment. The judge's role in the trial proceedings is to interpret the law. The jury's role is to decide the facts. There is no set rule as to when you can or cannot have a jury. The presence of a jury depends on the request of either of the parties involved.

The trial process works by putting the burden on the plaintiff (the party filing the suit) to present the evidence. After the plaintiff's attorney presents the case, the defendant's attorney responds and presents the defendant's case. After the defense has rested, there may be further examination of witnesses by either attorney. After the case is presented and arguments are given, the judge may render a decision. If there is a jury, the judge gives "charges" to the jury. These charges are generally prepared by the counsel for both sides under the direction of the judge. The charges that the judge reads are directions to the jury and explanations of what the state law is concerning the particular matter in controversy. It is the jury's job, then, to take the law and the facts as presented and to render a decision as to which party should prevail. It puts the burden on the jury to determine which of the witnesses was telling the truth, which of the witnesses may have been stretching the truth a bit, and, ultimately, what the facts actually were. If the jury comes back with a verdict for a party that is contrary to law, then the judge can overrule the jury and enter his own ruling.

Beyond the trial stage, the only question is whether there is a point of law in controversy. Since the jury has decided the facts, only points of law can be appealed to the appellate court. An appeal is made only to settle a question of law or incorrect ruling that a trial court may have made. There is no jury present beyond the trial court level. The appeal might be based on a rule of evidence, procedure, substantive law, jury charge, or other more technical legal point.

The process of appeals can be a relatively complicated process in regard to exactly what it takes to appeal to which court. In the state court system, there are proceedings in which you can appeal certain matters directly to the state supreme court, but most appeals go to the courts of civil appeals first. There are other rules for appeals from the courts of civil appeals to the state supreme court. The federal courts have similar, but not the same, rules. It is not pertinent to our discussion to go into detail over these matters, but it should be emphasized that the appellate process and the infinite amount of detail that arises during litigation make any litigation very complicated and difficult to predict. It has been said that when a case goes to court, no one wins. Considering the attorneys' fees that are paid, the emotions that are dealt with, and the time consumption and overloaded dockets that litigation promotes, the amount in controversy generally has to be fairly high before litigation is worthwhile.

Keeping in mind the foregoing basic substantive and procedural aspects of the law, one can appreciate the complexities that may arise in any given legal situation, particularly if any litigation should take place. It should also be kept in mind that the impact of the law is often flexible and most rules of the law are general rules, subject to exceptions and equitable interpretation. These are the major reasons why, when asking your attorney a question, it is so difficult to get a simple answer in response. All of these alternatives, both procedural and substantive, must stay ever-present in the practitioner's "areas of concern" so that he can competently represent and advise clients.

One might wonder how the details of all the foregoing information become available to the attorney. It is basically through research in a law library. Unlike any other type of library, a law library has an

Legal Research

almost never-ending supply of legal treatises, articles, statutes, opinions, and case law reports. Every case in the United States above the district court level is written and bound in volumes called *Reporters,* which, along with statutes, digests, and current treatises, must constantly be updated. Each volume is given a separate number as it is bound (most recent cases are reported in paperback volumes). Therefore, when searching for a case, one may find it cited:

Case v. *Case,* 376 P.2d 941 (Cal. App.–1936),

if it is a civil appeals court decision, or

Case v. *Case,* 376 S.W.2d 941 (Utah 1936),

if it is a state supreme court decision. Each of the foregoing examples indicates that the case is found in volume 376, page 941, of the *Southwestern Reporter,* second series. The material in parentheses refers to the court and years of decision. Statutes are normally cited as:

Rev. Civ. Stat. Ann., art. 6573a

which indicates that the statute is located in the civil statutes, Article 6573a. The statutes are updated with "pocket parts" located in the back of each volume, and are usually also available on CD-ROM.

As the student reads the following chapters, he or she will find a number of citations as authority for a particular point of law. These are not intended to dazzle or baffle the reader, but only to give additional sources of information for more in-depth study.

After this cursory introduction, one will find that the following chapters are more detailed and concern the more substantive aspects of real property law. For the layperson, it is important to recognize these problem areas and understand them as such, always keeping in mind that they should be avoided at all costs. Any advice, litigation, or negotiation of a client's rights should be left for the attorneys who are trained to handle such problems. It is the attorney's job to relieve real estate agents and other laypersons from shouldering this type of burden.

Real estate is rapidly becoming a field for true professionals. Similarly, real estate law is becoming more and more specialized.

SUMMARY

There are two sources of law: federal and state. Both sources have constitutional foundations. The source of law that affects property rights in greater detail is the statutes that are created by the state and federal legislatures. The city ordinances and federal regulations may apply the respective laws in even greater detail.

The modern court system is a blend of the courts of law and equity. The state civil court system consists of justice of the peace courts, county courts, district courts, courts of civil appeals, and the state supreme court. The federal court system consists of the federal district court, the circuit courts of appeals, and the United States Supreme Court. Jurisdiction of the various courts can change in any given case. The rules and procedures regarding jurisdiction are defined by the various statutes and consist of substantive as well as procedural laws concerning jurisdiction, trial, and appellate procedure. Basically, the jury decides all questions of facts, while the court (the judge) decides questions of law.

2

Estates in Land

An *estate in land* has been defined as the degree, quantity, nature, and extent of interest that a person has in real property, *Pan American Petroleum Corp. v. Cain,* 355 S.W.2d 506 (Tex. 1962). The estates in land that will be discussed in this chapter are *freehold estates* and *statutory estates. Freehold estates* are estates that manifest some title of real property. They include fee simple absolute, fee simple determinable, fee simple conditional, fee on condition precedent, and life estates. The laterally severed estates of mineral rights and air rights will also be discussed as freehold estates. The title to freehold estates is created in the deed or will and is not to be confused with, and should be distinguished from, statutory estates. *Statutory estates* are created by statute and vest in the person rather than in the land itself. These statutory estates will be discussed later in the chapter.

Not discussed under this topic will be leasehold estates (i.e., estates in which one has leasehold or tenant rights rather than legal title). Leasehold estates will be discussed in Chapter 15, "Landlord and Tenant Relationships."

As an introduction to the concept of freehold estates in land, one basic theory needs to be explained to help establish guidelines for further discussion.

FREEHOLD ESTATES

The basic theory is a restriction on ownership of real property, called the *Rule against Perpetuities.* This restriction, which has been adopted by all states, provides that no one entity can hold title to real estate for a period longer than the life of some person plus 21

Rule against Perpetuities

years and nine months. This also applies to contracts as interests in real estate. Rights of first refusal can't be perpetual, *Law* v. *Spellman,* 629 A.2d 57 (Me. 1993), nor options to purchase, *Proctor* v. *Foxmeyer Drug Co.,* 884 S.W.2d 853 (Tex.—App., 1994).

The reasoning behind the rule against perpetuities is the idea that land, by its nature, is unique, and cannot be held forever by any one interest. This theory has not always been accepted. For example, there is an opposing theory whereby a person could be the grantee of certain property, along with the "heirs of his body." This would enable the property to literally stay in a man's family until his bodily descendants ceased to exist. During this time in history, *primogeniture* (the right of the first male child to become legal title holder to the property upon the death of the father) and *entailments* (only heirs of the individual's body could get fee title to the property) were the common practice for real property owners, and wealthy families could effectively monopolize real estate holdings. This is not the case today.

The rule against perpetuities, then, encourages the free transferability and conveyance of property and prohibits the monopolizing and perpetual control of certain real estate interests. The rule is usually interpreted to prohibit unreasonable restraints on alienation, and means that any interest in real estate must vest in some grantee no later than 21 years after some life in being plus the normal period of gestation. It is important to remember that as we discuss real estate, this constitutional doctrine underlies all theories of real property, whether it deals with estates in land or ownership control, and it still continues to be one of the basic underlying theories in real estate law.

Types of Freehold Estates

We will explore virtually every type of freehold estate to give some insight into just how complicated legal titles and equity interests can become. The primary concepts to remember are that all freehold estates are *interests in real estate, of indefinite duration,* and *inheritable* by the heirs of the owner.

Fee Simple Absolute Estates. A fee simple absolute is the most complete ownership interest one can have in land. An individual can do whatever he pleases with fee simple absolute ownership, subject only to those rights reserved by the government and his duty not to interfere with the rights of other landowners. He does not have to satisfy any condition in order to retain ownership and cannot lose title because of the happening of some event over which he has no control. As we shall see later, retaining ownership of some types of fee estates is subject to such conditions and contingencies.

An estate in fee simple absolute is normally characterized as (1) having a duration that is indefinite as to time of termination, and (2) being inheritable by both the grantee's collateral and lineal heirs. This second requirement has created some controversy because of the common law derivation of our real property laws. It was held under common law that the conveyance to the grantee must be to the grantee and his heirs in order to ensure the inheritability of the estate and thereby confirm the estate in fee simple absolute. This created a conflict in the courts over the intent of the grantor and the tendency of the courts to complicate the land transactions, versus the ultimate goal of expediting the free transferability of real estate and simplifying the transfer of title to fee simple absolute estates.

In an effort to clarify these matters, 39 states have subsequently passed statutes that presume an estate to be in fee simple absolute unless clearly stated otherwise. In the remaining 11 states, nine have partially adopted this same theory.[1] These nine states are Arkansas, Delaware, Pennsylvania, South Dakota, Maine, New Hampshire, South Carolina, Vermont, and Florida. Some of these nine states have abrogated the common law rule with respect to wills, others with respect to deeds. Some have limited the common law rule in some respects to conveyances by both instruments.

Fee Tail Estates.   In contrast to fee simple absolute estates, consider the following granting clause language:

> From Able to Baker and the heirs of his body.

This is an example of the kind of language historically used in England to create an entailment. It triggered the rule of primogeniture under which the eldest son in each successive generation held a life estate in the land.

This fee tail ownership interest prevented free transferability of fee simple absolute ownership. As such, it had the capacity to impede economic growth and social progress. For example, developers wanting to build shopping centers are not interested in buying a fee tail estate because they would be buying only the ownership interest held by the current generation.

To avoid this possibility, most states flatly do not permit the creation of fee tail estates. Thus, the granting clause, "From Able to

---

[1] Two states, Connecticut and Louisiana, have not adopted any form of this presumption.

Baker and the heirs of his body," is interpreted in these states to give Baker a fee simple absolute ownership interest, with his heirs receiving nothing. On the other hand, some states interpret this as being somewhere between the old English entailment and a fee simple absolute. Their interpretation would give Baker a life estate, with the heirs of his body receiving a contingent remainder. This means the heirs would get a fee simple absolute title, contingent on their surviving Baker. If this interpretation is not wanted, the use of this language should be avoided.

The conflicting interpretations placed on the fee tail language illustrate why most states have now taken a stand against this form of title. Simply stated, it is not socially desirable to tie up land titles for long periods of time in such a manner that no one would want to buy the land. This would cause the creation of monopolies and could substantially hurt the rate of economic growth and social progress.

For these reasons, all states now have some version of the rule against perpetuities. Discussed earlier, one may recall that this requires any estate in land (this usually does not apply to potential interests, such as contingent remainders) must vest in someone within a period of time not to exceed the life of some person in being, plus 21 years and nine months. As a general rule, title cannot "linger," unvested, in a mere potential future interest. The important point to remember is that an attempt to create something in the nature of the old English entailment is generally null and void, and is not effective to create this kind of interest.

Some kinds of limitations, however, can be placed on subsequent grantees and do not violate the rule against perpetuities. The more common of these, fee simple determinable and fee simple conditional estates, will be discussed in the next two sections.

Fee Simple Determinable Estates.   Various states use slightly different rules and technical language in defining the fee simple determinable and the fee simple conditional estates in land.

In general terms, a *fee simple determinable* estate exists where the estate is limited to the happening of a certain event, and it is characterized by the automatic nature of its termination. When the stated event occurs, the estate is terminated and reverts back to the grantor by what is called an *eo instanti* reversion; that is, the estate *automatically* goes back to the grantor. This estate can also be referred to in some states as a *fee on conditional limitation*. An example of this type of estate would be one where the estate is created by the use of a deed or will, stating that the property will be conveyed as follows:

To the grantee so long as the fences are kept in repair.

Documents creating a determinable fee generally use the words "so long as," "until," or "during," which intend to limit the type of estate that is going to be created. Upon the happening of that certain stated event, the estate automatically reverts (is transferred back) to either the grantor or his heirs. Of course, it can go forward (in contrast to reversion), and vest in some third party, the remainderman, if one is provided for in the conveyancing instrument. In a fee simple determinable estate, this future interest is called an *executory interest*. The important thing to remember is that the grantee's estate is terminated *automatically* upon the happening of that certain stated conditional event.

Fee Simple Conditional Estates.   The *fee simple conditional* (also called the *fee simple on condition subsequent*) estate is very similar to a fee simple determinable estate. The authorities generally seem to agree that the basic distinction between a fee simple conditional and a fee simple determinable lies in the fact that the fee simple determinable has an *automatic* termination upon the happening of that event, but the fee simple conditional gives the reversionary interest or the remainderman the *right* to terminate the estate, rather than the automatic termination provided for by the fee simple determinable, *Field v. Shaw*, 535 S.W. 2d 3. This right of the grantor of reversion of the fee simple conditional estate is properly called the *right of reentry*, in contrast to the *eo instanti* reversion of the fee simple determinable estate.

An example of this right of reentry conveyance would be where a deed would convey the property in the following manner:

To the grantee, but this is on the express condition that fences are kept in repair.

This type of language, used in the fee simple conditional, implies that the grantor, his heirs, or assigns would have the right to reenter the property and take it back as a condition rather than a limitation of rights. However, the grantor can only terminate the estate if he takes the initiative to reenter the property within a reasonable time.[2] As in the fee simple determinable estate, if the estate has a

---

[2] In some states, statutes of limitation place a maximum time limit on what constitutes a reasonable length of time.

future interest, it is considered as creating an executory interest in the remainderman.

Fee on Condition Precedent Estates.   A fee on condition precedent is a title passed such that the title will not take effect in the named grantee until a condition is performed. For instance, a conveyance may be made as follows:

> To a grantee in fee simple on the condition precedent that he live to attain the age of thirty years.

In this case, the grantee gets a conditional title that will only be fully vested upon his attaining the age of 30 years as provided for in the deed. This principle is particularly applicable when there is no other consideration shown in the deed, or no other value has changed hands except this particular condition. If the condition precedent is not fulfilled within a reasonable or stated time period, title reverts back to the grantor or his heirs. In common law states, the fee on condition precedent estate creates a future interest in the grantee referred to as a *springing executory use.*

One often finds this type of estate utilized when the grantor is attempting to increase the value of his property by encouraging development of the adjacent property. In this situation, the grantor conveys the property with full title not vesting "until the grantee constructs a business within two years." Using this time limitation, the grantor forces the purchaser to build something on the adjacent property to enhance the value of his (the grantor's) property.

Life Estates.   Estates that are less than fee simple limit the grantee's title and rights to varying degrees. A *life estate* is an estate for the life of some person, and is almost always accompanied by a second estate termed *a remainder interest.*

A life estate lasts as long as the grantee's life. On the other hand, the remainder interest ensures that the remainderman will receive full title to the property at a future date (generally when the grantee/life tenant dies), and is called a *future interest, Collins* v. *New,* 558 S.W.2d 108; and *U.S.* v. *164.51 Acres of Land, More or Less, in Van Buren and Cliburne Counties, Arkansas,* 205 F. Supp. 202. To illustrate, suppose a granting clause in a deed conveys my house as follows:

> To my brother for his life; then upon his death to pass to my wife.

Clearly this divides what was full ownership into two entirely different estates: the brother's life estate and the wife's remainder interest.

No particular form of words is necessary to create a life estate. It is created by a deed or a will in which the grantor manifests an intention to convey to a person the right to possess, use, or enjoy the property during the period of the person's life.

It is also possible to convey a life estate to a grantee for the life of somebody else. Life estates measured by the life of another person are called life estates *pur autre vie.* For instance, an individual could convey a life estate to his brother for the life of his great-great-grandfather. The life estate then would terminate when the great-great-grandfather died, and the remainderman would then receive the property.

Although ordinary life estates are not inheritable, a life estate *pur autre vie* is, in the case where the possessory party dies before the measuring life. In the preceding example, if the brother predeceased the great-great-grandfather, the brother's interest would be inherited by his heirs.

Both a life estate and a remainder may be transferred separately from each other. When an ordinary life estate is conveyed, it is transformed into a life estate *pur autre vie.* Thus, the purchaser's interest is no greater and can last no longer than the life of the initial life estate holder. Depending on life expectancies and the financial risks involved, the life estate may be worth only a very small amount of money, whereas the remainder interest can be quite valuable, or vice versa.

At times the preferences and economic interests of the life tenant (life estate owner) and the remainderman may directly conflict. Therefore, it is important to understand the nature and extent of their respective rights. Neither party may encumber the property if it results in the waste, deterioration, or alienation (transfer) of the other's rights. For instance, if the life tenant allows the property to deteriorate during his or her occupancy, the value of the property may be lowered, which arguably is unfair to the remainderman. It would likewise be unfair for the remainderman to do anything that would adversely affect the rights of the life tenant or the value of the property to him.

Since the remainderman is a nonoccupant and a nontenant, he has less opportunity to create waste and deterioration in the property. However, both parties have the right to pledge, encumber, or convey their respective interests in the real estate as long as this does not result in waste, deterioration, or alienation of the other's interest.

Types of Remainders.   To further complicate matters, remainder interests can be of two types: (1) a vested remainder or (2) a contingent remainder. A *vested remainder* exists if at any moment during the continuance of the previous estate (in this case, the life estate) a specifically identified remainderman is ready to come into possession whenever that life estate terminates. For instance, a vested remainder would exist if a conveyance stated the following:

> To my brother for life, remainder to my wife.

A *contingent remainder,* on the other hand, requires some sort of fulfillment of a condition before it may vest. It may not specifically identify the remainderman, or it may depend on the happening of an uncertain event. An example of a contingent remainder interest would be as follows:

> A life estate to my brother for life, remainder to the children of my wife.

If my wife has no children at the time of my brother's death, the future interest would not vest at that time, but rather may create a *reversionary interest.* A reversionary interest, you may recall, is one that reverts to the grantor or his heirs. In the typical life estate, however, the grantor may not anticipate a reversionary interest. In such cases, title may pass to the heirs of the life estate holder. The law on this area varies from state to state.

In common law states, there is often a careful distinction between different types of vested and contingent remainders and what is termed a *shifting executory use* in the future interest. However, this type of in-depth legal discussion is better left to more sophisticated treatises on the subject.

Subsurface Estates   Subsurface rights are, by all means, a freehold estate and an interest in land, and an owner of a fee title may separate his estate on the surface from the minerals underneath and sell one type of estate (the subsurface) while reserving the other (the surface) for his own use and benefit. Even when the subsurface is leased, it is generally regarded as a conveyance, giving the grantee a determinable fee, so long as the subsurface is producing oil, gas, or other minerals.

Lateral Severance. It is important to understand that estates in land are generally considered to go to the center of the earth. Therefore, a separation of the mineral estate results in a *lateral severance* (separation) of the surface estate from the mineral estate. The grantor will continue to own the surface estate, whereas the grantee of the mineral interest will own or lease the subsurface estate. Lateral severance generally provides that the grantee or lessee of the mineral estate may acquire rights to drill for oil and gas or to mine certain minerals on the grantor's property, but that the grantor still owns the surface estate, subject to the rights of the mineral owner.

Interesting questions arise as to whether or not a substance is surface or subsurface, depending upon its proximity to the surface. Although the law varies from state to state, the general rule is that whoever has an interest in the subsurface has the right to go onto the property and extract it regardless of whether or not it is extracted by strip mining procedures or traditional mining techniques. Some states have held that when the substances are so near the surface that extraction depletes the land surface, there is no lateral severance and the substances belong to the surface estate.

Dominant Estates. The concept of lateral severance creates a conflict of estates between the surface owner's right to use the surface and the mineral owner's right to enter upon that surface to extract the minerals. The mineral owner is generally construed to have the *dominant estate.* This means he has the right to use the surface, reasonably, to exercise his rights to extract the minerals from the subsurface. Any subsequent purchaser of the surface rights of the property would get a fee title to that property, subject to the rights of the mineral owner. This may seem at first to be a disadvantage to the surface owner. Practically speaking, however, the surface owner often leases or sells the subsurface and will receive benefits from the mining of those minerals in terms of percentage of the payment or production of these minerals (called "royalties"), and perhaps even a cash "bonus" payment in addition to the lease payments for allowing the mineral owner to mine the subsurface minerals. These payments, or "royalty interests," are not real estate and the owner relinquishes his rights to explore the minerals for himself. The royalty interests are merely interests in the income off of the profits produced by the mining of those minerals.

In the event the surface owner does not wish to have the mineral owner on his property mining or extracting the minerals, he may reserve the sole rights to the surface estate, which may force the mineral estate owner to enter upon an adjacent property to

extract the minerals through various underground drilling or excavation methods.

Air Rights   There is another area of lateral severance that involves the ownership of *air rights*. Although the concept of air rights is self-explanatory to some extent, legal aspects of air rights tend to be nebulous
and difficult to describe. Generally, however, the concept of air
rights means that the surface owner has control over his own air
rights, subject to certain limitations.

The initial question of air rights came from owners of property who were adjacent to airports. It was understood that, between
the two private property owners (the privately owned airport and
the privately owned property abutting that airport), there had to be
a conflict of rights over the noise, pollution, and litter that accompanied the airplanes' taking off and landing, conditions that
adversely affected the adjacent property owners. This type of law
found its origin in the law of nuisance, where one property owner
would sue the adjacent property owner because of the nuisance
value and discomfort caused by the other property owner.

In more current times, and with municipal ownership of airports, we have found that there is a more complex problem
between the concepts of private ownership versus the public welfare. In the airport situation, we find that for the good of the public
certain ordinances are passed prohibiting the building of structures
adjacent to an airport because of both the danger to air traffic and
the discomfort of the people adjacent to the airport. The municipality generally exercises its power of eminent domain to acquire
adjacent property or to restrict use of the adjacent property to uses
that would be nondetrimental to the public airport purposes.

Overhead Structures.   Other air rights concepts have involved the
construction of overhead walkways, office buildings, and similar
structures across streets. Such structures may create pollution hazards, carbon monoxide build-up, and other unhealthy conditions if
not built properly. In these cases, of course, we have the conflict of
the private ownership of the building versus the public welfare of
people who have to live adjacent to or pass through the type of
environment this building might create.

Solar Rights.   Another concept of air rights is the right of adjacent
property owners to the sun. Although this has been a very old concept, one that generally was predicated on creating "tunnels" in
downtown areas, a new type of legal problem now becomes evi-
dent because of the use of solar energy.

Estates in land have previously been defined as the degree, quantity, nature, and extent of a person's ownership interest in real property. In many jurisdictions, statutes create additional estates, which exist concurrently with the estates previously mentioned. Since these estates are created by statute (rather than by possession and title), we will refer to these estates as *statutory estates*. The statutory estates to be considered are homestead, dower, curtesy, and community property.

Since ownership by community property is usually voluntary (marriage), it has both the characteristics of a legal estate and a type of co-ownership (see also discussion in Chapter 3). Table 2-1 summarizes which states recognize the various statutory estates.

STATUTORY ESTATES

The homestead is an estate in land created by statutory or constitutional provision. The primary purpose of homestead rights is to provide a secure asylum, one that the family cannot be deprived of by creditors. Such protection may extend to the family home, farm, or small business.

Homesteads

Criteria. Homestead exemptions are generally based on two basic criteria: (1) the existence of a family and (2) a place of residence. The family is normally construed to be two or more persons, with one member who is the head and has legal or moral obligations to support the other family members. The definition varies from state to state. The last bastion of great homestead rights is Texas, where these rights are constitutional as well as statutory. There a recently passed constitutional amendment extends homestead rights to single adult persons. Similar statutory provisions for homestead rights for single adults have been passed in Arizona, New Hampshire, New York, and Oklahoma.

The place of residence criterion generally requires that the home be the primary and principal residence of the family or single adult person, and is usually satisfied by the family being in possession of the home. Florida additionally requires an intent to create the homestead, *Sheaf* v. *Klose*, 75 S.E.2d 595 (Fla. 1954). Texas also requires intent, along with some other overt act to render the homestead rights operative. Homestead rights are not restricted to fee simple ownerships, but can exist concurrently with any right of occupancy.

Texas has additionally provided for a business as well as a residential homestead. Although the concept of a business homestead may seem awkward (since the family security doesn't appear to be protected), there has been no difficulty in enforcing this exemption there, *O'Neill* v. *Mack Trucks*, 542 S.W.2d 112 (Tex. 1976).

TABLE 2-1
Statutory Estates Existing in Different States

	Dower Right for Wife	Curtesy or Dower Right for Husband	Homestead Protection	Community Property
Alabama	x		x	
Alaska			x	
Arizona			x	x
Arkansas	x	x	x	
California			x	x
Colorado			x	
Connecticut				
Delaware				
Florida			x	
Georgia			x	
Hawaii	x	x		
Idaho			x	x
Illinois			x	
Indiana			x	
Iowa			x	
Kansas			x	
Kentucky	x	x	x	
Louisiana			x	x
Maine			x	
Maryland				
Massachusetts	x	x	x	
Michigan	x		x	
Minnesota			x	
Mississippi			x	
Missouri			x	
Montana			x	
Nebraska			x	
Nevada			x	x
New Hampshire			x	
New Jersey	x	x		
New Mexico			x	x
New York			x	
North Carolina			x	
North Dakota			x	
Ohio	x	x	x	
Oklahoma			x	
Oregon			x	
Pennsylvania				
Rhode Island				
South Carolina	x		x	

TABLE 2-1 Continued

	Dower Right for Wife	Curtesy or Dower Right for Husband	Homestead Protection	Community Property
South Dakota			x	
Tennessee			x	
Texas			x	x
Utah			x	
Vermont			x	
Virginia	x	x	x	
Washington			x	x
West Virginia	x	x	x	
Wisconsin	x	x	x	x
Wyoming			x	

However, as you may expect, there are limitations as to exactly what can be declared as one's homestead, usually expressed as a dollar amount or acreage limit. The homestead includes the property and the improvements thereon. Some states also include certain items of personalty, such as clothes, furniture, cemetery lots, cows, hogs, sheep, and chickens. Some of the more common limitations are shown in Table 2-2.

The homestead property can usually be foreclosed on for primary debts for acquisition and construction (mortgages, mechanics' liens, and property taxes assessed against the homestead), but is usually exempt from other types of debts and creditors. Moreover, upon sale of the property, the proceeds may be exempt from attachment by such other creditors for lengths of time from six months to one year, and the homestead rights can vest in the newly acquired property if it is acquired in a timely fashion. This makes it possible for a family to sell one home and acquire another without risking the loss of their home to creditors during the process of moving.

Creation. The manner of creating a homestead varies from state to state. California requires filing a declaration, *Taylor v. Madigan,* 53 Cal. App. 23d 945, whereas New Mexico, Ohio, Oregon, South Carolina, and Wisconsin provide only for a set-off of exempt property after execution of a levy on the debtor's property. The exemption arises automatically in Colorado, Texas, Vermont, and West Virginia. Massachusetts requires recordation.

TABLE 2-2
Sample Homestead Limitations Existing in Some States

State	Statute	Dollar Limit	Acreage Limit
Alabama	Sec. 6-10-2	$5,000	160 acres
Alaska	Sec. 09.38.010	$27,000	none
Arizona	Sec. 33-1101	$50,000	none
Arkansas	Rural Sec. 30-223	$800	no less than 80, no more than 160
	Urban Sec. 30-224	$2,500	no less than 1/4, no more than 1
California	Sec. 704.730	$45,000	none
Colorado	Sec. 38-41-201	$20,000 in excess of liens and encumbrances	none
Florida	Sec. 222.01	none	160 acres rural, 1/2 acre in city
Georgia	Sec. 51-101	$5,000	50 plus 5 per child under 16 yrs. old
Hawaii	Sec. 651-91	$20,000	none
Idaho	Sec. 55-1201	$25,000 in excess of mortgages, deeds of trust, liens of record	none
Illinois	Sec. 12-901	$7,500	none
Indiana	Sec. 34-2-28-1	$7,500	none
Iowa	Sec. 561.2	$500	up to 1 acre in city; up to 40 acres outside city
Kansas	Sec. 60.2301	none	up to 1 acre in city; up to 160 acres outside city
Kentucky	Sec. 427.060	$50,000	none
Louisiana	Title 20, Sec. 1	$15,000	160 acres
Maine	Title 14, 4422(1)	$7,500	none
Massachusetts	Chapter 188 Sec. 1	$50,000	none
Michigan	Sec 27.5285, 27.5286	$10,000	none
Minnesota	Sec. 510.02	none	up to 80 acres outside city; up to 1/2 or 1/3 inside city
Mississippi	Title 85 Sec. 3-21 and 3-23	$30,000 in excess of liens and encumbrances	160 acres
Missouri	Sec. 513.475	$8,000	none
Montana	Title 70 Sec. 32-104	$40,000	320 acres if used for agriculture purpose; 1 acre if not in a municipality; 1/4 acre if in a municipality
Nebraska	Sec. 40-101	$6,500	up to 160 acres outside city; 2 continuous lots in city

TABLE 2-2 Continued

State	Statute	Dollar Limit	Acreage Limit
Nevada	Sec. 155.010	$90,000	none
New Hampshire	Sec. 480:1	$5,000	none
New Mexico	Chap. 42 Sec. 10-9	$20,000	none
New York	C.P.L.R. 5206:1	$10,000	none
North Carolina	Sec. 1C-1601(a)(1)	$7,500	none
North Dakota	Title 47 Sec. 18-01	$80,000 in excess of liens and encumbrances	none
Ohio	Sec. 2329.66(A)(1), 2329.661	$5,000	
Oklahoma	Title 31 Sec. 1, 2, 5	$5,000	outside city 160 acres; no less than 1/4 acre in city
Oregon	Sec. 23.164, 23.240, 23.250, 23.160	$15,000	160 acres outside city; 1 block in city
South Carolina	Sec. 15-41-200	$5,000	none
South Dakota	Title 43 Sec. 31-1, 31-2	none	none
Tennessee	Sec. 26-2-301	$5,000	none
Texas (1982–83 on)	Const. Art. 16 Sec. 51	none	200 acres for family, 100 acres for individual, 1 acre in urban area
Utah	Sec. 78-23-3	$8,000	none
Vermont	Title 27, Sec. 101	$30,000	none
Virginia	Sec. 34-4	$5,000	none
Washington	Sec. 6.12.050	$20,000	none
West Virginia	Sec. 38-10-4	$7,500	none
Wisconsin	Sec. 815-20	$25,000	none
Wyoming	Title 1, Sec. 20-101	$10,000	none

Termination. Once a homestead is established, there is a presumption that it continues. It may be terminated if the parties so intend, however, and this is usually accomplished by alienation (sale or transfer), waiver, or abandonment.

Homestead rights can be waived (voluntarily relinquished) in most states as long as the waiver is properly acknowledged, in writing, and signed by both spouses. Since homestead rights are constitutional rights in Texas, the rights cannot be waived there. The ability to voluntarily relinquish rights may depend on the source of such rights (i.e., constitutional, statutory, contractual).

Homestead property sales must be executed and acknowledged by both spouses, because one spouse cannot waive homestead rights held equally by both spouses.

Abandonment is a difficult way to prove homestead termination. It involves cessation of use, together with a showing that there is a fixed intention by the claimants to never again return to the property. A temporary renting of the homestead, even if a new home is acquired, may not terminate the homestead rights in the prior home if the intent to abandon did not exist. This is often the case, particularly if the value of the second home exceeds the maximum homestead exemption but the first does not.

Dower and Curtesy   *Dower.*   Under common law, the widow from a valid marriage becomes entitled to an estate for life in one-third of all the land that the man had owned during "coverture" (provided that the man's estate was such that children born of the marriage might have inherited it). Upon marriage or upon acquisition of property by the husband after marriage, the wife acquires an "expectation" with respect to the land that the husband has acquired. This expectation is called *inchoate dower.* The prerequisites of this dower are simply: (1) that the man must be or have been owner of the property, (2) that he must have or have had an estate of inheritance, and (3) that this property was acquired during the marriage.

Qualifying ownership by the husband includes only present interests. Neither future nor possible reversionary interest qualifies for inchoate dower. It is not always clear whether a husband's equitable ownership interests are subject to dower. Although some jurisdictions allow it (e.g., Arkansas), others have statutes expressly prohibiting the attachment of dower to equitable estates (e.g., Hawaii). If all three requirements are met, inchoate dower takes on the characteristics of an encumbrance on title. It also constitutes an interest and an estate in land, often characterized as a future estate for life. Dower rights cannot be transferred except by the wife's consent. This creates an obvious problem for a husband wishing to convey real estate without his wife's joinder, since her dower interest is not transferred. For this reason, in those states where dower exists, it is always good practice for buyers and lenders to acquire the rights of both the husband and the wife or to require that the wife waive her right to the dower interest in the estate.

Dower rights can also be barred by agreement of the parties, by judicial proceedings, or in some jurisdictions by adultery of the wife. (The errant wandering of the husband appears to have been overlooked.)

Dower as an estate for life in one-third of the lands of the husband still exists in Alaska, Delaware, Georgia, Hawaii, Ohio, Rhode Island, Tennessee, Virginia, and West Virginia. Other states have enlarged the dower rights to one-half of the husband's property, or have restricted dower rights to some extent. Those states that still maintain a significant dower interest, although slightly modified from the common law one-third of the husband's estate, are Alabama, Arkansas, Kentucky, Maryland, Massachusetts, New Jersey, and Wisconsin. Because so many states have abrogated or modified common law dower, both dower and curtesy are included here as statutory estates.

Curtesy.   In a similar fashion to dower, under common law a husband also automatically receives an estate in all of his wife's freehold estates of inheritance. His estate is referred to as *curtesy*.

Under common law, the prerequisites for a valid curtesy include the following:

1. A valid marriage.
2. The wife's ownership of an estate of inheritance during the marriage.
3. The wife must have given birth to children capable of inheriting her estate.

Only three states retain curtesy as an estate for life in all of the wife's lands: Alabama, Rhode Island, and Tennessee. But curtesy still exists to some extent in Arkansas, Delaware, Hawaii, Maryland, Massachusetts, New Jersey, Ohio, Oregon, Virginia, West Virginia, and Wisconsin.

In the vast majority of jurisdictions both dower and curtesy have either been totally abolished or are gradually being phased out (see Table 2-1). Instead, other rights have been developed to protect spouses, with such rights generally not directly impacting on title to real estate.

Community Property

Community property law has its roots in the old Spanish community property system. Eight states originally followed the community property system: Arizona, California, Louisiana, New Mexico, Texas, Idaho, Nevada, and Washington (see Table 2-1).

Two basic types of property, *separate* and *community,* are recognized under the community property system. Property acquired by one spouse prior to marriage, or by gift, devise, or descent after marriage, is classified as separate property. In addition, compensation received for personal injuries is separate property in Louisiana, Texas, New Mexico, and Nevada.

Community property law basically provides for equal ownership by each spouse of all property acquired after marriage. These rights exist irrespective of whether the marriage was the result of a formal legal ceremony or of common law cohabitation. Community property rights terminate upon divorce or the death of either spouse.

All property acquired by the husband or wife during their marriage is presumed to be community property, so adequate records must be kept if one wishes to prove the existence of separate property. Community property is subject to the joint ownership, control, and disposition of both spouses.

Conflicts often arise concerning (1) property acquired after marriage by separate property funds, (2) income from separate property, (3) increases in property value after marriage, and (4) when a cause of action based on facts prior to the marriage results in a judgment for damages after the marriage.

Generally, creditors levy on a spouse's separate property for the separate contracts and obligations of that spouse before pursuing the community property interest. When a creditor of one spouse pursues community debts, the separate property of the other spouse is not liable for those debts.

With this general background, we now explore some of the more important differences in rules existing among community property states. Conflicts in determining whether property is separate or community are normally resolved in favor of community property unless the intention is clearly otherwise. Some states have enacted statutes to resolve this and the previously mentioned conflicts. Louisiana, for instance, has the presumption that any land acquired during the marriage in the name of the husband is conclusively presumed to be community property, *Lewis* v. *Clay*, 60 So.2d 78 (1952).

Texas adopts a somewhat different approach. It presumes all property acquired during marriage to be community property, but property owned in the name of one of the spouses is presumed to be under that spouse's sole control. However, this presumption can be rebutted by showing a different intent (*V.A.T.S.* Family Code § 5.241).

Conflict can arise in some states due to the differences in rules regarding property acquired before marriage but requiring maintenance with community funds. New Mexico and Texas hold that such property maintains its status as separate, but upon disposition, the community property has a right to be compensated for all maintenance expenditures. Louisiana holds a similar view depending on the time the title is acquired. On the other hand, California, Nevada, and Washington provide that such property becomes a mixture of separate and community property, with the precise division determined by the relative proportion of separate and community funds expended for and on the property. Arizona law on this question is even more complicated, because it has adopted part of each of the previously described approaches. All community property states permit any increase (appreciation) in separate property value to maintain its separate property identity.

Income derived from separate property is community property in Idaho, Louisiana, and Texas. In other states (specifically Arizona, California, New Mexico, Nevada, and Washington), income from separate property is classified as separate property.

To avoid some of the previously mentioned problems, some states have permitted the separate nature of property to be maintained by recording inventories as separate property in antenuptial and postnuptial agreements. The most severe interpretation problems occur when separate and community funds have been commingled to the extent that they are difficult to identify. Again, this emphasizes the need to maintain adequate records in order that the true character of property may be proven.

From a real estate agent's standpoint, an important legal question in community property states concerns who (either or both spouses) has the power to bind the community property. Louisiana, Nevada, and New Mexico still provide for the husband to manage the community estate. Arizona, California, Idaho, Texas, and Washington provide for equal control and management of community property, thereby giving each spouse the right to contract and bind the community property for debts and obligations, provided it is not done to defraud the rights of the spouse. The basic rule in all community property situations should be to require the joinder of both spouses in signing any instruments that attempt to convey any rights that might possibly be interpreted as community property, *Colorado National Bank of Denver* v. *Merlino*, 668 P.2d 1304 (Wash. 1983).

Common-Law Marriage. All community property rights hinge on whether the couple is married. There is little question in the case of a formal, ceremonial marriage (except for annulments). However, there is a serious question in states that recognize common-law marriages. Currently, Texas and Idaho are the only community property states that recognize the validity of common-law marriages. The requirements to create a common-law marriage are surprisingly meager in both Texas and Idaho. Texas, for instance, requires only (1) intent, (2) conduct leading others to believe they are husband and wife, and (3) cohabitation (with no time limit on cohabitation). If the last two requirements are met, the first is presumed. If *all three* are met, a common-law marriage exists that requires a divorce to dissolve. A whole lot of people there are married and don't know it! Could be complicated, too.

SUMMARY   Ownership interests in real property are called *estates*. There are two principal kinds of estates: leasehold and freehold estates. Leasehold estates last for a definite time period, whereas freehold estates are indefinite in length.

Freehold estates may be further divided into fee estates and life estates. A fee estate may be transferred to the next generation, but a life estate and the right to transfer it typically end with the death of the landowner. A life estate *pur autre vie,* on the other hand, is measured by the life span of someone other than the current life estate owner.

Creating a life estate involves dividing full (usually fee simple absolute) ownership into two parts: a life estate and a remainder. Remainders are of two types: vested and contingent. A vested remainder is a future ownership interest for which a definitely identified owner currently exists. A contingent remainder is one that will vest in the future but only if certain contingent events occur. The owner of a contingent remainder often is not fully identified when this ownership interest is created.

Fee estates are of three principal types: fee simple absolute, fee simple conditional, and fee simple determinable. A fee simple estate is the greatest private ownership interest one can have in real property. It consists of all possible property rights except those exclusively reserved by the state.

Conceptually, fee simple conditional (also known as a *fee simple on condition subsequent*) involves dividing a fee simple absolute into two parts. The part conveyed to the grantee is a fee simple conditional. The portion retained by the grantor is a right of entry. The right of entry means the grantor can get full title back if he goes to court and proves that the fee simple conditional ownership has failed to meet some condition placed on his continued ownership. A fee simple on condition precedent is similar in nature, but requires a condition to be met to create the ownership interest.

The fee simple determinable also can be thought of as dividing a fee simple absolute into two parts. The part received by the grantee is a fee simple determinable. The ownership interest retained by the grantor is a possibility of reverter. Under this type of ownership, full fee simple absolute title will automatically revert to the grantor upon the happening of some specific but contingent event.

Several other estates in land, known as statutory or legal estates, also exist in certain states. These include homestead rights,

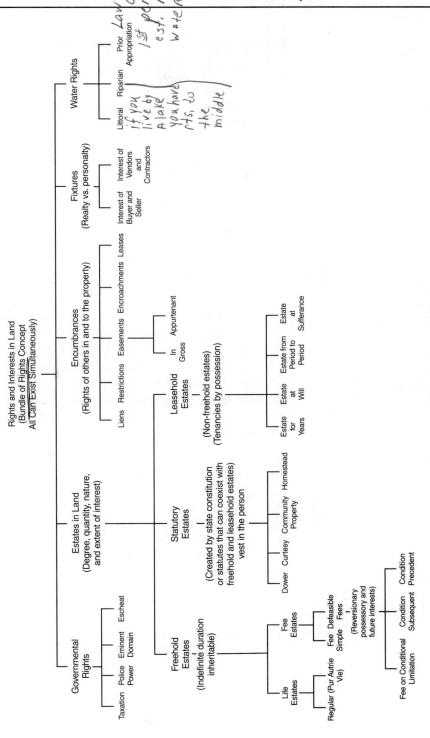

Figure 2-1 Interests in Real Estate

Handwritten notes (top of figure): Prior Appropriation — Law in Colorado 1st person est. rts to water

Littoral Riparian — if you live by a lake you have rts to the middle

dower, curtesy, and community property. Homestead rights are basically designed to protect the family by preventing general creditors from being able to force the family home to be sold in order to collect debts owed to them.

Under common law a wife receives a life estate in one-third of all the real estate owned by her husband during their marriage. This interest, known as dower, still exists in various forms in some 16 states. Curtesy, the common law equivalent of dower for husbands, is now found in 13 states.

Nine states now follow the law of community property, in which both spouses are equal owners of property even if the document of title names only one as owner. Each spouse may also own separate property if acquired before marriage or by gift or inheritance during marriage.

DISCUSSION QUESTIONS

1. Why is it important to recognize and be aware of the various kinds of estates that may be created in land?

2. Suggest several reasons why you should require both spouses to sign a deed transferring real estate to you, even though only one spouse is listed as the sole owner of the land involved.

3. Explain the differences between homestead rights and community property rights.

4. Which statutory estates exist in your state?

5. Contrast a fee simple conditional with a fee simple determinable.

3

How Ownership Is Held

Ownership of real estate must be vested in a specific, identifiable legal entity. Some person, company, or organization maintains legal control over real estate and is held to be responsible for activities and obligations arising as a result of that ownership and control. A group of people, or an individual, contemplating a purchase of real estate, will want to give serious consideration as to how the ownership of that real estate should be held. This normally requires sound legal advice because the means of ownership dictates the scope of control and liabilities of that ownership—liabilities that may have far-reaching, and sometimes unexpected, legal complications.

The entities of ownership discussed in this chapter will include ownership in severalty, tenancy in common, joint tenancy, corporations, partnerships, limited partnerships, and trusts. Each type of ownership will be discussed in its purest, most basic form to simplify its unique characteristics.

Sole ownership, also called *ownership in severalty,* is the easiest form of ownership to understand because it is simply individual ownership. One person is the owner. He has sole control over the use and possession of the property, as well as sole and unlimited liability for all obligations arising out of ownership. Ownership in severalty is available in all states.

SOLE OWNERSHIP

In co-ownership, also called *concurrent ownership*, two or more people directly share title to real estate. Some important characteristics of all types of co-ownership include the following:

CHARACTERISTICS OF CO-OWNERSHIP IN GENERAL

1. Each co-owner generally has the right to convey his ownership interest separately from those of other co-owners.
   (An exception exists for tenancies by entireties.)

2. Each co-owner has the right to insist on partitioning (physically dividing) the property (again, tenancies by entireties
   may be an exception). Once physical division has
   occurred, each co-owner becomes the sole owner of one of
   the component parts.

   Alternatively, if physical division is not feasible, the
   property may be sold via forced sale and the proceeds
   divided proportionately among the co-owners, *Nordhausen
   v. Christner,* 338 N.W.2d 754 (Neb. 1983).

3. Each co-owner is deemed to have possession of the entire
   tract. That is, if one is in possession, he cannot adversely
   possess against the other co-owner.

4. With the exception of tenancies by entireties, the individual fractional ownership interests need not be equal.

Different states may authorize from one to three kinds of co-
ownership. These three are tenancy in common, joint tenancy, and
tenancy by entireties (see Table 3-1). Each of these co-ownership
forms generally has the preceding four characteristics. The important differences of each are now discussed.

Tenancy in Common.   Tenancy in common can best be defined as
multiple ownership of real estate in undivided interests. There is
no requirement that the fractional undivided interests be equal.

Tenancies in common are characterized by *unity of possession,*
i.e., all the co-tenants (co-owners) have the right to be in possession. All the co-tenants do not have to occupy the real estate at one
time, however. Possession by one co-owner is deemed to be possession by all co-owners.

A tenancy in common is often the appropriate ownership form
when a person dies without a will and title descends to his heirs.

Since one's co-ownership interest in a tenancy in common is
inheritable, at death it is transferred to heirs of the co-owner's
choice. Inheritability assures that at the death of any co-owner, his
family will be protected to the extent possible. It is in an effort to
protect the family that all real estate transfers involving co-owner-
ships are presumed to create a tenancy in common in some states[1]

---

[1] Exceptions often exist in states recognizing tenancies by entireties. To protect
spouses, the law in these states may presume that any conveyance to a married couple creates a tenancy by entireties rather than a tenancy in common.

TABLE 3-1
Availability of Selected Ownership Entities, by State

	Tenancy in Common	Joint Tenancy	Tenancy by Entireties	Community Property	Adopted UPA[1]	Adopted ULPA[2]	L.L.P.	L.C.
Alabama	x	x			x	x	x	x
Alaska	x	x	x		x	x		x
Arizona	x	x		x	x	x	x	x
Arkansas	x	x	x		x	x		x
California	x	x		x	x	x		x
Colorado	x	x			x	x		x
Connecticut	x	x			x	x		x
Delaware	x	x	x		x	x	x	x
Florida	x	x	x		x	x		x
Georgia	x	x			x	x	x	x
Hawaii	x	x			x	x		x
Idaho	x	x		x	x	x		x
Illinois	x	x			x	x		x
Indiana	x	x	x		x	x		x
Iowa	x	x			x	x	x	x
Kansas	x	x			x	x	x	x
Kentucky	x	x	x		x	x		x
Louisiana				x	x		x	x
Maine	x	x			x	x		x
Maryland	x	x	x		x	x	x	x
Massachusetts	x	x	x		x	x		x
Michigan	x	x	x		x	x	x	x
Minnesota	x	x			x	x	x	x
Mississippi	x	x			x	x	x	x
Missouri	x	x	x		x	x		x
Montana	x	x			x	x		x
Nebraska	x	x			x	x		x
Nevada	x	x		x	x	x		x
New Hampshire	x	x			x	x		x
New Jersey	x	x	x		x	x	x	x
New Mexico	x	x		x	x	x		x
New York	x	x	x		x	x		x
North Carolina	x	x	x		x	x	x	x
North Dakota	x	x			x	x		x
Ohio	x				x	x	x	x
Oklahoma	x	x	x		x	x		x
Oregon	x		x		x	x		x
Pennsylvania	x	x	x		x	x		x
Rhode Island	x	x	x		x	x		x
South Carolina	x	x			x	x		x

TABLE 3-1 Continued

	Tenancy in Common	Joint Tenancy	Tenancy by Entireties	Community Property	Adopted UPA[1]	Adopted ULPA[2]	L.L.P.	L.C.
South Dakota	x	x			x	x		x
Tennessee	x	x	x		x	x		x
Texas	x	x		x	x	x	x	x
Utah	x	x			x	x	x	x
Vermont	x	x	x		x	x		x
Virginia	x	x	x		x	x	x	x
Washington	x	x		x	x	x		x
West Virginia	x	x			x	x		x
Wisconsin	x	x	x	x	x	x		x
Wyoming	x	x	x		x	x		x

[1] Uniform Partnership Act.

[2] Uniform Limited Partnership Act.

unless the legal documents clearly show that a different form of co-ownership was intended. The states authorizing tenancy in common ownership are shown in Table 3-1.

Rights of Parties. Under a tenancy in common, the co-owners have certain obligations to each other. When only one is in possession, the relationship between the possessor and other co-owners is generally construed to be that of landlord and tenant. However, if a co-owner receives more than his proportionate share of rents (for instance, if the property is income-producing), he is obligated to pay the other co-owners their proportionate part, and he must give them a full accounting upon request.

On the other hand, if one co-owner's possession clearly contradicts the rights of the other owners, the former may be construed to be an adverse possessor. Under these circumstances, it may be proper to institute eviction proceedings against him.

More difficult questions are posed when unmarried adults of the opposite sex co-habitate. Courts may imply a right to an accounting, *Marvin v. Marvin*, 557 P.2d 106 (Cal. 1976); *Cook v. Cook*, 691 P.2d 664 (Ariz. 1984); *Beal v. Beal*, 557 P.2d 507 (Ore. 1978).

Liabilities. Nothing prohibits a co-owner from encumbering, selling, or leasing his proportional ownership interest as long as the rights of the other co-owners are not adversely affected, *Gillmor v. Gillmor*, 694 P.2d 1037 (Utah 1984).

Importantly, a co-owner's obligations to third-party creditors extend only to his proportionate undivided interest in the real property. If a co-owner's interest is transferred to a creditor, the creditor simply becomes a tenant (owner) in common with the other co-owners. However, if the property is encumbered by a single mortgage signed by all the co-owners, in some states the creditors may seek collection from one or all of the co-owners, jointly or severally (individually). In such a case, the co-owner who ultimately pays the debt has the right to be reimbursed by the others.

The direct ownership aspect of tenancies in common permits marketability of the property to be temporarily affected by the death or divorce of a co-owner/investor. It also results in unlimited liability and a possible loss of other assets if the investment proves to be a poor one. However, tenancies in common do allow for tax-sheltering because all losses and gains are reported on the co-owner's individual income tax return.

Joint Tenancy

The major difference between a joint tenancy and a tenancy in common is that joint tenancy is characterized by a right of survivorship. This means that the interest of a deceased co-owner is automatically transferred to the surviving co-owners, often without the need for probate proceedings. Since an individual generally is more interested in taking care of his own family rather than seeing to the well-being of his co-investors, a joint tenancy is the form of ownership often used for co-owners who are members of the same family. A tenancy in common is generally a more appropriate form of co-ownership to use when one is investing with nonfamily members.

Because a joint tenancy often operates to transfer title without formal probate proceedings, in some states it is referred to as a "poor man's will." However, it does not affect distribution of assets held under other forms of ownership; so it should never be viewed as a substitute for a will.

The rights and liabilities of joint tenants are essentially identical to those of tenants in common.

Creation.   Recall that in order to protect families, most states presume that any conveyance to multiple owners (other than a married couple) creates a tenancy in common. This legal presumption must be rebutted in order to create a joint tenancy. In the deed that creates this ownership entity, it is usually written in explicit terms, such as:

> To Able and Baker as joint tenants and not as tenants in common.[2]

Although lesser language may prove the intent to create a joint tenancy, expensive litigation may be required to determine what type of ownership has been created. For this reason, the language used should be specific and precise, and the recommendation of legal counsel should be carefully followed.

Questions may arise whether joint tenancies between husband and wife can exist in community property states. (That is, will the community property rules prevail for all transactions involving married couples?) Most community property states permit the joint tenancy to exist, provided that it is specifically created and consists solely of one spouse's separate property (see Table 3-1).

Under common law a joint tenancy was created by the presence of the four "unities": the unities of interest, title, time, and possession. Basically this means that each joint tenant's interest in the real estate must:

1. Be of the same type (interest).
2. Occur by the same conveyance (title).
3. Commence at the same time (time).
4. Be held in the same undivided possession (possession).

In some states, statutes have been enacted that may eliminate the need to meet all four unities in order to create a joint tenancy.

Termination.   A joint tenancy may be terminated if one of the co-owners (1) voluntarily conveys his interest to a third party or (2) involuntarily permits a creditor to obtain a judgment against and execution on his ownership interest. In either case, the party acquiring the co-ownership interest becomes a tenant in common with the other joint tenants. If only one other joint tenant exists, the co-ownership form is converted to a tenancy in common. See Figure 3-1.

At the death of one joint tenant, the right of survivorship *always* conveys title to the surviving co-owner(s). This holds true even if a different disposition is directed in one's will, because the right of survivorship takes precedence over the will. For this reason, if an individual wishes to change the distribution implied by

---

[2] See Richard R. Powell, *Powell on Real Property,* ed. Patrick J. Rohan (New York: Matthew Bender & Company, Inc.), § 616.

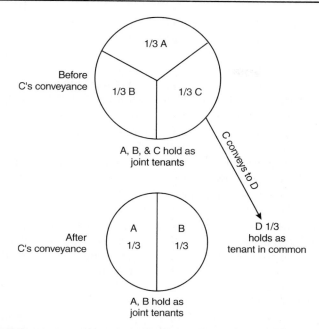

**FIGURE 3-1   Illustration of the Effect of Transferring an
Individual Interest in a Joint Tenancy**

a joint tenancy, he must modify the form of ownership during his
lifetime.[3]

Family members investing together under a joint tenancy need
to be aware of its impact on marketability, limited liability, and tax-
sheltering opportunities. Direct ownership with right of survivorship means that marketability may be affected by the divorce but
not by the death of a co-owner. Otherwise joint tenancy is identical
to a tenancy in common in that such direct ownership facilitates
tax-sheltering but does not provide limited liability.

A *tenancy by entireties* is basically a joint tenancy between husband   *Tenancy by Entireties*
and wife. The basic requirements are that:

1. The previously discussed four unities exist.
2. The two co-owners be married to each other.

---

[3] A possible exception exists where the joint tenants have executed a joint and
mutual will, because this type of will creates a contract between or among the joint
tenants.

As in joint tenancy situations, when one spouse dies, that individual's ownership interest is automatically transferred to the other by right of survivorship.

As shown in Table 3-1, the tenancy by entireties form of co-ownership exists in 22 states: Alaska, Arkansas, Delaware, Florida, Indiana, Kentucky, Maryland, Massachusetts, Michigan, Missouri, New Jersey, New York, North Carolina, Oklahoma, Oregon, Pennsylvania, Rhode Island, Tennessee, Vermont, Virginia, Wisconsin, and Wyoming, *Harris* v. *Crowder,* 322 S.E.2d 854 (W. Va. 1984). There are varying degrees of acceptance and use of this form of ownership within these states. It is generally concluded that a tenancy by entireties cannot exist in community property states.

The tenancy by entireties form of ownership arose as a method to protect the wife. For this reason the signatures of both husband and wife are necessary to convey any interest (partial or full ownership) in property held as tenants by entireties. An exception may exist when one is the agent for the other, *Harris* v. *Crowder, supra.*

This type of ownership is gradually becoming less prevalent nationally, for two principal reasons. The first reason is that women are increasingly achieving greater legal rights and independence, *West* v. *First Agricultural Bank,* 419 N.E.2d 262 (Mass. 1981). The second is that in many states the law prevents creditors of one spouse from attaching tenancy by entireties property to satisfy debts owed them, *Fairclaw* v. *Forrest,* 130 F.2d 829 cert. den., 318 U.S. 756, 63 S. Ct. 530, 1943. This logically creates a property immune to the separate creditors of either spouse. (Exceptions exist if the conveyance creating the tenancy by entireties was made as an attempt to defraud creditors.) On the other hand, if both spouses are jointly liable for a debt, property owners as tenants by entireties may be levied on by their creditors.

The increasing ability of husbands and wives to obtain credit individually has caused many lenders concern because of the difficulty of collecting debts where the spouses own essentially all property as tenants by entireties. This, in turn, has also contributed to the decrease in numbers of states authorizing this type of co-ownership.

Tenancies by entireties may be terminated by death, divorce, or annulment. In the case of divorce or annulment, the two former spouses generally become tenants in common. One case has held that this is so even when one spouse "feloniously kills" the other. See *Hicks* v. *Boshears,* 846 S.W.2d 812 (Tenn. 1993). On occasion a court may exercise the power to order partition of the estate and permit each tenant to hold sole ownership of a specific portion of the real estate.

Tenancies by entireties are identical to joint tenancies with respect to marketability being affected by divorce but not death, tax-sheltering being available, and a co-owner's liability being unlimited.

Corporations as an ownership entity are probably affected by more statutory provisions than any other type of ownership. Corporations are complicated in nature, and it is important that the basics of the corporate structure be understood before further legal aspects of corporation ownership and control of real estate are discussed.

Organization. Three basic classes of individuals are involved in the organization of all corporations: officers, directors, and shareholders.

Shareholders are, in fact, the owners of the corporation. A corporation normally raises its money for capital and initial ownership costs by selling shares to the shareholders. The shareholders, after advancing the money for the corporation's initial costs, ultimately control the corporation by voting their shares at the annual shareholders' meeting. At the annual shareholders' meeting, the shareholders also elect the board of directors. The business and affairs of the corporation are managed by this *board of directors,* who are not required by law to be residents of the state, or even shareholders of the corporation. The officers of the corporation are elected by the board of directors. The *officers and agents* of the corporation (including employees) have the authority to perform the duties of the management of the corporation on a day-to-day basis and as may be determined by the board of directors. The corporation may then return the shareholders' investments through payment of dividends, normally paid quarterly. The diagram in Figure 3-2 graphically illustrates these functions.

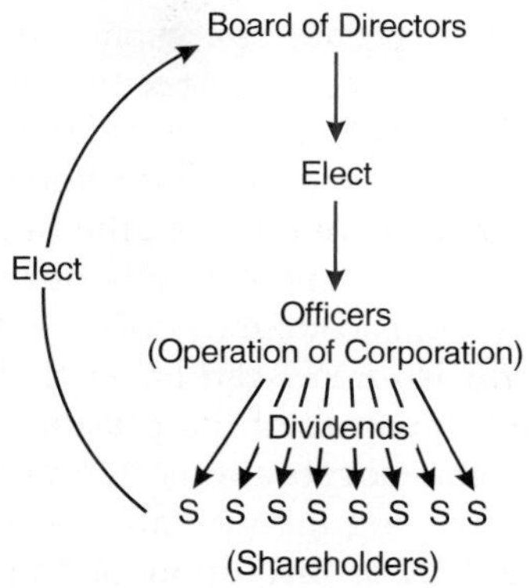

FORMS OF BUSINESS ORGANIZATION

Corporations

FIGURE 3-2 Corporate Organization

Creation.   A corporation is created upon filing of the charter with the office of the secretary of state, and paying the statutory filing fee. The corporation's charter, though fairly general, requires certain disclosures, such as the amount of capital funds (e.g., $1,000) in services performed, money, or assets; names of the incorporators, first officers, and directors; and the number of shares authorized to be distributed. After the corporation has been formed, the only requirement to maintain the corporate entity is to pay its corporate franchise tax each year.

If a corporation is formed in another state, it is deemed to be a "foreign" corporation. A foreign corporation may qualify to do business in another state by registering with the secretary of that state, designating a resident agent for service of process, and paying the applicable annual franchise fees similar to the ones that domestic corporations pay. This provides a means by which a corporation organized in one state (the vast majority of major corporations are organized under the laws of the State of Delaware) can do business in another state and not necessarily have to be organized under the laws of that state.

Although creation of a corporation may appear to be deceptively simple, it is important to realize that this normally requires the services of an attorney who is experienced in corporation law. There are additional statutory requirements for shareholders' and directors' meetings, minutes to be kept, bylaws, and other ancillary documents and functions required by law but which are not part of the simple filing of the corporate charter. These additional requirements, along with others involving corporate ownership (particularly in the field of real estate), require the expertise of individuals well-versed in the areas of corporate and real estate law.

Corporate Real Estate.   Since all aspects of corporations are so carefully controlled by statute, it is only logical that the ownership and management of corporate real estate are also controlled by statute. Corporations are given the specific power to purchase and acquire real property, as well as the specific statutory power to sell same. However, there is a significant difference between selling property and assets of a corporation in the regular course of business, and the sale of all, or substantially all, of the corporation's assets. Sales in the regular course of business (a real estate development company, for instance) can effect the conveyance of real estate simply by the signature of the president, vice president, or attorney-in-fact of the corporation. Although not necessarily required, a deed conveying a corporation's real property should also be accompanied by a resolution of the board of directors authorizing said sale, although the conveyance may be achieved without the resolution under certain conditions. If the sale of the real estate consists of substantially all of the assets of the corporation, however, ratification by a substantial majority (e.g., two-thirds or three-fourths) of the shareholders is required before such conveyance can be made.

Additionally, several miscellaneous corporate real estate ownership statutes exist in most states. For instance, a corporation cannot purchase real estate unless its ownership is necessary to enable the corporation to do business in that state (or to secure a debt in due course of business, as in buying land at a foreclosure sale to protect its interest). Time limits are usually placed on land ownership not held for this purpose.

The reason for these rules is that they make the creation of real estate-related monopolies less likely. Since most corporations are created to last forever, they theoretically involve "perpetual" ownership of real estate. Such perpetual ownership has the capacity to impede social progress, and so historically such ownership has not met with judicial favor. Furthermore, statutes usually do not permit private corporations to acquire land by purchase, lease, or otherwise when their stated main purpose is the acquisition and ownership of real estate. However, a blanket exception often exists for land located inside incorporated cities.

At the same time, it is clear that corporate real estate ownership has substantially expanded in recent years. Moreover, it can readily be concluded that prohibitions against corporate real estate ownership have not been enforced in most states. Since state attorneys general usually have the responsibility to enforce these laws, presumably they have not encountered situations in which corporate ownership of real estate is against the public interest.

Liabilities.   Since the corporation owns all property and conducts all business in its own name, the shareholders are not personally liable for corporate debts and obligations. This holds true as long as all statutory requirements are complied with, no fraud exists, and corporate business affairs and/or assets are not intermingled with the business and personal affairs of individual shareholders. This "shield" between the corporation and its shareholders also prevents a corporation from being held liable for shareholders' personal obligations. In many small business corporations, however, major shareholders may be required to personally cosign corporate notes as a condition of a loan. To this extent, the corporate form of business does not provide unlimited protection against liability if the corporation should be unable to repay the cosigned loan.

Advantages of Corporate Ownership. The advantages of doing business as a corporation vary, depending on the objectives of the shareholders and the nature and size of the business. For small, closely held businesses, recent research suggests three primary advantages: (1) facilitation of family estate planning, (2) lowering of income taxes, and (3) limited liability. Since cosigning requirements may largely negate the limitation on liability, it may be of less importance in small, closely held corporations.

Although different shareholder circumstances and objectives may lead to different results, several estate-planning possibilities work well when the family business is under corporate ownership. The first reason is that one is able to *maintain control* of the business (51% of the voting stock) while decreasing the taxable value of one's estate via gifts of minority stock interests. A second reason is that fractional ownership interest may be discounted below fair market value for estate tax purposes. A third reason is to pass future appreciation in corporate asset valuation to the next generation free of estate and inheritance taxes via the judicious use of common and preferred stock and lifetime gifts of the latter to heirs. Corporations also have superior pension and retirement plan opportunities.

Disadvantages of Corporate Ownership. It has often been stated that the corporate ownership of real estate is not a desirable form of ownership because of the technical problems that result through the corporate tax laws and the structures of organization within the corporation itself.

One of the biggest drawbacks of corporate ownership is the problem of double taxation. Income from real estate, profits from tax-free exchanges, capital gains benefits, and depreciation benefits—all normally considered attributable to real estate tax-shelter techniques—are benefits accrued on behalf of the corporation, not on behalf of the shareholders. Therefore, the corporation gets the extra tax benefits and tax shelter, not the shareholders. To further complicate matters, all income of the corporation is taxed twice if it is distributed to the shareholders. The corporation is taxed once on its real estate income. Then, if there are any excess profits to be distributed to the shareholders, these profits are distributed in the form of dividends, which are taxed a second time and are reflected on the shareholder's individual income tax return. Therefore, as a tax shelter, corporations are generally not considered the best form of ownership for real estate purposes.

Further problems in corporate ownership result from the technical requirements of state law pertaining to corporate ownership, distribution of securities, and disclosure to shareholders, as well as the requirements of other statutes pertaining to shareholders' and directors' obligations that are peculiar to corporate law.

A third difficulty of corporate ownership, particularly if the corporation is a large one, involves the infrastructure of the corporation itself. For example, it is not always clear to outsiders as to who has the authority to negotiate contracts, attend closings, and sign papers on behalf of the corporation. There has been further concern over the fact that it takes too much time for a corporation to operate from the initial negotiations between parties to the final ratification by shareholders and directors, plus the never-ending complications that "committees" create in the corporate process. A number of theories contend that corporations, as owners and managers of real estate, can never operate as fast as individuals or partnerships, and therefore they are not one of the better methods of owning, acquiring, and developing real estate. These theories are based on the assumption that decisions cannot be made quickly enough to satisfy the real estate market. It should be pointed out, however, that a number of extremely large corporations own, operate, and develop real estate very profitably because of the corporation's strength and stability, qualities that generally are not affected by the cyclical tendencies normally incident to the real estate industry as a whole.

Subchapter S Corporations

For many years the Internal Revenue Code has recognized an ownership called a subchapter S corporation. Basically, a subchapter S corporation is a recognized corporation under state statutes, but for income tax purposes it is treated similarly to a partnership. The income and losses for the corporation in any given year pass directly through to the shareholders, and therefore there is no "double taxation" disadvantage which the law recognizes in regular corporations.

Federal legislation passed in 1996 (it became effective January 1, 1997) significantly expanded a person's eligibility to use a subchapter S corporation, so that these corporations may become a more popular vehicle for real estate investment. In general, a small business corporation can elect subchapter S status under Section 1362(a)(1) of the Internal Revenue Code by unanimous vote of all of its shareholders. It may have only one class of stock, although the law does provide for differences in voting rights. Therefore, that one class of nonvoting stock could provide a situation similar to that of limited partnerships, where all partners are entitled to a share of the profits but their ability to manage the business entity is limited. If a person becomes a shareholder after the election is filed, his consent is not required unless he owns more than 50% of the corporation's stock.

There are some limitations, however. It must be a domestic corporation (not incorporated in another state). There can be no more than 75 shareholders permitted in the corporation and sub-chapter S status will terminate if 25% of the corporation's income is from passive sources for three consecutive years. There are also special rules concerning the pass-through of income and capital gains and losses. As a rule, ordinary losses cannot pass through to a shareholder to the extent that they exceed his basis in the stock; however, he is allowed to carry them forward indefinitely to create a tax deduction in future years.

In short, the new legislation appears to create the best of both worlds, and an investor can insulate himself from liability as a corporate shareholder but can take advantage of the tax benefits, which are similar to those of a partnership, as long as the corporation remains reasonably active and doesn't concentrate its income on passive sources. If one is anticipating this method of holding property, however, it is imperative that he seek competent legal and tax advice to help the corporation avoid some of the peculiar pitfalls of the application of corporate statutes, as well as to help it cope with the unique requirements of the Internal Revenue Code as they apply to subchapter S corporations.

Partnerships A partnership is generally defined as "an association of two or more persons to carry on as co-owners a business for profit." There are three basic partnership entities available: general partnerships, joint ventures, and limited partnerships. There has been a widespread adoption of the Uniform Partnership Act and the Uniform Limited Partnership Act, creating a great similarity in partnership law in almost all states.

General Partnership. By 1997, all states had adopted the Uniform Partnership Act (see Table 3-1). It contains comprehensive provisions relating to the creation, operation, and dissolution of general partnerships. A general partnership is one in which all partners are jointly and severally (individually) liable for partnership obligations. Where one partner is required to pay an entire partnership obligation, he has a "right of contribution" under which other partners can be forced to pay their proportional share of the obligation.

Creation. There are no specific statutory guidelines necessary for the creation of a partnership; a written or oral agreement is not necessarily essential. A partnership is normally inferred when there is a clear intention to create a partnership, and when the partners in fact have a co-ownership with the intention of sharing profits or losses on a particular business venture. Any estate in real property may be acquired in the partnership name or the names of individual partners and any property bought by the partnership or acquired by the partnership, by purchase or otherwise, is considered partnership property. Once so acquired, the estate can be conveyed only in the partnership name. As a matter of form, the purchase or conveyance of partnership property generally includes the name of the partnership and then lists each of the partners individually, so that there is no mistake as to who is liable for the partnership's debts or obligations.

Once it has been determined that a partnership has been created, the law tends to support the maintenance and continuity of that partnership. It is important to understand that each partner actually gets three distinct rights:

1. His rights in *specific partnership property,*
2. His *interest in the partnership,*
3. His *right to participate in the management* of that partnership.

Of these three interests, the only one that may be considered community property (and therefore subject to a spouse's interest) is the partner's interest in the partnership. A partner's rights to specific partnership property and his right to management in the partnership are separate property and cannot be conveyed or assigned without the consent of all the members of the partnership. Similarly, a person cannot become a partner in a partnership without the consent of all the other partners.

Partnership law creates a very high duty of care and trust that each partner owes to the other partners. This relationship of trust is termed a *fiduciary* relationship. Each partner is an agent for the whole partnership and can bind the partnership to any obligations incurred in the usual course of business. For instance, where title to real property is in the partnership name, any single partner may convey title to such property by conveyance executed in the partnership name. Similarly, a single partner can incur a partnership debt or other contractual obligation without the joinder of the other partners.

Although some of these conditions may seem rather onerous, the basic reason for this regulation and total obligation of the partners revolves around the obligations and liabilities to which the partners are bound, pursuant to the provisions of the Uniform Partnership Act. Since every act of the partner for carrying on, in the usual way, the business of the partnership binds the partner-

ship totally, each of the partners is liable jointly and severally; that
is, the partnership is liable and each of the partners is liable individually for the entire obligation of the partnership. The partnership is bound by the partners' acts, even if they are wrongful, and
even if one of the partner's acts amounts to a breach of trust
between the partners.

Advantages.   The advantages of a partnership are basically the
pooling of resources and liabilities so that, at least theoretically, no
one partner bears the brunt of all the losses and all partners share
in their respective areas of expertise. Another advantage is that all
losses to the partnership, as well as all profits, are passed through
directly to each of the partners individually. Although the partnership itself is required to file a federal tax return, the payment of
all taxes or deduction of all losses is proportionately applicable to
the individual partners' tax returns. This is in contrast to corporate
or trust ownership, where there are less advantageous elements of
taxation. Since real estate is given special tax benefits to owners
(depreciation allowances, capital gains tax treatment, tax-free
exchange, and installment sale benefits), it is sometimes very
important for tax purposes that these losses and deductions be
able to pass to the individual purchasers rather than to an ownership entity, which provides no direct benefits to the individual's
tax return.

Joint Venture.   A joint venture is a partnership, sometimes more
appropriately called a *joint adventure.* This is a particular type of
partnership where two or more partners jointly pursue a specified
project. They are not simply in business for a profit, as is the typical definition of partnerships as a whole. Rather, they are in business for profit from a particular project. The more typical joint venture situations involve two partners, one of which is a financial
partner, the other of which is a managing partner. The financial
partner is generally a lending institution, insurance company, or
other financially strong investment group. The managing partner
is generally a very experienced developer who has had a long
track record of building certain types of projects. The financial
partner (company or institution) normally visualizes a chance for
more profits than simply the return on its investment capital if it
owns half of the project. The developer visualizes no financing
worries or funding problems while the project proceeds to final
completion. Both partners, of course, have mutual dependencies
on each other by sharing risks, but they also have those certain
areas of expertise that lower those risks. Joint ventures are usually
very sophisticated transactions, although they can be as small as

two brokers agreeing to work together and share a commission on a particular sale. Legally, a joint venture generally is governed by the same rules as partnerships, although one partner cannot bind the other except on that one project.

Limited Partnerships. Limited partnerships have been a very effective tool for real estate ownership and investment. They have been of such long-standing acceptance that this method is considered by many professionals to be one of the more stable means of ownership, as well as one of the most beneficial. The law in this area is reasonably well settled and is generally understood by most investors, and therefore has been effectively utilized in very large types of investments, some of which have been syndicated using large numbers of investors and have been offered for sale by large stock brokerage firms.

Forty-five states have adopted the Uniform Limited Partnership Act (see Table 3-1). A limited partnership is statutorily defined as a partnership formed by two or more persons under the provisions of the Act and having as members one or more *general partners* and one or more *limited partners.* The limited partners, as such, are a separate class of partners and are not bound by the obligations of the partnership to third parties as long as the formalities of the limited partnership agreement and applicable statutes are complied with.

Creation. The creation of a limited partnership involves a certain amount of formality and structure. Two of the instruments needed to properly create a limited partnership are the *certificate of limited partnership* and the *limited partnership agreement.*

There must be a *certificate of limited partnership* filed with the secretary of state that discloses the nature of the business, the name of the partnership, the principal place of business of the partnership, who the partners are, the rights of the limited partners as to assignment, admission of additional limited partners, etc. This type of disclosure allows a private investor, or creditor, to look into the organization of the partnership and determine who the partners are before making any decisions to loan money to or to invest in the limited partnership. Since these disclosures are required, much secrecy and questionable dealings by a limited partnership are eliminated. All of the information contained in the certificate of limited partnership generally is available via a phone call to the secretary of state's office.

The certificate of limited partnership is usually a condensation of the information and obligations contained in another instrument, the *limited partnership agreement.* This agreement, signed by all of the general and limited partners, sets out the obligations of each of the partners. The agreement typically sets out in greater detail the information contained in the certificate of limited partnership. It also specifies the obligations of each partner, events of default, dissolution procedures, and other pertinent information relating to the internal structure and operation of the limited partnership. An investor is well-advised to have his attorney review all such documents prior to signing them.

Liabilities. One of the more attractive aspects of ownership by limited partnership is the limited liability it provides for the limited partners. The general partner in a limited partnership has all the liabilities of the partner in a general partnership, that is, joint, several, and total. The limited partners, however, are not bound by any of the obligations of the partnership, and none of the limited partner's assets are considered liable for partnership debts or liabilities. In theory, the only risk the limited partner takes is the loss of his contribution. However, it should not be overlooked that the limited partner does have statutory liability to the partnership for the difference between his contribution as made and any unpaid contribution that he agreed to make in the future. So where a limited partner may not be liable to third-party creditors, he may be personally liable (both by statute and by the terms of the limited partnership agreement) to his other partners for his contributions to the partnership. Limited partners, because of the nature of their contribution, are sometimes given preferential returns on their contribution. However, they cannot get a return on their investment until *all of* the obligations of the partnership have been met. The limited partnership's interest is generally assignable, subject to the restrictions in the limited partnership agreement and the certificate of limited partnership.

Advantages. The advantages of a limited partnership are self-explanatory. The main advantage, of course, is the limited liabilities of the limited partners as far as business obligations of the partnership to third parties are concerned. As stated previously, the limited partner's liability to a third party is limited to his contribution to the partnership and the obligations for additional contribution, but he may also have a personal liability to the other partners for his contributions.

Tax benefits are, of course, an additional advantage to limited partnerships. Partnerships, as stated previously, are not taxed as a partnership, but the profits are normally passed through to the individual partners, who get the benefits of whatever tax savings, investment credit, or depreciation benefits accrue to the partnership. Therefore, at least in theory, the limited partner gets all the benefits of tax-sheltered real estate investments with virtually no liability except for his contribution to the partnership.

Disadvantages. The main disadvantage to a limited partnership is that there is total reliance by the limited partners on the expertise and management capabilities of the general partner. Although the general partner enjoys joint, several, and total liability, one normally expects that the general partner selected will be one of prudent and capable past experience. There have been recent attempts to make the general partner a corporation, thereby limiting the liability of the general partner as well as that of the limited partners. Although this is not in itself illegal, it should be understood that certain tax consequences may arise as a result of this type of organization. The Internal Revenue Service sometimes feels that if the general partner is a corporation, the limited partners are, in effect, shareholders rather than limited partners. The Internal Revenue Service, then, would look on the partnership as a corporation that would be taxed as a corporation rather than as a limited partnership. The guidelines and criteria of the Internal Revenue Service can sometimes be very technical, and one's accountant should always be consulted when considering this type of investment.

A second disadvantage revolves around the Securities and Exchange Commission. Limited partnerships, being investments, can be considered to be securities, and, if so, must be filed either with the state securities board or with the Securities and Exchange Commission. Filing is always a requirement unless the limited partnership falls under one of the two basic exemptions provided by the Securities and Exchange Act or under a single exemption provided by the state securities board. The scope of these exemptions will be discussed in Chapter 17, "Regulation of Real Estate."

A third disadvantage is that in filing a certificate of limited partnership, there is a certain amount of disclosure of personal business that an individual may not want the public to know. There are times when a private investor may prefer not to have his interest known to the public when making real estate investments. If this is the case, limited partnerships may not be the most effective tool of investment.

In addition to the required disclosures, certain costs are involved in forming limited partnerships. To file the certificate of limited partnership with the secretary of state, the law provides that you might pay, for example, 1/2% of the amount of cash contributed by each limited partner, as well as of his additional contributions. This may involve a substantial amount of money, although most states put minimum and maximum cash limits to file the certificate of limited partnership.

The last disadvantage to be discussed is one important to all investors and brokers anticipating this type of investment: control. It is statutorily provided that only general partners are allowed to take part in the control of the business. If any limited partner assumes the position of taking control of the business or taking part in any significant management of the partnership, he will become a general partner and liable as a general partner. This principle applies even though the limited partner may assume such control in good faith and in the best interest of the partnership. Therefore, when a client or investor is interested in taking part in the business of the limited partnership, he may be well advised to keep his involvement to a minimum or he may be construed as a general partner.

Limited Liability Partnership

Most states have amended their statutes to provide for the creation of limited liability partnerships. A partner in a registered limited liability partnership is not individually liable for debts and obligations of the partnership arising from errors, omissions, negligence, incompetence, or malfeasance committed in the course of partnership business by another partner, or a representative of the partnership, not working under the supervision or direction of the first partner at the time the errors, omissions, negligence, incompetence, or malfeasance occurred, unless the first partner directly involved had knowledge of the misconduct at the time of the occurrence.

To register a limited liability partnership, the partnership must file an application with the secretary of state stating the name of the partnership, the address of its principal place of business, the number of partners, and a brief statement of the business in which the partnership engages. The registered limited liability partnership's name must contain the words "registered limited liability partnership" or the abbreviation "L.L.P. " as the last words or letters of its name. The registered limited liability partnership must carry a specified amount of liability insurance of the kind that is designated to cover the kinds of errors, omissions, negligence, incompetence, or malfeasance for which liability is limited.

Limited Liability Company

There has been legitimate, and probably justified, concern over liabilities of defendants in a business environment. One understands that if a person is harmed, there should be an ability to recover from the wrongdoer. Yet many juries are awarding significant sums of money, and pursuing personal liability for officers and directors of corporations because of their duties of care in the business entity (including real estate brokers!).

By 1997, all state legislatures had adopted legislation of historical significance, authorizing limited liability companies. There will be a lot of case law and perhaps amendments to the statutes forthcoming in the next few years.

Creation.   In general, any natural person of 18 years of age or older can act as organizer of a limited liability company by signing the articles of organization of the company and giving a copy of the articles to the secretary of state. The articles of organization generally include:

1. The name of the limited liability company,
2. The period of duration, which may not exceed 30 years from the date of filing with the secretary of state,
3. The purpose for which the limited liability company is organized (which may include any or all lawful business),
4. The address of the principal place of business and the name of the initial registered agent in the state,
5. The names of the managers or members who are to manage the company.

The secretary of state then issues a certificate of organization, and the existence of the limited liability company begins at that time.

In general terms, a member or manager of a limited liability company is not liable for debts, obligations, or liabilities of the company. A membership interest is considered to be personal property and the member has no interest in specific limited liability company property.

Operations of a Limited Liability Company.   Most states require that the limited liability company name must include the word "Limited" or the abbreviation "Ltd." or "L.L.C." It must maintain the registered office and registered agent (similar to a corporation). All real or personal property owned or purchased by the limited liability company shall be held and owned, and the conveyance shall be made, in the name of the company. All instruments and documents providing for the acquisition, mortgage, or disposition of the limited liability company shall be valid and binding upon the company if they are executed by one or more persons acting as manager or member (if the management of the company is retained by the members).

Note that limited liability companies are neither corporations, partnerships, nor limited partnerships. They are a totally new theory of ownership and, as stated previously, there is a lot of law yet to be made in this area.

Most limited liability statutes clearly permit professional limited liability companies to be used by architects, attorneys, doctors, accountants, and certain other professionals.

OWNERSHIP BY TRUSTS

There are three major types of trust ownership: (1) *testamentary* or *inter vivos trusts*, (2) *land trusts*, and (3) *real estate investment trusts.*

Organization

As in corporate ownership, we must understand the basics of how a trust form of ownership operates before going into each of the individual types of trusts. Trusts generally have a *trustor*, sometimes called a *settlor*, who establishes the trust. Ownership and control of the trust are held by the *trustee*, who holds the trust in name only for the true owners, the *beneficiaries* of the trust. Normally, once a trust has been established by the trustor, it is usually irrevocable (and if irrevocable, it must be set out in the trust instrument). Title stays in the name of the trustee until the assets of the trust (called the *corpus*) are ultimately distributed to the beneficiaries. The income from the trust can be distributed to the beneficiaries at varying intervals depending on the trust instrument. Trusts per se do not pay taxes if the income is distributed to the beneficiaries, because the income is taxed as it is distributed to the beneficiaries. When the corpus of the trust and other undistributed income vest in the beneficiaries, however, the entire amount is taxed at that time, and this tax can be substantial. Figure 3-3 may help explain how the trust form of ownership generally operates.

According to the laws of most states, the trustee individually is not liable for debts or obligations of the trust. As in corporate ownership, however, when a third party deals with a person who operates as a trustee, such party is bound by law to understand that the trust is not individually liable under most circumstances. The only liability is to the assets of the trust, although the trustee has a fiduciary obligation to administer the trust properly, and he or she can be held personally liable to the beneficiaries for not protecting the beneficiaries' respective interests.

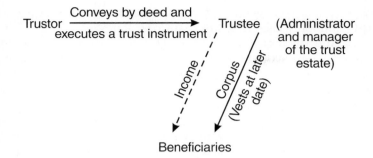

FIGURE 3-3   Trust Organization

Testamentary and *inter vivos* trusts are normally trusts set up for the benefit of the beneficiaries for estate purposes of the trustor. The Rule against Perpetuities (Chapter 2) dictates that the period that the trust may exist is limited to approximately 21 years after the death of the trustor at the time the trust was created, plus any actual period of gestation (this period is typically 21 years, plus nine months after the death of the trustor). If the beneficiaries are children or grandchildren of the trustor, the trustor generally sets up the estate in a trust so that only the income will be taxed, and the income and benefits of that trust will be managed professionally by a bank trust department or by some other responsible entity. The corpus of the estate will vest in the settlor's grandchildren (probably at a lower tax rate, depending on their incomes when it vests) and will provide for their well-being, expenses, and usual standard of living.

Testamentary and Inter Vivos Trusts

As previously discussed, real estate held by a trustee in this capacity is subject to very high fiduciary obligations between the trustee and beneficiaries. The only personal liability involved is that of the trustee to the beneficiaries, and not to third-party creditors. If a trustee has mismanaged the assets or acted in bad faith, the beneficiaries have a cause of action against the trustee. Real estate conveyed, sold, mortgaged, or encumbered on the part of the trustee, therefore, must be done only in good faith and in the exercise of sound business judgment. The trustee binds the assets of the trust for whatever obligations may be incurred.

A second type of trust becoming increasingly popular is the land trust. It is not ordinarily used as a principal part of an estate plan, but rather is set up solely as a real estate ownership entity. A land trust is sometimes referred to as an "Illinois land trust" (see

Land Trusts

below), and is somewhat analogous to the Massachusetts business trust commonly used in many East Coast states.

Land trusts typically involve real estate syndications. The syndicator may become the trustee (or the trustee may hire him as a property manager), and the other investors are the beneficiaries. Land trust agreements must be carefully drawn and must fully set out the rights and liabilities of all parties.

The original Illinois land trust was quite simple. Under it the trustee's only duty was to convey title when the land was sold. In some states this arrangement was interpreted as not creating a trust at all because one basic trust requirement is that a trustee must have (periodic) active duties to perform. This is a primary reason why the laws enabling the use of land trusts are not well settled in some states.

However, where favorable interpretations exist, land trusts enjoy increasing popularity. Their advantages include anonymity for investors, limited liability, continuous marketability, and no initial public registration costs.

Real Estate Investment Trusts

The real estate investment trust was specifically provided for by federal statute in the form of an amendment to the Internal Revenue Code. The new provision enables the ownership and development of large real estate interests by a trust for the benefit of large numbers of investors while maintaining the tax benefits of real estate ownership for each investor. In these cases, the promoter or developer is the trustor, and the assets of the trust are the investors' cash. The trust is generally administered by a board of trustees (who are professional real estate consultants), and the beneficiaries are, of course, the investors.

Real estate investment trusts for a number of years prospered very heavily in the real estate investment market and sold shares as over-the-counter stocks or were registered on the New York Stock Exchange or American Stock Exchange. This form of real estate ownership encouraged the small investor to invest small amounts of money in very large projects. Unlike other investments on the stock market, however, the small investor could enjoy all the tax shelter benefits of real estate ownership in addition to the income from the project. In theory, this turned out to be one of the true booms in the real estate industry because it provided a large amount of capital and equity dollars to buy and develop projects from private sources (small individual investors). However, in the early to middle 1970s, a number of mismanagement, overextension, and negligence problems arose as a result of the boom in real estate investment. This caused a decline in real estate investment trusts. Other reasons for the decline are unusually complicated because they involve not only the technicalities of real estate law, but also technicalities pursuant to stock exchange registration, disclosures required by the Securities and Exchange Commission, and certain theories of economics and finance. However, the basic premises under which real estate investment trusts were originally formed are still good, and these trusts will probably become strong once again, perhaps under a little more strict federal regulation. These requirements, coupled with the additional requirements of the Internal Revenue Service and the Securities and Exchange Commission, make this a relatively complicated method of real estate ownership. However, its effectiveness should not be underestimated.

A chart showing the various methods of ownership is shown in Figure 3-4.

SYNDICATIONS

Group investments in real estate are referred to as *syndications.* They may be created under any form of ownership except ownership in severalty.

There are several economic reasons contributing to the popularity of real estate syndications. First, they may represent profitable ventures which many individual investors alone would not have the financial capacity to handle. Second, by investing in several syndications rather than in one real estate tract, an investor can "diversify his investment portfolio" and can minimize his financial risks. Third, the syndicator (the person organizing and marketing the real estate syndication) may hire or provide management expertise that the individual investor does not have. Finally, each investor may be able to contribute some skills to the "ripening," development, and sale of the property (e.g., architects, lawyers, engineers, etc.), thereby permitting out-of-pocket costs to be minimized.

Different investors have different reasons for investing and varying concerns about the investment itself. However, research has disclosed that most investors have one or more of three principal objectives in mind when they select a legal entity for their form of ownership:

1. Investors are interested in keeping the title *marketable* at all times. In particular, they do not want the death or divorce of a fellow investor to tie up the title to such an extent that a profitable sale cannot be made in a timely manner.
2. Investors are interested in protecting their other assets and

keeping them intact in case this investment turns sour. Stated alternatively, investors often select a form of ownership that provides *limited liability.*

Where a particular form of ownership does not provide limited liability, investors may partially protect other assets through the use of nonrecourse financing. This technique provides limited liability for real estate debt, but not for third-party injuries suffered while on the real estate (although insurance policies can protect against the latter). Moreover, nonrecourse financing may also create income tax liabilities when one walks away from a deal. So clearly nonrecourse financing is not always a perfect substitute for limited liability.

3. Finally, many investors prefer real estate investments with *income tax-shelter* potential. Traditionally, an income tax shelter refers to an investment that (1) provides currently deductible losses that can be set off against ordinary income on the investor's personal income tax return, and (2) yields a long-term capital gain upon disposition.

Of course, no one wants to suffer a real economic loss; so paper losses in the form of depreciation deductions are one of the tax-sheltering attractions of real estate. Tax sheltering is possible any time deductible losses are passed through from the legal entity owning the real estate to the individual investor to be reported on his personal income tax return.

Tax sheltering is important only if an investor has income from other sources from which deductions may be subtracted. For example, a $1 deduction can save an investor anywhere from nothing (when he has no other income to deduct it from) to 70 cents (when he is in the 70% tax bracket). Clearly it is of greater importance to those with high incomes than to those with low incomes.

Because of the importance of these three investment objectives, our discussion of the various forms of real estate ownership includes the capacity of each form to satisfy these objectives (see Table 3-2).

SUMMARY   Ownership of real estate must always be vested in a specific, identifiable legal entity. This entity may be sole ownership, tenancy in common, joint tenancy, tenancy by entireties, general partnership, joint venture, limited partnership, regular corporation, subchapter

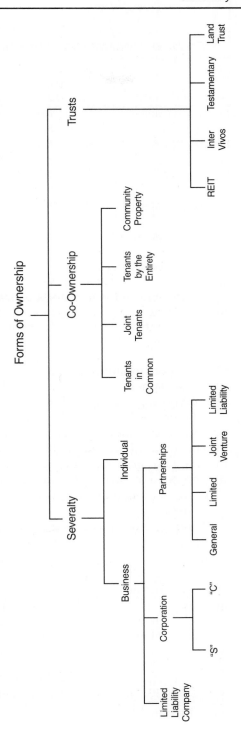

FIGURE 3-4   Real Estate Ownership

TABLE 3-2
Forms of Ownership and Selected Investment Criteria

Form of Ownership	Marketability in case of Death	Divorce	Limited Liability	Tax Shelter	Other Comments
Tenancy in common	No	No	No	Yes	
Joint tenancy	Yes	No	No	Yes	
Tenancy by entireties	Yes	No	No	Yes	
Regular corporation	Yes	Yes	Yes	No	
Subchapter S corporation	Yes	Yes	Yes	Yes	Limit of 75 investors
General partnership (joint venture)	?	?	No	Yes	
Limited partnership	Yes	Yes	Yes	Yes	
Regular trust	Yes	Yes	Yes	?	Provides investor anonymity
Land trust	Yes	Yes	Yes	?	
Real estate investment trust	Yes	Yes	Yes	Yes	

S corporation, testamentary or *inter vivos* trust, land trust, or real estate investment trust. Each may be an appropriate choice, depending on the circumstances and investor objectives.

Alternative forms of ownership may be evaluated for their capacity to provide desired business operating characteristics or investment attributes, or both. Although difficult to measure, important business operating attributes include the degree of control possessed by owners; the ease and efficiency in creating, operating, and terminating the business; business continuity; and differing state and federal income tax treatment.

Three specific objectives are often sought by investors when selecting a real estate ownership entity: continuous marketability of title, limited liability, and income tax-sheltering opportunities.

The tenancy in common form of co-ownership offers tax sheltering but does not insulate other assets from liability if the investment should go sour. Further, it does not provide continuous marketability when a co-owner dies or gets divorced. Because the ownership interest of a co-owner is inheritable by his heirs, this co-ownership form may be useful when real estate is held by business associates.

Joint tenancies work best when the co-owners are all members of the same family. This is because the right of survivorship automatically transfers a deceased co-owner's interest to the surviving joint tenants. The investment attributes of joint tenancies are quite similar to those of a tenancy in common, except that a co-owner's death is less disruptive with respect to continuous marketability.

The tenancy by entireties also is characterized by a right of survivorship but can only be held by a married couple. Some states have discontinued or limited this co-ownership form because tenancy by entireties property often cannot be attached to satisfy debts owed to separate creditors of either spouse.

All states have specific rules affecting corporate ownership and operation of real estate. Since a corporation owns the real estate and the shareholders own the corporation, conceptually investors may think of this an "indirect" ownership. In turn, this effectively limits a shareholder/investor's liability for corporate obligations, and vice versa. Furthermore, a corporation does not die or get divorced, so continuous marketability is maintained. However, the corporation itself is a tax-paying entity, so ordinary losses and long-term capital gains cannot be passed through to shareholders. Thus, corporations do not facilitate tax-shelter investments, but they may assist in minimizing taxes on income generated by an ongoing business.

Subchapter S corporations are named after a specific subchapter in the Internal Revenue Code. They are identical to regular corporations except they are taxed as partnerships. This means they pay no taxes themselves, but rather all income and/or losses are reported by corporate shareholders and/or employees. They offer investors continuous marketability, limited liability, and tax-shelter potential. However, they do have several disadvantages, including an upper limit of 75 shareholders.

Testamentary and *inter vivos* (lifetime) trusts are occasionally used in real estate syndications, but they are taxed as regular corporations. In those states where they have been authorized, land trusts are increasing in popularity. On the other hand, real estate investment trusts are less popular than in the early seventies, and are not a strong economic force in today's market.

General partnerships do not provide the limitation on liability sought by many investors. However, they generally do provide both continuous marketability and tax-shelter opportunities. A joint venture is identical to a general partnership with respect to its investment characteristics.

Limited partnerships generally are the most popular form of ownership for real estate syndications. They provide continuous marketability, pass-through of income tax treatment, and limited liability to limited partners. As with all forms of ownership, sound legal advice is essential if the desired results are to be achieved.

Eight states follow community property rules, which generally take precedence over other ownership rules. In essence, the community property rules discussed in Chapter 2 may modify the discussion found here.

DISCUSSION
QUESTIONS

1. Continuous marketability of title, limited liability, and income tax shelter are generally considered the three most important considerations in selecting an optimal investment entity. What other considerations are important to you as an investor?

2. If your primary concern is operating a real estate-based business (as opposed to a passive, long-term real estate investment), what are some major factors to consider when selecting a legal form of business organization?

3. Under what general circumstances would you prefer to use the tenancy in a common type of co-ownership? The joint tenancy? The tenancy by entireties?

4. If you have a large group of investors, is it possible to select a single form of co-ownership or business organization that will satisfy all of them?

4

Fixtures and Easements

Fixtures and easements each have one common characteristic that enables them to be discussed in the same chapter: They both involve rights that a third party may have in another owner's real estate. Fixtures involve the rights that a materialman, supplier, seller, or purchaser may have in certain appliances or appurtenances to one's real estate. Easements, on the other hand, involve the rights of a third party to the use of an access across another individual's real estate.

There is a large number of different laws applicable to the concept of fixtures, making the exact meaning of the term "fixture" as used in every case difficult to define. A *fixture* has been defined by case law as an article or personalty that has been attached to the real estate so that it becomes real estate, *W.O. Co.* v. *Benjamin Franklin Corp.*, 562 F.2d 1339 (1st Cir., 1977). Statutorily, it has been determined that goods are "fixtures" when they become so related to particular real estate that an interest in them arises under the real estate law of the state in which the real estate is situated. See the Uniform Commercial Code, Section 9.313.

FIXTURES

The difficulty in the determination of fixtures results from the change in the nature of articles that are to become fixtures. For instance, a light fixture is very clearly an item of personalty (properly called *chattel*) that one may buy at a store that sells lights. However, once the fixture has been bolted into the ceiling and has been established as a part of the particular decor of a dining room, one might expect that it will become part of the real estate. Similar

Realty to Personalty—
Personalty to Realty

problems occur with drapes, certain types of shelving, carpeting, and many other objects that can be affixed to real estate in one form or another. On the other hand, there is an equal difficulty in determining the characteristics of items that are real estate and then become personalty. There are interesting applications of this concept in the oil and gas law, where the minerals are considered part of the real estate, but once they reach the wellhead or are extracted from the ground, they are considered personalty, to be sold by the owners as a nonreal estate item. Similarly, it is easy to envision a house being destroyed and several items of realty being converted for personal use and sold at auctions, garage sales, and even lumber and brick yards.

This problem can be further complicated by the fact that the conveyancing instruments utilized for realty and personalty are entirely different. Real estate is normally conveyed by the use of a deed, will, or other conveyancing instrument, whereas items of personalty are normally transferred by an instrument called a *bill of sale*. A copy of a bill of sale is shown in Figure 4-1.

For more confusion, additional complications can arise in fixtures depending on who is claiming an interest in those fixtures. Once it has been determined that an item is a fixture, real estate law applies, along with certain mechanics' and materialmen's liens, statutes, and certain laws relating to mortgages. If an item is not a fixture the Uniform Commercial Code (adopted by 49 of the 50 states), applies to rights of parties, and the real estate law does not. A party may also qualify to claim an interest in an item both as an item of realty and as an item of personalty. Therefore, the law of fixtures must include certain applications of mortgage law, real estate liens, and fixture filing provisions of the Uniform Commercial Code. It is through the interrelationships of these three areas of the law that one can determine who has the right to a particular item, after it has been determined whether or not that item is a fixture.'

Now that total confusion has set in, it is important to discuss the determination of a fixture and then attempt to untangle the problem of priorities once the concept of fixture is fully understood.

Determination of a Fixture

In most real estate sales, the key concern in the determination of a fixture generally involves a fact situation when a prospective purchaser is buying real estate, normally a home, and this purchaser expects certain items to remain with the real estate because he considers them to be fixtures. The homeowner, however, having installed a fixture, may fully expect to remove it and take it with

BILL OF SALE

THE STATE OF TEXAS §
§   KNOW ALL MEN BY THESE PRESENTS:
COUNTY OF HARRIS §

THAT I.M. Seller and wife, Happy Seller, of the County of Harris and State aforesaid, for and in consideration of the sum of Ten and No/100 Dollars ($10.00) to it in hand paid by N. Debted and wife, May B. Debted, the receipt of which is hereby acknowledged, have Bargained, Sold and Delivered, and by these presents do Bargain, Sell and Deliver, unto the said N. Debted and wife, May B. Debted of the County of Harris and State of Texas all of the following described personal property in Harris County, Texas, to-wit:

1)   One High Performance Central Air Conditioning Unit, Model No. 694, Serial No. SE3469R739

2)   Deluxe Woodburner One Freestanding Stove, Model No. 3, Serial No. WRS86543

FIGURE 4-1   Bill of Sale

And it does hereby bind themselves, their successors and assigns to forever Warrant and Defend the title to the aforesaid property unto the said N. Debted and wife, May B. Debted, their heirs and assigns, against the lawful claim or claims of any and all persons whomsoever.

EXECUTED this the 28th day of February, 19xx.

SELLER

_____

I.M. SELLER

_____

HAPPY SELLER

THE STATE OF TEXAS   §
                           §
COUNTY OF HARRIS   §

The foregoing instrument was acknowledged before me on this the 28th day of February, 19xx, by I.M. Seller and wife, Happy Seller.

_____

NOTARY PUBLIC, STATE OF TEXAS

FIGURE 4-1   *Bill of Sale Continued*

him to his new residence. It is at this point that we set the stage (a stage found in many home sales) to determine whether an item is a fixture. Inevitably, the criteria revolve around the situations as they occur, and the facts seem to differ in every case.

The basic criteria of fixture determination in most states were adopted from *Teaff* v. *Hewitt,* 1 Ohio St. 511 (1853), an 1853 Ohio case, which set them out as follows:

1. *Mode of annexation.* The first method of determining whether or not an item is a fixture is by the manner in which the article is attached to the real estate, *George* v. *Commercial Credit Corp.,* 440 F.2d 551 (7th Cir., 1971). It is easy to see that wallpaper, for instance, is attached to the real estate in such a manner that it is certainly meant to stay with the property when the property is sold. The same is generally true of shelves that have been built into the wall of the house. At the opposite end of the spectrum, however, we have pictures, hanging plants, swag lamps, and furniture. The questionable areas, of course, in this particular method can be quite large. Light bulbs, for instance, are certainly attached to the real estate but are easily removable, as are drapes, light switch plates, carpeting, and light fixtures that have been attached to the ceiling.

2. *Adaptation.* A second method for determining whether or not an article is a fixture depends on the character of the article and its adaptation to the real estate. It is certainly easy to determine that a lamp or freestanding stove would not have to be used in just one place; they could readily be removed and be used in another residence. However, these examples should be contrasted with custom-made drapes, custom-built bookcases, and even movable, matching kitchen counters, which have been made for a particular home. All of these items can easily be seen to be movable but probably would not have an equally effective use in another home.

   Therefore, adaptation, combined with the mode of annexation of the article, forms the basis for the third method, which is the intention of the parties.

3. *Intention.* The intention of the parties is, of course, the ultimate fact situation: What did each of the parties—the home purchaser and the homeowner—really intend to transfer when their earnest money contract was signed? The question of intention is inferable from the acts of the parties and the nature of the article, and incorporates the

first two methods—the mode of annexation and the adaptation to real estate—because all of these particular factors come into the minds of the purchaser and seller as they enter into their negotiations, *George* v. *Commercial Credit Corp., supra.*

In utilizing these three criteria, preference is given to the question of intention in deciding what constitutes a fixture. The question of intent is not a question of law but of fact, as created by the conduct of the parties. The intent should be clearly expressed in the earnest money contract. There can never be enough emphasis given to the care a real estate agent must utilize in representing either party in a contractual negotiation.

Alternatives to Intent, Adaptation, and Mode of Annexation Tests. Not all states follow the three-test combination of intent, adaptation, and mode of annexation. Three alternative fixture tests are sometimes used.

1. The *institutional test* has been adopted in Pennsylvania, Vermont, South Carolina, and a few other states, wherein items are fixtures if they are necessary to the enjoyment of the land. Like intent, this becomes a question of factual interpretation and has not resulted in decisions much different from those found in states following the previously discussed three-test combination.

2. Louisiana has adopted the *immovables by destination theory,* wherein it must be determined whether an item was to be part of the real estate upon its final annexation to the realty, La. Civ. Code Arts. 468, 469. Again, similar fixture determinations are found under this test.

3. *Removal without material injury* is still another fixture test used in most states by creditors, contractors, material suppliers, mortgagors, and sellers. This test classifies an item as a fixture if its removal will cause material damage to the building, *First National Bank* v. *Whirlpool,* 517 S.W.2d 262 (Tex. 1974), and Uniform Commercial Code, Section 9.313(l)(A). If the item can be removed without material damage, it may be subject to prior claims of materialmen, suppliers, and vendors of that particular fixture. The important point is that even if the real estate buyer and seller fully agree (intend) that an item is a fixture, it still may be classified as a chattel and be subject to prior existing security interests.

To help explain the conflict that may be created by installing the fixture, it must be understood that when personalty (chattel) is purchased on credit, the seller of that item may protect his interest in it by recording his lien interest in that chattel pursuant to the statutes contained in the Uniform Commercial Code. These liens are commonly called UCC liens (named after the Uniform Commercial Code) and "chattel mortgage" liens. For instance, if a homeowner purchased a new central air conditioning unit and did not pay cash for same, the seller of that unit may wish to reflect that he still has an interest in the air conditioning unit because it has not been fully paid for. As the item is purchased, the purchaser would sign a promissory note for payment, a security agreement (a copy of which is shown in Figure 4-2), and two financing statements (the financing statements are commonly called *UCC-1 forms*). The seller would record his interest in that chattel by filing the financing statements or security agreement in two places: (1) in the UCC lien records in the county clerk's office in the county of the purchaser's residence, and (2) in the office of the secretary of state. When a UCC lien has been properly recorded, it is considered to be "perfected," and the public is legally on notice of that vendor's interest in the air conditioning unit. A copy of the UCC-1 Financing Statement is shown in Figure 4-3. A subsequent purchaser, for his own protection, is supposed to search the records of the county and determine that no such liens exist against the real estate he is about to purchase.

When it is anticipated that the collateral will be affixed to real estate, there are additional provisions for filing the UCC liens in the fixture records of the county in which the real estate is located, as well as in the office of the secretary of state. This type of lien is also referred to as a *UCC lien,* and its recordation is termed a *fixture filing.* A copy of a UCC-1 Financing Statement for fixtures is shown in Figure 4-4.

It has long been determined under the Uniform Commercial Code that a perfected security interest in fixtures has a priority over the conflicting interest of an encumbrance or owner of the real estate when the security interest is:

1. A purchase money interest; or
2. The fixture filing is perfected before the interest of the encumbrance or owner is of record; or
3. The fixture is readily removable factory or office machines; or
4. The lien is prior in time to any other conflicting security interest.

Security Interests

SECURITY AGREEMENT

_____
Debtor's Name   Street Address

_____
City   County   State

(hereinafter called in accordance with the terms and provisions of the Uniform Commercial Code – DEBTOR) for

value received hereby grants to _____
                                        Secured Party's Name

(hereinafter called in accordance with the terms and provisions of the Uniform Commercial Code – SECURED

PARTY) whose address is _____ ,
                         Street   City, County, and State

a security interest in and mortgages to SECURED PARTY the following described property (which hereinafter is

referred to as COLLATERAL) to-wit:

FIGURE 4-2   Security Agreement

(Note — If COLLATERAL is crops, or oil, gas or minerals to be extracted, or timber to be cut, or if COLLATERAL is to become a fixture, describe in the above space following the description of the COLLATERAL the real estate concerned, and give the name of the record owner hereof.)

to secure DEBTOR'S note to SECURED PARTY dated _____, 19____, for $_____.

DEBTOR warrants and covenants: (Note—Place checkmark (√) or DEBTOR'S initials in the blank space before each statement which applies to this agreement.)

____ COLLATERAL is to be used for personal, family, or household purposes.

____ COLLATERAL is to be used in business other than farming operations.

____ COLLATERAL is equipment used in farming operations, or farm products, or accounts, contract rights or general intangibles arising from or relating to the sale of farm products by a farmer.

____ COLLATERAL is accounts or contract rights and the records concerning same are kept at

_____

or if left blank at address given for DEBTOR.

____ COLLATERAL is a fixture attached to or to become a fixture attached to the above described land.

____ COLLATERAL is being acquired by DEBTOR from SECURED PARTY or is being acquired with the proceeds of the advance evidenced by this agreement.

____ DEBTOR'S residence is at the above address.

____ DEBTOR'S residence is at

_____

____ COLLATERAL will be kept at DEBTOR'S residence.

____ COLLATERAL will be kept at

_____

____ DEBTOR'S chief place of business is in the county of DEBTOR'S residence.

____ DEBTOR'S chief place of business is at

_____

FIGURE 4-2 Security Agreement Continued

75

The warranties, covenants, terms and agreements on the reverse side hereof are incorporated herein and made a part hereof for all intents and purposes. DEBTOR and SECURED PARTY as used in this Security Agreement include the heirs, executors or administrators, successors or assigns of those parties.

Dated _____

_____
Signature of DEBTOR

FIGURE 4-2 Security Agreement Continued

IMPORTANT — READ INSTRUCTIONS ON BACK BEFORE FILLING OUT FORM — **DO NOT DETACH STUB**

THIS SPACE FOR USE OF FILING OFFICER

FINANCING STATEMENT — FOLLOW INSTRUCTIONS CAREFULLY
This Financing Statement is presented for filing pursuant to the Uniform Commercial Code and will remain effective, with certain exceptions, for 5 years from date of filing.

A. NAME & TEL. # OF CONTACT AT FILER (optional)	B. FILING OFFICE ACCT. # (optional)

C. RETURN COPY TO: (Name and Mailing Address)

D. OPTIONAL DESIGNATION [if applicable]: | LESSOR/LESSEE | CONSIGNOR/CONSIGNEE | NON-UCC FILING |

1. DEBTOR'S EXACT FULL LEGAL NAME - insert only one debtor name (1a or 1b)

1a. ENTITY'S NAME: **BUYER BEWARE**

OR

1b. INDIVIDUAL'S LAST NAME	FIRST NAME	MIDDLE NAME	SUFFIX

1c. MAILING ADDRESS	CITY	STATE	COUNTRY	POSTAL CODE
4736 Madison	Houston	TX		

1d. S.S. OR TAX I.D.#	OPTIONAL ADD'NL INFO RE ENTITY DEBTOR	1e. TYPE OF ENTITY	1f. ENTITY'S STATE OR COUNTRY OF ORGANIZATION	1g. ENTITY'S ORGANIZATIONAL I.D.#, if any	NONE

2. ADDITIONAL DEBTOR'S EXACT FULL LEGAL NAME - insert only one debtor name (2a or 2b)

2a. ENTITY'S NAME:

OR

2b. INDIVIDUAL'S LAST NAME	FIRST NAME	MIDDLE NAME	SUFFIX

2c. MAILING ADDRESS	CITY	STATE	COUNTRY	POSTAL CODE

2d. S.S. OR TAX I.D.#	OPTIONAL ADD'NL INFO RE ENTITY DEBTOR	2e. TYPE OF ENTITY	2f. ENTITY'S STATE OR COUNTRY OF ORGANIZATION	2g. ENTITY'S ORGANIZATIONAL I.D.#, if any	NONE

3. SECURED PARTY'S (ORIGINAL S/P or ITS TOTAL ASSIGNEE) EXACT FULL LEGAL NAME - insert only one secured party name (3a or 3b)

3a. ENTITY'S NAME: **CAVEAT VENDOR, INC.**

OR

3b. INDIVIDUAL'S LAST NAME	FIRST NAME	MIDDLE NAME	SUFFIX

3c. MAILING ADDRESS	CITY	STATE	COUNTRY	POSTAL CODE
3737 Arnold	Houston	TX		

4. This FINANCING STATEMENT covers the following types or items of property:

One (1) Deluxe Woodburner One Freestanding Stove, Model No. 3, Serial No. QRS86543.

5. CHECK BOX [if applicable] | This FINANCING STATEMENT is signed by the Secured Party instead of the Debtor to perfect a security interest (a) in collateral already subject to a security interest in another jurisdiction when it was brought into this state, or when the debtor's location was changed to this state, or (b) in accordance with other statutory provisions [additional data may be required]

7. If filed in Florida (check one) | Documentary stamp tax paid | Documentary stamp tax not applicable |

6. REQUIRED SIGNATURE(S)

Buyer Beware

8. | This FINANCING STATEMENT is to be filed [for record] (or recorded) in the REAL ESTATE RECORDS Attach Addendum [if applicable]

9. Check to REQUEST SEARCH CERTIFICATE(S) on Debtor(s) [ADDITIONAL FEE] (optional) | All Debtors | Debtor 1 | Debtor 2 |

(1) FILING OFFICER COPY — NATIONAL FINANCING STATEMENT (FORM UCC1) (TRANS) (REV. 12/18/95)

Reorder from Hart Forms & Services, Inc.
800-223-HART (111691)

FIGURE 4-3   Financing Statement

IMPORTANT — READ INSTRUCTIONS ON BACK BEFORE FILLING OUT FORM — **DO NOT DETACH STUB**

THIS SPACE FOR USE OF FILING OFFICER

FINANCING STATEMENT — FOLLOW INSTRUCTIONS CAREFULLY
This Financing Statement is presented for filing pursuant to the Uniform Commercial Code
and will remain effective, with certain exceptions, for 5 years from date of filing.

A. NAME & TEL. # OF CONTACT AT FILER (optional)	B. FILING OFFICE ACCT. # (optional)

C. RETURN COPY TO: [Name and Mailing Address]

D. OPTIONAL DESIGNATION [if applicable]: ☐ LESSOR/LESSEE ☐ CONSIGNOR/CONSIGNEE ☐ NON-UCC FILING

1. DEBTOR'S EXACT FULL LEGAL NAME - insert only one debtor name (1a or 1b)

1a. ENTITY'S NAME: **Buyer Beware**

OR 1b. INDIVIDUAL'S LAST NAME | FIRST NAME | MIDDLE NAME | SUFFIX

1c. MAILING ADDRESS	CITY	STATE	COUNTRY	POSTAL CODE
4736 Madison	Houston	TX		

1d. S.S. OR TAX I.D.#	OPTIONAL ADD'NL INFO RE ENTITY DEBTOR	1e. TYPE OF ENTITY	1f. ENTITY'S STATE OR COUNTRY OF ORGANIZATION	1g. ENTITY'S ORGANIZATIONAL I.D.#, if any ☐ NONE

2. ADDITIONAL DEBTOR'S EXACT FULL LEGAL NAME - insert only one debtor name (2a or 2b)

2a. ENTITY'S NAME

OR 2b. INDIVIDUAL'S LAST NAME | FIRST NAME | MIDDLE NAME | SUFFIX

2c. MAILING ADDRESS	CITY	STATE	COUNTRY	POSTAL CODE

2d. S.S. OR TAX I.D.#	OPTIONAL ADD'NL INFO RE ENTITY DEBTOR	2e. TYPE OF ENTITY	2f. ENTITY'S STATE OR COUNTRY OF ORGANIZATION	2g. ENTITY'S ORGANIZATIONAL I.D.#, if any ☐ NONE

3. SECURED PARTY'S (ORIGINAL S/P or ITS TOTAL ASSIGNEE) EXACT FULL LEGAL NAME - insert only one secured party name (3a or 3b)

3a. ENTITY'S NAME: **Caveat Vendor, Inc.**

OR 3b. INDIVIDUAL'S LAST NAME | FIRST NAME | MIDDLE NAME | SUFFIX

3c. MAILING ADDRESS	CITY	STATE	COUNTRY	POSTAL CODE
3737 Arnold	Houston	TX		

4. This FINANCING STATEMENT covers the following types or items of property:

One (1) High Performance Air Conditioning
Unit, Model No. 694, Serial No. SE3469R739.

The above goods are, or are to become,
fixtures on March 1, 1997.

5. CHECK BOX [if applicable] ☐ This FINANCING STATEMENT is signed by the Secured Party instead of the Debtor to perfect a security interest (a) in collateral already subject to a security interest in another jurisdiction when it was brought into this state, or when the debtor's location was changed to this state, or (b) in accordance with other statutory provisions [additional data may be required]

7. If filed in Florida (check one) ☐ Documentary stamp tax paid ☐ Documentary stamp tax not applicable

6. REQUIRED SIGNATURE(S) Buyer Beware   Caveat Vendor, Inc.

By: By: Dewey Cheatham, President

8. ☒ This FINANCING STATEMENT is to be filed [for record] (or recorded) in the REAL ESTATE RECORDS Attach Addendum [if applicable]

9. Check to REQUEST SEARCH CERTIFICATE(S) on Debtor(s) [ADDITIONAL FEE] [optional] ☐ All Debtors ☐ Debtor 1 ☐ Debtor 2

Reorder from Hart Forms & Services, Inc.
800-223-HART (111691)

(1) FILING OFFICER COPY — NATIONAL FINANCING STATEMENT (FORM UCC1) (TRANS) (REV. 12/18/95)

FIGURE 4-4   Fixture Financing Statement

The legal ramifications of chattel mortgages and fixture filings can be rather far-reaching. However, it is very important that all real estate agents understand the complications and conflicts that can arise if a UCC lien is of record in the county courthouse affecting the property that the agent may be attempting to sell or list.

Once a chattel mortgage is perfected, it is released by the use of a UCC-3 form for termination of a security agreement. A copy of a UCC-3 form is shown in Figure 4-5.

The conflicts of mechanics' and materialmen's liens and mortgagees' liens have special applications to other areas of real estate law and will be discussed in greater detail in later chapters.

Trade Fixtures

There is a special class of fixtures, termed *trade fixtures*, which are articles that enable a tenant to carry on his business for trade. One normally finds the concept of trade fixtures in landlord-tenant situations when the tenant installs certain fixtures for his own use and benefit and for his own specific business purposes.

With few exceptions, the concept of trade fixtures is well settled in the law. The parties' rights are usually set out in a lease or other contractual obligation between the parties. The general rule is that all trade fixtures are ordinarily removable during or at the expiration of the tenant's term of occupancy, provided they can be completely removed without material or permanent injury to the building, *Kaczmarek* v. *Mesta Machine Co.*, 324 F. Supp. 298 (D.C. Pa. 1971). Unless otherwise specified in the contract, the fixtures must be removed within a reasonable time after the termination of the tenant's occupancy. "Reasonable," as in other cases, is a question of fact for a jury to decide. In the event the tenant does *fail* to remove the trade fixtures within a reasonable period of time, he forfeits his rights to those improvements and they become the property of the landlord.

Although this concept may seem to be simple and hardly worthy of explanation, one must remember that even when the rights are set up by terms of a written agreement between the parties, conflicts may arise and can create difficult situations. In at least one case, "fixtures and floor coverings" were determined by the court to include permanent floor coverings and various built-in items that could not be removed without material damage to the premises, *Haverfield Company* v. *Siegel*, 366 S.W.2d 790 (Tex. Civ. App.—San Antonio, 1963). There are always exceptions!

EASEMENTS

An *easement* is generally defined as the right acquired by one person to the use of the land of another for a special purpose. If you

IMPORTANT – READ INSTRUCTIONS ON BACK BEFORE FILLING OUT FORM – DO NOT DETACH STUB

THIS STATEMENT IS PRESENTED TO A FILING OFFICER FOR FILING PURSUANT TO THE UNIFORM COMMERCIAL CODE.

1. DEBTOR (IF PERSONAL) LAST NAME	FIRST NAME	M.I.	1A. PREFIX	1B. SUFFIX

Buyer Beware

1C. MAILING ADDRESS	1D. CITY, STATE	1E. ZIP CODE

4736 Madison — Houston, Texas

2. ADDITIONAL DEBTOR (IF PERSONAL) LAST NAME	FIRST NAME	M.I.	2A. PREFIX	2B. SUFFIX

2C. MAILING ADDRESS	2D. CITY, STATE	2E. ZIP CODE

3. SECURED PARTY (IF PERSONAL) LAST NAME	FIRST NAME	M.I.

Caveat Vendor, Inc.

3A. MAILING ADDRESS	3B. CITY, STATE	3C. ZIP CODE

3737 Arnold — Houston, Texas

4. ADDITIONAL SECURED PARTY (IF ANY)

4A. MAILING ADDRESS	4B. CITY, STATE	4C. ZIP CODE

5. ORIGINAL FINANCING STATEMENT NUMBER	5A. ORIGINAL DATE FILED	6. CHECK IF APPLICABLE [X]	THIS FINANCING STATEMENT CHANGE IS TO BE FILED IN THE REAL ESTATE RECORDS. NO. OF ADDITIONAL SHEETS PRESENTED _____.
	Feb. 32, 1978		

7. A. ☐ AMENDMENT – THE FINANCING STATEMENT BEARING THE FILE NUMBER SHOWN ABOVE IN ITEM 5 IS AMENDED AS SET FORTH IN ITEM 8 BELOW. (INSTRUCTION B.7(A))

B. ☐ TOTAL ASSIGNMENT – ALL OF SECURED PARTY'S RIGHTS UNDER THE FINANCING STATEMENT HAVE BEEN ASSIGNED TO THE ASSIGNEE WHOSE NAME AND ADDRESS ARE SET FORTH IN ITEM 8 BELOW. (INSTRUCTION B.7(B))

C. ☐ PARTIAL ASSIGNMENT – SOME OF SECURED PARTY'S RIGHTS UNDER THE FINANCING STATEMENT HAVE BEEN ASSIGNED TO THE ASSIGNEE WHOSE NAME AND ADDRESS ARE SET FORTH IN ITEM 8 BELOW. A DESCRIPTION OF THE COLLATERAL SUBJECT TO THE ASSIGNMENT IS ALSO SET FORTH IN ITEM 8 BELOW. (INSTRUCTION B.7(C))

D. ☐ CONTINUATION – THE ORIGINAL FINANCING STATEMENT BETWEEN THE FOREGOING DEBTOR AND SECURED PARTY BEARING THE FILE NUMBER AND DATE SHOWN IN ITEM 5 AND 5A IS CONTINUED. THE ORIGINAL STATEMENT IS STILL EFFECTIVE. (INSTRUCTION B.7(D))

E. ☐ PARTIAL RELEASE – THE SECURED PARTY RELEASES THE FOLLOWING COLLATERAL DESCRIBED IN ITEM 8 BELOW WHICH IS DESCRIBED IN THE FINANCING STATEMENT BEARING THE FILE NUMBER SHOWN IN ITEM 5 ABOVE. (INSTRUCTION B.7(E))

F. ☒ TERMINATION – THE SECURED PARTY(IES) OF RECORD NO LONGER CLAIMS A SECURITY INTEREST UNDER THE FINANCING STATEMENT BEARING THE FILE NUMBER SHOWN IN ITEM 5 ABOVE. (INSTRUCTION B.7(F))

8.

9. SIGNATURE(S) OF DEBTOR(S)	THIS SPACE FOR USE OF FILING OFFICER (DATE, TIME, NUMBER, FILING OFFICER)

CAVEAT VENDOR, INC.

SIGNATURE(S) OF SECURED PARTY(IES)

By: Dewey Cheatham, President

10. Return copy to:

NAME
ADDRESS
CITY
STATE
ZIP

FIGURE 4-5   Release of Financing Statements

would like to dazzle your friends with your brilliance, you may choose to describe easements as "incorporeal hereditaments" because they are, in fact, incorporeal (intangible) rights that may be inherited. Each easement carries with it the right to reasonable use, but only reasonable use, such that it is necessary, convenient, and as little burden to the owner of that real estate as possible. It can even be changed to accommodate that reasonable use through the conduct of parties, *Porter* v. *Kalas,* 597 A.2d 708 (Pa. Super., 1991). An easement right carries with it only user privilege and not any privilege of ownership. A mere easement can *never* be transposed into fee simple title or a feasible claim of title to the real estate.

Easements are generally categorized into two types: (1) an easement appurtenant and (2) an easement in gross. An *easement appurtenant* is an easement created for the benefit of another tract of land. There must be two different owners involved, one being the owner of the estate over which the easement crosses; this is called the *servient estate.* The other owner owns the property that the easement serves; this is called the *dominant estate.* Figure 4-6 illustrates how the appurtenant easement concept can be applied. Because of the nature of an appurtenant easement (it benefits a particular piece of property), an appurtenant easement is considered to be a covenant running with the land; that is, the right to use that easement passes along with the title to the dominant estate. This helps assure the dominant estate's continued usefulness.

    An *easement in gross,* on the other hand, is an easement that does not normally benefit any particular piece of property but benefits only the individual owner for his particular use. The holder of a commercial easement in gross usually has the right to sell, assign, or devise it, provided it is used for the same general purpose, *State of Washington Wildlife Preservation, Inc.* v. *State and Its Department of*

Appurtenant versus in Gross

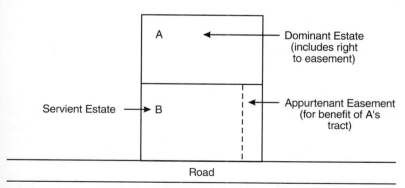

FIGURE 4-6 Estates Created by an Appurtenant Easement

Natural Resources, 329 N.W.2d 543 (Minn. 1983). However, an easement in gross for personal use normally terminates with the dissolution of the entity that has the right to use that easement. This type of easement is generally a right-of-way easement for power companies, gas transmission companies, flood-control authorities, and other governmental and quasigovernmental authorities. It should be emphasized that if the court is in the position of determining whether an easement is an easement in gross or an easement appurtenant, the court will generally attempt to find that it is an easement appurtenant, since easements in gross are not favored under the law. An easement in gross is generally in writing and is agreed to by all parties; it is often acquired by eminent domain proceedings by some condemning authority.

Creation Creation of an easement can be either express or implied, written or oral. Easements are normally created in one of six ways: (1) by express grant, (2) by express reservation, (3) by implication, (4) by prescription, (5) by reference to a plat, or (6) by estoppel. We will discuss each of these methods individually.

Easement by Express Grant. If an express easement is made by an agreement between the parties (easement by express grant), it has to follow the normal formalities of any real estate instrument and be in writing, properly subscribed by the party to be charged, with adequate legal description, acknowledged (if it is to be recorded), and properly delivered. Since it is granting a real property interest, the word "grant" may be a key factor. It may distinguish a grant of easement (a real property interest) instead of a mere license (a personal property interest), *Stratis* v. *Doyle,* 575 N.Y.S.2d 400 (N.Y. App. Div., 1991). An easement by express grant is the simplest and most direct method of creating an easement: the intent of parties is obviously clear, the use is properly set out, and it includes termination and other pertinent terms requested by the respective parties. If recorded, the instrument can meet all the requirements of constructive notice for the parties' own protection, as well as for the protection of third parties.

Easement by Express Reservation. An easement created by express reservation in a deed is also an express easement. However, the details and terms of an easement created in this manner are often left out, because the use of an easement reserved in a conveyance by a deed is usually appurtenant and necessary for either the property being conveyed or for the real estate contiguous thereto. For instance, property owner A may be willing to sell his frontage to property owner B but will reserve an easement to himself for access to the remainder of his property. The property over which the easement crosses still vests fee title unto the grantee but reserves the right to reasonable use to the grantor. Note that this is usually not an exception to title but rather a property right reserved out of the conveyance passed by the deed. A more detailed discussion of exceptions and reservations in deeds will be discussed in Chapter 8, "Conveyances."

Easement by Implication. An easement by implication (sometimes referred to as an easement by necessity), is one that is not in writing. It is usually imposed by a court in the form of an equitable remedy to provide access to a landlocked parcel of real estate. This is normally an easement that has been in continuous use for some time but was not created by any agreement in writing between the parties affected. However, before a court will impose such an easement by implication, certain criteria must be met to justify the court's intervention:

1. The prior use of the easement must be apparent and obvious by the party seeking to enforce his easement right.
2. The prior use must also have been reasonably continuous. This does not mean that the party must have used it every day, but he must have used it often enough to establish a certain continuity of use.
3. The use of that easement must be reasonably necessary to a fair and enjoyable use of the dominant estate.
4. There must have originally been a unity of ownership of the dominant and servient estates immediately prior to the easement being created, *U.S.* v. *O'Connell*, 496 F.2d 1329 (2nd Cir., 1974).

In the typical situation surrounding an easement by implication, two owners have an oral agreement for the use of an easement to a landlocked parcel of real estate that was originally owned by one of the two parties. When the oral agreement is breached, the aggrieved party petitions the court for intervention.

Easement by Prescription. An easement by prescription is one that has been obtained and is held by a claimant against the wishes of the landowner. It is very similar and analogous to obtaining title to property by adverse possession. However, remember that adverse possession and easement by prescription are entirely different concepts. An easement, as stated previously, never ripens into fee simple ownership, but adverse possession does. The requirements to create an easement by prescription are understandably a little more difficult than those required to create an easement by implication. A claimant's right to this easement is generally imposed by a court, as is the case in an easement by implication. The requirements for an easement by prescription may include the following:

1. The use of the easement must be adverse, open, notorious, and hostile to the interest of the landowner over which the easement passes. This does not mean that the claimant must have used the easement under artillery fire or carrying a sack of grenades, but the landowner must have been clearly against the creation and use of said easement.

2. The use of the easement must be exclusive to the claimant and not available to the public.

3. The use of the easement must have been uninterrupted and continuous for a period of at least ten years, *Engel* v. *Rhen Marshall*, 292 N.W.2d 301 (Neb. 1980), *Nature Conservancy* v. *Machipongo Club, Inc.*, 571 F.2d 1294 (4th Cir., 1978).

An easement by prescription can be acquired on privately owned lands by either a private individual or, in some states, by the public. In practice, however, a private citizen generally is not permitted to acquire an easement by prescription on publicly held lands or on lands owned by charities. Most often this type of easement is acquired by one private landowner against another.

Easement by Reference to a Plat.   An easement can be created by reference to an existing subdivision plat. It is quite common for subdivision developers, when laying out a subdivision, to record that subdivision's plat in the county in which the subdivision is located. The legal descriptions to a given lot, block, and section can then be made by reference to the plat rather than by the more complicated metes and bounds system. It logically follows that as the developer changes the legal description to a piece of property by filing a subdivision plat, he may also create easements for water mains, gas distribution lines, road rights-of-way, and other types of easements that are similarly created by governmental and quasi-governmental authorities through the promulgation of official city, county, and state maps that delineate flood-way areas, flood-control districts, power lines, and major utility distribution systems.

Easement by Estoppel.   *Estoppel* is a rather elusive legal concept that alludes to a claim made an affirmative defense to a cause of action when the defendant has been induced into doing an act by the plaintiff. This concept is sometimes called *promissory estoppel.* An easement by estoppel normally occurs when a party, by oral agreement, has granted a right to an easement in his land upon which the other party has relied in good faith and has expended money—money that would be lost if the right to use and enjoy that easement is revoked by the promisor. Since the owner of the dominant estate relied on the servient tenant's promise for using that easement, equity normally prohibits the owner of the servient estate from preventing the dominant owner's use of that easement. The only requirements for creating an easement by estoppel are that:

1. The representation must have been communicated to the promisee or owner of the dominant estate.
2. The representation must have been believed by that promisee.
3. There must have been a reliance on such promise to the detriment of the dominant estate owner, *Exxon Corp.* v. *Schutzmaier,* 537 S.W.2d 282 (Tex. Civ. App.—Beaumont, 1976).

The nature of an easement by estoppel is one that is imposed by equity because of the bad faith evidenced by the promisor in granting an easement and then attempting to take it back after the promisee has relied on his promise. The strong equitable nature of this particular type of easement is such that the same strict and conclusive rules of law as an easement by implication, which has many of the same characteristics, do not apply. As in the case of all other easements, generally, the use of this easement can only be reasonable use that is necessary and convenient and of as little burden to the servient estate as possible.

Easements by Necessity.   There has often been confusion between easements by implication and easements by *necessity.* They are not the same, and they need to be discussed in more detail to emphasize the differences. For an easement by necessity to exist, it must be shown that:

1. There was a unity of ownership with the alleged dominant and servient estates.
2. The roadway is a necessity, not a mere convenience.
3. The necessity existed at the time of the severance of the

two estates, *Othen* v. *Rosier,* 226 S.W.2d 622 (Tex. 1950), *Koonce* v. *Brite*, 663 S.W.2d 451, 452 (Tex. 1984), *Morrell* v. *Rice*, 622 A.2d 1156 (Me. 1993).

No one can have an easement by necessity over the land of a stranger. Therefore, there must be some conduct between the dominant and servient estates that creates the easement right. A tract's being landlocked, by itself, does not create the necessity. The courts have further held that the necessity required must be a "strict" necessity, providing the only access to the dominant tenant's property. It cannot exist just because a road is impassable. *Duff* v. *Matthews, supra.* Note that in this type of easement there is no requirement that the easement be apparent or continuously used. An easement by necessity probably has its best application in situations when the servient owner claims abandonment, but there is no other access to the dominant estate.

Termination   If it has been determined that an easement has been properly created and is in existence, even if it is an oral easement created by implication, by estoppel, or by prescription, the termination of that easement, as in the termination of most other property rights, must meet certain requirements before that termination becomes effective. The methods of terminating an easement are release, merger, failure of purpose, and abandonment.

Release.   As an easement can be created by an express reservation or express grant, it can also be released by express agreement of termination between the parties involved. The same care in drawing the instrument for creating the easement should also be taken in the termination of that easement. There may be rights created that could be overlooked when the release is drawn, and such an oversight may inadvertently create a cloud on the title.

Merger.   Merger is accomplished when the owner of the dominant estate purchases the servient estate or vice versa and therefore owns fee simple title to the entire property and no longer has any use for the easement. Figure 4-7 will help to illustrate this matter more clearly. Note that properly owner A has the dominant estate and property owner B has the servient estate that is encumbered by the easement. Recall that the easement is a right that vests in the dominant estate. Although property owner B still owns the land encumbered by the easement, it logically follows that when property owner A acquires property owner B's interest to the fee title to the property, the rights in the easement and his

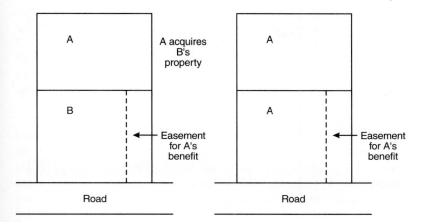

FIGURE 4-7   *Termination of an Easement by Merger*

rights to the fee title of the real estate merge, and the easement terminates.

Failure of Purpose.   Easements are normally created for a particular purpose, whether express or implied. It is within this purpose that guidelines are established for reasonable use. When the purpose for an easement fails, so does the easement. An illustration of this would be a road that was created to cross property because there was no other access to the dominant estate. When a new road is constructed along a public right-of-way that provides other access to the dominant estate such that the easement is no longer needed, it may be reasonably assumed that the servient owner may terminate the easement for failure of purpose. It is interesting to note that due to the failure of purpose doctrine, it is, at least theoretically, possible to have a perpetual easement. For instance, consider an easement for flood-control drainage or public street access. Once the easement has been created by a third party or governmental authority, the doctrines of merger and release will probably never be satisfied, and one would have to rely on the failure of purpose doctrine for a party to effectively terminate the easement. Without some change in condition, these easements would effectively last forever.

Abandonment.   An easement can be terminated by abandonment. However, as in the terminations of all other real estate rights, abandonment is difficult to prove and is not an easy method of termination. There must be proof of an intent of the party using the easement to abandon that easement before it can be properly terminated. This abandonment must be proved by the person attempting to terminate the easement rights, and must be established by clear and satisfactory evidence. Mere nonuse, by itself, does not constitute abandonment, *Penn. Cent. Trans.* v. *Pirate Canoe Club Inc.*, 463 F.2d. 127 (2nd Cir., 1972). It is not difficult to see that the burden of proof in a situation constituting abandonment requires much more effort than the failure of purpose or merger doctrines that can be proved without regard to intent.

Prescription.   An easement may be either created or terminated by prescription. The same elements of proof are required. In essence, an easement is terminated by prescription when the servient tenant openly and continuously prevents the dominant tenant from using it for the required period of time. He might do this where an access road easement is involved, for example, by placing a locked gate at each end of the road. He has no right to do this, and clearly it is adverse to the dominant tenant's interests. Thus, the dominant tenant can and should seek a court injunction to force the gates to be unlocked and prevent the termination of the easement via prescription.

SUMMARY   Both fixtures and easements involve rights to real estate that may be held by persons other than the real property owner.

Under the law of fixtures, anything permanently attached to the real estate is considered real property. Classification of an item as real property or a chattel is important because this affects the manner of transferring title (deed or bill of sale) and the procedure that creditors must follow to obtain a security interest in such property. This area is complicated further by the fact that personal property may be converted to real property and vice versa.

Because nothing is permanently attached to real estate in the sense that it is impossible to remove, other judicial tests have been developed to assist in determining when an item of property is a fixture. These tests may vary slightly from state to state, but generally include the following features:

1. The mode of annexation.
2. The character and adaptation to real estate.
3. Whether the item was intended to become part of the real estate.
4. Whether the items are necessary to the enjoyment of the real estate.
5. Whether the item could be removed without material injury to the property.

These rules determine what is transferred under a contract of sale for "real property," and also the procedure that a creditor must follow in order to create a security interest (lien) in chattels and fixtures. Generally a creditor must file the financing statements or security agreement in the local county land records office in the case of fixtures, and at some central location such as the office of the secretary of state in the case of chattels.

The order of recording basically determines the order of payment (priority) when two or more chattel lien creditors are competing for limited debtor funds. The same is true for competing fixture liens creditors.

When insufficient funds exist to pay both the real property mortgagee and a fixture lien creditor, the latter generally receives priority even though his lien may be recorded after the real estate mortgage. The reasoning is that the mortgagee would consent to the addition of the fixture because it increases the value of his security in the long run.

Whereas the law of fixtures involves the classification of property as real or personal, an easement is a nonpossessory right to use another's land for some special purpose. There are two major types of easements: an easement appurtenant and an easement in gross. An easement appurtenant is one created for the benefit of another, often adjoining, tract of land. The tract being benefitted is called the dominant estate; the tract burdened by the easement's existence is the servient estate. An easement in gross benefits a particular person or business rather than another tract of land. An example is an easement for electrical transmission lines.

Easements may be created in six different ways: by express grant, express reservation, implication, prescriptive right, reference to a plat, or estoppel. An express grant of easement is generally created by a written agreement, following the normal formalities of any real estate legal instrument. An easement created by reservation in a deed typically involves the conveyance of highway frontage while reserving an easement across it for access to an otherwise landlocked tract. Easements by implication are implied and formalized by a court when demanded by principles of fairness and good conscience. Easements by prescription are not the result of a formal conveyance but rather result from continuous nonpossessory use adverse to the fee simple absolute owner's interest, for a specific period of time (usually ten years). Recording a subdivision plat showing the existence of easements in the local county land records office is another method of creating an easement. The final method of creating an easement, by estoppel, involves one party inducing the other to change his economic position. This type of easement is created by court decision when necessary to avoid unfair results.

In order to keep title to real estate clear and unclouded, termination of an easement should be given just as much attention as creating one. Easements generally may be terminated in any one of five ways: release, merger, failure of purpose, abandonment, and prescription. A release is simply an express (preferably written) agreement between the dominant and servient tenants to terminate their easement. Merger, on the other hand, results any time the dominant and servient estates come into common ownership. The easement then disappears and legally merges back into a fee simple absolute because there is no reason for its continued existence. Similarly, an easement is terminated for failure of purpose when the basic reason for its presence ceases to exist. If the dominant tenant's intent to abandon can be proven, an easement is also terminated in this fashion. Finally, if all elements are present to prove a prescription right has been acquired, an easement may be terminated by continuously and adversely preventing the dominant tenant from using his easement for the legally required time period.

DISCUSSION QUESTIONS

1. In what way are easements and fixtures similar?
2. What judicial tests does your state employ to determine whether an item is a chattel or a fixture?
3. Is the law logical that determines which competing lien creditors should be paid first?
4. List as many examples as you can of an easement in gross.
5. What is the legal logic behind the doctrine of merger as a method of terminating an easement?

5

Real Estate Brokerage and Management

Real estate brokers and salespersons are regulated by state statutes. Although these statutes may vary from state to state, they have the common purpose of protecting the public from fraud and misrepresentation by dishonest or incompetent persons. Such regulatory statutes have generally been held to be constitutional, *State* v. *Polakow's Realty Experts,* 10 So. 2d 461, cert. den. 391 U.S. 750 (1942), and *Haas* v. *Greenwald,* 237 P.38, aff'd. 275 U.S. 490 (1927).

These statutes are designed to regulate entry into the industry as well as to regulate the professional conduct of licensed brokers and salespersons. Many states have upgraded their educational requirements in an effort to further professionalize the industry. Hopefully, this increases the quality and level of services to real estate buyers and sellers.

Most real estate licensing acts are administered by state agencies called real estate commissions or departments of real estate. These agencies are generally composed of industry and public members and have the ultimate responsibility for determining licensing standards, holding public hearings, and otherwise taking administrative actions to determine whether licenses should be suspended or revoked. The regulations of these agencies have the force of law, and they serve to administratively enforce the canons of professional ethics and conduct that have been legislated for real estate licenses. Failure to meet statutory and regulatory standards of conduct usually is grounds for license suspension or revocation.

In order to further protect the public against financial loss from a licensee's unscrupulous and incompetent dealings, state real estate agencies generally have one of two requirements:

STATE REAL ESTATE COMMISSIONS/ DEPARTMENTS

1. Either they require every licensee to be bonded so that recovery is assured for legitimate complaints involving improper conduct on the part of licensees,
2. Or they establish a statewide recovery fund financed by assessments paid by brokers and salespersons.

Under either system, if a licensee is not financially able to reimburse the damaged party for the losses he has caused, recovery may be had against the statewide recovery fund or the licensee's bond. Both systems can work well. The general public is protected so long as unrealistically low recovery limits are not placed on either the bond or the recovery fund.

LICENSING STATUTES

The most common form of state regulation in the real estate industry is made up of the licensing requirements established for the brokers and salespersons. All states have adopted licensing statutes, and most seem to be increasing their requirements and standards in an effort to upgrade the professional standards of the industry. Although the statutes and regulations vary from state to state, many follow the general format of a model real estate license law published by the License Law Committee of the National Association of Real Estate License Law Officials. This model law includes the following major features:

1. Specific definitions, including those of *real estate broker* and *salesperson.*
2. Persons and transactions exempt from brokerage licensing requirements.
3. Eligibility requirements for licensees.
4. Delineation of the state real estate commission and its function.
5. Standards for suspension or revocation of licenses.
6. Other miscellaneous requirements (which vary from state to state) such as legal actions to recover sales commissions, civil rights matters, prohibitions against real estate agents practicing law, and contractual authority of brokers and salespersons.

The licensing laws are intended to be all-encompassing, and their basic purpose is to protect the public. With this in mind, courts tend to liberally construe licensing law provisions against the practitioner and in favor of the consumer.

Real estate is usually defined to include both leasehold and freehold estates in land, and all tangible improvements thereon. Thus, licensure is generally required for a wide variety of real estate transactions.

Real estate broker normally refers to any person, association, partnership, or corporation who for another and for a fee, commission, or other valuable consideration lists, sells, purchases, exchanges, leases, rents, or collects rent for the use of real estate or who attempts or who offers to perform any such function or who advertises or holds himself out as engaging in any of these activities.

Real estate salesperson is any person licensed to perform on behalf of any licensed real estate broker any act or acts authorized to be performed by a real estate broker.

A broker-salesperson or *associate broker* is generally defined as a person who has a broker's license, but is employed by another broker.

Generally, eligibility requirements for real estate licensure are quite similar in all states. Usually an individual must be a citizen of the United States (or a lawfully admitted alien), at least 18 years of age, and for some fixed time period be a legal resident of the state in which he is applying for a license. The license applicant generally must also satisfy the commission as to his honesty, trustworthiness, and competency.

Competency is most often established by an examination prepared and administered by the real estate commission. In order to enforce the rules and regulations and further assure competency of licensees, the commission usually inspects and accredits proprietary real estate educational programs and courses and establishes standards for accreditation of all such programs in the state. Education and experience requirements for broker and salesperson licensure are set out in Table 5-1.

Most state real estate licensing acts permit certain real estate transactions to be consummated by unlicensed persons, such as the following:

1. An attorney at law.
2. An attorney in fact under a duly executed power of attorney authorizing the consummation of a specific real estate transaction.
3. A public official in the conduct of his official duties.

TABLE 5-1
Real Estate Education and Experience Requirements

State	Salesperson License		Broker License		
	Education Requirement	Continuing Education	Education Requirement	Experience Requirement	Continuing Education
Alabama	45 hours	Yes	60 hours	2 years	Yes
Alaska	20 hours	Yes	35 hours	2 years	Yes
Arizona	90 hours	Yes	180 hours	3 years	Yes
Arkansas	60 hours	Yes	None	2 years	Yes
California	135 hours	Yes	360 hours	2 years	Yes
Colorado	72 hours	Yes	120 hours	2 years	Yes
Connecticut	30 hours	Yes	90 hours	2 years	Yes
Delaware	93 hours	Yes	168 hours	5 years	Yes
District of Columbia	45 hours	Yes	135 hours	2 years	Yes
Florida	63 hours	Yes	135 hours	1 year	Yes
Georgia	75 hours	Yes	135 hours	3 years	Yes
Hawaii	45 hours	Yes	91 hours	2 years	Yes
Idaho	90 hours	Yes	180 hours	2 years	Yes
Illinois	30 hours	Yes	90 hours	1 year	Yes
Indiana	54 hours	Yes	108 hours	1 year	Yes
Iowa	60 hours	Yes	120 hours	2 years	Yes
Kansas	30 hours	Yes	54 hours	2 years	Yes
Kentucky	96 hours	Yes	336 hours	2 years	Yes
Louisiana	90 hours	Yes	240 hours	2 years	Yes
Maine	39 hours	Yes	168 hours	1 year	Yes
Maryland	45 hours	Yes	135 hours	2 years	Yes
Massachusetts	24 hours	No	54 hours	1 year	No
Michigan	40 hours	Yes	130 hours	3 years	Yes
Minnesota	90 hours	Yes	30 hours	2 years	Yes
Mississippi	60 hours	Yes	150 hours	1 year	Yes
Missouri	60 hours	Yes	108 hours	1 year	Yes
Montana	60 hours	Yes	120 hours	2 years	Yes
Nebraska	60 hours	Yes	240 hours	2 years	Yes
Nevada	90 hours	Yes	1,050 hours	8 years	Yes
New Hampshire	None	Yes	None	1 year	Yes
New Jersey	75 hours	No	225 hours	3 years	No
New Mexico	60 hours	Yes	180 hours	2 years	Yes
New York	45 hours	Yes	90 hours	1 year	Yes
North Carolina	30 hours	Yes	120 hours	2 years	Yes
North Dakota	30 hours	Yes	90 hours	2 years	Yes
Ohio	120 hours	Yes	240 hours	2 years	Yes
Oklahoma	90 hours	Yes	165 hours	2 years	Yes
Oregon	90 hours	Yes	150 hours	3 years	Yes

TABLE 5-1 Continued

| State | Salesperson License | | Broker License | | |
	Education Requirement	Continuing Education	Education Requirement	Experience Requirement	Continuing Education
Pennsylvania	60 hours	Yes	300 hours	3 years	Yes
Rhode Island	None	Yes	90 hours	1 year	Yes
South Carolina	30 hours	Yes	90 hours	3–5 years	Yes
South Dakota	40 hours	Yes	100 hours	2 years	Yes
Tennessee	60 hours	Yes	120 hours	3 years	No
Texas	180 hours	Yes	900 hours	2 years	Yes
Utah	90 hours	Yes	120 hours	3 years	Yes
Vermont	None	Yes	8 hours	1 year	Yes
Virginia	60 hours	Yes	240 hours	3 years	Yes
Washington	60 hours	Yes	180 hours	2 years	Yes
West Virginia	90 hours	Yes	180 hours	2 years	Yes
Wisconsin	72 hours	Yes	108 hours	None	Yes
Wyoming	30 hours	Yes	60 hours	2 years	Yes

EXPLANATION: Hours are clock-hours in the classroom; experience requirement is experience as a licensed real estate salesperson; continuing education refers to education required for license renewal. Some states credit completed salesperson education toward the broker education requirement.
SOURCE: National Association of Real Estate License Law Officials. Check with any specific state for any subsequent changes.

4. A person acting officially as a receiver, trustee, administrator, executor, or guardian.

5. A person acting under a court order or under the authority of a will or a written trust instrument.

6. A salesperson employed by an owner in the sale of structures and land on which said structures are situated, provided such structures are erected by the owner in the due course of his business.

7. An on-site manager of an apartment complex.

8. A person involved in transactions embracing the sale, lease, or transfer or any mineral or mining interest in real property.

9. An owner or his employees in renting or leasing his own real estate, whether improved or unimproved.

10. A person handling transactions involving the sale, lease, or transfer of cemetery lots.

Generally, when a nonexempt person acts as a real estate broker or salesperson without obtaining a license, he is guilty of a misdemeanor. Such misdemeanors usually are punishable by a fine or imprisonment.

Real estate licensing acts generally make it unlawful for a person to hold himself out as a broker or to engage in the business of real estate brokerage without first being licensed by the state real estate commission. He cannot collect a commission unless he is licensed. It is also unlawful for any salesperson to act or attempt to act as a real estate agent *unless* he is associated with a licensed real estate broker. Furthermore, the salesperson cannot accept compensation from any person other than the broker under whom he holds his license.

Changing Agency Relationships

There has been a major change in licensing acts in the last few years. Most of the real estate licensing acts have been set up to reflect agency law (i.e., the broker is the agent of the principal) with resulting fiduciary duties (discussed later). The original licensing statutes presumed that the real estate agent represented the seller through the use of a listing agreement. The advent of buyer brokerage, however, created a new focus on the licensing statutes to emphasize employment agreements (versus listing agreements) and duties of buyer representation. Many states have also amended their statutes to provide for statutorily enabled dual agency, or an even newer concept of *intermediary, designated broker, facilitator,* or *limited agency* status. These new statutes attempt to create legislated relationships and often redefine the duties of care between a principal and agent, as well as duties to third parties.

All states still require a sponsoring broker for licensees. The intermediary-designated broker type of statutes create new issues. Under these statutes, a sponsoring broker has the authority to appoint, or designate, one of its agents to represent the seller and another one to represent the buyer. What is the liability of the sponsoring broker in the event there's misconduct on the part of the sponsored agent? Some states create a dual agency concept for the broker; other states don't mention a liability of the sponsoring broker at all, other than the obligation to remain impartial. Courts may overlook the statutory protections created by these statutes and revert back to the common law when they find that a party has been legitimately damaged as a result of misconduct of the licensee. Remember, the purpose of the licensing laws is to protect the public, not the brokers.

LISTING AGREEMENTS

The real estate broker's employment is usually evidenced by a contract called a *listing agreement.* This contract may be expressed or implied, although a minority of states require that the broker's employment contract be in writing in order to recover a commission. These states are Arizona, California, Connecticut, Hawaii, Idaho, Indiana, Kansas, Kentucky, Louisiana, Maryland, Michigan, Minnesota, Montana, Nebraska, New Jersey, New Mexico, Ohio, Oklahoma, Oregon, Texas, Utah, Washington, and Wisconsin. Alaska and Rhode Island provide that the brokerage contract must be in writing to be enforceable as a part of their statute of frauds. The other states have held that an oral contract of employment is enforceable, although there is always the difficult problem of proof between parties to an oral contract. Oral contracts are never advisable.

The contract is generally governed by the law of the place where it is made, rather than the state where the land is located (although the latter may be relevant in some cases). See Powell §938.13, n.106 and cases cited therein.

As in all other real estate contracts, the listing agreement must be sufficient to enforce performance. A listing agreement, or memorandum thereof, is normally considered to be specific enough when it:

Legal Sufficiency

1. Is in writing and is signed by the person to be charged the commission.
2. Promises a definite commission will be paid, or refers to a written commission schedule.
3. Specifies the name of the broker to whom the commission is to be paid.
4. Either itself or by reference to some other existing writing identifies with reasonable certainty the land to be conveyed, *Campbell* v. *Mutual Service Corp.* 263 S.E.2d 202 (Georgia 1979).

If the written agreement does not contain the required information, it must refer to an existing agreement or form from which the information can be obtained. If there is no listing agreement, or memorandum therefore, an obligation to pay the broker's commission contained in the earnest money contract may be specific enough to enforce payment, *Maloney* v. *Strain,* 410 S.W.2d 650 (1966), and *Showcase Realty, Inc.* v. *Whittaker,* 559 F.2d 1165 (1977).

Most real estate brokers prefer to use standard form listing agreements supplied by local trade associations in order to keep their

Types of Listing Agreements

rights clearly specified and defined. Standard listing agreements are generally considered to be of five types: (1) exclusive right to sell, (2) exclusive agency to sell, (3) open listing, (4) net listing, and (5) multiple listing. A sample standard form of listing agreement is shown in Figure 5-1. The content of each form may vary slightly from state to state because of differences in state law and brokerage practices.

Exclusive Right to Sell.   Under the exclusive right to sell listing the real estate broker is employed to sell the property, and the property owner is specifically prohibited from selling the property himself without paying the broker a commission. With this agreement the broker is entitled to a commission if anyone sells the real estate during the term of the listing agreement, even though the broker himself may have had nothing to do with the sale, *Arthur H. Richland Co.* v. *Harper,* 302 F.2d 324 (4th Cir. 1962), and *Flynn* v. *LaSalle National Bank,* 137 N.E.2d 71. This type of listing gives the broker protection against "back door" dealings by others in the profession, or by the owner himself.

Because of the assurance of collecting a commission if a sale occurs, brokers with this type of listing generally are more willing to advertise and otherwise spend time and money in an attempt to sell the property. This in turn may increase the probability that the property will be sold within a reasonably short time period.

Exclusive Agency to Sell.   In the exclusive agency to sell, the owner again employs the broker to sell the property. However, the owner reserves the right to sell the property himself and does not have to pay the broker a commission if he (the owner) is able to sell his own land, *Flynn* v. *LaSalle National Bank, supra.* The broker can, however, collect a commission on a sale consummated as a result of anyone else's efforts except those of the owner.

Open Listing.   An open agency listing merely gives the broker a nonexclusive right to sell the property. A landowner may sign an open agency listing with several different brokers but only the broker who first produces a ready, willing, and able buyer is entitled to a commission. No broker will receive a commission if the owner sells the property himself. When the property is sold, the sale terminates the authority of all the brokers.

Open agency listing agreements are effective to enforce the payment of a commission but do not encourage a broker to expend substantial funds in an attempt to make a sale. Furthermore, serious conflicts may arise as to whether a broker under an open

EQUAL HOUSING
OPPORTUNITY

TEXAS ASSOCIATION OF REALTORS®
RESIDENTIAL REAL ESTATE LISTING AGREEMENT
EXCLUSIVE RIGHT TO SELL

REALTOR

THIS FORM IS FURNISHED BY THE TEXAS ASSOCIATION OF REALTORS®
FOR USE BY ITS MEMBERS. USE OF THIS FORM BY PERSONS WHO ARE NOT MEMBERS
OF THE TEXAS ASSOCIATION OF REALTORS® IS NOT AUTHORIZED
©Texas Association of REALTORS®, Inc., 1995

1. **PARTIES:** The parties to this agreement (this Listing) are _____
_____ (Seller) and _____
_____ (Broker). In consideration of services to be performed by Broker, Seller appoints Broker as Seller's sole and exclusive real estate agent and grants to Broker the exclusive right to sell the Property for the price and on terms described below.

2. **PROPERTY:** The Property is legally described as:_____
_____ in the City of _____,
_____ County, Texas, known as _____
_____ (address and zip code),
or as described on an attached exhibit, together with the following items, if any: curtains and rods, draperies and rods, valances, blinds, window shades, screens, shutters, awnings, wall-to-wall carpeting, mirrors fixed in place, ceiling fans, attic fans, mail boxes, television antennae and satellite dish with controls and all equipment, permanently installed heating and air-conditioning units and equipment, window air conditioning units, built-in security and fire detection equipment, plumbing and lighting fixtures (including chandeliers), water softener, built-in kitchen equipment, garage door openers with controls, built-in cleaning equipment, all swimming pool equipment and accessories, shrubbery, landscaping, permanently installed outdoor cooking equipment, built-in fireplace screens, artificial fireplace logs, and all other property owned by Seller and attached to the above described real property except the following property which is not included: _____
_____ The Property ❑ is ❑ is not subject to a mandatory membership in an owners' association and its assessments and requirements. (Note: If Property is a condominium see Condominium Addendum). All property described above is called "the Property."

3. **LISTING PRICE:** Seller lists the Property for the gross amount of $_____ (Listing Price) and agrees to sell the Property for the Listing Price or for any other price Seller may accept. A sale of the Property may be financed through any one or a combination of the following terms: ❑ conventional loan; ❑ F.H.A. insured loan; ❑ V.A. guaranteed loan; ❑ a loan under the Texas Veteran's Housing Assistance Program; ❑ assumption of an existing note; ❑ cash; ❑ a loan financed by Seller; or through such other terms as Seller may accept. Seller shall pay all typical closing costs charged to sellers of residential real property in Texas, including loan discount points and prepayment penalties (sellers' typical closing costs are those set forth in the residential earnest money contracts promulgated by the Texas Real Estate Commission). **NOTICE: Broker does not guarantee that the Property will be appraised or sold for the Listing Price nor does Broker guarantee any net amount Seller might realize from the sale of the Property.**

4. **TERM:** This Listing shall commence on _____ (Commencement Date) and shall terminate at 11:59 p.m. on _____ (Termination Date). If on the Termination Date there is a pending contract for the sale of the Property, in whole or part, in effect between Seller and a buyer and the transaction described in such a contract has not closed, Broker's Fee is earned and shall be payable according to paragraph 7. If Seller enters into a binding written contract to sell the Property before the Commencement Date, this Listing shall not commence and shall be void.

5. **ASSOCIATION AND FILINGS:**

(a) Association: Broker is a member of the _____ Association or Board of REALTORS® (the Association) and is bound by its rules.

(b) Filing of Listing (choose (1) or (2)):

❑ (1) Broker shall file this Listing with the following Multiple Listing Services (MLS) or other listing services: _____ within the earlier of: (i) the time required by the rules or regulations of the named MLS or listing service; or (ii) 4 days after the Commencement Date of this Listing. Seller authorizes Broker to place the Property on a computerized system of public access through a program of the MLS or other listing service. Seller authorizes Broker, upon a final and closed sale of the Property, to submit information about this Listing, the sale of the Property, and contract terms, to the named MLS or listing services for publication to subscribers for market evaluation or appraisal purposes and for disclosure of such information to such persons as Broker deems appropriate, including the appraisal district. Any information or data, including information about a sale, shall become the property of the named MLS or listing services for all purposes. **NOTICE: Submission of information to MLS insures that persons who use and benefit from MLS also contribute information.**

❑ (2) Broker shall not file this Listing with a Multiple Listing Service or any other listing service.

(c) Cooperation with other brokers: Cooperating with and compensating other brokers means that Broker will allow other brokers to show the Property to prospective buyers and if another broker procures an acceptable offer, Broker will pay the other broker part of the Broker's Fee described in paragraph 7(a). Broker shall offer cooperation and compensation (choose only one): ❑ only to buyer agents; ❑ only to subagents of Broker; ❑ to both buyer agents and Broker's subagents. Broker will determine the terms and conditions of offers to cooperate with and compensate other brokers.

6. **AGENCY RELATIONSHIPS:**

(a) Seller acknowledges receipt of the attached exhibit entitled **"Information About Brokerage Services"**, which is incorporated in this Listing for all purposes.

(b) Broker shall exclusively represent Seller in negotiations for the sale of the Property unless Seller authorizes Broker, as set forth below, to act as an intermediary in the event Broker also represents a buyer who offers to purchase the Property (choose (1) or (2)).

FIGURE 5-1 Standard Listing Agreements

☐ (1) <u>Intermediary Relationship Authorized</u>: Seller authorizes Broker to show the Property to prospective buyers Broker has agreed to represent. If Broker represents a buyer who offers to buy the Property, Seller authorizes Broker to act as an intermediary between the buyer and Seller, to present any offer such buyer may wish to make, and to assist both Seller and buyer in negotiations for the sale of the Property. Broker's compensation shall be paid by Seller as provided in paragraph 7. If **Broker acts as an intermediary between Seller and a buyer, Broker:**

(i) may not disclose to the buyer that the Seller will accept a price less than the asking price (Listing Price) unless otherwise instructed in a separate writing by the Seller;

(ii) may not disclose to Seller that the buyer will pay a price greater than the price submitted in a written offer to Seller unless otherwise instructed in a separate writing by the buyer;

(iii) may not disclose any confidential information or any information Seller or the buyer specifically instructs Broker in writing not to disclose unless otherwise instructed in a separate writing by the respective party or required to disclose the information by the Real Estate License Act or a court order or if the information materially relates to the condition of the Property;

(iv) shall treat all parties to the transaction honestly; and

(v) shall comply with the Real Estate License Act.

If Broker acts as an intermediary, Broker may appoint a licensed associate(s) of Broker to communicate with, carry out instructions of, and provide opinions and advice during negotiations to Seller and appoint another licensed associate(s) for the same purposes to the buyer.

☐ (2) <u>Intermediary Relationship not Authorized</u>: Broker shall exclusively represent Seller and may not act as an intermediary between Seller and a buyer. Seller understands *(choose (i) or (ii))*:

☐ (i) Broker exclusively represents sellers of real property and does not represent buyers.

☐ (ii) Broker represents both buyers and sellers of real property. However, Broker shall not show the Property to any buyer Broker represents.

(c) Broker shall not knowingly during the term of this Listing or after its termination, disclose information obtained in confidence from Seller except as authorized by Seller or required by law. Broker shall not disclose to Seller any information obtained in confidence regarding any other person Broker represents or may have represented except as required by law.

7. BROKER'S FEE:

(a) Seller shall pay Broker a fee of *(complete (i) or (ii))*: (i) $ _____; or (ii) _____% of the sales price; in cash in _____ County, Texas when Broker's Fee is earned and payable. In the event of exchange or breach of this Listing, the Listing Price shall be the sales price for purposes of computing Broker's Fee.

(1) <u>Earned</u>: Broker's Fee shall be earned when any one of the following events occurs during the term of this Listing: (i) Broker individually or in cooperation with another broker procures a buyer who enters into a contract with Seller to buy the Property; (ii) Broker individually or in cooperation with another broker procures a buyer ready, willing, and able to buy the Property at the Listing Price and on terms stated in paragraph 3 or at any other price and on terms acceptable to Seller; (iii) Seller sells, exchanges, agrees to sell, or agrees to exchange the Property to anyone at any price on any terms; or (iv) Seller breaches this Listing.

(2) <u>Payable</u>: Once earned, Broker's Fee shall be payable, either during term of this Listing or after its termination, at the earlier of any one of the following events: (i) the closing and funding of any sale or exchange of the Property; (ii) Seller's refusal to sell the Property; (iii) Seller's breach of this Listing; or (iv) at such time as otherwise set forth in this Listing. Broker's Fee shall not be payable if a sale of the Property does not close or fund as a result of: (i) Seller's failure, without fault of Seller, to deliver a title policy to a buyer; (ii) loss of ownership due to foreclosure or other legal proceeding; or (iii) Seller's failure to restore the Property, as a result of casualty loss, to its previous condition by the closing date set forth in a contract for the sale of the Property.

(b) If a buyer, with whom Seller has entered into a contract for the sale of the Property during the term of this Listing, breaches such a contract and Seller receives earnest money or a portion thereof as liquidated damages, Seller shall pay Broker one-half of such amount, but not to exceed Broker's Fee stated in paragraph 7(a).

(c) If Seller collects the sales price and/or damages either by suit, compromise, settlement or otherwise from a buyer who breached a contract for the sale of the Property entered into during the term of this Listing, Seller shall pay Broker, after deducting attorneys' fees and other expenses of collection, an amount equal to one-half of the amount collected after deductions or the full amount of the Broker's Fee described in paragraph 7(a), whichever is less.

(d) If within __180__ days after the termination of this Listing (the Protection Period), Seller enters into a contract to sell the Property or sells, exchanges or otherwise transfers a legal or equitable interest (excluding a lease with no right to purchase) of the Property to any person whose attention has been called to the Property by Broker, any other broker, or Seller during the term of this Listing, Seller shall pay Broker the Broker's Fee stated in paragraph 7(a), provided Broker, prior to or within five (5) days after the termination of this Listing, has sent to Seller written notice specifying the names of the persons whose attention has been called to the Property during the term of this Listing. If during the term of the Protection Period such sale, exchange or transfer occurs while the Property is listed exclusively with another Texas licensed real estate broker, this paragraph shall not apply and Seller shall not be obligated to pay Broker's Fee. The term "person" shall be broadly construed to include any individual or entity in any capacity.

8. BROKER'S AUTHORITY: Broker shall make reasonable efforts and act diligently to sell the Property. Seller authorizes Broker or Broker's associates to: (a) advertise the Property by means and methods as Broker determines; (b) place a "For Sale" sign on the Property in compliance with any State and local laws, rules, ordinances, restrictions, or covenants; (c) remove from the Property all other signs offering the Property for sale or lease; (d) furnish comparative marketing and sales information about other properties to prospective buyers; (e) disseminate information about the Property to other brokers and their associates; (f) enter the Property at reasonable times to show the Property to prospective buyers; (g) authorize other brokers and their associates, home inspectors, appraisers, and repair personnel to enter the Property at reasonable times to show the Property to prospective buyers or for other

FIGURE 5-1 Continued

pertinent purposes; (h) obtain information from any holder of any note secured by a lien on the Property; (i) upon a final and closed sale of the Property, disclose the sales price and terms of sale to other brokers, appraisers, or other real estate professionals; and (j) accept earnest money and deposit the earnest money in trust in accordance with the terms of the earnest money contract. Broker is not authorized to execute any document in the name of or on behalf of Seller with respect to the Property.

9. SELLER'S REPRESENTATIONS AND ADDITIONAL PROMISES:

(a) Seller represents that: (1) Seller has fee simple title to and peaceable possession of the Property and all its improvements and fixtures thereon, unless rented, and the legal capacity to convey the Property; (2) Seller is not now a party to a listing agreement with another broker for the sale, exchange or lease of the Property; (3) no person or entity has any right to purchase, lease, or acquire the Property by virtue of an option, right of first refusal, or other agreement; (4) there are no delinquencies or defaults under any deed of trust, mortgage, or other encumbrance on the Property; (5) the Property is not subject to the jurisdiction of any court; and (6) all written information relating to the Property provided to Broker by Seller is true and correct.

(b) Seller shall: (1) cooperate fully in good faith with Broker to facilitate the showing and marketing of the Property; (2) not rent or lease the Property during the term of this Listing without the prior written approval of Broker; (3) not negotiate with any prospective buyer who may contact Seller directly, but refer all prospective buyers to Broker; (4) not enter into a listing agreement with another broker for the sale, exchange or lease of the Property to become effective during the term of this Listing; (5) furnish to a buyer of the Property an owner's policy of title insurance in the amount of the sales price at Seller's expense; and (6) provide Broker with copies of all leases or rental agreements, if any, pertaining to the Property and advise Broker of any tenants moving in or out of the Property.

10. SELLER'S DISCLOSURE NOTICE AND RESIDENTIAL SERVICE CONTRACTS:

(a)   Section 5.008 of the Texas Property Code requires a seller of residential real property of not more than one dwelling unit to deliver a Seller's Disclosure Notice to a buyer on or before the effective date of a contract for the sale of the Property (unless otherwise exempt). Seller authorizes Broker and Broker's associates to furnish prospective buyers and other brokers with a copy of the attached Seller's Disclosure Notice. Seller represents that the attached Seller's Disclosure Notice was completed to the best of Seller's knowledge and belief and that Seller has disclosed all known material defects and material facts affecting the Property in the attached Seller's Disclosure Notice. Seller agrees to amend the Seller's Disclosure Notice if any material change occurs during the term of this Listing. Seller shall protect, defend, indemnify and hold harmless Broker, Broker's associates, and any other brokers or their associates of and from any damages, costs, attorney's fees or expenses arising from Seller's failure to disclose any material or relevant information or the giving of any incorrect information to Broker, Broker's associates, any other brokers or their associates, or prospective buyers.

(b)   Residential service contracts (home warranties) are available from residential service companies licensed under Article 6573b, Texas Civil Statutes. A residential service contract is an agreement whereby the residential service company may, under the terms of the agreement, repair or replace all or any part of the appliances, or electrical, plumbing, heating, cooling, or other systems. Seller ❑ accepts ❑ waives a residential service contract during the term of this Listing.

11. BACK-UP OFFERS: Broker shall not be obligated to continue to market the Property after Seller has entered into a binding contract to sell the Property. If a subsequent or back-up offer for the sale of the Property is submitted to Broker after Seller has entered into a binding contract to sell the Property, Broker ❑ shall ❑ shall not submit the subsequent or back-up offer to Seller. If Broker is to submit subsequent or back-up offers, Seller shall specifically provide in any contract for the sale of the Property with a buyer that Seller may receive and negotiate subsequent or back-up offers.

12. KEYBOX:

NOTICE: A keybox is a locked container placed on the Property in which a key to the Property is placed. Keyboxes make it more convenient for cooperating brokers and their associates, home inspectors, appraisers, and repair personnel to facilitate the showing, inspecting, and repairing of the Property. The keybox is locked and opened by a special combination, key, or a programmed access card so that whoever possesses the special combination, key, or the access card to the keybox has access to the Property at any time, even in Seller's absence. The use of the keybox will probably increase the number of showings, but involves risks (such as unauthorized entry, theft, property damage, or personal injury). Neither the Association nor MLS requires the use of a keybox. Please discuss the advantages and disadvantages of keyboxes with your Broker, insurance agent, and/or attorney.

(a)   Broker ❑ is ❑ is not   authorized to place a keybox containing a key to the Property on the Property.

(b)   If a keybox is authorized, Seller shall protect, defend, indemnify and hold harmless Broker, Broker's associates, and other brokers and their associates, the Association, MLS, any listing service, and any keybox provider of and from any damages or claims arising from the use of a keybox including, but not limited to, damages to or loss of real or personal property or personal injury not caused by Broker's negligence. Seller shall assume all risk of any loss, damage, and injury. Broker advises Seller to obtain personal property insurance.

(c)   If the Property is occupied by a tenant at any time during this Listing, Seller shall furnish Broker a written statement, signed by all tenants, authorizing the use of a keybox or Broker may remove any keybox from the Property.

13. LIMITATION OF LIABILITY: Broker and any other broker shall not be responsible in any manner for personal injury to Seller resulting from acts of third parties or loss or damage of personal or real property due to vandalism, theft, freezing water pipes, and any other damage or loss not caused by Broker's negligence. If the Property is or becomes vacant during the term of this Listing, Seller shall notify Seller's casualty insurance company and request a "Vacancy Clause" to cover the Property. Broker shall not be responsible for the security of the Property nor for inspecting the Property on any periodic basis. Seller shall protect, defend, indemnify, and hold harmless Broker, Broker's associates, any other brokers and their associates, and the Association of and from any damages, costs, attorneys' fees, and expenses arising from acts of third parties or loss or damage of personal or real property due to vandalism, theft, freezing water pipes and any other damage not caused by Broker's negligence.

14. ESCROW AUTHORIZATION: Seller authorizes, and Broker may so instruct, any escrow or closing agent authorized to close a transaction for the purchase or acquisition of the Property to collect and disburse to Broker the Broker's Fee due under this Listing.

FIGURE 5-1   Continued

15. IRS: The Internal Revenue Service (IRS) requires a closing agent to report the gross sales price, Seller's tax identification number and other required information to the IRS. Seller shall provide to any closing agent such information at the time of closing. IRS requires a buyer of real property to withhold a percentage of the sales price from Seller if Seller is a foreign person. A foreign person includes nonresident aliens, foreign corporations, foreign partnerships, foreign trusts, or foreign estates. In most sales, Seller will be required to deliver an affidavit that Seller is not a foreign person. Seller certifies that Seller ☐ is ☐ is not a foreign person.

16. SPECIAL PROVISIONS:

17. MEDIATION: The parties agree to negotiate in good faith in an effort to resolve any dispute related to this Listing that may arise between the parties. If the dispute cannot be resolved by negotiation, the dispute shall be submitted to mediation before resorting to arbitration or litigation. If the need for mediation arises, the parties to the dispute shall choose a mutually acceptable mediator and shall share the cost of mediation equally.

18. ATTORNEYS' FEES: If Seller or Broker is a prevailing party in any legal proceeding brought as a result of a dispute under this Listing or any transaction related to or contemplated by this Listing, such party shall be entitled to recover from the non-prevailing party all costs of such proceeding and reasonable attorneys' fees.

19. NOTICES: All notices shall be in writing and effective when hand-delivered, mailed, or sent by facsimile transmission to:

Broker at _____   Seller at _____
Phone ( )_____   Phone ( )_____
Fax ( )_____   Fax ( )_____

20. AGREEMENT OF PARTIES: Addenda and other related documents which are part of this Listing are: Information About Brokerage Services; ☐ Seller's Disclosure Notice; ☐ _____
This Listing contains the entire agreement between Seller and Broker and may not be changed except by written agreement. This Listing may not be assigned by either party without the written approval of the other party. This Listing is binding upon the parties, their heirs, administrators, executors, successors, and permitted assigns. All Sellers executing this Listing shall be jointly and severally liable for the performance of all its terms. The laws of the State of Texas shall govern the interpretation, validity, performance, and enforcement of this Listing. Should any clause in this Listing be found invalid or unenforceable by a court of law, the remainder of this Listing shall not be affected and all other provisions of this Listing shall remain valid and enforceable to the fullest extent permitted by law.

21. ADDITIONAL NOTICES:

(a) **Broker's Fees, or the sharing of fees between brokers are not fixed, controlled, recommended, suggested, or maintained by the Association of REALTORS®, MLS, or any listing service. The amount a seller agrees to pay a broker is negotiable.**

(b) **Fair housing laws require the Property to be shown and made available for sale to all persons without regard to race, color, religion, national origin, sex, disability or familial status.**

(c) **Whether a keybox is authorized or not, Seller is advised to safeguard and/or remove jewelry and other valuables located in the Property.**

(d) **If the Property was built before 1978, federal law requires that before a buyer is obligated under a contract to buy the Property, the Seller shall: (1) provide the buyer with a lead hazard information pamphlet (as prescribed by EPA); (2) disclose the presence of any known lead base paint or hazards (including providing the buyer with any lead hazard evaluation report available to Seller); and (3) permit the buyer to conduct a risk assessment or inspection for the presence of lead base paint hazards. A contract for the sale of Property built before 1978 must contain a statutorily prescribed Lead Warning Statement to the buyer.**

(e) **Broker cannot give legal advice. This is intended to be a legally binding agreement. READ IT CAREFULLY. If you do not understand the effect of this Listing, consult your attorney BEFORE signing.**

_____   _____   _____   _____
BROKER'S PRINTED NAME   LICENSE NO.   SELLER'S SIGNATURE   DATE

By: _____   _____   _____   _____
    BROKER'S or ASSOCIATE'S SIGNATURE DATE   SELLER'S SIGNATURE   DATE

                                                      _____
                                                      SELLERS' SOCIAL SECURITY NUMBERS OR TAX I.D. NUMBERS

FIGURE 5-1 Continued

agency listing is in fact the "procuring cause" in making a sale. This may be a problem, particularly when an open agency listing has been given to several brokers.

In those areas where a multiple listing service (MLS) is prevalent, the use of open listings is relatively rare. MLS provides the desired exposure to several brokers (and, thus, a large number of potential buyers), while protecting the broker's exclusive right to a commission.

Net Listing.   A net listing agreement can technically be used in any listing agreement. The term *net listing* refers to the manner of calculating the brokerage commission due rather than to the broker's rights to sell the property. In a net listing agreement the commission is not specified but rather determined by the excess of the total sales price over the owners' desired sales price for the real estate. For instance, an owner may require that a broker sell the property for whatever price will net $35,000 for the owner. The broker, then, is free to sell the property for whatever price the open market may bring, knowing that out of the sales price, the first $35,000 will go to the owner; then the closing costs must be paid; and if any monies are left over, these funds will go to the broker as his commission.

Although a net listing can be lucrative, most brokers prefer to rely on a percentage of the sales price for the purposes of convenience and to avoid any conflict of interest with the property owner. For example, if a broker walks away from a closing with more money than the property owner, questions may be raised as to how well the property owner was represented in the sale. For this reason net listings are considered unethical and/or illegal in some states.

Multiple Listing.   A multiple listing agreement normally involves an exclusive right to sell held by a broker who is a member of the local real estate board and/or of the multiple listing service (MLS). Technically, it should be thought of as a marketing method rather than a type of listing agreement. Since all member brokers have an equal right to sell the property, an MLS generally provides a broad exposure to a large number of potential buyers. Commission fees are split between the listing and selling brokers who brought about the sale, *Frisell* v. *Newman,* 429 P.2d 864, 868. Since the listing broker will receive a portion of the fee regardless of who makes the sale, he is generally willing to advertise and otherwise spend time and money that might lead to a sale.

LEGAL ACTIONS TO RECOVER COMMISSIONS

In most written agreements, both parties promise to perform some service or do some act. Thus attorneys refer to these as *bilateral* contracts. A listing agreement, on the other hand, may be thought of as a *unilateral contract* because only one party promises his performance. That is, the owner promises to pay the broker a commission if the broker sells his property at a certain price and within a certain time period. On the other hand, the broker makes no promises and incurs no obligations other than to use his best efforts to market the property. He cannot be sued if he fails to sell the property because he has not promised to make a sale.

A unilateral contract is completed and the contractual obligation fulfilled when the broker produces a ready, willing, and able buyer to purchase the property according to the terms of the listing agreement. Thus, the broker completes his part of the contract by performance rather than by making promises contained in the listing agreement. Therefore, the broker's right to a commission arises when he produces a ready, willing, and able buyer on the terms specified in the listing agreement, even though the seller may decline to execute the contract for sale. This also includes consummation of sales during "override" periods, after the listing has been terminated and the broker is entitled to commissions for sales closed which were solicited during the listing period, *United Farm Agency of Wisconsin, Inc.* v. *Klasen,* 334 N.W.2d 110 (1983). Some states still require some causal relationship, however, during these extension periods, *Chapman Co.* v. *Western Nebraska Broadcasting Co.,* 329 N.W.2d 107 (Neb. 1983).

A real estate broker's right to a commission is also conditioned on several other factors. First, any person bringing an action for a commission must be a duly licensed real estate broker or salesperson at the time he sold the real property. Second, there must have been an agreement for the payment of the commission. This requirement is often satisfied if there is a listing agreement or if the promise to pay the commission is clearly set out in the earnest money contract, *Maloney* v. *Strain, supra.* Third, under the terms of some listing agreements, the broker must show that he was the *procuring cause* of the sale. Depending on the type of listing agreement and its precise terms, if the broker produces a ready, willing, and able buyer he is entitled to his commission if these three requirements are met.

In some states the broker is also required to advise the purchaser in writing that he should either have the abstract covering the real estate examined by an attorney or obtain a policy of title insurance, *Jones* v. *Del Anderson and Associates,* 539 S.W.2d 348 (1977). Furthermore, if the broker fails to do so, he may be legally prevented from collecting a commission otherwise earned.

Regardless of the legal requirements, it is always good practice to advise a purchaser of the options available to help assure that he is acquiring a good and clear title to the real estate. The age of consumerism is clearly upon us!

Many cases have arisen in which the seller has refused to pay a commission because a contracted sale was never consummated. Generally, the closing of the sale is *not* the factor determining whether the broker is entitled to a commission. Rather, the broker is entitled to a commission if he produces a buyer who is ready and able to buy pursuant to the terms of the listing agreement. If the seller backs out of the deal, he has breached the terms of the listing agreement and owes the broker a commission. The fact that the sale has not been consummated is not the fault of the broker, and the broker will be entitled to his commission, *Duckworth* v. *Field,* 516 F.2d 952 (5th Cir. 1975). Furthermore, court decisions have held that when the purchaser backs out of the agreement and the seller chooses not to enforce specific performance, the broker still has earned his commission, *Davidson* v. *Suber,* 553 S.W.2d 430 (1977). In many states, if a broker is required to sue the seller, he is also entitled to reimbursement for his attorney's fees, although this may depend on the terms of the listing agreement.

Filing suit to recover commissions due is generally the only effective remedy that a broker has against a seller who has breached his contract. In most states, the broker has no interest in the real estate (there's an interest in the <u>transaction</u>, not the real property), and therefore cannot put a lien on it or in any other way "slander" the title of the seller's real property. Moreover if title to the seller's real estate becomes clouded as a result of a broker's intentional act, the broker may be liable for significant damages.

There are some circumstances under which the broker is not due a commission for unconsummated sales, even though he provided a willing and able buyer pursuant to the terms of the contract. For instance, a "special agreement" between the broker and seller may override the terms of both the listing agreement and the earnest money contract. A clear illustration of this is when the agreement provides that the broker be paid out of the sale proceeds, *DeFranceaux Realty Group, Inc.* v. *Leeth,* 391 A.2d 1209.

A broker may have difficulty, however, in obtaining a commission for an option agreement. An option agreement is not an earnest money contract, but rather a contract executed by the optionor which gives the optionee the right (not the obligation) to purchase the property at a later date. This is discussed in greater detail in Chapter 7. The law is well settled in Texas that if a purchaser produced by the broker enters into a mere option agreement, the broker will not be entitled to a commission. *Moss & Raley*

v. *Wren,* 120 S.W. 847 (Tex. 1909), *John Dull & Co.* v. *Life of Nebraska Insurance Co.,* 642 S.W.2d 1 (Tex. Civ. App.—Houston, 1982). In order to prevail for a commission under an option contract there must be a closing. It is only at that point that a ready, willing, and able buyer has been procured in an option agreement. Leasing commissions are payable in basically the same manner. It has already been determined in Texas that a lease is a sale within contemplation of the Real Estate Licensing Act, *Moser Company* v. *Awalt Industrial Properties, Inc.,* 584 S.W.2d 902 (Tex. Civ. App.— Amarillo, 1979), although another case holds differently, *Collins* v. *Beste,* 40 S.W.2d 788 (Tex. App.—Ft. Worth, 1992). The only difficulty is when the leasing commission is paid over a long period of time. Lease commissions are not a covenant running with the land, and if the existing landlord sells the property, the new purchaser is not liable for the lease commission payments. *Dauley* v. *First National Bank of Fort Worth,* 565 S.W.2d 346 (Tex. Civ. App.—Ft. Worth, 1978). Therefore, it is probably advisable that the broker should get a cash commission payment for obtaining the lessee's lease even if it has to be discounted.

SPECIAL PROBLEM AREAS

There are certain problem areas unique to the real estate brokerage business. They deserve special discussion so as to make real estate agents and others more aware of them and hopefully avoid the worst pitfalls.

Real Estate as a Security

Group investments in real estate, often called *syndications,* present a potential licensing problem for real estate brokers who market them. Irrespective of the form of ownership used by the syndication (e.g., corporation, limited partnership, etc.), real estate may be legally classified as a security if the investors expect a *profit* through the *efforts of a third party, SEC* v. *Howey,* 329 U.S. 819. If the interest sold is legally deemed a security, the broker may find he cannot maintain an action for a commission sale unless he has a securities broker's license, *Lyon* v. *Stevenson,* 135 Cal. Rptr. 457 (Cal. 1977), and *Ness* v. *Greater Arizona Realty, Inc.,* 572 P.2d 1195 (Arizona 1978).

In its simplest form, the legal logic is that a stockbroker cannot recover a commission if he sells real estate unless he has a real estate broker's (or salesperson's) license. Correspondingly, a real estate broker should not be able to recover a commission from the sale of securities unless he has a securities broker's license.

Truth in Lending

Federal truth-in-lending legislation presents another possible source of legal difficulty for some real estate brokers. If the broker should be determined to be "in the business of making loans," Regulation Z requires him to make a full disclosure of all loan costs to a consumer. This may occur when a real estate broker personally finances real property sales, *Eby* v. *Reb Realty*, 495 F.2d 646. The Federal truth-in-lending legislation is discussed in greater detail in Chapter 11.

When a real estate broker hires sales personnel to represent his brokerage company in seeking listings and negotiating real estate transactions, something that is far too often overlooked is whether or not that sales agent should be classified as an *independent contractor* or as an *employee.*

Employees versus Independent Contractors

The broker normally assumes that the sales agent will be an independent contractor because there are a number of advantages, from the broker's point of view, favoring independent contractor status of the sales personnel. These advantages generally include a smaller amount of paperwork and fewer records to maintain on behalf of the broker; no office hours are required to be kept; and the sales personnel are more motivated to sell if they work on a commission-only basis. There also are tax savings to the firm because there are no social security and unemployment taxes to be paid by the firm, and the system tends to promote more professionalism and advantages for more experienced sales agents. The independent contractor status basically provides for a more professional, harder working, motivated sales agent because there is no limit to his potential income, and there are fewer controls on the individual's time and effort.

If classified as an employee, on the other hand, the individual salesperson may not be as well motivated since the basic check amount is the same every month regardless of whether or not any results are achieved. Furthermore, the employing broker's overhead remains relatively constant but quite high. Accounting and bookkeeping become more expensive because of the larger amount of paperwork and office records required. Added costs of social security taxes and unemployment benefits as well as other requirements by the federal government that apply to employees generally must also be considered.

This issue has been greatly simplified for the services of real estate agents. *The Tax Equity and Fiscal Responsibility Act of 1982* provides a safe harbor to eliminate the vast majority of conflicts that have existed for real estate agents. The new federal law is an addition to the Internal Revenue Code, and provides that a qualified real estate agent shall not be treated as an employee nor shall the person for whom such services are performed be treated as an employer. The key to compliance with the statute revolves around the definition of qualified real estate agents. It includes any individual who is a salesperson if (1) such individual is a licensed real estate agent; (2) substantially all the remuneration is directly related to sales rather than to the number of hours worked; and (3) the services are performed pursuant to a written contract between such individual and the person for whom the services are performed and such contract provides that the individual will not be treated as an employee with respect to such services for federal tax purposes.

This has been held to apply to real estate appraisal services as well, *Internal Revenue Code,* §3508.

Brokers versus Lawyers   In many states substantial controversy has arisen between brokers and lawyers in delineating the proper role of each. In some instances "statements of principles" or "broker-lawyer accords" have been jointly developed in an effort to define their respective roles in a real estate transaction. These documents basically define the broker's obligation to negotiate a transaction and to be well informed on real estate market developments in order to provide good advice to his client's business judgment, *New Jersey State Bar Association* v. *New Jersey Association of Realty Boards,* 461 A.2d 1112, mod. 467 A.2d 577 (1983). The lawyer, on the other hand, is to use his best efforts to proceed diligently to the conclusion of the transaction and to prepare the required documents.

A statement of principles does not have the binding force of law. However, there are sound reasons for its substantive contents, and better relationships will result between brokers and lawyers when the principles are adhered to. Brokers should not attempt to give legal advice, and lawyers generally should not advise clients on the fair market value of real estate. Likewise, in those states where attorneys are permitted to sell real estate on a commission basis, they should not attempt to force the broker to split the commission on the sale of real property unless they actively contributed to making the sale. In most states, brokers have the legal right to fill in simple blanks in form contracts.

In short, the relationship between a professional broker and a professional lawyer should be complementary, and neither profession should make even the slightest attempt to downgrade the other before, during, or after a real estate transaction is made.

Antitrust Laws   Antitrust laws may seem to have a limited impact on the individual licensee; however, they create an increasing concern for brokers, Realtor boards, and Multiple Listing Services (MLS).

There are several common names for the antitrust statutes and their subsequent amendments. The two that have the most far-reaching impact on real estate are the *Sherman Antitrust Act* (15 U.S.C.A. §l et seq) and the *Clayton Antitrust Act* (15 U.S.C.A. §12 et seq). The provisions of these Acts are enforced by the Federal Trade Commission and the Department of Justice. The basic theory of antitrust laws is that monopolies and dominance in any industry are against the pubic interest and the free flow of goods and services through interstate commerce.

Sherman Act.   Pertinent provisions of the Sherman Antitrust Act prohibit unreasonable restraint of trade and monopolies. This Act was "specifically intended to prohibit independent businesses from becoming 'associates' in a common plan which is bound to reduce their competitor's opportunity. ... " This has been interpreted by the Supreme Court of Pennsylvania as prohibiting a Board of Realtors® from excluding a licensee from MLS membership, even for cause. *Collins* v. *Main Line Board of Realtors,* 304 A.2d 493 (Penn., 1973). While the Pennsylvania case is a complicated one, its primary holding is well reasoned, and the U.S. Supreme Court declined to hear an appeal.

Clayton Act.   The Clayton Act is not as broad in scope as the Sherman Act and seeks to reach specified practices that have been held by courts to be outside the scope of the Sherman Act, but that Congress considered to adversely affect free competition. It specifically deals with price discrimination, acquisitions and mergers, and exclusive dealing arrangements. The Clayton Act was passed to complement the Sherman Act, although both can be violated at the same time.

One pertinent part of the Clayton Act that may affect real estate brokers is the aggressive acquisition of smaller brokerage offices by larger ones. If a very large brokerage office moves into a new area of the state and their acquisition of smaller real estate companies significantly lessens the competition in the area, it may be a merger or acquisition that results in the violation of Section 7 of the Clayton Antitrust Act.

Price Fixing.   One of the key areas of concern for real estate licensees has been *price fixing,* which is generally defined as the setting of prices by an industry at an artificial level. Price fixing, whether good or evil, express or implied, is *illegal per se.* In theory, prices must be set by competitors only, and not by any agreement between or among competitors.

Two recent decisions have been made in the area of antitrust law as it pertains to real estate brokers. Both involved a conspiracy to set prices. In the first case, six corporate and three individual defendants were convicted of conspiracy to fix real estate commissions in Montgomery County, Maryland (commission rate at 7%) in violation of Section 1 of the Sherman Act. The facts in this case indicated that there was, in fact, a conspiracy. There was even testimony in the case that some brokers took a 6% listing and one of the conspiring brokers called the 6% broker to inform him of his mistake. There was further testimony that the conspiring brokers called each other to be sure that they were "holding the line" for setting a new, higher commission rate, *United States* v. *Foley,* et al., 598 F.2d 1323 (1979).

The second case was a United States Supreme Court case decided in 1980. The more serious question in this case was whether or not real estate brokerage constitutes interstate commerce. If real estate brokerage does involve interstate commerce, it automatically establishes federal jurisdiction and antitrust jurisdiction for the Federal Trade Commission. If it does not, it will mean that the regulation of real estate brokerage will remain primarily a state matter and therefore not be subject to federal antitrust jurisdiction.

The Supreme Court discussed the possibility that the courts may consider the broker's activities within the flow of interstate commerce because of the movement of their clients into and out of the state, and the broker's assistance in securing financing and title insurance. The Supreme Court remanded the case to the trial court to determine whether or not, by the facts of the case, the broker's activities were within the flow of interstate commerce. This greatly emphasizes how critical the facts of each case are. If the jury can determine from this case that the broker's activities are substantially affected by interstate commerce or substantially affect interstate commerce, it could set a very important precedent for the federal government's regulation of brokerage activities. In many cases it could even supersede state law as it pertains to real estate brokerage, *McLain* v. *Real Estate Board of New Orleans,* 100 U.S. 512 (U.S. Sup. Ct., 1980).

As in all areas of the law, particularly those involving very sophisticated federal laws, arguments on both sides of these issues are very good. The public needs to be protected against restraints on trade and price fixing in order to increase competition and to prevent conspiracy. However, as all licensees know, very few businesses are as competitive as the real estate business. It is probably fair to say, again, that the decisions yet to be made in this area will be determined largely by the facts of each case and by how the respective federal laws apply to those facts.

Boycotting.   There has also been complex litigation in recent years over *boycotting* practices by Boards of Realtors® and their subsidiary MLS systems in refusing to allow membership to real estate licensees. Rather than the *per se* rules of illegality, courts have tended to invoke the *rule of reasonableness* to determine whether or not the boycotting did, in fact, restrain trade. *United States* v. *Realty Multi-List, Inc.,* 629 F.2d 1351 (5th Cir., 1980). The rule-of-reasonableness standard acknowledges the anticompetitive effect of excluding members, but also acknowledges the competitive effects of MLS, and the ability of its members to provide better service because of the existence of the MLS system.

In alleging a restraint of trade by boycotting, the complaining party must show that a concerted effort to boycott exists in an attempt to monopolize a segment of the market. This must be more than just refusing to deal with another licensee. Before a Board of Realtors® can be boycotting, for instance, it must be proved to be the conduct of the board, rather than just a few of its members. *Park* v. *El Paso Board of Realtors,* 764 F.2d 1053 (5th Cir., 1985). Reasonable requirements for membership, then, are not necessarily anticompetitive. Requiring members to attend orientation courses, pay dues, and maintain a residency can provide a reasonable basis for allowing membership. However, arbitrary exclusions from the board or MLS systems because applicants are part-time brokers, or can't pay an unreasonably high membership fee, could be construed to be exclusionary conduct.

It should also be noted that the membership requirements of MLS and other Realtor® trade organizations can also be protected through copyright laws. These laws can help by refusing access to certain publications to nonmember brokers, *Supermarket of Homes, Inc.* v. *San Fernando Valley Board of Realtors,* 786 F.2d 1400 (9th Cir., 1986).

Tying Claims

A tying claim requires that a consumer be tied to a particular product. For instance, if a broker agrees to perform his services for no charge, on the condition that you are required to use him at some future date for another transaction, regardless of his quality of services, he has tied himself into the transaction. The tying arrangements can be analyzed under either the *per se* rule or the rule of reason, but are generally analyzed under the rule of reason. The general criteria for tying arrangements are: (1) that there are two separate products, a tying product and a tied product; (2) that those products are in fact tied together—that is, the buyer was forced to buy the tied product to get the tying product; (3) that the seller possessed a sufficient economic power and the tying product to coerce buyer acceptance of the tied product; (4) the involvement of a non-insubstantial amount of interstate commerce in the market of the tied product.

Tying has surfaced in two separate issues. In *King City Realty, Inc. v. Sun Pace Corporation*, 633 P.2d 784 (Ore. 1981), a listing contract provided that the defendant would purchase seven lots, but included a list-back under which the defendant agreed to list exclusively with the plaintiff realty company for resale of all of the lots purchased by the defendant under the agreement after construction of houses on such lot. In *Thompson v. Metropolitan Multi-List, Inc.*, 934 F.2d 1566 (11th Cir., 1991), the court held that tying the multiple listing service to a real estate board membership may also constitute an unfair competition and therefore an antitrust violation.

SUMMARY   Real estate brokers and salespersons are affected in their everyday activities by a large number of state and federal laws. One of the major laws to which they are subject is their own state real estate licensing law. This law serves two different purposes. First, it serves to regulate entry into the real estate brokerage industry by setting out eligibility requirements and requiring examinations so as to help assure the general public that it will be served by people with a minimum degree of competency. Second, it serves to further protect the public by regulating broker/salesperson conduct in certain respects. State real estate commissions have been established and have the legal responsibility of enforcing both licensing and professional conduct within the industry.

Financial protection is afforded the general public against licensees' financial misconduct either by bonding requirements or through a statewide recovery fund. In either case, to the extent possible recovery must first be had from the licensee whose improper conduct caused the loss.

State real estate commissions also generally oversee punishment for unlicensed or unauthorized persons who engage in real estate brokerage activities. Usually these violations constitute misdemeanors and may be punished by fines and/or by short-term imprisonment.

State real estate licensing laws and/or statutes of fraud generally set out conditions that a real estate licensee must meet before he can recover a commission on a real estate transaction. The typical requirement is a document, often a listing agreement or an earnest money contract, signed by the party to be charged (sued).

At least five different types of listing agreements may be employed by real estate brokers, depending on the legal rights that the parties desire to create. These five types are the exclusive right to sell, the exclusive agency to sell, open listing, net listing, and multiple listing. If a sale is made by anyone, including the landowner, during the time period specified in an exclusive right to sell listing, the broker is entitled to a commission. Under an exclusive agency to sell listing, the landowner cannot list the property with other brokers but can reserve the right to sell it himself without liability for a commission. An open listing gives a broker a nonexclusive right to sell under which he can earn a commission only by selling the property. A net listing may be used for any of the three previous types of listings and states the prices that the seller will accept. If the broker can sell the property for a greater amount, he can keep the excess as his commission. A multiple listing normally involves an exclusive right to sell being given to a broker who is a member of a multiple listing service (MLS). This exposes the property to a large number of potential buyers (the clients of all brokers belonging to the MLS) and involves a commission split between the listing and selling brokers.

In general, in order to collect a commission a broker must be duly licensed; have a written memorandum of agreement involving the subject property and signed by the seller; perhaps advise the purchaser of the need to either have an abstract examined by his attorney or procure an owner's title insurance policy; and, depending on the type of listing agreement, show that he either produced a ready, willing, and able buyer or that he was the procuring cause of a sale.

The law of agency determines many important legal relationships between broker and seller. A broker is a special agent of the seller, and he can bind the seller only in the limited manner set out in the agreement. He is under a fiduciary relationship to act in the best interests of the seller. Further, a broker owes the seller the duties of performance, loyalty, reasonable care, and an accounting of all monies received and disbursed.

Real estate brokers also have certain legal duties to prospective purchasers. These include a duty not to make material misrepresentation about the property or otherwise make false promises likely to induce a prospective purchaser to buy the property.

Real estate brokers who sell interests in a syndication are not entitled to a commission unless they have a securities broker's license. This is because real estate is legally classified as a "security" when an investor expects a return from the efforts of a third party, such as a general partner/syndicator.

The legal relationship between a broker and his sales personnel may be either employer-employee or employer-independent contractor. Most brokers prefer creating the latter relationship because it permits them to avoid social security and unemployment taxes, as well as avoiding extra bookkeeping requirements. To create an employer-independent contractor status, brokers can remunerate their salespersons only on a commission basis, and, among other requirements, they cannot require salespersons to attend periodic sales meetings.

A legal area of continuing concern is the proper role of both brokers and lawyers in real estate transactions. Brokers should not give legal advice, and lawyers should not comment on the condition or value of the property unless employed to do so. All legal documents should be drafted by lawyers, although brokers do have the authority to fill in simple blanks in approved form contracts.

A final legal area in which brokers must maintain continuing diligence is in avoiding antitrust laws. They particularly must guard against restraint of trade and price-fixing restrictions. Where common commission rates are charged in a community, these should be the result of competition between realty firms rather than the result of an agreement to charge the same rate.

DISCUSSION QUESTIONS

1. What reasons can be cited justifying the need for state real estate commissions?

2. In your state, what are the requirements for collecting a commission on the sale of real estate?

3. What are the requirements for obtaining a salesperson's license in your state? A broker's license?

4. In your locality, will most salespersons be classified as employees or as independent contractors? Why?

6

The Law of Agency

The changing provisions of the real estate licensing acts, as well as generally accepted provisions for employment contracts, have underscored the technicalities of the law as they apply to real estate brokerage. The law of agency has long been considered by courts as the fundamental relationship between clients and brokers. Historically, the real estate agent was hired by the seller to assist in marketing and sales. The concepts of buyer brokerage, dual agency, and intermediary have added new dimensions to the traditional theories. To simplify the issues, let's first consider those traditional relationships. The parties necessary to agency relationship are the *principal* (the *seller*, also called the *client* and *owner* of the property), the *agent* (the *broker*), and third parties (the *buyer*, *customer*, or *purchaser*).

One can be deemed to be an agent of a principal through written or verbal authority. Brokers frequently think that the person who pays the commission is the principal. Who pays the commission is not determinative. The agency can even arise if the agency relationship is specifically rejected, because a jury may make the ultimate decision, *Wilson* v. *Donze*, 692 S.W.2d 734 (Tex. Civ. App.—Ft. Worth, 1985).

CREATION OF THE AGENCY RELATIONSHIP

Another factor also becomes important in creating the agency relationship, and that is determining *when* the agency relationship arises. There has been convincing authority in other states that the agency relationship can arise before any written agreements are signed, because confidences can be exchanged in the earliest stages of negotiating the listing agreement! See *Lyle* v. *Moore*, 599 P.2d 336 (Mont. 1979).

Types of Authority   Agency relationships are classified according to the authority given to the agent to represent the principal, or to the agent's authority represented by the principal to a third party. These types of agency include agency by actual authority, agency by ostensible authority, and agency by ratification.

Ageny by Actual Authority.   Agency by *actual authority* exists when the agent is employed by the principal by either an express or an oral contract. This type of agency generally outlines in detail what authority the agent has to act on behalf of and to bind the principal. When this is specifically given to an agent either in writing or verbally, it is considered to be *express authority.* Along with express authority there is often created a certain amount of *implied authority.* Implied authority is the right to do certain acts on behalf of the principal even though the acts may not have been specified in the contract. This authority may arise from custom in the industry, common usage, or conduct of the parties (an inference or implication as to the agent's right to act). An example of implied agency would be a listing agreement that does not specify that the broker has a right to put a sign in the yard offering the house for sale. However, it is customarily recognized that the broker may erect a sign in the front of the house offered for sale. The same might also be true of hours for showing the house, or means of advertising the house for sale. These are not things usually set out in the listing agreement, but the authority to do these things arises as implied authority because of common custom and usage in the industry.

In the traditional marketplace, a real estate agent is usually employed to represent the seller. An agent can also be employed to represent the buyer, however, creating the fiduciary duty to the purchaser rather than to the seller, *Tatum v. Preston Carter Co.,* 702 S.W.2d 186 (Tex. 1986).

Agency by Ostensible Authority.   Agency by *ostensible authority* exists because the principal intentionally or negligently causes a third party to believe that another was his agent, even though that agent may not actually be employed by the principal. If the third party reasonably believes that the agent is employed by the principal, the principal is bound by the act of his agent.

It is important to remember that an agent possessing apparent authority has no actual authority at all. If, however, the principal cloaks the agent in the authority to act in his behalf, or negligently gives him the authority by failing to exercise proper control over him, the agency relationship arises, *Hall v. Halamicek Enterprises, Inc.,* 669 S.W.2d 368 (Tex. Civ. App.—Corpus Christi, 1984). It should be emphasized that declarations of the agent alone are not sufficient, and it must be *acts of the principal* which create the apparent authority. Creation of agency through this type of conduct has also been called an *agency by estoppel* or *agency by apparent authority.*

A cautious licensee should also note that other states have held that, notwithstanding the existence of a listing agreement, an agency by ostensible authority can create an agency for a purchaser in some circumstances. *Little* v. *Rohauer, 707* P.2d 1015 (Colo. App., 1985). This could create the classic dual agency situation, discussed later in this chapter.

Agency by Ratification.   An *agency by ratification* is an agency that occurs *after the fact.* For instance, if an agent secures a contract on behalf of the principal and the principal subsequently agrees to the terms of the contract, the courts may hold that the agency was created as of the time the initial negotiation was transacted. The critical factors in determining whether a principal has ratified an unauthorized act by his agent are the principal's knowledge of the transaction and his actions in light of such knowledge. If the principal fails to repudiate the unauthorized transaction, it gives rise to an agency by ratification, *Cox* v. *Venters,* 887 S.W.2d 563 (Ky. App., 1994).

Agency Coupled with an Interest.   An *agency coupled with an interest* is a particular type of agency relationship in which the agent has an interest or estate in the property as part or all of his compensation. An agency coupled with an interest is generally considered to be irrevocable, although it may be terminated pursuant to an express agreement between the parties. It may not be terminated by unilateral act on behalf of the principal, however. This has created interesting questions in the use of guaranteed sales plans. If the broker creates an agency coupled with an interest and there is no sale, it may create an irrevocable agency.

Agency Liabilities

One of the significant factors in any agency relationship is the liability that the agent or the principal may impose on the other. (We will talk about the duties of these parties to each other for the remainder of this chapter.) If the duties are not met, however, it is important to know where the ultimate liability will lie between the principal and agent once the agency relationship has been created. Recent court rulings seem to indicate a strong trend toward suing licensees for other liabilities as a result of their agency, such as misrepresentation as to encumbrances, *Stone* v. *Lawyers Title Ins. Corp.,* 554 S.W.2d 183 (Tex. 1977); *Ingalls* v. *Rice,* 511 S.W.2d 78 (Tex. Civ.

App.—Houston, 1974); terms of an agreement, *Newsome* v. *Starkey,* 541 S.W.2d 468 (Tex. Civ. App.—Dallas, 1976); slandering title, *Walker* v. *Ruggles,* 540 S.W.2d 470 (Tex. Civ. App.—1976); failure to disclose defects, *Smith* v. *National Resort Communities, Inc.,* 585 S.W.2d 655 (Tex. 1979); failing to inform the client as to apprecia- tion in value of this property, *Ramsey* v. *Gordon,* 567 S.W.2d 868 (Tex. Civ. App.—Waco, 1978); engaging in conduct which consti- tutes real estate fraud, *McGaha* v. *Dishman,* 629 S.W.2d 220 (Tex. Civ. App.—Tyler, 1982); and even expressions of opinion, *Trenholm* v. *Ratcliff,* 646 S.W.2d 927 (Tex. 1983).

Special Agency. There are two types of agency relationships: a special agency and a general agency. The relationship between a listing broker and the principal is normally deemed to be a *special agency.* In a special agency, the principal is not responsible for the acts of the agent. The broker's responsibility is limited to market- ing the house. If a misrepresentation is made to the third party, it is probably made by the broker, since there is no relationship in con- tract or tort between the purchaser and seller prior to the earnest money contract being signed. In practice, the seller has little, if any, control over the conduct of the agent. Therefore, these misrepre- sentations will result in the broker being liable for them rather than the seller. So, in a special agency relationship, the principal is not responsible for the acts of his agent. This results in the agent being primarily liable in tort law (money damages for misrepresentation or negligence) to third parties, and to the principal in contract law (in the event he breaches any of his duties of care or misrepresents anything to the seller because of his fiduciary relationship).

General Agency. More difficult problems occur when there is a general agency relationship. In a *general agency* relationship the principal is always responsible for the acts of his agent as long as that agent is acting within the scope of his duties. In the typical list- ing situation, a general agency relationship exists between the salesperson and his sponsoring broker. The salesperson is the agent of the sponsoring broker and a *subagent* of the principal. The general agency relationship creates a wide scope of authority for the salesperson, who signs contracts on behalf of his principal and binds the principal on matters within the scope of his duties on a daily basis. In the general agency situation, if the agent makes a misrepresentation to the purchaser, the sponsoring broker is responsible for the acts of his agent and the third party sues the sponsoring broker rather than the sales agent. This may be partic- ularly harsh when an agency has been created by ostensible authority or ratification (the principal may have an agent and not know it!). Remember, he is responsible for those acts regardless of how the agency was created.

A disturbing trend is developing in law that may be converting special agencies to general agencies under certain circumstances. If a seller benefits from the fraud, or the seller knew of the fraud and did not reject the benefits of that fraud, he may be jointly and severally liable for misrepresentations made by his real estate agent, *Century 21 Page One Realty* v. *Naghad*, 760 S.W.2d 305 (Tex. App.—Texarkana, 1988).

DUTIES OF THE AGENT TO THE PRINCIPAL

The agent acts in the capacity of a *fiduciary.* That is, there is a duty of *trust, confidence,* and *honest business dealing* that is owed to his principal. There will probably be communications between the principal and agent that could not be disclosed to third parties without breaching that fiduciary relationship. An example of this would be a principal who chooses to list his house for a $100,000 sales price but informs the broker that he would probably take $80,000 from a qualified purchaser who offers good terms. The agent is, of course, under a fiduciary capacity not to disclose anything that would be adverse to the interest of his principal. There are issues, though, that may need to be discussed in detail with the seller.

Performance

The term *performance* (often referred to as *obedience)* indicates that the broker will use his best efforts and diligence to market his principal's property for the highest price then obtainable, *Riley* v. *Powell*, 665 S.W.2d 578 (Tex. Civ. App., 1984). Moreover, he will obey the principal's instructions as to asking price, condition of the property, and marketing practices in accordance with the broker's scope of authority, *Interstate Employment System* v. *Hall* 24, 257 P. 1075, and *Slaughter* v. *Jefferson Federal Savings and Loan Association,* 361 F. Supp. 590.

Most state real estate licensing acts specifically set out standards or obligations of performance for real estate brokers. Some are owed to the sellers, and others are owed to the general public. The following is a list of acts that the broker should probably *not* engage in:

1. Making a false promise likely to influence, persuade, or induce any person to enter into a contract or agreement when he (the licensee) could not or did not intend to keep such promise.
2. Soliciting, selling, or offering for sale real property under a scheme or program that constitutes a lottery or deceptive practice.

3. Acting in the dual capacity of broker and undisclosed principal in a transaction.

4. Placing a sign on real property offering it for sale, lease, or rent without the written consent of the owner or of his authorized agent.

5. Negotiating or attempting to negotiate the sale, exchange, lease, or rental of real property with an owner or lessor, knowing that the owner or lessor had a written outstanding contract granting exclusive agency in connection with the property to another real estate broker.

6. Offering real property for sale or for lease without the knowledge and consent of the owner or of his authorized agent, or on terms other than those authorized by the owner or his authorized agent.

7. Publishing, or causing to be published, an advertisement including, but not limited to, advertising by newspaper, radio, television, or display that is misleading, or is likely to deceive the public, or in any manner tends to create a misleading impression, or fails to identify as a licensed real estate broker or agent the person causing the advertisement to be published.

8. Establishing an association, by employment or otherwise, with an unlicensed person who is expected or required to act as a real estate licensee, or aiding or abetting or conspiring with a person to circumvent the requirements of the real estate license act.

9. Employing conduct that constitutes dishonest dealings, bad faith, or untrustworthiness.

10. Acting negligently or incompetently in performing an act for which a person is required to hold a real estate license.

Loyalty   The duty of loyalty is probably the most easily breached fiduciary capability. It includes not only the broker's duty to put the principal's interest above that of his own, but also an all-encompassing obligation of full disclosure to the principal of all pertinent facts known to the broker. This has been held to include such material disclosures as:

1. Disclosing to the principal that there is a potential buyer; eliminating "double escrow" or "flip" closings where the agent profits at the expense of his principal, *Southern Cross Industries, Inc. v. Martin*, 604 S.W.2d 290 (Tex. Civ. App.—

San Antonio, 1980), and *State of Nevada, Department of Commerce, Real Estate Div.* v. *Soeller,* 656 P.2d 224.

2. Failing to disclose that the value of the property has increased during the listing period, *Ramsey* v. *Gordon,* 567 S.W.2d 868 (Tex. Civ. App.—Waco, 1978).

3. Failing to disclose purchaser's financial status when the seller is financing the transaction, *White* v. *Boucher,* 322 N.W.2d 560 (Minn. 1982).

4. Failure to disclose any disputes which might affect a principal's decision as to whether or how to act, *Owen* v. *Shelton,* 277 S.E.2d 189 (Va. 1981).

5. Failure to tender the client an offer to purchase, *Virginia Real Estate Commission* v. *Bias,* 308 S.E.2d 123 (Va. 1983).

6. Failure to disclose that a listing agreement is an exclusive right to sell listing agreement, *Lyle* v. *Moore,* 599 P.2d 336 (Mont. 1979). See also *Jothann* v. *Irving Trust Co.,* 270 N.Y.S. 721 (N.Y. Sup. Ct. 1934), where the court held that the fiduciary relation arises during negotiation of the listing agreement.

7. It has also been shown that it is not enough just to offer to disclose information. The broker is obligated to advise his principal fully of all facts within his knowledge that could be reasonably calculated to influence the principal's actions, *Hercules* v. *Robedeaux, Inc.,* 329 N.W.2d 240 (Wis. Civ. App., 1982).

8. Failure to disclose information which may be material to the subject matter of the agency (receiving additional commission from another party), *Hurney* v. *Locke,* 308 N.W.2d 764 (S.D. 1981).

What information to be disclosed is as important as the obligation to disclose. When coupled with the various consumer protection acts, cases seem to point to the fact that the broker should disclose all that he should know about a transaction, although he would not be held to a duty of care of knowing information that was not reasonably within his realm of knowledge, *Hercules* v. *Robedeaux, Inc., supra,* and *Easton* v. *Strassburger,* 199 Cal. Rptr. 383 (Ct. App., 1984).

Full Disclosure

The duty of loyalty also includes the broker's duty of *full disclosure* to his principal. The amount of information which needs to be disclosed appears to be total. *Janes* v. *CPR Corporation,* 623 S.W.2d 733

(Tex. Civ. App.—Houston, 1981); see also *Kinnard* v. *Homann,* discussed later in this chapter. There have been a number of cases, however, in which the courts have determined that full disclosure was not made and held the agent liable for breach of his fiduciary capacity. For instance, if the real estate appreciates in value and the broker buys the property during the listing period himself while failing to disclose that appreciation in value, a liability has been created for the broker. One of the most obvious forms of nondisclosure is the flip sale. In this transaction the broker may find himself liable if he acquires the property from his principal and sells it for a higher price to a prospective purchaser on the same day or soon thereafter, *Southern Cross Industries, Inc.* v. *Martin,* 604 S.W.2d 290 (Tex. Civ. App.—San Antonio, 1980). A broker must also disclose if the agent owns an interest in the purchaser, *Nix* v. *Born,* 890 S.W.2d 635 (Tex. App.—El Paso, 1993).

Frightening cases have come out of courts of other states, which might indicate a trend toward more disclosure than the broker might expect. In one case there was a disputed closing and the seller's broker dutifully "held his ground" to demand an interest payment from the purchaser which was said to be under protest. The purchaser ultimately sued to have his interest refunded and lost his claim. However, the seller sued the broker for his commission, plus the expenses of defending the lawsuit, on the grounds that the broker had breached his contractual and fiduciary duties in closing subject to the purchaser's protest. The court found that the broker had followed the *letter* of the instructions given to him by the principal, but had violated the *spirit* of those instructions by failing to inform the seller of the dispute over the interest amount, *Owen* v. *Shelton,* 277 S.E.189 (Va. 1981). A similar result was reached in a Montana case in which the Montana Supreme Court held that the broker breached his fiduciary relationship with his client by failing to make a full disclosure to his client of the contract with the broker (the listing agreement). The court held that the fiduciary relationship between a broker and his client includes a full and understandable explanation to the client before having him sign a contract, particularly when the contract is with the broker himself. Basically, the court held that the broker had a fiduciary relationship with his client before he was an agent, *Lyle* v. *Moore, supra.* So it would be perhaps part of a broker's disclosure to reveal the nature and extent of his broker's fees to the client before he signs the client listing contract. In the *Lyle* v. *Moore* case, the client alleged he did not understand the extent of an exclusive right to sell listing agreement when he ultimately sold his property to his sons.

This duty of disclosure has also been held to include submitting an offer to purchase, although it is limited to that. The broker has no control over the decisions as to who the property will be sold to. *Shore* v. *Thomas A. Sweeney & Associates*, 864 S.W.2d 182 (Tex. App.—Tyler, 1993). A broker should disclose, however, all facts within the agent's knowledge that could reasonably be calculated to influence the principal's actions. *Hercules* v. *Robedeaux, Inc., supra*. The licensee's explanation of various aspects of the transaction must be commensurate with the education and understanding of the principal. *Mallory* v. *Watt*, 594 P.2d 629 (Id. 1979).

Sales Information. A particularly sensitive issue exists as to whether or not a licensee may disclose information about the real property sales price or terms of the sale. While in many cases this may be deemed to be confidential information, real estate license acts often provide that a licensee, or not-for-profit real estate board, may provide information about real property sales prices or terms of the sale for purposes of facilitating, selling, leasing, financing or appraising real property. In such event, any entity providing this information shall not be held liable to any other person as a result of providing the information, unless this disclosure is specifically prohibited by statute or written contract.

Specific Disclosure Issues

HIV Issues. Similarly there was a concern about whether or not AIDS or HIV-related viruses infecting occupants of real property should be disclosed. The more traditional theory, at least at this time, is that a person infected with AIDS or an HIV-related virus is considered to be handicapped and therefore belongs to a protected class of people such that the handicap need not be disclosed. It also provides a basis for discrimination under the Fair Housing Act.

Death. Some state legislatures have enacted provisions for death occurring on the property. A real estate licensee may have no duty to inquire about, disclose, or make representations concerning a death on the property which was a result of suicide, natural causes, or accidents unrelated to the condition of the property. Apparently, disclosures would still have to be made if death occurred as a result of murder, condition of the premises, or unnatural causes. This is still a major concern, however. There are a lot of purchasers who will not buy a house in which a death has occurred, regardless of the reason. In many cases, their reluctance to purchase is based on cultural or religious factors. If a buyer has an inquiry concerning death on the premises, it is probably best to discuss it with the seller. A truthful disclosure may save the expense of litigation in the future, even with a successful outcome.

Generally, it has been held by courts that a real estate broker, as an agent, owes the duty to his principal of performance, loyalty, reasonable care, and an accounting for all monies received with regard to the transaction.

Lead-Based Paint. The final rule was issued from the Environmental Protection Agency concerning lead-based paint disclosures.

What Is Required? Before ratification of the contract for sale or lease:

1. Sellers and landlords must disclose known lead-based paint and lead-based paint hazards and provide available reports to buyers or tenants.
2. Sellers and landlords must give buyers and renters the EPA/CPSC/HUD pamphlet titled *Protect Your Family from Lead in Your Home.*
3. Homebuyers will get a ten-day period to conduct a lead-based paint inspection or risk assessment at their own expense, if desired. The number of days can be changed by mutual consent.
4. Sales contracts and leasing arrangements must include certain language to ensure that disclosure and notification actually take place.
5. Sellers, lessors, and real estate agents share responsibility for ensuring compliance.

Note that the rule does not require testing, removal, or abatement of lead-based paint, nor does it invalidate leasing and sales contracts.

The statute targets housing built prior to 1978, and specifically does *not* cover the following:

1. Housing built after 1977,
2. Zero bedroom units, such as efficiencies, lofts, and dormitories,
3. Leases for less than 100 days, such as vacation houses or short-term rentals,
4. Houses exclusively for the elderly (unless there are children living there),
5. Housing for the handicapped (unless there are children living there),

6. Rental houses which have been inspected by a certified inspector and found to be free of lead-based paint,

7. Houses being sold because of foreclosure.

Agent Responsibilities. There are specific requirements for real estate agents under the final rule. The agents must ensure that:

1. Sellers and landlords are aware of their obligations,

2. Sellers and landlords disclose the proper information to buyers and tenants,

3. Sellers give buyers the ten-day opportunity to conduct an inspection (or other mutually agreed-upon period),

4. The lease, which is a sales contract, includes proper disclosure language and proper signatures,

5. He complies with the law if seller or landlord fail to do so.

Although the regulations are lengthy, they can be easily summarized. If one is selling property, the owner should:

1. Give buyers the pamphlet,

2. Give buyers the opportunity to test for lead, if desired,

3. Disclose all known lead-based paint and lead-based paint hazards in the house (and provide buyers with any available reports),

4. Include standard warning languages in the attachment of the contract,

5. Complete and sign statements verifying completion of requirements,

6. Contain the signed acknowledgment *for three years.*

If one of the renters moves out, he should:

1. Give renters the pamphlet to disclose all known lead-based paint and lead-based paint hazards in the dwelling unit (and provide renters with any available report) (the pamphlet must also be provided when the lease is renewed),

2. Have running language in the lease referring to an attachment for a complete and signed statement verifying completion of requirements which must be kept *for three years.*

The RESPA Final Rule. HUD has published a new "final rule" addressing controlled business arrangements, referral fees, computerized loan origination systems, and other related issues under RESPA. The final rule is accompanied by three "Statements of Policy": 1996-1, 1996-2, and 1996-3. The final rule became effective on October 7, 1996.

The 1992 rules created broad exemptions for payment of referral fees. The new final rule withdraws these broad exemptions and then creates new exemptions for payments to "managerial employees" and employees who do not provide settlement services. A "managerial employee" is one who does not routinely deal directly with consumers and who hires, directs, assigns, promotes, or rewards other employees or independent contractors, or is in a position to formulate, determine, or influence the policies of the employer.

The new final rule, in general terms, provides an exemption for employees who are not in a position of "trust" with regard to the consumer and who therefore are not in a position to exert influence or steer the consumer to a related entity. In addition the only payments that can be made are from the employer to the employee. An affiliated company may not make these referral fee payments.

Statement of Policy 1996-1: Computer Loan Origination Systems (CLOs). The final rule withdrew the existing blanket exemption for CLOs. The rule eliminated the Appendix E disclosure requirement of the 1992 rule, as well as the exemption for borrower payments to CLOs. The statement of policy does not define a CLO, but refers to it as "a computer system that is used by or on behalf of a consumer to facilitate a consumer's choice among alternative products or settlement service providers in connection with the particular RESPA-covered real estate transaction." The rule merely attempts to describe the existing practices of service providers. The technology is evolving so rapidly that it is difficult to provide guidance on unspecified practices.

Any payments made to a CLO must bear a reasonable relationship to the value of the goods, facilities, or services provided. RESPA places no restrictions on the pricing structure of CLO as long as the payments are not referral fees and are reasonably related to the services provided.

When a CLO is used in a controlled business arrangement (CBA), the RESPA regulations on controlled business arrangements apply. A controlled business arrangement does not violate RESPA if three conditions are met:

1. When consumers are referred from one business entity to an affiliated business entity, a written disclosure of the affiliated relationship must be provided.

2. There can be no required use of the affiliated company.

3. The only thing of value received by one business entity from other business entities in the controlled business arrangement is a return on an ownership interest or franchise relationship.

Statement of Policy 1996-2: Sham Controlled Business Arrangements (CBAs).   This statement makes it clear that Congress did not intend for the controlled business arrangement (CBA) to be used to promote referral fee payments to sham arrangements or sham entities. If the entity is not a bona fide provider of settlement services, then the arrangement does not meet the definition of a CBA. In determining whether or not a CBA is a "sham" the Department of Housing and Urban Development weighs ten factors in light of the specific facts that indicate whether or not an entity is a bona fide provider.

In determining a permissible return on an ownership interest or franchise relationship, the Department of Housing and Urban Development considers roughly four factors.

This portion of the rule is basically simple. In a true controlled business relationship, disclosed fees are specifically allowed. If one attempts to set a "sham" relationship with an affiliated company that doesn't provide legitimate services and may attempt to disguise referral fees under "returns on ownership," it will be disallowed as a violation of RESPA.

Statement of Policy 1996-3: Rental of Office Space, Lock-outs, and Retaliation.   In this statement, HUD acknowledges that the rental payment that is higher than the ordinary rental paid for facilities can constitute a kickback in violation of the Section 8 prohibition of referral fees. When HUD is faced with a complaint that a person is renting space to a person who is referring business to that person, HUD examines the facts to determine whether the rental payment bears a reasonable relationship to the market value of the rental space provided or is a disguised referral fee. The market value of the rental space may include an appropriate proportion of the cost for all the services actually provided to a tenant, such as secretarial services, utilities, telephones, and other office equipment. HUD interprets the existing regulations to require a "general market value" as a basis for the analysis. If the rental payments paid by the tenant exceed the general market value of the space provided,

HUD will consider the excess amount to be payment for the referral of business in violation of Section 8(a) of RESPA.

Another form of referral fee can be a lock-out. A *lock-out* arises when a settlement service provider prevents other providers from marketing their services within a setting under that provider's control, for instance, in a situation in which the rental rate to a particular settlement service provider (title company) could lead to other settlement service providers being "locked out" from access to the referrals of business, or from reaching the consumer.

A third prohibition includes *retaliation.* Retaliations occur when a settlement service provider raises negative consequences for an agent to refer business to another settlement service provider. For instance, a real estate broker that imposes quotas or referrals to a particular lender or title company on its agents, under the threat of dismissal, is engaging in retaliation. See 61 FR III.

It is safe to say that the 1994 rule, which revises and replaces the 1992 rule, will probably be revised again. As times change, business practices change, and settlement services become more competitive. The only thing constant is change!

Reasonable Care   The duty of *reasonable care* generally implies competence and expertise on the part of the broker. He has a duty to disclose knowledge and material facts concerning the property and cannot become a party to any fraud or misrepresentation likely to affect the sound judgment of the principal. In procuring a purchaser, the broker obviously has a duty to discover whether or not that purchaser is financially able to pursue the transaction. The broker should also disclose any material changes in property values so that his principal may stay fully informed at all times.

The broker further has a duty to make sure that all material facts of a transaction are disclosed to his principal. However, the broker may not give legal interpretations of the documents involved in a transaction. To give legal interpretations of an instrument is practicing law without a license. There are other provisions in most state licensing acts that provide for license revocation if the duty of reasonable care has been breached, such as the following:

1. Making a material misrepresentation, or failing to disclose to a potential purchaser any latent structural defect or any other defect known to the broker or salesperson. Latent structural defects and other defects do not refer to trivial or insignificant defects but refer to those defects that would be a significant factor to a reasonable and prudent purchaser in making a decision to purchase.

2. Pursuing a continued and flagrant course of misrepresentation or making of false promises through agents, salespersons, advertising, or otherwise.

3. Having knowingly withheld from or inserted in a statement of account or invoice, a statement that made it inaccurate in a material particular.

4. Failing or refusing on demand to furnish copies of a document pertaining to a transaction dealing with real estate to a person whose signature is affixed to the document.

Accounting

The duty of *accounting* is provided for generally in requiring that any money accepted as earnest money must be placed in a proper escrow account within a reasonable amount of time. This duty of accounting would also apply to failure to report undisclosed commissions or failure to disclose the true purchase price of the seller's property. This type of conduct, of course, represents the severest type of fraud and misrepresentation. These subjects are discussed in almost every provision of the Texas Real Estate Licensing Act.

The areas that deal specifically with escrow and accounting for funds are set out in the various states' licensing acts, which often prohibit:

1. Either accepting, receiving, or charging an undisclosed commission, rebate, or direct profit on expenditures made for a principal;

2. or, failing within a reasonable time to deposit money received as escrow agent in a real estate transaction, either in trust with a title company authorized to do business in this state, or in a custodial, trust, or escrow account maintained for that purpose in a banking institution authorized to do business in this state;

3. or, disbursing money deposited in a custodial, trust, or escrow account, as provided in Subsection (Y) before the transaction concerned has been consummated or finally otherwise terminated.

DUTIES OF THE PRINCIPAL TO THE AGENT

Similar to the duties previously specified, the principal owes certain duties to the agent. While these duties are not nearly as concrete and so distinctly spelled out by state statutes, the duties are important in determining the rights of the agent when the principal fails to live up to his obligations as created by the agency relationship. These duties are:

1. Performance.
2. Compensation.
3. Reimbursement.
4. Indemnification.

Performance *Performance* is normally considered to be an agent's obligation; however, the principal is expected to do whatever he reasonably can to help accomplish the purpose of the agency.

Compensation *Compensation* is normally specified in the listing agreement or in the employment contract. In most real estate situations, even if the contract is contingent on the closing of the sale, if the agent can produce a ready, willing, and able buyer, he is entitled to be paid.

Reimbursement *Reimbursement* implies that the principal must reimburse the agent for expenses made on the principal's behalf. This does not mean that the principal has to reimburse the agent for the costs of advertising, entertainment, and other costs of doing business. Those are clearly the agent's responsibility. However, in the event of an absentee landlord or seller, the agent is often required to perform minor repairs and incur other small expenses in order to keep the property in good condition. When these expenses are made in good faith and within the scope of the agent's authority, he is entitled to reimbursement from the principal for funds expended on the principal's behalf.

Indemnification *Indemnification,* in these days of consumer awareness, is becoming more and more important for the agent. This duty arises when the agent suffers a loss through no fault of his own while performing his duties on behalf of the principal, such as an innocent misrepresentation by the broker when he is performing acts on behalf of the principal. As previously discussed, the agent is almost always liable when he makes a misrepresentation to a third party. However, if this misrepresentation has in fact been represented to the broker who was carrying out his activities in good faith, relying on a representation made by the principal, the agent may be reimbursed for his losses if the principal has in fact misrepresented those items to his agent. This would often include concealed defects and representation as to the quality and condition of the property.

In addition to a broker's responsibility to act in his principal's best interests, he also has certain legal duties to prospective purchasers. Basically, these duties are to engage in fair and honest business dealings, to disclose property defects, and to disclose his (the broker's) interest in the real estate, if any.

BROKER'S DUTIES TO PROSPECTIVE PURCHASERS

Although the broker owes a duty of performance to his principal, he cannot be a part of any fraud on behalf of his principal. If his principal should request that he misrepresent certain material defects, the broker should terminate his listing agreement and refuse to engage in any such acts.

A broker is also liable to purchasers for material misrepresentations and/or false advertising, *People* v. *The Alpert Corp.*, 660 P.2d 1295 (Colo. Ct. App., 1982), and particularly for failure to disclose any material defects that affect the buyer's good judgment and sound business practice. Misrepresentations for which brokers have been held liable include the following:

1. The defense of "puffing" has effectively been wiped out when it results in liability to the third party, *Ridco, Inc.* v. *Sexton*, 623 S.W.2d 792 (Tex. Civ. App.—Ft. Worth, 1981).

2. An agent has been held liable in representing that a home builder built homes of good construction and that the home builder was on an "approved builder list," *Lakeway Real Estate Corporation* v. *Whittlesey*, No. 9086 (Tex. Civ. App.—Texarkana, Dec. 28, 1982).

3. Representing that title was free and clear on property, *Ingalls* v. *Rice*, 511 S.W.2d 78 (Tex. Civ. App.—Houston, 1974), and *Stone* v. *Lawyers Title Insurance Corp.* 554 S.W.2d 183 (Tex. 1977).

4. Representing the agent's "opinion" as to the value of future use of the property, *Trenholm* v. *Ratcliff*, 646 S.W.2d 927 (Tex. 1983).

5. Misrepresenting the square footage of a house, *Cameron* v. *Terrell and Garrett*, 618 S.W.2d 535 (Tex. 1981).

6. Misrepresenting that there were drainage and sewage problems with a result and obligation to disclose all material facts not reasonably ascertainable to the buyer, *McRae* v. *Bolstad*, 646 P.2d 771 (Wash. Civ. App., 1982).

7. Misrepresenting the location of land, *Fulton* v. *Aszman,* 446 N.E.2d. 803 (Ohio App. 1983).

8. Failure to disclose is equally as harmful, as when a broker fails to disclose that murders occurred in the house, *Reed* v. *King,* 193 Cal. Rptr. 130 (1983).

   Even an innocent misrepresentation has rendered a broker liable. One case held that real estate brokers are licensed professionals, possessing superior knowledge of the realty they sell and the real estate market generally. Prospective purchasers recognize this expertise and tend to rely on a broker's representations. Just as purchasers are entitled to rely on an owner's representations . . . purchaser should be entitled to rely on the broker's representations, *Bevins* v. *Ballard,* 655 P.2d 757 (Alaska 1982).

In the age of consumerism, some states have enacted deceptive trade practice laws and consumer protection acts that are a further potential source of liability for real estate brokers, *People* v. *The Alpert Corp., supra; Cameron* v. *Terrell & Garrett, supra,* and *Attorney General* v. *Diamond Mfg. Co.,* 327 N.W.2d 805 (Mich. 1982). Such acts may call for brokers to even pay treble damages, plus the damaged party's attorney's fees, when a material misrepresentation of fact has been made. Treble damages may even be granted for *innocent* misrepresentations in some states, such as when the seller gave the broker incorrect information about square footage, the presence of structural defects, etc. Great duties of care are placed on brokers under these circumstances.

A common difficulty has been determining how much information should be disclosed to the purchaser without disclosing the confidences of the seller. A simple rule is that a broker should disclose anything that would make a material difference to a prudent purchaser in his decision making; for instance, a licensee cannot conceal any confidential information which could cause potential harm to a prospective purchaser. Some states now provide for a *seller's disclosure statement.* The form is usually signed by both parties to the transaction and, at least theoretically, enables the *seller* to make the disclosure to the purchaser rather than putting the burden on the real estate broker.

COOPERATING BROKERS

Other problems arise when we talk about the duties of care, liabilities, and obligations of the cooperating broker. Cooperating brokers are usually subagents, and do not have a contractual relationship with the principal and, in many cases, may *think* they represent the purchaser. There are a number of unanswered questions as consumers become more sophisticated and more real estate transactions are co-oped between brokers. There are confusing issues as to whether or not one broker (the co-op) can make a misrepresentation which will create a liability for the listing broker. *Sullivan* v. *Jefferson,* 400 A.2d 836 (N.J. App., 1979). There are further theories of brokers conspiring to sell the property at a cheaper price so that they can get their commissions rather than actively representing the seller to try to achieve the highest price possible, *Lester* v. *Marshall,* 352 P.2d 786 (Col. 1960). There is also the ever-present problem of the couple who come into the broker's office and say "Help us find a house." It is difficult to explain to them (after showing them 467 houses) that you actually work for the seller and are trying to achieve the highest price the market will bear.

The high degree of fiduciary care that an agent owes to his principal coupled with the "real world" function of trying to facilitate a real estate transaction might seem to complicate the duties of care a broker would owe to the seller. One should recall that the fiduciary relationship developed between the listing broker and the owner of the property creates the fiduciary duty of *full and complete disclosure* of absolutely *everything* the agent knows, and this should include information that the buyer has chosen to divulge to the real estate broker, *Kinnard* v. *Homann,* 750 S.W.2d 30 (Tex. App.—Austin, 1988). This presumably would include all information given to him by the buyer. It should also be pointed out that even if the buyer gives *confidential* information to the broker, the broker still has the duty to disclose that to the seller or he runs the risk of breaching his fiduciary duty of loyalty.

Please remember that the broker has a duty of disclosure to the purchaser of anything which may materially affect the purchaser's decision, such as latent structural defects, but it is not a fiduciary duty to disclose everything the broker knows. The difficulty arises, then, when a buyer voluntarily discloses confidential information to the broker because he is not aware of the broker's complete fiduciary duty to the seller. In many cases, the buyer thinks the real estate broker represents him while the buyer is in the process of looking for a house. This has created many conflicting and difficult situations. After all, shouldn't the buyer be assisted also?

BUYER BROKERAGE

An interesting alternative is the concept of *buyer brokerage*. In this situation the broker represents the purchaser and not the seller, contrary to the typical listing situation. The buyer hires the broker to represent him, creating a single agency and fiduciary duty solely to the buyer. It should be noted that there are a number of serious concerns if you are going to undertake buyer brokerage. The first is the fiduciary duty owed to the *buyer,* not the seller. The buyer brokerage employment is procured by utilizing a buyer representation agreement which employs the broker.

Duties of Care   One would presume that the duties of care of a broker as a buyer's agent would be the same as that of a seller's agent (performance, accounting, reasonable care, and loyalty). It should be pointed out, however, that the functions are somewhat different. In representing a seller, the broker is supposed to try to get the highest price in the marketplace, *Riley* v. *Powell, supra.* In representing the buyer, it is arguable that the broker's duty should be to get the lowest price in the marketplace, or at least a reasonable price, not the highest price the market will bear. There may be additional duties concerning the market analysis for the benefit of the buyer. Diligently inquiring as to the potential use of the property for the buyer's benefit, and other duties of performance and obedience, may be different from the duties owed to the seller. For instance, if the buyer requests the toughest inspector in town, does the broker have the duty to recommend or seek out that inspector? What if the buyer discloses a particularly devastating negotiating strategy to beat down the seller? What if the buyer directs the broker to insert meaningless contingencies in the contract so the buyer can have an easy out? There is at least some authority that indicates a buyer's broker has the duty to inquire as to zoning and deed restrictions as they pertain to the property, *Lewis* v. *Long & Foster Real Estate, Inc.,* 584 A.2d 1325 (M.D. App., 1991). Another case has held that the broker has the fiduciary duty to confirm the property meets with the client's standards or to disclose that no such investigation has been made, *Salhutdin* v. *Valley of California, Inc.,* 29 Cal. Rptr.2d 463 (App., 1994). The easier answer to all of these questions is that the duties of care of buyer's brokerage have not really been clearly defined either under case law or under traditional theories of agency as applied in the practical marketplace. Buyer agency is a new concept, and, as such, there are many unanswered questions.

A key thing to remember, however, is that who pays the commission is not determinative. A broker can represent either party, get paid by either or both parties, provided that all commissions are disclosed. Some sellers may argue that they are paying the commission and expect the brokers to represent them. The buyers' counterargument is that the seller is including the broker's commission in the sales price; therefore, the buyer is paying it indirectly. If the seller has built a commission payment into his sales price, who gets that commission should logically not be of concern, as long as the property is marketed and the deal is made. The split of commissions between the brokers is merely that: an agreement between brokers. The seller and buyer are not normally a part of that agreement.

As stated previously, who pays the commission is not determinative of who the agent represents so long as the compensation is disclosed. It would be anticipated that listing brokers would still be willing to split their commissions under the MLS system. If, however, a listing broker refuses to split the commission because of a buyer's representation of a purchaser, the buyer's broker would have to look to the purchaser or some other source (whatever that is!) for recovery. Remember that a cooperating broker does not have an agreement with a seller and therefore may not be able to sue him for a commission, *Boyert* v. *Tauber,* 834 S.W.2d 60 (Tex. 1992).

Compensation

As previously mentioned, real estate brokers have traditionally represented sellers. The development of the concept of buyer brokerage has indicated a niche in the marketplace for buyers who feel they want representation, or for buyers who have particularly close relationships with real estate brokers, such that a buyer agency is almost presumed (relative, business partner, close friend, previous working relationship).

    Real-life issues, however, complicate this situation. If a potential buyer walks into a broker's office looking for a home and wants buyer representation and employs the broker to be the buyer's agent, can the broker show his own listings to that buyer? Recall that this creates a fiduciary duty owed to both the buyer and seller, and the resulting potential conflict. Note that the seller's broker has the duty to get the highest price on the market for the seller; the buyer's broker focuses on buying product—obtaining the real estate which best fits the buyer's needs, and maybe for a lower price. As seller's agents, brokers may feel tempted by the prospect of a buyer slipping away because they cannot present them with their own listings. What results is the pressure to represent both parties, and become a dual agent.

DUAL AGENCY

Initially, the interests of the buyer and seller do not seem to be antagonistic, but as negotiations begin to become more adversarial, a dual agent has an unusual (and not well defined) standard of care. Many state real estate license acts prohibit dual agency except

Duties of Care

in certain circumstances. In order to act as a dual agent, the agent should: (1) provide the parties with agency disclosure forms, (2) obtain written consent of all parties to the transaction, and (3) disclose the source of expected compensation to all parties.

All of these disclosures can be made in the broker's listing agreement or by a representation agreement which authorizes a broker to act as agent to more than one party to a transaction, provided that the agreement sets forth the dual agency conflict in conspicuous, bold, or underlined print.

In general terms, a real estate broker who acts as an agent for more than one party to a transaction must:

1. Not disclose to the buyer or tenant that the seller or landlord will accept a price less than the asking price unless otherwise instructed in a separate writing by the seller or landlord.

2. Not disclose to the seller or landlord that the buyer or tenant will pay a price greater than the price submitted in a written offer to the seller or landlord unless otherwise instructed in a separate writing by the buyer or tenant.

3. Not disclose any confidential information or any information a party specifically instructs the real estate broker in writing not to disclose unless otherwise instructed in a separate writing by the respective party or required to disclose such information by law.

4. Treat all parties to the transaction honestly and impartially so as not to favor one party or work to the disadvantage of any party.

In addition, the real estate broker shall use due diligence to assist the parties in understanding the consents, agreements, or instructions under which the real estate agent is permitted to represent more than one party to a transaction.

It is extremely important that a real estate company have a written policy on agency and the types of agency that it will accept. This policy should carefully articulate the required responsibilities of each agent and the sponsoring broker. It should list the required disclosure forms and when they are required. If a company represents both buyers and sellers, early disclosure to buyer and to seller that there is a possibility of dual agency is imperative.

In Minnesota, a court ruled that although a real estate firm's disclosures of dual agency relationships complied with state laws on agency disclosure, the firm's disclosure was inadequate because it failed to meet the requirements of common law. In *Dismuke* v. *Edina Realty, Inc.,* 1993 WL3 27771 (Minn. Dist. Ct.), a group of listing sellers sued Edina, claiming there was no informed consent to the dual agency. They complained that the firm's statement in its usual purchase contract concerning dual agency had not adequately informed them of the company's potential conflict while utilizing dual agency in their transactions. Edina had adopted the policy that the listing agent represented the seller and that the selling agent acted as an independent contractor representing the buyer. This policy was also stated on their sales contracts. There may be a problem of public misconception, however.

Conflicts

While in many ways the market seems to be demanding the utilization of dual agency, there are many disturbing situations. Can a real estate broker remain impartial when one of the parties is a long-time friend or close relative? What if the buyer discloses a devastating negotiating strategy meant to "bargain hard" for the best deal? If a licensee attempts to encourage one of the parties, is impartiality lost? A similar conflict occurs when one of the parties discloses confidential information (which the statute says must never be disclosed to the other party) that the licensee knows will make a material difference to that other party. Briefly stated, the statute does not deal with a lot of real-life situations that create potential conflicts. If the broker is going to attempt to represent both sides, he must be strongly cautioned. Even though the licensee may think he is impartial, one of the parties may not perceive it that way.

SINGLE AGENCY

Single agency is another agency concept that has developed recently. In a single agency situation, a broker would be limited to representing only one party in any given transaction. In this situation, the buyer may employ the broker, but the broker could not show the buyer any of the broker's own listings. Similarly, a seller may request that the broker have 100% allegiance to him, and not show his home to any buyers that the broker represents. In either of these cases, a segment of the market will be omitted. For instance, the broker should explain to the seller that if he cannot show the property to any buyers that the brokerage company represents, it may eliminate a potential buyer for that listing. In the opposite situation, the buyer would have to be informed that the broker will not show any of his own listings to the buyer, so the broker may want to show all the broker's listings before being employed by the buyer.

INTERMEDIARIES/ DESIGNATED BROKERAGE

State legislatures have introduced a new concept into real estate brokerage law called an intermediary, facilitator, or designated agent, defined as a broker who is employed to negotiate a transaction between the parties, and for that purpose may be an agent for the parties to the transaction. This may allow a licensee to opt out of the agency relationship.

Under most state statutes, a real estate broker who acts as a designated agent between the parties:

1. Should not disclose to the buyer or tenant that the seller or landlord will accept a price less than the asking price unless otherwise instructed in a separate writing by the seller or landlord.

2. Should not disclose to the seller or landlord that the buyer or tenant will pay a price greater than the price submitted in a written offer to the seller or landlord unless otherwise instructed in a separate writing by the buyer or tenant.

3. Should not disclose any confidential information or any other information parties specifically instruct the real estate broker in writing not to disclose unless otherwise instructed in a separate writing by the prospective party, or a court order, or if the information materially relates to the condition of the property.

4. Should treat all parties to the transaction honestly.

If a real estate broker obtains the consent of the parties to act as a designated agent, the broker may appoint, by providing written notice to the parties, one or more licensees associated with the broker to communicate with and carry out instructions of one party and one or more other licensees associated with the broker to communicate with and carry out instructions of the other party or parties, so long as the parties consent and authorize the broker to make the appointment, which is presumably done in the listing agreement.

The net effect of these statutes is yet to be determined. We have not yet been able even to see the final results of the dual agency legislation. It does pose some interesting questions, however. Does a party have to consent to the particular licensee who is appointed to represent him? What if the sponsoring broker (intermediary) appoints a licensee to work with a party and they don't get along? Presumably, they could simply appoint another licensee, if there is one in that broker's office. The statute also provides that the duties of a licensee acting as an intermediary supersede or are in lieu of the licensee's duties under common law or any other law; however, no duties are defined under the statute other than the previously referenced five duties (which are really no different from those required of a dual agent, discussed previously). Presumably, a licensee could be both a dual agent and an intermediary, the way some state statutes are currently written.

MIDDLEMEN

One exception to the agency theory has been the middleman concept. In a pure middleman situation, the broker brings the buyer and seller together, and may receive a commission for it, but represents neither party. If such a transaction is contemplated, it is very important that the broker be a mere middleman. If the court, or the jury, construes that the agent is acting on behalf of either party, he owes fiduciary duties to that party even though he is a middleman, *West* v. *Touchstone,* 620 S.W.2d 687 (Tex. Civ. App.—Dallas, 1981).

It may well be more difficult to be a middleman than to be a party's agent. A few other states have created a statutory provision for a transactional broker. It has not yet been determined, though, whether this limits the broker's liability, nor has there been any clear definition as to what the limited scope of the broker's duties is. For instance, if the broker provides fewer services (which seems to be necessary in this case as well as in dual agency) should the broker be compensated the same amount?

MANAGEMENT RESPONSIBILITIES

Brokers also have legal responsibilities when they contract to manage real estate. These responsibilities may involve both the handling of management service contracts and the proper maintenance of the property so that a third party is not negligently injured.

One of the major liability problems facing a broker is whether he can be held personally liable to pay for goods or services bestowed on the project he is managing. In other words, if a third party suffers damages, should the seller of the goods sue the principal, the agent, or both? Basically, the law of agency covers the situation as follows:

1. When an agent (broker) acts on behalf of a principal who is known to the service company performing the work, and the agent is acting within the scope of his authority, the principal is liable and the agent is not. Furthermore, the supplier of goods and services has a duty to inquire as to the agent's authority, *Morris & Co.* v. *Hardy & Co.,* 3 F.2d 97. It follows that since the principal chooses his agent,

employs him, and instructs him as to his scope of authority, he should be liable for the agent's acts. This theory is called the doctrine of *respondent superior*.

2. If the agent (broker) indicates to suppliers of goods and services that he has the authority to bind his principal for specified work, the principal will be required to pay under the theory that the broker apparently (ostensibly) had the authority to make the agreement with the service company. However, if the actual authority to bind his principal did not exist (i.e., the agent was acting outside his scope of authority), the principal can recover the damages paid the service company from the agent/broker.

3. If the broker discloses that he is an agent but does not disclose the identity of the principal, the broker generally will be considered personally liable on the agreement. The legal logic is that the supplier is advancing goods or services only on the broker's good name and promise to pay, even though he knows the broker is acting only as an agent. A supplier of goods or services should not expect to be paid by a principal when he does not know who that principal is or anything about the principal's ability to pay.

4. If the principal and the agency are both undisclosed, the agent/broker must pay for any goods or services for which he contracts because the supplier logically was depending on his credit when such goods or services were delivered.

As a final thought, the agent is *always* liable if he commits an act constituting deceit or fraudulent misrepresentation. Even if the supplier of goods and services sues the principal and recovers, the agent would be liable to the principal. Strong national trends to liability tend to hold both parties responsible anyway, *Mongeau* v. *Boutelle*, 407 N.W.2d 352 (Mass. App., 1980).

TERMINATION OF AGENCY

Once it has been determined that an agency agreement exists, there are two basic ways it can be terminated:

1. By acts of the parties.
2. By operation of law.

Termination of an agency agreement by acts of the parties can be accomplished by either party or by both parties. If both parties agree to terminate the agency agreement, it is simple to agree to the termination by *mutual consent*. The termination can also be accomplished by *completion of the agency objective* (i.e., the property being sold) or by expiration of the stipulated length of time as set out in the listing agreement or agency contract.

Termination of the contract by one of the parties tends to be more complicated. A principal may unilaterally *revoke* the agency or listing agreement at any time if he has cause to do so. If he does not have cause to do so and his reasons appear to be arbitrary, the agent has the right to recover the reasonable value of his services and reimbursement for his agency expenses. Conversely, the agent can *renounce* the contract if he feels that the principal is not helping him to complete his agency objective. The agent may then be liable for damages if the agent does not have just cause to terminate the contract. In both cases, what is just cause is a fact question that has to be determined by a jury. In either case this creates, at best, a difficult situation.

Termination of the agency relationship by operation of law occurs upon the *death* of either the principal or the agent, *insanity* of either party, or *change of law*. Since the agency contract is a contract for personal services and is often purely unilateral, the death of either party terminates the obligations of either party. This can always be modified, however, if the broker is a corporation, the seller is a corporation, or either are entities rather than natural persons (e.g., a trust or limited partnership). Similarly, insanity of either party limits the contractual capacity of either party to the point that the principal–agent relationship cannot be completed. Of course, determinations and definitions of sanity are difficult to determine. If a change of law (called *supervening illegality*) makes a contract become illegal, any contract that is illegal is void. An excellent example of this arose in the recent case of *Centex Corporation* v. *Dalton*, 840 S.W.2d 952 (Tex. 1994). In that case, the listing broker earned a substantial commission by negotiating the sale of several savings and loans. While the transaction was pending, however, Congress made the payment of commissions to brokers for this type of sale illegal. The broker was then denied his commission because of supervening illegality. It was legal initially, but became illegal during the pendency of the transaction.

Once the confidential relationship is established, it cannot just be disregarded or ignored. If the agent takes advantage of the principal because of this "insider" information, or if he advises someone else to do so, he still may breach his fiduciary duty. Therefore, even if the agency terminates, the fiduciary duty may not end, *Swallows* v. *Laney*, 691 P.2d 874 (N. Mex. 1984). For instance, a broker cannot become a principal on the same transaction and shed his fiduciary obligations. The agency relationship is presumed to continue once it is established, *Southern Cross Industries, Inc.* v. *Martin, supra.* The agency liabilities may continue far beyond the termination of the agency relationship.

The law of principal and agent has always been difficult. There are a number of fact situations that are always involved, making trial proceedings difficult. It is important to note that the expanding duties to third parties are currently drawing the most attention and controversy pertaining to broker liability. Many attorneys consider this to be a trend and a substantial change to the existing theories of agency law.

SUMMARY   The parties necessary to establish an agency relationship are the principal, the agent, and third parties. An agency relationship can be created by actual authority, ostensible authority, or by ratification. The agent owes certain duties to his principal, including the duties of performance, reasonable care, loyalty, and accounting. The principal owes the agent the duties of care including performance, compensation, reimbursement, and indemnification. The agent also owes duties of care to third parties. The primary duty of care to third parties is honesty and integrity, although there are other requirements of disclosure pursuant to the Texas Real Estate Licensing Act.

In a special agency, a principal is not responsible for the acts of his agent. In a general agency, the principal is responsible for the acts of his agent. The agency relationship may be terminated by acts of parties or operation of law.

DISCUSSION   1. What types of agency relationships are recognized in your state?
QUESTIONS
               2. If your state has a statute that allows for intermediary or designated brokers, does the sponsoring broker incur liability if the agents give conflicting advice?

               3. Can an agent represent both a buyer and a seller at the same time? Discuss potential conflicts.

               4. Discuss the effect of the newest federal laws. Do they justify the cost of enforcement?

Contracts for the Sale of Real Estate

The law of contracts is one of the most complex areas of the law to study. Contracts normally used in real estate include listing agreements, earnest money contracts, installment land contracts, leases, easement agreements, deeds, mortgages, security agreements, liens, construction contracts, and partnership agreements. A complete discussion of the law of contracts would require many volumes for a thorough study and explanation, so for the purposes of this chapter, the discussion of contract law will be centered around the creation and construction of contracts generally; then earnest money contracts, option contracts, and installment land contracts will be discussed.

A contract can be most simply defined as an agreement between competent parties, made on a sufficient consideration, to do or not to do a particular legal act or thing.

CONTRACTS GENERALLY

Four essential elements must exist for a contract to be present. They include *competent parties, legal subject matter, consideration* for the promises contained in the contract, and *mutual assent.*

Creation

Competent Parties.   The general rule of law is that all parties to a contract have read it and understood it. This is true even if they are "slow" or are illiterate. Certain persons do not have full contractual capacity, however. These are minors, mental defectives, and persons under the influence of drugs or alcohol.

 For purposes of determining contractual capacity, minors are defined by most states as people who have not yet attained the age of 18. Contracts executed by a minor are generally considered to be voidable at the option of the minor. This power of voiding the contract lies only with the minor; the option is not available to the other contracting party if he is not a minor. Therefore, anyone who contracts with a minor always contracts at his peril with the possibility that the minor may chose to avoid his contract. However, when the minor achieves the legal age, and continues to perform on the contract, it then becomes valid and binding.

Contracts with the mentally infirm can be either void or voidable. If the person has been adjudicated to be insane, the contract is void, since the person never had capacity to enter into the contract. When such an adjudication has not been made, however, the contracting party must prove his temporary insanity, mental infirmity, or senility. The contract then becomes voidable at the option of the infirmed party, his agent, or guardian. Proof of temporary insanity may be difficult, since it may have been temporary, or not "apparent" to the third party dealing with the allegedly insane claimant.

Parties under the influence of drugs are generally treated the same as people who are mentally incapacitated. Cases permitting avoidance when the party voluntarily becomes under the influence, however, are rare. It is only when the party is induced at the instigation of the other contracting party prior to entering into the contract that the courts may allow avoidance.

Legal Subject Matter. A contract for an illegal purpose is void and the law treats the contract as if it were never created. Therefore if a contract is for an illegal purpose, to commit a tort, or to violate public policy, the courts treat it as if it never existed.

Consideration. People often think of consideration as the money or good exchanged by the parties. Legally, however, consideration is defined as the obligation that each party makes to the other in order to make the contract enforceable. It is sometimes defined as something of value given in exchange for a promise. Alternatively, it is sometimes said that a benefit and a detriment must exist for each promise contained in the contract. To determine whether the essential element of consideration is present, it is helpful to first determine whether a contract is unilateral or bilateral in nature.

In a *unilateral contract,* only one party makes a promise, and the other party completes his half of the contract by performance. A listing agreement might be thought of as an example, because only one party (the seller) makes a promise. He conditionally promises to pay a commission if the broker produces a ready, willing, and able buyer, but the other party (the broker) does not promise to sell the property. He accepts the offer (promise to pay a commission) when he secures a ready, willing, and able buyer, because this is the performance that is anticipated by the offer. Thus, the legal requirement of consideration for each party is then present.

A common example of a *bilateral contract* is an earnest money contract in which the seller promises to sell and the buyer promises to buy the described real property. The seller suffers a detriment on his promise, in that he must give up the land. The buyer realizes a benefit on this same promise, because he will receive the land. The buyer experiences a detriment on his promise to buy, because he must give up his money. At the same time the seller benefits, because he receives the money.

The law generally does not concern itself with the "sufficiency" of the consideration, so long as it is present. Even "love and affection" can be sufficient, *Rose v. Elias*, 576 N.Y.S.2d 257 (N.Y. App.—Div., 1991). On the other hand, if there is great disparity between the values of the bargain received by each party, a court of equity may grant relief to avoid treating one party unfairly. When this occurs, it is because fairness and good conscience dictate that one party should be relieved of his legal obligation. The important point to remember is that the sufficiency of the consideration generally does not prevent a contract from being created, although it may give grounds for equitable relief.

Mutual Assent.   *Mutual assent* is an essential prerequisite to the formation of a contract, and is often the most difficult factor to determine. There must have been a "meeting of the minds" between parties, meaning that they must objectively have appeared to have reached an agreement on all material items in the contract. Since this involves acts of the parties, the determination of mutual assent is usually a question of fact and is completed by the process of *offer and acceptance, Eisenburg v. Continental Cas. Co.,* 180 N.W.2d 726 (1970).

Offer.   The person making the offer is called the *offeror.* The person to whom the offer is made is called the *offeree.* To be effective, the offer must meet certain legal requirements. It must be: (1) communicated to a specific offeree, (2) intended to be a serious offer, and (3) definite and certain enough to be accepted by the offeree. That is, its communication must be such that it creates a *power of acceptance* in the offeree. It can't be merely an invitation for offers (as in a newspaper advertisement). It can't be made in jest, while a person is drunk, or as a "dare," since this destroys the requisite intent. It must also be specific so that the offeree, in exercising his power of acceptance, knows exactly what he is accepting. In most real estate situations, the offer is usually completed upon submitting the earnest money contract, signed by the purchaser, to the seller.

Termination of Offers. At this point, no contract is in existence, only the unilateral offer extended by the offeror. If an offer has been made, it can be terminated prior to acceptance by the offeree by (1) the acts of the parties or (2) operation of law. While one of the following criteria can terminate an *offer,* it does not necessarily terminate a contract.

Acts of the parties depend on the conduct of the offeror and offeree. If no time is specified, the offer remains open for a reasonable period of time, and the offeree may accept this offer within that reasonable time period. If there is a specified time period, the offer terminates when the time period has expired. Similarly, an offer may be terminated by the offeror *revoking* his offer, prior to its being accepted, by *rejection* of the offeree or by the offeree's partially rejecting a contract (perhaps changing some of the terms), which creates a *counteroffer.*

An offer may also be terminated by operation of law prior to acceptance by the offeree. The law terminates the offer upon the *death* of the offeror or offeree prior to the acceptance, *insanity of* either of the parties prior to acceptance, *bankruptcy* of either party, or *a change in the law* that renders the contract illegal.

Acceptance. If an offer is accepted, mutual assent has been achieved. In determining whether or not there was an effective *acceptance* of the contract, the points generally considered are those of *intent*, the *manner* of acceptance, the *timeliness* of the acceptance, and whether or not that acceptance was *unconditional.*

Intent (also one of the main criteria for an effective offer) speaks to the intent of the parties' bargain. Did the person accepting the contract intend, by his words and conduct, to create a contractual relationship by accepting the offer?

The *manner of acceptance* is also important. There must not have been any jest, qualification, or proposed change in the offeree's mind or in the manner in which he accepted the offer. The offeree must also have been the party to whom the offer was made, not someone who simply may have overheard the offer being made.

The concept of *timeliness* alludes to the time in which the contract is to be performed. The offeree must have accepted the offer within a reasonable period of time, and before the offer was revoked either by act or by operation of law. If the contract is unilateral (as in a listing agreement), the offeree must have performed his part of the contract within a reasonable period of time in order to make it enforceable against the offeror.

To effect a proper acceptance, there also must be an *unqualified, unconditional acceptance* of the offer, which must be communicated to the offeror. Any acceptance that is not an acceptance of the whole offer becomes conditional acceptance, and a conditional acceptance becomes a *counteroffer,* which terminates the original offer, *Allen R. Krause Co. v. Fox,* 644 P.2d 279 (Ariz. 1982). Therefore, the contract is not completed until the offeror (counterofferee) has accepted the counteroffer to complete the agreement, *First Development Corp. of Kentucky* v. *Martin Marietta Corporation,* 959 F.2d 617 (6th Cir. 1992).

Defenses to Mutual Assent. One often finds that there has been a written contract, signed by all parties, which leads to the assumption that the requirement of mutual assent has been satisfied and that a contract is valid. However, this is not necessarily the case. Either party may wish to assert, at a later date, that he entered into the contract as a result of *fraud, mutual mistake* of material fact, *duress, menace, undue influence,* or because of some act of the other party which constitutes *misrepresentation* or deceit. If proven, this could be a valid defense to the formation of the contract and the contract would be voidable because the essential element of mutual assent did not, in fact, exist. These defenses need to be explained in a little more detail to help describe how they can arise. Fraud in real estate consists of:

1. False representation of a past or existing material fact, when the false representation is:
   a. Made to a person for the purpose of inducing that person to enter into a contract, and
   b. Relied on by that person in entering into that contract, or
2. False promise to do an act, when the false promise is:
   a. Material,
   b. Made with the intention of not fulfilling it,
   c. Made to a person for the purpose of inducing that person to enter into a contract, and
   d. Relied on by that person in entering into that contract.

The measure of actual damages suffered by the aggrieved party is the difference between the value of the real estate as represented or promised and its actual value in the condition in which it is delivered at the time of the contract. Any person who commits the fraud is additionally liable to the person defrauded for exemplary damages which exceed the amount of the actual damages by an enormous amount. In order for fraud to exist, there must usually be an intent to induce the defrauded party. This is often very difficult to prove.

Mutual mistake of material fact is the assertion that the parties were both in error as to some integral fact in the contract. A discrepancy in price alone does not constitute material mistake, however. It must be a factor that materially affects the performance of the parties such as the amount of property to be purchased. It is not grounds for relief if only one of the parties made a mistake, unless the mistake is of such great consequence that to enforce the contract would be unconscionable.

Duress is the use of physical force to induce a party to sign a contract, whereas *menace* is the mere threat (mere threat?) of physical violence. One would think that when the samurai sword is pointed at your kidney, it is menace; when the sword touches, it is duress.

Undue influence results from a breach of trust or fiduciary capacity, such as when a broker fails to inform his principal of an increase in value of the property or "convinces" an innocent consumer to accept an unfavorable contract.

Misrepresentation or deceit has a whole new meaning since the passage of the various state Consumer Protection Acts. It is sufficient to say only that the aggrieved party could probably avoid his contractual obligation if the other party violated these sacrosanct pillars of legislation.

It is important to remember that even if the foregoing defenses to mutual assent are not true allegations, the lawsuit that can result can be a lengthy and difficult proceeding. In the meantime, the property may be "tied up" so that no sale can occur.

Delivery.   There is often a question arising as to whether delivery is required in contracts. Physical delivery is usually not required. The key terms to remember are the "offer" and "acceptance," which constitute the mutual assent. The contract is generally considered to be enforceable when the acceptance of the offer has been communicated to the offeror. This must occur prior to the offer being revoked. Since the intent of the parties can usually be determined during this period of mutual assent, the requirement of delivery isn't material.

RULES FOR THE CONSTRUCTION OF CONTRACTS   Once it has been determined that a legal contract has been formed, the court will make every effort not to strike down the contract unless it was illegal or was made under fraud, duress, or mistake.

The underlying theory is that if two parties care enough to make a binding contract, and each performs to some extent on that contract, there must have been sufficient intent to warrant enforcement of that contract. As an introduction to contracts, it is helpful to understand some basic "rules of thumb" that courts generally use in interpreting and construing the intent of contracts.

Reasonable Time

There is a general rule in the law that if the time is not specified, the contract must be performed within a "reasonable" period of time. What is "reasonable" is usually a fact question for the jury to decide and is said to be such time as is necessary and convenient to do what the contract requires to be done, and as soon as circumstances will permit. It never means an unnecessary delay and needs to be determined by the jury as it applies to the facts of the particular case.

Validity

Contracts are always construed in favor of upholding the contract. Forfeitures of contracts are not favored in the law, and if given an equal choice, the court will always choose to uphold the contract rather than strike it down. If two contracts seem to conflict, or two provisions of one contract seem to conflict, the court will attempt to construe them so that each will be permitted to stand.

Four Corners Doctrine

Another standard construction of contracts is called the *four corners doctrine*. This doctrine states that the instrument must be read in its entirety. No particular provision may be lifted out of context and be construed on its own merits. When you are reading each provision in the contract, every other provision of that contract must be kept in mind also, so that no inequitable constructions will be made on a clause or paragraph contrary to the intent of the rest of that contract. This also applies to separate instruments executed at the same time for the same purpose (deed, deed of trust, and note, for instance), and in the same transaction. They are to be read and construed together.

Interlineations, "Fill-in-the-Blanks"

All interlineations (writing between the lines) of contracts are deemed part of that contract and stand on an equal footing with the remainder of the contract. The same is true of addendums or other instruments that are incorporated by reference in the contract, or attached to the back thereof. There is a difficult problem of proof when there are interlineations and addendums. Good practice suggests that when an interlineation, addendum, or an incorporation by reference is made, said interlineation should be initialed by all parties to the contract. In addition, all addendums, or documents incorporated by reference, should be indicated on the face of the contract. Addendums to the document should also be initialed, indicating that all parties to the contract knew which documents were being incorporated.

Against Maker   When a contract is unclear or ambiguous, and both possible interpretations stand on an equal footing, the court will construe the instrument most strictly against the party who drafted it and is responsible for the language used. This does not mean the court chooses to penalize the person who drew the contract, but merely that in a case of reasonable doubt as to interpretation, the equities will be construed against the drafter of the ambiguous contract.

Parol Evidence Rule   In construing a contract, as well as in courtroom proceedings, one of the critically important factors in determining interpretations of contractual instruments is what is termed the *parol evidence rule.* Simply explained, the parol evidence rule stands for the theory that when an agreement has been reduced to writing, parol evidence (oral or additional writings) is not admissible in court to add to or vary the promises contained in the original instrument. However, the contract must be clear and certain as to its terms, and not ambiguous in order for the parol evidence rule to apply.

This rule is critically important when drafting earnest money contracts. There is very often underlying intent in areas of financing, fixtures, and repairs, which can be agreed to orally and with the best of intentions. However, when one party fails to perform on an implied or oral agreement (even though the agreement may have been considered an important part of the earnest money contract), the court will not allow this evidence to be introduced so that it can construe the terms of the earnest money contract if it is otherwise unambiguous. To be found to be unambiguous, only one meaning must clearly emerge in interpretation of the provision, *Laguarta, Gavrel, & Kirk, Inc.* v. *R & P Enterprises*, 596 S.W.2d 517 (Tex. Civ. App.—Houston, 1979). In other words, a person can say whatever he wishes, but if it is not in the contract, he will have a very difficult time of proof and enforcement when it gets to court.

An often overlooked area of the parol evidence rule is that of modifying existing contracts. If the subsequent modification or amendment of an existing unambiguous contract does not properly incorporate or amend the previous contract, it is considered a new and separate agreement and cannot be used as evidence to construe the terms of the original contract. To properly amend a previous contract, one must achieve the same formalities as making the original contract; that is, there must be a meeting of the minds, both parties must execute it, and they must have all of the other attributes as if the agreement were a new contract, *Mandril* v. *Kasishke,* 620 S.W.2d 238 (Tex. Civ. App.—Amarillo, 1981).

Printed versus Typed

When a contract uses a printed form contract and typed provisions are put into the contract that conflict with a statement in the form of the contract, the typed provisions will control over the printed provisions, since it was the language the parties used and should carry more weight than that of the printed form. The same is true of a handwritten provision versus a typed or printed provision in a contract. The changes usually imply the intent of the parties, possibly done as a last-minute change, to give more effect to prior provisions in the contract, or to clarify them.

Effective Date

The standard rule for the effective date of the contract is *not* when the contract is delivered (this is true of deeds and leases, but not of contracts generally). The contract takes effect when it is dated or when both parties have signed it.

The foregoing general rules are by no means conclusive, since each fact situation can, of course, impose its own equities and variations. Inevitably, conflicts will arise, and even the foregoing general rules can conflict in many situations. In one case, the court had to construe a conflict between the foregoing general rules when a real estate broker used a form contract on which he typed special provisions. The court had to decide which rule should be applied: the rule that says that typed matter controls over printed matter, or the rule that says the contract should be construed against the maker (the broker). In this particular case, the court held that the rule should be applied that typed matter controls over printed matter instead of the rule of construction against the author, *Quad Construction, Inc.* v. *Wm. A. Smith Contracting Co.,* 534 F.2d 1391 (10th Cir., 1976). Unfortunately, this type of problem with earnest money contracts comes up far too often, and great care should be taken to avoid such situations.

Legal Effect

There is a lot of confusion as to the validity of a contract once it has been agreed to. In determining the validity and enforceability of a contract, it is generally construed to have one of four legal effects. It may be *valid, void, voidable,* or *unenforceable.*

A *void* contract is a contract that never existed, and therefore has no legal effect. These contracts lack one of the essential contract elements (legal subject matter, competent parties, consideration, or mutual assent) to the extent that the parties knew, or should have known, that it was void on its face. Therefore, a contract for an illegal act is void, as is a contract with a person judicially declared to be insane. Similarly, a forged contract is void, as the party signing the contract was not the legitimate party to enter into the contractual obligation.

The vast majority of contracts held to be not valid are held to be *voidable.* These contracts do not have a patent defect which renders the contract void, but have latent defects which can be discovered upon further inquiry and disclosure of additional facts. In some states, contracts by minors are considered to be voidable at the option of the minor, as are those involving a party determined to be insane at the time of the contract's execution. In the latter case, the insane is not an adjudicated insane (making the contract void), but one who is later determined to be insane or temporarily insane at the time he signed the contract. Similarly, the law in most states looks at contracts in violation of the statute of frauds as voidable when the statute of limitations for the contracts' enforcement has expired. When the jury determines that there has been a valid defense to mutual assent (fraud, duress, menace, undue influence, misrepresentation), the contractual obligations are voidable and can be avoided at the option of the aggrieved party.

The law generally recognizes that if contracts are not performed on within the statutory period (generally two years for oral agreements and four years for written agreements), the contract is no longer enforceable by either party. There is a similar equitable doctrine called *laches,* which is a period of unreasonable delay in enforcing a contract, causing detriment to the other party. Instead, of a statutory period, however, the period of time is what is "reasonable." That is, if the contract is not performed within a reasonable amount of time, the doctrine of *laches* may be imposed by a court to render the contract unenforceable. Laches cannot be asserted against a governmental entity, however.

The major difference between a contract that is voidable and one that is unenforceable lies in the fact that if an unenforceable obligation has been performed, it may not be avoided. A voidable contract can be avoided for performance if the proper facts can be proven. The remedy for an unenforceable contract is cancellation, while the remedy for a void or voidable contract is reversion, which restores the parties to their former positions.

Contracts may be oral or express, although in matters involving real estate, each state has a law that requires some contracts be in writing in order to be enforceable, commonly called a *statute of frauds.*

The statute of frauds provides that any agreement as described in that statute is not enforceable unless the promise or agreement, or a memorandum of it, is (1) in writing and (2) signed by the person to be charged with the promise or agreement or by someone lawfully authorized to sign for him. The contracts and agreements in a statute of frauds that are specifically pertinent for real estate transactions are (1) a contract for the sale of real estate, (2) a lease of real estate for a term longer than one year, or (3) an agreement that is not to be performed within one year from the date of making the agreement, (4) a promise or agreement to pay a commission for the sale or purchase of (a) an oil or a gas mining lease to an oil or gas royalty, (b) minerals, or (c) a mineral interest. The statute applies to modification of contracts, as well as to the contracts themselves.

The contract for the sale of real estate is more commonly called an *earnest money contract* and needs to be discussed in greater detail.

The earnest money contract is by far the most important instrument that a real estate agent comes into contact with in the general day-to-day business of real estate practice. Earnest money contracts are, of course, binding obligations; they normally involve substantial amounts of money and very often control the biggest investment a family makes in its lifetime. It simply cannot be overemphasized how important this document is.

Despite their importance, in many instances earnest money contracts are drafted by real estate agents rather than by attorneys. Since attorneys have more formal and specific training in drafting contracts, there has been some objection to the drafting of contracts by real estate agents in almost all states. In most cases, the problem has been resolved by permitting real estate agents to fill in blanks in approved form contracts, *Chicago Bar Association* v. *Quinlan & Tyson, Inc.,* 214 N.E.2d 771 (1966). Using other than the standard approved form can be interpreted as practicing law without a license. Such decisions have come about in order to make sure that the general public is protected from innocent but mistaken acts that can cause substantial financial damage. On the other hand, using approved standard forms is a practical necessity if real estate agents are to conduct business in a normal manner.

Oral Contracts. Recall that there is a general requirement that all contracts affecting the transfer of real estate must be in writing, in

EARNEST MONEY CONTRACTS

Requirements of Earnest Money Contracts

order to comply with the statute of frauds. We will depart from this basic underlying theory just enough to prove that there are exceptions to every rule. There is such a thing as an *oral earnest money contract* (horror of horrors!). There are basically three requirements to enforce an oral earnest money contract, and these all must exist simultaneously, *Hooks* v. *Bridgewater,* 229 S.W.2d 1114 (Tex. 1921), *Richardson* v. *Taylor Land & Livestock Co.,* 17 P.2d 703 (Wash. 1946), and *DuPont Feedmill Corp.* v. *Standard Supply Corp.,* 395 N.E.2d 808 (Ind. 1979):

1. There must be payment of the consideration, whether it be in money or services.
2. The possession of the subject property must be taken by the purchaser.
3. The purchaser must have made payment and valuable improvements on the property with the seller's consent.

While the reader is scratching his head in bewilderment, we will attempt to explain a fact situation under which an oral earnest money contract could be enforced:

> Vendee agrees to pay vendor $10,000 as full purchase price for vendor's house. Vendee moves in, takes possession of that house, and then constructs some valuable improvement to that property with the vendor's consent. Vendor subsequently tries to renounce the sale and get his property back.

The courts find that an oral contract which meets the three requirements (or some combination thereof, depending on the state) is valid and enforceable because to do otherwise might work a fraud on the purchaser. Logically, a person would not do all three acts—part payment, possession, and adding permanent and valuable improvements—unless he believed that he had an enforceable contract to purchase the property. Therefore, to avoid an unfair result, the court enforces the oral earnest money contract, but only under very limited circumstances. Oral earnest money contracts not meeting the requirements of either the statute of frauds or the doctrine of part performance are often considered to be voidable.

Express Contracts.   Express contracts are, of course, written contracts. As our discussion comes back to more identifiable current business practices, it should be pointed out that in earnest money contracts, as in all other real estate instruments, courts have established specific and basic requirements that must be satisfied before such contracts will be considered to be enforceable. These requirements are as follows:

1. *There must be a written instrument* (the only exception is the one noted above).

2. *The instrument must be signed by the party to be charged.* This means that the person against whom the instrument is being enforced must have signed the contract; for instance, if *A* and *B* contract to sell real estate, and only *A* has signed the contract, it can reasonably be assumed that *B* could enforce the contract against *A*, but *A* could not enforce the contract against *B* until *B* signs the contract. With one signature on the contract, it is now a standing offer, which *B* can accept at any time by simply signing his name (provided that this was within the guidelines of acceptances described above).

3. *There must be evidence of an intent to convey an interest in the real estate at some time in the future.* This requirement generally meets the consideration guidelines in that one party offers to give up his money while the other party offers to convey his interest in some real estate at a future date.

4. *There must be an identifiable grantor and grantee.* The grantor and grantee must be identifiable and be competent as described earlier.

5. *The subject matter to be conveyed must be identifiable.* This is a requirement of a proper legal description, so that there can be no mistake as to which property is the subject matter of the contract.

Once these formalities have been met, the contract is considered specific enough to be enforceable in a court of law.

Provisions of Earnest Money Contracts

As real estate agents know, most earnest money contracts go into much greater depth than the foregoing requirements, and a much more in-depth discussion of each of these requirements is necessary to clarify and understand the need for each of these provisions.

Legal Descriptions. All earnest money contracts must describe the property to be conveyed so that it may be identified with reasonable certainty by a person familiar with the locality, *Foster* v. *Bullard*, 496 S.W.2d 724; *Ruth* v. *Crane*, 392 F. Supp. 724 (D. Pa. 1975). The legal description generally is contained in the earnest money contract itself, although it may refer to another instrument containing the legal description. Generally, land may be identified either by the rectangular survey method or by metes and bounds.

Rectangular Survey Method. The rectangular survey method of land description is used in 30 states: Alabama, Alaska, Arizona, Arkansas, California, Colorado, Florida, Idaho, Illinois, Indiana, Iowa, Kansas, Louisiana, Michigan, Minnesota, Mississippi, Missouri, Montana, Nebraska, Nevada, New Mexico, North Dakota, Ohio, Oklahoma, Oregon, South Dakota, Utah, Washington, Wisconsin, and Wyoming. This system originates from two imaginary lines: one is called the *base line* and runs east-west; the other is the *principal meridian* and runs north-south.

There are several base lines and several principal meridians found in different places in the country. In general, the single base line and single principal meridian closest to the area in question are used as starting points to describe the land in that locality. Starting from these two lines, a grid is formed from which all land can be located and described by survey. The lines that run east-west in this grid are referred to as *township lines*. Beginning at the base line, township lines exist at six-mile intervals. The land located between township line number one and the base line is in township one; the land located between township lines number one and number two is located in township two, etc. Here the use of the term "township" has no relation to political subdivisions called *townships* that exist in many states.

The lines running north-south in the grid also are located at six-mile intervals. These are measured from the principal meridian and are called *range lines*. The area between range line number one and the principal meridian is said to be located in range one; the land between range lines number one and number two is located in range number two, etc. In this way, a grid is formed by the intersecting township and range lines, as illustrated in Figure 7-1.

In Figure 7-1, the line denoted R1W refers to range line number one located *west* of the principal meridian. The line labeled R1E refers to range line number one located *east* of the principal meridian. Similarly, the letters N and S following the township line number identify a particular township line as being *north* or *south* of the base line.

As illustrated in the figure, the grid formed by the township and range lines is six miles on each side. Each square within this

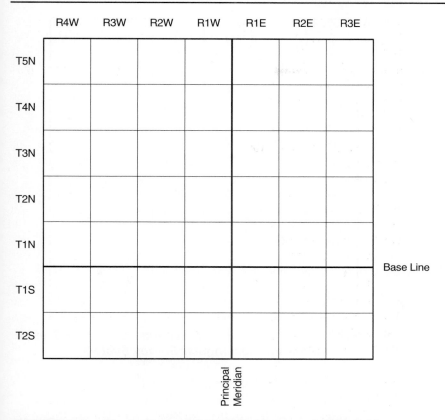

FIGURE 7-1 *Illustration of Township Lines and Range Lines under the Rectangular Survey System*

square is then divided into 36 *sections*. Each section is one mile square and contains 640 acres. These sections are identified by number as illustrated in Figure 7-2.

Since the grid formed by the township and range lines is square and the earth is round, allowances must be made so that our survey system will conform with the curvature of the earth. This is done by a "lot" system. This means that certain sections contain what are usually called *lots*. These lots may contain either more or less than 640 acres. They generally are located in sections 1-7, 18, 19, 30, and 31.

A section can be further divided into quarters in order to assist in locating a given tract of land. For example, if someone owns the 160-acre tract that comprises the northwest quarter of a certain section, it might be described as follows.

6	5	4	3	2	1
7	8	9	10	11	12
18	17	16	15	14	13
19	20	21	22	23	24
30	29	28	27	26	25
31	32	33	34	35	36

**FIGURE 7-2   Illustration of the Section Numbering System
under the Rectangular Survey System**

> The Northwest Quarter of Section 17, Township 51
> North, Range 20 West of the Fifth Principal Meridian,
> located in Acme County, Missouri, and containing
> 160 acres, more or less.

Thus, under the survey system one can describe any tract of land, regardless of its shape and size. If the land is irregularly shaped, one can still describe it by first starting at a corner of a section (or quarter section) and specifying how to locate one corner of the tract, and then tracing the tract's boundaries by stating the directions and distances between points on its perimeter. An example of a small, regularly shaped tract might be as follows.

> Starting at the Northeast corner of Section 17, then
> South 575 feet and then West 300 feet to the point of
> beginning; then South 300 feet, then West 400 feet
> then North 300 feet, then East 400 feet to the point of
> beginning; all located in Section 17, Township 51
> North, Range 20 West of the Fifth Principal Meridian,
> in Acme County, Missouri.

Metes and Bounds System. In lieu of the rectangular survey method, land may also be described by the metes and bounds (sometimes called *monuments*) system. Here distances and directions around the tract are recited, with tangible monuments often being referred to at the corners and/or along one or more sides. These tangible monuments might include such items as trees, streams, roads, stakes, buildings, and so forth. Since monuments may be destroyed, moved, or gradually shifted, they should be described as completely as possible in order to aid in locating boundaries several years hence.

Financial Considerations. When an earnest money contract is contingent upon the buyer securing a loan, the buyer impliedly promises to make application for the loan and to diligently pursue obtaining the loan. If the buyer fails to exercise this diligence, or causes a cancellation of his loan, he may not recover his earnest money because of his failure to obtain that loan, *Bushmiller* v. *Schiller,* 368 A.2d 1044 (Md. 1977), *Makofsky* v. *Cunningham,* 576 F.2d 1223 (5th Cir., 1978).

However, if the sale is other than one for cash, it probably involves an assumption of or "subject to" existing seller financing. When such is the case, it is very important that all the terms of the purchase price are clearly set out. These requirements would usually include the down payment, the terms of the note (to be assumed or to be newly incurred), and the identification of the type of mortgage to be utilized.

On the other hand, if the purchaser is having difficulty securing financing, he has a right to terminate the contract at his option. There have been several cases in which the seller has attempted to take advantage of the buyer's inability to obtain financing to cancel the contract. Financing contingencies tend to run in favor of the purchaser. It only makes the contract avoidable at the purchaser's option in the event financing is not obtained. The seller cannot take advantage of this contingency—only the party who benefits from the contingency can take advantage of it.

For the purchaser, these requirements help to operate as a full disclosure of the indebtedness charged against the property. The seller is also assured that the purchaser is capable of completing the sale because he (the purchaser) is fully apprised of all obligations he is about to undertake.

Title Matters. In the absence of an agreement otherwise, the buyer is entitled to a *marketable title* when the real estate is transferred to him. A marketable title is generally considered to be one free of encumbrances and free of any third-party rights or interests incompatible with the full enjoyment and ownership of the property. It is not a perfect title, but one generally considered to be reasonably free of any hazards of litigation.

Any encumbrances on the title affecting marketability should be spelled out in the contract so that the purchaser will be aware of them. He may waive his right to object to such encumbrances if he signs the contract acknowledging that the title may be passed with the encumbrances included. Encumbrances may include any matter that affects the title to the real estate, such as the reservation of mineral rights, restrictions on use and ownership, leases, mortgage liens, easements, restrictions, encroachments, and possibly even threatened condemnation proceedings.

In many states real estate agents are required to disclose certain title matters to purchasers before they can institute a lawsuit for their commission. To fully protect their rights in these states most agents use standard form contracts, which contain the appropriate caveats on title matters, *Jones* v. *Del Anderson and Associates, supra.* Usually it is sufficient to advise the purchaser that he should either (1) secure an abstract of title and employ an attorney to give an opinion as to the quality of his prospective title, or (2) purchase an owner's title insurance policy.

If a title company is to be used, the normal procedure in most states is for the seller to purchase the title policy (it is his certification that the title is good), but it is usually the purchaser's prerogative as to which title company to use. The purchaser is the one who is having the title insured. Therefore, he should be careful to select a title company that he knows is solvent, reputable, and accommodating to his needs.

Earnest Money. Earnest money is generally defined as a representation of a buyer's good faith—a deposit of money to show the buyer is "earnest" in presenting the offer. There is no legal requirement for earnest money in a contract. It has also been held that even the deposit of the earnest money is not a condition precedent to performance, *Hudson* v. *Wakefield*, 645 S.W.2d 427 (Tex. 1983). However, it is often customary to put in a certain amount of earnest money, both to enforce consideration and to assure the seller that the purchaser is, in fact, serious about buying the property. Provisions in most earnest money contracts provide that in the event that a purchaser does not perform, the earnest money should go to the seller as liquidated damages. Normally, if the seller defaults, the earnest money is returned to the purchaser. The amount of escrow deposited, or the requirement of where the escrow is deposited, is normally not a legal matter, but rather one of negotiation between the parties.

When the earnest money is deposited, the title company, as a neutral third party, frequently serves as the escrow agent. However, other parties may perform this function if it is acceptable to the parties. One party's attorney, a broker, or a financial institution can serve this same function.

Another consideration concerning the earnest money provision of the contract may involve the type of earnest money to be used. Earnest money deposits don't need to be in cash, and often include a letter of credit, a certificate of deposit, a check or bank draft, or even a promissory note, made due and payable upon the date of closing.

A significant factor concerning the deposit of earnest money involves the escrow agent's obligation to protect the earnest money. Regardless of the facts surrounding a default in an earnest money contract, most escrow agents are very reluctant to release the earnest money to either party without the other party's written consent. No matter how blatant or obvious the breach of the contract may be, one will seldom find that an escrow agent will readily forward the earnest money to either party unless he (the escrow agent) is adequately protected by some other agreement, affidavit, bond, or other assurance. It is all too often that a party simply backs out of a sale, but will not sign a written consent to allow the earnest money to be forwarded to the other party. When this happens, there is very little available to the aggrieved party as a remedy except the courthouse.

Representations. There are often representations in earnest money contracts that the property is in good condition. These representations are sometimes supported by a further representation that the seller will complete the repair of certain items in the house, or building, or whatever might be the subject of the sale. There are distinct differences between a representation and a warranty. A representation may hinder the closing or create certain verbal adversities, whereas a warranty generally gives the purchaser a certain damage claim, *Fant v. Howell*, 547 S.W.2d 261 (Tex. 1977).

Although the number of representations or warranties that could be contained in earnest money contracts is as vast as the imagination can conceive, great care should be taken by the agent to see that both parties have their representations very clearly stated. There should be specific provisions made for remedies in the event one of the representations is not true, or is not performed as required by the contract.

Recent case law has taken the issue of misrepresentations to new levels of controversy. In general, a cause of action is created for *misrepresentation* (either intentional or negligently made) as well as *failure to disclose* latent defects. Common misrepresentations include structural issues, such as the poor condition of a sewage system, *Anderson* v. *Harper,* 622 A.2d 319 (Pa.—Super., 1993), leaks in the house, *Colgan* v. *Washington Realty Co.,* 879 S.W.2d 686 (Mo. App., 1994), the building being declared uninhabitable, *Shimmons* v. *Mortgage Corp. of America,* 520 N.W.2d 670 (Mich. Ct. App., 1994), or faulty inspection, *Runsford* v. *Valley Pest Control, Inc.,* 629 So.2d 623 (Ala. 1993), *Smith* v. *Mitchell,* 911 S.W.2d 427 (Tex. App.—San Antonio, 1995).

One possible way of overcoming the problem of misrepresentation is to allow the buyer to purchase the property "as is." The results of the as is cases vary widely, although a pattern seems to be developing. Parties still have the right to bargain, and when the buyer agrees to take the property as is, some courts might presume that the buyer got a better price as a part of the bargain. It would therefore be unfair to hold a seller liable for misrepresentation if that seller accepted a lower sales price as part of the bargain. This is particularly true if the buyer is given the unrestricted right to inspect. See *Prudential Insurance Company of America* v. *Jefferson Associates, Ltd.,* 896 S.W.2d 156 (Tex. 1995), *Layman* v. *Binns,* 35 Ohio St. 3d 176 (Oh. 1988).

The right to buy as is is generally qualified, though, and not totally caveat emptor. Courts will seldom enforce an as is clause if there has been fraud, concealment, fraudulent misrepresentation, or affirmation misrepresentation. See *Prudential, supra., George* v. *Lumbrazo,* 584 N.Y.S.2d 704 (N.Y. App.—1992), and *Brewer* v. *Brothers,* 611 N.E.2d 492 (Oh. App. [12th Dist.], 1992).

Representations and covenants are often omitted altogether by granting the purchaser a right of inspection prior to the closing.

Closing.   "Closing" is the term normally given to the process of consummating the sale of real estate. Provisions pertaining to a closing generally specify a date, any automatic extensions if needed, and an absolute date by which the closing must take place or the contract becomes voidable at the option of either party. Specific provisions provided for under closing conditions normally include right to possession of the real estate (which usually is not given until the seller has received all of his funds), and requirements for the documentation needed at the closing (usually including the deed, mortgage procedures, assignments, bills of sale, and application of escrow funds). There may be additional provisions for surveys, delivery of title policy, and allocation of expenses to be borne by each party. The expenses include the attorneys' fees, brokerage fees, survey fees, inspection fees, proration of taxes, utilities, and insurance, and recording and escrow fees.

Time Is of the Essence.   Unless a contract clearly indicates that time is of the essence, it will not be construed to be so, *Tannenbaum v. Sears, Roebuck and Co.,* 401 A.2d 809 (Penn. 1979). However, in an option contract, time is always of the essence, *Cummings v. Bullock,* 367 F.2d 182 (9th Cir., 1966), although the stipulated time limit may be extended by agreement of the parties. Unless time is a critical factor in closing, funding, or possession, it is not of the essence. This phrase should never be used otherwise, since it can enable a party to avoid the contract when anyone (even a third party) may not meet a time constraint.

Assignment.   Unless otherwise provided for, contracts for the sale of real property are assignable. However, when the sale is to be made on credit or other condition of personal performance by one of the parties, the contract is normally not considered to be assignable unless made specifically assignable by its terms, *Farrell v. Evans,* 517 S.W.2d 585 (Tex. Civ. App.—Houston, 1974).

Contingencies.   Purchasers often desire to tie up the seller's property for a "free look" by putting unreasonable or frivolous contingencies in the contract for sale. These contingencies may be solely at the purchaser's option, such that the purchaser has no obligation at all. For instance, the purchaser may make his contract:

> ... contingent upon the approval of purchaser's attorney. In the event said approval is not obtained, this contract shall become null and void, at the purchaser's option.

This type of contingency contains no time for performance, does not name the attorney, and gives no rights at all to the seller.

Such contingencies are not only vague and ambiguous, but may also be complicated by unexpected legal problems. If there is a contingency, the law generally imposes a standard of reasonable diligence on the purchaser, regardless of the terms of the contract. If the terms are too one-sided, the court may even refuse to enforce them because of a lack of mutuality and construe them to be an option to purchase, not a contract for sale. Similarly, if one of the parties causes the default (intentionally causing the refusal of financing, for instance), the court will enforce the performance and not allow that party to benefit from his own default. Trying for the "free look" is not always as simple as it may seem.

Remedies for Default   When a buyer or seller fails to carry out some material part of his earnest money contract, this is referred to as a *default* or *breach of contract*. Several different remedies may be available to the aggrieved party when the other defaults on the contract.

These remedies may be judicial or nonjudicial in nature. *Judicial remedies* refer to those that require a lawsuit to obtain. *Nonjudicial remedies,* on the other hand, are provided for in the contract and represent an attempt by the parties to avoid the necessity of court action in case default occurs.

Nonjudicial Remedies.   Two principal nonjudicial remedies are arbitration and liquidated damages. In *arbitration,* the parties include a provision in their contract that calls for them to submit any disputes to "binding arbitration." Basically, this means they agree to be bound by the arbitrator's decision, so that the time and expense of a lawsuit may be avoided. Their contract generally either names an arbitrator or specifies how the arbitrator will be selected. A common provision here is that each party may choose one arbitrator, the two arbitrators so selected shall choose a third, and a majority vote of the three is binding on the parties. Arbitrators generally are experts in the field who can expedite a dispute settlement fairly, quickly, and efficiently.

A second method to avoid court action involves placing a *liquidated damages* clause in a contract. In essence, it sets out how damages will be calculated in case either party defaults on his contractual obligations. A common use of this clause calls for the seller to retain the earnest money as liquidated damages if the buyer defaults. See *Leet* v. *Totah,* 620 A.2d 1372 (Md. App. 1993).

Occasionally, the defaulting party will refuse to carry out the remedy imposed by the liquidated damages clause. For this reason, two rules have been developed governing the enforceability of liquidated damages provisions. First, in order to be enforceable, a liquidated damage clause basically must have represented an honest attempt by the parties to determine the damages that would result if the contract were breached. Second, in some jurisdictions there is the additional requirement that the clause will be enforceable only under circumstances in which it would be difficult if not impossible to estimate the actual damages that would occur (in case of default). For example, suppose an earnest money contract involves an $80,000 duplex and calls for a $1 million liquidated damages payment to the seller if the buyer defaults. Clearly this is not a reasonable attempt to determine damages resulting from breach because $1 million in damages will not result from an $80,000 contract. Courts call this a *penalty* clause and generally refuse to allow one party to hold a penalty clause over the other's head as a club to ensure that he performs a contract. Good practice suggests that it is better to use the term *liquidated damages* rather than the term penalty in a contract.

Does the fact that the parties call their provision a "liquidated damages" clause mean that it will be legally interpreted as such? To answer this, we can pose another question: "Does calling an elephant a giraffe make it a giraffe?" Clearly the answer is no, so irrespective of whether the parties call their provision a "penalty" or "liquidated damages" clause, the determinative factor will be whether it constitutes an honest attempt to determine future damages for contractual default.

Judicial Remedies—Damages. Although nonjudicial remedies are being used more often, judicial remedies still constitute the major avenues of recovery in many instances.

Recall that a legal action is one that seeks money damages. Basically, what is being requested is reimbursement for financial losses that occurred because the other party defaulted on the contract. For example, suppose Bill Buyer defaults on a contract to buy Blackacre from Sam Seller at the contract price of $100,000. In this case, the best price (fair market value) that Sam can get from another purchaser is $90,000. Thus, he suffered at least $10,000 in damages when Bill defaulted. Sam may also be entitled to other damages caused by Bill's breaking the contract, such as additional interest on his investment, property taxes, property insurance premiums, and perhaps duplicate real estate brokerage commissions.

Take another example. Suppose Bill defaults on his contractual obligations as in the example, but Sam can sell the land elsewhere for $110,000. In this case he did not suffer any financial damage by Bill's default (in fact, he was $10,000 better off because of it), so legally he is entitled only to nominal damages (usually one dollar), *Smith* v. *Mady*, 194 Cal.Rptr.42 (1983). However, he may still be entitled to retain the earnest money as liquidated damages if the contract so provides.

There are two kinds of damages, general and special. *General* damages are usually defined as "the natural and necessary result of a breach of contract." In our example, Bill knew that certain damages would naturally and necessarily result if he broke the contract. Although he may not have known the exact amount, he knew (or the law will imply that he knew) that the resulting damages would be at least the difference between the sale price and the fair market value of the property.

Special damages, on the other hand, are "the natural but *not* the necessary result of a breach of contract." To illustrate, suppose Sam Seller was planning on taking his real estate sales proceeds and quickly investing them in another profitable venture. If Bill defaults on the contract, Sam will also lose the opportunity to make a profit on the other venture. The lost profit on that venture might be thought of as special damages. This naturally resulted when Bill defaulted on his contractual obligations. However, Bill may not have known that they would necessarily result. For this reason Bill is usually held liable for special damages only when he knew that his default would cause Sam to lose money in another specific venture. He is, however, always liable for general damages.

Specific Performance.   There may be times when the aggrieved party must have the contract carried out, rather than be paid damages. In this case, he may be able to institute a lawsuit for *specific performance.* However, since specific performance is an equitable action, it can be brought only if the legal remedy (the payment of money damages) is not adequate to compensate him for his losses. This requirement may also be met when the subject matter to be received is unique or not readily available elsewhere. Real estate is almost always considered unique. See *Kalinowski* v. *Yeh,* 847 P.2d 673 (Hawaii App., 1993).

In some states only the buyer can seek to force specific performance. This is because the item he is to receive (real estate) is legally unique, whereas the item received by the seller (money) is not. Other states will permit both parties to seek specific performance under the theory that if one party has a judicial remedy, it is only fair that the other party have the same remedy. Specific performance is not an easy remedy to successfully prosecute. Some contracts provide that specific performance may not be sought, and both parties agree that money damages may be the only remedy, *Brewer* v. *Meyers,* 545 S.W.2d 235, *Tourea* v. *Alderman,* 211 F. Supp. 865 (Or. 1962).

As an equitable remedy, the party seeking specific performance must also have acted in good faith and not personally have materially breached the contract. Furthermore, the essential terms of the contract must be expressed with reasonable certainty, *Pitts* v. *Marsh,* 567 P.2d 843 (Kan. 1977), *Melaro* v. *Mezzanotte,* 352 F. 2d 720 (D.C. Cir. 1965), adequate damages must be virtually impossible to ascertain, and not granting specific performance must result in irreparable harm and hardship on the party seeking specific performance, *Cowman* v. *Allen Monuments, Inc.,* 500 S.W.2d 223 and *Leasco Corp.* v. *Taussig,* 473 F.2d 777 (2nd Cir. 1972).

Rescission: Fraud and Misrepresentation.   Rescission is a judicial remedy that asks a court to declare a contract voidable. Thus, to rescind a contract is to cancel it and set it aside just as though it had never been made. The court has the alternatives of (1) seeking restitution of the parties' various interests (that is, to put them back in the same position that they were in prior to entering into the contract), or (2) it may order forfeiture of funds to the seller if the purchaser defaulted. In the latter case, the contract is still rescinded, but the purchaser would have lost any funds expended to date.

Rescission may be proper when one party materially misrepresented facts, which served to induce the other to enter into a contract with him, or there is a mutual mistake between the parties, *Bar-Del v. Oz, Inc.,* 850 S.W.2d 855 (Ky. Ct. App., 1993). Under certain circumstances, misrepresentation of value may also be grounds for rescission.

To illustrate *misrepresentation of fact,* suppose a seller tells a prospective buyer that the roof of a commercial building is leakproof. However, in actual fact the roof may have serious leakage problems. If this statement induces the prospective buyer to purchase the property, the seller's liability depends on which of three distinctly different types of conduct are involved, as listed below.

1. *Fraud* is the most serious case and involves a willful intent to deceive. When proven, it is grounds for rescission in all states.

2. *Negligent* misrepresentation is not intentional, but rather involves a representation of fact about something that a reasonable and prudent seller would have checked before making. It is grounds for recovery of damages in some states and under some circumstances.

3. The third type of factual misrepresentation, *conscious ignorance,* lies somewhere between fraud and negligence, and is also grounds for recovery in some states. It is present when a seller realizes he does not know whether a statement is true or false but makes it anyway. This is quite similar to fraud but does not require proof of a willful intent to deceive.

Misrepresentation of value involves statements by a seller about value. Such statements may be grounds for rescinding a contract if the prospective buyer relied on them and thereby was induced to enter into the contract. Clearly, however, there are instances in which the buyer does *not* rely on the seller's statement about value. We often expect a seller to inflate the value, which is known as "puffing," so that many times it is our own judgment about the value that makes us decide to buy. The important point to remember is that a misrepresentation of value *must have induced* the buyer to make the contract before rescission will be permitted. Generally, this occurs only when the seller is in a superior position to know what the value is, or when the prospective buyer believes the seller is in a superior position to judge value.

The Merger Doctrine   It is a well understood point of law that the earnest money contract is a contract for sale and performs precisely that function. Most contracts for sale contain a provision that the written contract must embody the entire agreement of the parties and that there is no other oral or written agreement between the parties. This provision is commonly called a *merger provision*; it is enforced by excluding parol evidence, unless the intention of the parties indicates otherwise, *Humber* v. *Morton*, 426 S.W.2d 554 (Tex. 1968) and *Spatz* v. *Nascone*, 364 F. Supp. 967 (1973). Once the sale has been closed and the deed has been transferred, the earnest money contract has no force or effect whatsoever on either party, because the purpose of the contract (the sale) has been fulfilled.

One may often find that an earnest money contract has certain representations and warranties that are intentionally specified to extend beyond the closing (properly termed *survive the closing*). However, unless these provisions are carefully drawn and unless the parties understand the intention to survive the closing, such provisions will not survive. Upon closing, it is normally determined that the terms of the earnest money contract are merged into the deed, or other instrument executed at the closing, and any cause of action for representation or warranties must be on the basis of the deed, rather than on the basis of the earnest money contract.

There has been erosion of this doctrine of merger in the past few years because of builder's warranties and agreements to perform services. The most recent cases are indicating that merger depends upon the intent of the parties, which is a fact issue. So, in the case of builder's or contractor's warranties, the doctrine of merger may not apply.

OPTION CONTRACTS   An option contract is an agreement by which the owner of a property gives another the right to purchase his property at a fixed price, on specified terms, within the time specified within the option contract, *State* v. *Clevenger*, 384 S.W.2d 207, *Kalamazoo County* v. *City of Kalamazoo*, 257 N.W.2d 260 (Mich. 1977). This agreement creates an irrevocable offer to sell the property at a fixed price. It requires consideration before the contract can be binding, although the parties may agree that the payment for the option can be applied to the purchase price in the event the option is exercised, *Granger Real Estate Exchange* v. *Anderson*, 145 S.W. 262, *Haire* v. *Cook*,

229 S.E.2d 436 (Ga. 1976). The option contract is normally signed only by the seller (optionor) because he is the only party to be charged in performance. It should be noted, however, that since the purchaser has no obligation to perform, he gets no title of any kind to the property (neither equitable nor legal), and time is always of the essence in an option contract.

There has been some litigation in recent years concerning the difference between an option contract and an earnest money contract in which the seller's sole remedy is to accept the earnest money as liquidated damages. The legal difference between the two instruments is insignificant. In fact, courts have even held that if the seller's only contractual remedy in the event of the purchaser's default in an earnest money contract is retention of the earnest money, the agreement constitutes an option rather than a bilateral agreement for sale, *Broady* v. *Mitchell*, 572 S.W.2d 36 (Tex. Civ. App.—Houston, 1978). The same is true of one-sided or vague contingencies (see the "Contingencies" section earlier in this chapter). So in an option contract, the only effective remedy is the buyer's right to force the seller to specifically perform. The seller has no right to force the buyer to specifically perform. As a more practical matter, however, most real estate agents feel that the earnest money contract without the specific performance provision is more acceptable in the typical business setting.

INSTALLMENT LAND CONTRACTS

An installment land contract is a contract for the sale of real estate that extends over a long period of time. It is called an *executory contract*, because the terms of the contract are not to be completed in the near future. This contrasts with an *executed* contract in which the terms of the contract are satisfied as of signing (e.g., a deed). The installment land contract is also called a *contract for deed*, and it is precisely that. It is a contract entered into between the buyer and seller to deliver a deed at some future date. This contract may last ten years or longer, depending on the terms.

An installment land contract has been likened to a marital agreement in that the parties have just entered into an agreement for a long period of time which may produce adverse results that they had not anticipated at the time they made the deal. There is very little difference between a vendor–buyer relationship under an installment land contract situation and a landlord–tenant relationship except that the purchaser (unlike the lessee) expects to gain title to the property at some future date. The seller retains *legal title*, and the purchaser gets an *equitable title* to the property. All of the purchaser's rights to the property are defined by that contract, just as a lessee's rights are defined by a lease.

Disadvantages There are several major pitfalls for the buyer in an installment land contract. First of all, there is usually no escrow required for the deed instrument. Second, there is normally no warranty that the seller can deliver a free and clear title. Third, there is very seldom any provision for a title insurance policy. Fourth, in the event of default by the buyer, the seller merely tears up the contract for sale, and there is no recordable interest that the purchaser can use to protect himself. Fifth, if the seller dies, becomes mentally incompetent, goes bankrupt, moves back to Indiana, neglects to pay his income tax, fails to keep up the payments on the mortgage governing the property, suffers an adverse judgment, refuses to pay off creditors, or transfers his interest to a six-year-old Native American boy in Broken Bow, Oklahoma—it may cause real legal complications for the installment land purchaser, *Haarman* v. *Davis,* 651 S.W.2d 134 (Mo. 1983).

There are disadvantages for the seller also. The buyer may destroy the premises; he may be habitually late in his payments and rely on his statutory redemption right (discussed later) to stay late on his payments; if the seller continually accepts late payments, he may lose his right to accelerate the payments; or the purchaser may have work performed on the property, giving the contractor a lien right.

An exhaustive review of installment land sales contracts is covered in Warren, "California Installment Land Sales Contracts," *U.C.L.A. Law Review,* Vol. 9 (1962), 608. Another excellent review of installment land sales contracts is covered by John Mixon, "Installment Land Contracts, A Study of Low-Income Transactions, with Proposals for Reform and a New Program to Provide Home Ownership in the Inner City," *Houston Law Review,* Vol. 7 (1970), 523.

Default and Remedies In the event the installment land contract is breached by the purchaser, the remedies of a vendor generally include rescission, eviction, suit for price, damages for the breach, and possibly suit for specific performance; but his most useful remedy is that of simple forfeiture of title and all payments by the purchaser, *Randall* v. *Riel,* 465 A.2d 484 (N.H. 1983). If the seller can declare the installment land contract forfeited, he can simply remove the tenant purchaser and sell the house to someone else. Although it is true that the purchaser under an installment land contract does get a certain identifiable equity interest in the property (the right to purchase same), most installment land contracts provide that the contract itself is not recordable, and therefore it is difficult for the purchaser to record his interest to protect himself and to put third parties on notice, as required by most recording acts. In such a case, the purchaser may want to assign his interest in the contract to a friendly party, and record the assignment, or he may do some work on the house and record a mechanic's and materialman's lien in order to be sure that his interest is properly reflected into the records of the real property.

In an effort to remedy the difficult situations often created by installment land contracts, state legislatures have passed statutes providing for certain redemption periods in the event of a contractual default. Since the statutes are basically remedial in nature, the courts tend to lean toward the side of the purchaser, *De Leon* v. *Aldrete,* 398 S.W. 2d 160, which forced the vendor who exercised his right of forfeiture to make restitution under the principles of equity and to reimburse some funds that the purchaser had expended on the residence, or to prevent unjust deficiencies, *Dalton* v. *Acker,* 450 N.E.2d 289 (Ohio 1983). In addition, some courts have held that these statutes apply retroactively to contracts entered into prior to the passage of the statute, *Hiddleston* v. *Nebraska Jewish Ed. Soc.,* 186 N.W.2d 904 (Neb. 1971).

There may also be prohibitions against forfeiture and acceleration of an installment land contract if the vendor has made a practice of accepting late payments in the past, and if no installments were delinquent at the time the vendor attempted to effect forfeiture, *Fox* v. *Grange,* 103 N.E. 576 (1913).

There are also mortgage aspects to installment land sale contracts. In some states installment land sales contracts are used as a substitute for a mortgage so that the time and expense of judicially foreclosing a mortgage may be avoided. Foreclosure is not required for default under an installment land sales contract because the seller still holds title—a large degree of protection.

Of course, the horrors of installment land contracts are supported by a number of stories and fact situations, such as the following:

1. A property owner purchased a lot from a resort subdivision developer on an installment land contract. He subsequently paid the full price for the lot and received a deed subject to the underlying indebtedness that the developer incurred to develop the subdivision. When the developer defaulted on his mortgage, the lender foreclosed. The property owner, even though he paid the full price for his lot, lost all of his interest in the property because of the underlying and prior indebtedness incurred by his vendor.

2. A lot purchaser purchased a lot in a subdivision with a very low down payment and very low monthly payments.

After calculating the price of his lot and the amount of his monthly payments, he determined that his monthly payments were not even enough to pay the interest and debt service on the lot. He, in effect, could pay his installments the rest of his life and never acquire the lot. One must remember that he signed a contract for this purchase, and all the construction and basic elements of interpretation of that contract must be complied with.

3. Since the installment land contract is seldom recorded, there have been repeated situations in which a developer has sold the same lot to several different people. None of the subsequent purchasers are on notice, nor under a duty to be on notice, because of the requirements of the recording act.

Unfortunately, the installment land contract has been a very useful tool for the unscrupulous land developer. However, installment land contracts, by themselves, are not necessarily bad if the vendor is acting in good faith. They are a very common tool for financing low-income housing, and, if properly used, are probably the best means of such financing. The mortgage aspects of installment land contracts will be discussed in greater detail in Chapter 10, "Mortgages."

Although this chapter is not intended to be an exhaustive review of all the provisions that may be contained in contracts, it must be remembered that each contract stands on its own and must be read very carefully to determine the rights of the parties involved. Whenever a party signs a contract, he is deemed by law to have read and understood all the provisions, even if that party is illiterate. It is always wise to have a party's attorney review his contract. This puts the burden of interpretation and reliance on the attorney, and not on the broker, who may be liable for misrepresentations, as well as being prohibited (by statute) from the practice of law. If a broker's client relied on certain representations or promises made by the real estate broker or sales agent (conditions that were not met by the broker), said agent may further be liable for deceptive trade practices, and violations of the respective state's consumer protection act.

SUMMARY   For a contract to exist, four essential elements must be present: competent parties, legal or proper subject matter, mutual assent, and consideration.

As a general rule an oral contract is just as valid as a written one. However, in order to avoid the possibility that one party might take unfair advantage of another, all states have a statute of frauds which generally requires contracts involving the transfer of interests in real estate to be evidenced in writing and be signed by the party to be charged in order to be enforceable.

In interpreting contracts, several rules of thumb have been developed. Generally courts will bend over backward to find that a contract exists, unless an agreement is illegal or was made under fraud, duress, or mistake. Where two contracts exist, an interpretation will be sought that permits both to be effective. Moreover, all interpretations should be made only after examining the entire document, and individual sections should not be reviewed out of context with the rest of the instrument. Writing found between the lines, addendums, and other legal instruments attached or incorporated by reference have equal importance to all other contractual material and often are the best evidence of the parties' intent. Finally, unclear or ambiguous provisions generally are interpreted against the party who drafted them.

The parol evidence rule is an important factor in reaching a final interpretation of contractual agreements. It prevents the introduction of evidence about prior contradictory oral agreements, which makes it doubly important for the parties to read written contracts carefully before they sign them.

Earnest money contracts are the most important legal documents with which real estate agents come into contact. Because of the legal significance of these contracts and their potential financial impact on buyers and sellers, most states generally give lawyers the sole legal authority to draft an entire earnest money contract. Brokers can, however, fill in simple blanks in standard form contracts and can add facts relating to business details that are not legal in nature. Failure to observe this restriction may constitute the unauthorized practice of law by a real estate broker.

Although most earnest money contracts must be in writing in order to be enforceable, the doctrine of part performance makes oral contracts enforceable under certain circumstances. Depending on the state, oral earnest money sales contracts may be enforceable when all, part, or various combinations of three legal requirements are present—that is, when (1) part payment (in money or services) of the purchase price has been made, (2) when the purchaser is in possession of the real estate, and (3) when the purchaser has made payment and valuable improvements to the property. The doctrine of part performance considers these items to be sufficient evidence of the existence of a contract so that no fraud would occur if the oral contract were enforced.

In order to be enforceable an earnest money contract must also describe with reasonable certainty the real property to be conveyed. Generally this is done by the rectangular survey method in some 30 states, whereas the metes and bounds method is used in the original 13 states, other New England and Atlantic Coast states (except Florida), Kentucky, Tennessee, Texas, and West Virginia.

Earnest money contracts generally specify that the title to be delivered must be marketable.

Not all earnest money deposits involve cash. They may include letters of credit, certificates of deposit, checks, bank drafts, or promissory notes due at closing. In any event, the seller generally has the right to keep the earnest money if the contract is not carried out because of the fault of the buyer. Similarly, if the cause of the contract not being completed is the seller's fault, the earnest money will be returned to the buyer. An independent escrow agent generally holds and disburses the earnest money.

When the earnest money contract is "closed" or carried out, the appropriate deeds, money, and promissory notes are exchanged. Earnest money contracts generally cease to have any legal effect when closing (settlement) is complete. Although certain representations and warranties contained in the contract may "survive the closing" and retain their legal effect under limited circumstances, their continued legal effectiveness is generally best assured by placing them in the deed used to transfer title.

If either party defaults or fails to carry out his obligations under the earnest money contract, both nonjudicial and judicial remedies may be available to the innocent party. Nonjudicial remedies are provided for in the contract in an attempt to avoid the time and expense of going to court. The major nonjudicial remedies include binding arbitration and liquidated damages. Judicial remedies include lawsuits for money damages in an amount at least equal to the difference between the contract price and fair market value, and specific performance where the other party is forced to carry out his specific contractual obligations.

An earnest money contract calls for transferring title to the buyer at closing (settlement), and provides for any mortgage and financial obligations to be incurred at that time. An installment land sales contract, on the other hand, requires the buyer to completely pay for the contract over a long time period prior to receiving title. For that reason it is sometimes properly referred to as a *contract for deed.*

An installment land sales contract is used as a substitute for a mortgage in some states in order to avoid the time and expense of judicially foreclosing a mortgage that is in default. No foreclosure proceedings are necessary under the contract arrangement because the seller still holds title to the property. This generally is more than sufficient protection against a default on payment.

Installment land sales contracts can be somewhat unfair to buyers if default occurs after the buyers have paid a substantial portion of the purchase price. Also, the seller's personal financial problems during the payment period could cause bankruptcy or other complications preventing conveyance of full or clear title. For these and other reasons, installment land sale contracts are of questionable enforceability in some states.

Contracts, both earnest money and installment land sales, may be rescinded and canceled under certain circumstances. The circumstances may include misrepresentation of the fact or value when the misrepresentation induced the other party to enter into a contract. Depending on the state, rescission for factual misrepresentation may be proper for any of three kinds of misrepresentation: fraudulent, negligent, or conscious ignorance.

Rescission for misrepresentation of value is more difficult to achieve because often buyers do not rely on sellers' assertions about value. Since buyers expect some "puffing" of the price, legally reliance can be claimed only when the seller is in a superior position, or when the buyer believes the seller is in a superior position, to determine value.

DISCUSSION QUESTIONS

1. What is the practical effect of classifying as voidable all contracts executed by minors?

2. What kinds of real estate contracts are required to be in writing by your state's statute of frauds?

3. Buyers may purchase land using either earnest money contracts or installment land sale contracts. Logically, which might be more advantageous to them? Why?

4. What features of installment land sales contracts are attractive to sellers?

5. What are the advantages and disadvantages of each of the judicial and nonjudicial remedies available when an earnest money contract is broken?

8
Conveyances

For centuries there has been a legal and practical method by which an owner can convey, alienate, transfer, or dispose of his interest in real estate; he can have it conveyed in his absence, or even without his consent. It was obviously apparent from the initial concepts in individual real estate ownership that something had to evidence title, and something had to transfer that title, short of armed combat. The types of conveyances discussed in this chapter will be *voluntary conveyances*, which encompass deeds and wills (wills are a voluntary means of conveyance, although the means to effect that conveyance may not be so voluntary), and *involuntary conveyances*, which include adverse possession, condemnation, foreclosure, intestacy (death of the owner leaving no will), tax sales, escheat, dedication, and transfer by natural causes.

A deed is a written instrument by which a landowner transfers the ownership of his land. The quality of title that the landowner (grantor) conveys to the purchaser (grantee) is controlled by the type of deed utilized, by the warranties included, and by the restrictions and exceptions to the title contained in that deed.

VOLUNTARY CONVEYANCES

Deeds

Types of Deeds. Before getting into the legal requirements, details, and interpretations of deeds, one should be familiar with the different types of deeds in order to establish the proper basis for more in-depth discussion. The types of deeds to be discussed, in their descending order of warranty, are general warranty deeds, special warranty deeds, trustee's deeds, court-ordered deeds, deeds of bargain and sale, and quitclaim deeds.

General Warranty Deed. The general warranty deed is the most widely used deed and usually assures the highest possible warranties recognized by the laws of the respective states. It typically states that the grantor will "warrant and defend" the title against "all persons whomsoever." It promises both that the title being conveyed is free of encumbrances and that all covenants cover the entire chain of title. The terms *warrant* or *general warranty* indicate slightly different warranties, depending on local statutes. Sixteen states provide for five common law covenants to be implied in the conveyance: (1) the covenant of seizin (explained below), (2) the right to convey, (3) freedom from encumbrances, (4) quiet enjoyment, and (5) general warranty. These 16 states include Colorado, Florida, Illinois, Indiana, Kansas, Michigan, Minnesota, Mississippi, New York, Oklahoma, and Wyoming. Three other states (Massachusetts, New Hampshire, and New Mexico) have four of the same warranties but omit the covenant of quiet enjoyment.

Most other states limit their warranties to two covenants: (1) a covenant that the grantor has good title and power to convey same (covenant of seizin) and (2) a covenant that there are no encumbrances on the premises that would adversely affect the purchaser (covenant against encumbrances). These states generally provide that the use of the words *grant, bargain and sell, convey,* or any variation of the use of these words typically triggers the existence of these two covenants. There are some variations, such as in the state of Missouri, where the use of these words also implies the covenant of further assurances.

Special Warranty Deed. A special warranty deed uses basically the same language as the general warranty deed. A special warranty deed differs significantly, however, in that the warranty extends *only to the grantor.* That is, the grantor does not warrant validity of the chain of title beyond himself. Rather, he only promises that title is good against all claimants whose title acquisition occurred "by or through me," *Tanglewood Land Co., Inc.* v. *Wood,* 252 S.E.2d 546 (Va. 1979). This type of deed contains the same covenants and warranties as the general warranty deed. Special warranty deeds have been recognized by case law in most states, and have been authorized by statutes in Colorado, New Hampshire, Rhode Island, Arizona, Delaware, and Virginia.

Special warranty deeds are frequently used by trustees in bank trust departments, major corporations, and governmental entities. These owners generally have held the property for a particular purpose that has since expired. They now wish to sell the property to a new owner but do not want to be bound by whatever discrepancies in title may have plagued the property prior to their ownership. At the same time, they are quite willing to promise that the title passed by and through them is good, and that they have not clouded or encumbered title to that property.

A special warranty deed may be just as effective as a general warranty deed in conveying clear title. However, clearly it gives the grantee fewer warranties and effectively causes him to waive his rights against the grantor as to any prior existing encumbrances. There is, of course, always a risk that such encumbrances may materialize at some future date.

Trustee's Deed.   In those states using a deed of trust to establish a security interest in land (discussed further in Chapter 10), a trustee's deed is in effect a foreclosure deed.

The trustee's warranty typically binds the landowner rather than the trustee. This is because the trustee is generally liable only in his representative capacity, so judicial recovery can be had only against the trust assets (if any). The trustee normally operates as a pure nominee (legal title holder) for and on behalf of the "beneficial owners," as discussed in Chapter 3.

The title conveyed by a trustee's deed is perfectly valid and contains all the covenants of a general warranty deed. However, these covenants bind the previous owner, not the trustee. And, usually, the title passed is subject to any encumbrances superior to those of the beneficial owner. The only risk to the grantee is whether the trustee acted in the proper capacity in executing the deed.

Court-Ordered Deed.   A court-ordered deed or sheriff's deed is a deed given pursuant to a court order or by a forced sale by execution (that is, a creditor has forced the property to be sold to collect a debt owed him by the property owner). The conveyance is accompanied by a warranty covering only the right, title, interest, and claim that the debtor/defendant had in the property sold.

Bargain and Sale Deed.   In most states the bargain and sale deed contains no warranties at all and is sometimes called a deed without warranty. However, it has a particular value in that it does purport to convey the grantor's interest in his real property. Therefore, the after acquired title doctrine (discussed later in this chapter) generally applies to bargain and sale deeds. Bargain and sale deeds usually do not contain the words *grant* or *convey*. Recall that this language reflects general warranties in many states; so the absence of these words is significant.

Quitclaim Deed.   The quitclaim deed is a deed by which the grantor quitclaims unto the grantee all of his right, title, and interest to the property. Under a quitclaim deed, the grantor does not claim to have any interest in the property described, but is only saying that if he does have an interest in it, he "quits" it in favor of the grantee.

Quitclaim deeds have a valuable use in clearing up clouds on title. A title company or abstractor, in searching the chain of title to a property, may determine that some heir or some grantee in the chain of title may have some interest in that property as the result of a previous transaction. Often, however, this heir, or possible title holder, does not know that he has any interest (and maybe he does not actually have any). Therefore, to clear up this cloud on the title, the title company will request that this "possible heir" execute a quitclaim deed, which contains no warranties whatsoever and is not binding as to any warranties on the grantor. The individual with the outstanding interest can then convey the interest, if there is any, but without worry that anybody will hold him to any type of warranty as to the title that is being conveyed.

An interesting thing about quitclaim deeds is that since there is no warranty or representation of ownership, one can literally give a quitclaim deed to anything. For instance, one can quitclaim the Brooklyn Bridge to convey whatever right, title, and interest one had, if any, in the Brooklyn Bridge to the grantee. It is a perfectly valid deed, and if the grantee is willing to pay consideration for it, the grantee obtains whatever right, title, and interest that the grantor happens to have in the Brooklyn Bridge (which, of course, is nothing beyond what the normal taxpayer has).

It is important to understand, however, that if a person conveys his house to somebody by virtue of a quitclaim deed (or by any of the other kinds of deeds described herein), whatever right, title, and interest he has in his house are certainly conveyed along with that deed, *Erickson* v. *First Natl. Bank of Minneapolis*, 697 P.2d 1332 (Mont. 1985). The only difference is the warranty of the grantor. Therefore, a quitclaim deed can pass good title if the grantor has good title at the time of the conveyance. Most courts hold, however, that the grantee under a quitclaim deed is on notice that the grantor is not even claiming to hold title, and can't be a bona fide purchaser for value. See *Polhemus* v. *Cobb*, 653 So.2d 964 (Ala. 1995).

Requirements of a Deed.   It is important that real estate professionals be familiar with the legal requirements of deeds, if for no other reason than to discuss these requirements with attorneys and to recognize when a serious problem exists.

The statutory requirements for a deed are generally quite simple. Most states require that the deed be in writing, be subscribed (signed) by the grantor(s), and be properly delivered. "Delivered" is a key word. If the deed is not properly delivered, it is not a valid conveyance.

In addition to delivery, a deed has one other unique requirement: it must show a *present* intent to convey (whereas an earnest money contract contains a *future* intent to convey). It is this change in intent to convey, from future to present, that logically merges the terms of the earnest money contract into the deed.

In general, case law has held that a deed is a contract and it must have the essential elements of a contract (offer, acceptance, consideration, and mutual assent) before it can be judicially supported. Deeds and earnest money contracts also share the following requirements:

1. It must be a written instrument.
2. It must be signed by the party to be charged.
3. It must contain operative words of grant showing intent to convey an ownership interest.
4. It must contain an identifiable grantor and grantee.
5. The subject matter to be conveyed must be described or identifiable.

Of course, the terminology, format, and net effect of earnest money contracts and deeds are entirely different. In many states there has been considerable discussion as to why a real estate broker generally has the authority to fill in the blanks of an earnest money contract but not the blanks in a deed (in some states he also has this authority). There is a certain finality in a properly executed and delivered deed. A mistake in it can only be corrected by a correction deed or by subsequent trips to the courthouse seeking to have the deed judicially reformed. Mistakes on an earnest money contract, on the other hand, can often be renegotiated, changed, or rescinded with considerably less effort and legal formality.

To keep these statutory and case law requirements from appearing too simple, one must realize that each of these requirements, of course, has further requirements. It is not so simple to determine who an identifiable grantor or grantee may be, what constitutes delivery, and so forth. So to make these matters more clear, we will attempt to discuss each of these requirements to help determine how any given fact situation may affect each of these requirements.

Requirements of Grantor and Grantee. The *grantor* is, of course, the owner and seller of the property. The grantor must have sufficient mental capacity to reasonably understand the transaction, or else the deed is voidable. The name of the grantor must appear on the document, but it is not necessary that it appear on the body of the deed. The name of the grantor could be just a signature, but it must be somewhere on the instrument, and the grantor must be identifiable.

It is a generally accepted practice to put the marital status of the grantor into the deed so that the grantee will be on notice of any conflicts of community property laws that may arise as a result of a husband conveying his property without the joinder of his wife, or vice versa. Louisiana and Massachusetts even have statutes that require deeds to state whether the parties are single, married, or widowed.

Similar concerns exist in states where homestead requirements are important. Many states require that the husband and wife must join in the conveyance of homestead property, and some exclusion must be made if there is no joinder. For instance, in many deeds, one may find the grantor to be: "E. T. Grant, not joined herein by my spouse as this constitutes no part of my homestead." There are relatively few states in which a spouse can transfer land without the joinder of the other spouse.

Additional questions about legal capacity arise when a grantor is a business entity. A corporation, for instance, should specify the state of incorporation and its authority to transact business in the state where the property is located. Partnerships should effectively disclose all the partners as well as the name of the partnership entity. When an individual conveys a property in the capacity of a "trustee" or "agent," it is acknowledged that he is not acting on his own behalf. Thus, no disclosure is required under these circumstances.

A deed must also have an identifiable *grantee*; if it does not, it is void—not voidable, but void. If the instrument does not purport to convey property to any particular grantee, it simply is not a conveyance. The grantee, of course, must be a legal entity. This does not preclude, of course, the deed being put into the hands of an agent for delivery at a later date. For instance, it can be left with any third-party escrow agent with the provision that it is to be delivered to "the first person who donates $5,000 to my church" or with some other such contingency. Providing it was properly delivered to the agent, such a conveyance would be considered valid because of the relation back doctrine, discussed later. An interesting note is that the grantee must be alive; a dead man cannot be a grantee. If the grantee dies before the deed is delivered, the conveyance is void.

Intent to Grant Title. The requirement of intent to grant title can be construed both from the consideration recited and from the words of conveyance found in the deed. Consideration is a requirement for contracts generally, and is interpreted as part of the intent to convey. However, consideration occupies a peculiar position in the law of deeds in most states in that valuable consideration is *not* essential to effect the conveyance of real estate. Montana, North Dakota, and West Virginia even have statutes eliminating the necessity of reciting consideration in deeds. However, consideration may be stated and, if so, is evidence of the intent to convey title. At the opposite extreme is Nebraska, where actual consideration must be stated.

By way of example, "$1," "$10," "love and affection," and "support and maintenance" are all types of consideration and are evidence of the intent to convey property. Such words of conveyance or token amounts are frequently used to denote transfer of property to a relative or loved one. As a gift or donation they are sufficient to show both intent to grant title and consideration. Consideration of "$1" or "$10" is sufficient in almost all states, including those states and instances where valuable consideration is required. The nominal amount also creates the ambiguity to circumvent the parol evidence rule where needed.

However, in a few states, although the preceding examples show *intent* to convey, they do not legally constitute "valuable consideration." The reason that such terminology as "$10 and other good and valuable consideration" may not be legally sufficient is that it does not clearly reflect true mutuality of agreement between the grantor and grantee, *Crane* v. *Glenney,* 352 S.W.2d 773. If a conveyance is contested by a third party, some cases suggest that the consideration, *at law,* must be substantially equal to value. On the other hand, the inadequacy of price must be extreme to obtain relief in equity unless coupled with concealment or misrepresentation.

Legal Description. The deed must have an adequate legal description. Although there is a large gray area as to what constitutes an adequate legal description, the general maxim is that the property must be sufficiently described so that it is reasonably certain which property is being conveyed. If the description of the real property is so indefinite that it cannot be identified with some certainty, the deed is void, *Town of Brookhaven* v. *Dinos,* 429 N.E.2d 830 (N.Y. 1980).

Signature of Grantor. The deed must be signed by the grantor to be valid. Additionally, where marital rights, community property, or a homestead is involved, the deed should also be signed by the spouse to assure that he or she retains no rights in the property being transferred. The signature requirements may also be satisfied by the grantor making his mark, *Aberdeen Oil Co., v. Goucher,* 362 S.W.2d 20 (Ark. 1962), or by signature of the grantor's authorized agent. A forged deed is void, *Bellaire Kirkpatrick Joint Venture v. Loots,* 826 S.W.2d 205 (Tex. App., 1992).

The grantee generally need not sign the deed. Rather, his possession of the deed shows acceptance of delivery and is sufficient to hold the grantee to any responsibilities or liabilities expressed in the deed.

Seals.   Only a few states currently require that a document be sealed in order to effect a valid conveyance. Even when a seal is required in these jurisdictions, unsealed instruments may be effective between the parties, or in an equitable proceeding. Those states requiring seals are Connecticut, Delaware, Illinois, Massachusetts, New Hampshire, New Jersey, North Carolina, South Carolina, Virginia, Wisconsin, and the District of Columbia.

Delivery.   An important but often misunderstood requirement of a deed is that it must be properly delivered and accepted by the grantee, *In re Estate of Ault,* 609 N.E.2d 568 (Ohio Ct. App., 1992). Generally, recording a deed in the county land records office is prima facie evidence that proper delivery has been effected. The date of the deed's delivery becomes the date of the deed's effectiveness, *Dolores Land Corp. v. Hillsborough County,* 68 So.2d 393 (Fla. 1953).

The more serious delivery problems arise when a grantee refuses delivery or there is a partial delivery of the deed to several grantees. In addition, there may be a fact question as to whether or not delivery to a third person as agent for the grantee is a proper delivery, or whether the agent can operate in that fiduciary capacity. The particular facts involved play a key role in determining the question of delivery, and the questions of law generally hinge on these facts. If the deed is placed in an escrow, delivery might take place at that time, if the grantee then has the final control over delivery. However, mere delivery to a third party passes no title if the grantor did not intend for that delivery to be effective as a conveyance.

Acknowledgment.   An acknowledgment by a notary public or appropriate public official is not necessary for the valid conveyance of real estate, but it is a prerequisite to being able to record a deed in most states. Even if an otherwise valid deed is not acknowledged, it is still good and binding between the parties, *Gordon* v. *Gordon*, 398 N.E.2d 497 (Mass. 1979). However, as an unrecordable instrument it will not give public notice of ownership interests to third parties, and thereby may permit them to acquire rights in the same property. This possibility is discussed in greater detail in the following chapter.

After Acquired Title Doctrine. To give proper effect to certain conveyances, the courts have developed an equitable doctrine that is termed the *after acquired title doctrine.* This doctrine basically sets out that if the grantor conveys the property to the grantee, when, in fact, the grantor did not have title to same, title would be conveyed whenever the grantor subsequently obtained title. The theory is that the grantor is estopped from claiming a title that he has been assumed to convey.

For instance, grantor *A* conveys a property to grantee *B* by general warranty deed. Grantor *A*, at the time of conveyance and delivery of the deed, does not have title to the mineral rights of the property; however, he has every expectation of obtaining same. Although there are a number of fact questions involved in a problem like this, the after acquired title doctrine stands for the principle that when grantor *A* does acquire the mineral rights, the conveyance of those mineral rights will be valid to the first grantee *B* because of the grantor's initial conveyance. The subsequently required property rights will pass immediately to the grantee, and be binding on the original grantor. Note that the after acquired title doctrine does *not* apply to quitclaim deeds, because quitclaim deeds do not purport to convey title to real estate; however, the doctrine does presumably apply to bargain and sale deeds. It is for purposes of this after acquired title doctrine that a bargain and sale deed is often used instead of a quitclaim deed. If there is a question of grantor's title in a bargain and sale deed, it may be later clarified by the after acquired title doctrine concept. The same is not true of a quitclaim deed.

The after acquired title doctrine also is very effective in eliminating problems of fraudulent conveyance. If a grantor induced the grantee to enter into a transaction and conveyed the property to grantee while the property was still under contract to the grantor, the law would not allow the grantor to obtain title to the property adverse to the present grantee's interest.

Exceptions, Covenants, and Reservations in Deeds. You may recall that, if an estate is not expressly limited, the law presumes fee simple title. Exceptions, covenants, and reservations are limitations on the title being passed from the grantor to the grantee.

These two types of limitations are significantly different. *Exceptions* are deficiencies in the existing title as part of the grant, which are excepted at the time of the conveyance; that is, they are deficiencies in the title that the grantor has at the time of conveyance. Exceptions would include easements, mineral rights held by third parties, rights-of-way, deed restrictions, or other encumbrances on the grantor's property. They would be excepted from the legal title conveyed because they are not part of the fee title that the grantor holds.

A *reservation,* on the other hand, is a paragraph in a deed creating or reserving an interest to the grantor out of the title being conveyed. Reservations might be mineral rights reserved to the seller. For instance, the grantor would convey the surface of some property but reserve the mineral rights to himself. Often an easement may be reserved to the grantor, by selling the frontage but reserving an easement for the grantor's benefit across the property being conveyed in the grantor's deed. All exceptions and reservations are part of the deed and are enforced under purely contractual principles.

Covenants are clauses in deeds which are usually given or received as consideration for the transfer of title. For instance, a deed may contain a covenant that as part of the conveyance the grantee agrees not to construct any noxious or odorous industrial plants on the property. Other covenants have often included prohibitions for construction of slaughtering houses, chemical plants, waste water facilities, cesspools, and the like. Since they are a part of the consideration of the conveyance, these covenants are enforced by theories of contract law. As such, they are enforced by injunctive relief or suit for damages. A breach of a covenant, however, does not result in a loss of title. For a loss of title to occur, you may recall, one must give a deed with a condition in it, as discussed in Chapter 2.

Wills

The conveyance of property by virtue of a will is a voluntary conveyance in that the person conveying the property by will (the "testator") does purport to convey his property to a definite grantee. In the strict application to real estate law, conveyance by wills need not be discussed in any great depth, especially as the vast majority of the law involved in this area is best considered in other works on probate law and estate planning. However, it is important to understand the basics of wills as these pertain to certain real estate interests.

The law basically recognizes three types of wills:

1. A *witnessed will,* one in writing signed by the testator and attested by the statutorily required number of credible witnesses.

2. A *holographic will,* one written wholly in the handwriting of the testator, which may or may not be witnessed.

3. A *nuncupative will* (an oral will) declared by a testator during his last illness before the proper number of witnesses, and later reduced to writing.

In most states only a written, properly witnessed will can be used to transfer title to real estate. Holographic wills may be used to transfer title when properly witnessed, but a nuncupative will normally cannot transfer title to real estate.

Generally, except in the case of a will contest or other probate complications, title to the entire estate of the deceased passes immediately (at death) by *devise* to the named heirs (properly termed *devisees*), subject to the settling of the affairs of that estate. The conveyance is formally executed by the executor named in the will to administer the estate. Death does not usually terminate a bilateral contract, and it may be important to real estate brokers to use listing, earnest money, and other contracts that bind both the parties and their "heirs or assigns."

It is particularly important for a real estate agent to acknowledge the fact that complications may exist in the estate of the deceased and to be sure that all listing agreements, contracts, and all other legal instruments pertinent to any real estate involved in the estate are signed by all heirs at law or beneficiaries of the will, to protect both the real estate agent and the purchaser in any subsequent transaction. When an estate is involved, it is very important that the broker rely on the decedent's lawyers to assure proper compliance with any legal technicalities.

Dedication

The final type of voluntary conveyance to be discussed is *dedication.* Dedication refers to the giving or donating of private land for public use. Generally there are two methods by which land can be dedicated to public use: (1) the statutory method and (2) the common law method.

Under the *statutory* method of dedication, one simply follows the statutory procedure and executes a deed transferring the property to some public body. The deed clearly shows how much land was dedicated to public use.

But it is also possible for property to be dedicated to public use by the common law method. Under this method, even if no deed is executed, dedication will be effective if two requirements are met. First, it must be shown that the landowner *intended* to dedicate the property to public use. Second the dedication must have been *accepted*. The acceptance may be in the form of a resolution made by the appropriate governmental entity, or it may be indicated by the public (the group that the grant was intended to benefit) making *some* use of the land. This use need not continue over any definite period of time.

Common law dedication can be readily distinguished from prescriptive rights (discussed with easements). With common law dedication, the landowner *intends* for the public to use the land, whereas the use is *adverse* (without consent) under a prescriptive right. Likewise, for common law dedication to occur, the public need only make *some* use of the land. Conversely, this use must continue for the statutory period of time (usually ten years) under the prescriptive rights doctrine. This distinction may be important in many instances.

INVOLUNTARY CONVEYANCES

Involuntary conveyances are generally categorized as those over which the grantor has little or no control. Their existence is usually set out in statutes (as in eminent domain, escheat, and intestacy), but discretionary actions of third parties are sometimes important factors (e.g., in tax sales, adverse possession, and foreclosures).

Eminent Domain

Eminent domain refers to the legal power of government to take private property for public use. For example, the government might acquire a strip of land for the purpose of constructing a new highway, but the owner will be paid for it. This process is called *condemnation* regardless of whether actual court action is involved.

Eminent domain generally does not arise from any specific power granted in either the federal or state constitutions. Rather, most authorities say it is an *inherent* power of government. That is, even though the power is not specifically granted by the constitution, the law has long implied its existence simply because government could not operate efficiently without it.

If the power did not exist, government could only buy lands that the owners had offered for sale. This would result in a highly inefficient system of roads and highways, increased utility costs because of the miles of extra cable required to provide service, and so forth. A government must have the power of eminent domain in order to efficiently serve its citizens. However, as an inherent power, eminent domain is limited by both the state and federal constitutions. The limitations on this power exist for the protection of private individuals and constitute the primary source of disputes between the parties to a condemnation proceeding.

Who Has the Power? The U.S. Congress and the state legislatures have the primary authority to exercise the power of eminent domain. This authority may be delegated to other governmental units, such as city or county governments, federal and/or state agencies, or in certain instances, private corporations (e.g., public utilities).

Projected Use of the Land. Assuming that such authority has been granted to an agency, there are two other limitations imposed by the applicable state or federal constitutions. The first is the requirement that the land be taken for *public use.* Public use means that the public must derive a benefit from the taking. It is not necessary that the land be open to the general public or that the general public have a direct right to use it. Property may even be taken for trade purposes or for the benefit of some private group, *Hawaii Housing Authority* v. *Midkiff,* 104 S.Ct.2321 (1984). There has even been authority that football teams could constitute public use, *City of Oakland* v. *Oakland Raiders,* 646 P.2d 835 (Cal. 1982).

Right to Just Compensation. The broadest and most important limitation on eminent domain is the right of the landowner to receive "just compensation" for property taken and special damages incurred because of the taking. As we shall see, the term special damages has a different meaning under eminent domain law than it has under contract law. The factors generally used to determine just compensation result in what the courts refer to as *net damages.* In many states the three specific elements used to determine net damages are (1) *fair market value,* (2) *special damages,* and (3) *special benefits.*

If a landowner's tract of land is taken, he is entitled to the fair market value of the land as damages. However, if only a partial taking occurs, the damages are computed by first determining the value of the entire tract of land, and then subtracting the value of the land remaining after the taking.

If the value of the remaining land is increased because of the public improvement, the damages will be correspondingly less. If the value of the land remaining is decreased because of the public improvement, then the damages will be increased. The increase in value to the remaining land often is referred to as *special benefits.* Similarly, the decrease in value of the remaining land often is referred to as *special damages* (note the new and different meaning of special damages under eminent domain law).

The first element to be considered is *fair market value.* Fair market value is what a willing buyer would pay a willing seller for a tract of land. This means that no payment is required for feelings of personal loss one might have in giving up the land. The landowner is treated as if he were willing to sell. On the other hand, this value does not refer to the price the land might bring if the seller were forced to sell in order to pay his debts.

Land being condemned is valued as if it were being employed in its most profitable use at the time of the taking. For example, suppose a tract of land is currently being used for agricultural purposes, but it is located so as to permit residential development. If its fair market value for residential purposes is greater than its value for farming at the time the land is condemned, and if the jury decides it is adaptable to such use, the owner is entitled to be paid on the basis of its value for residential use. However, the owner is *not* entitled to be paid on the basis of what the property would be worth *after* the public improvement occurs.

Generally, a landowner must also be paid for special damages to his property. This usually results when there is a taking of only part of the property. Special damages may result as a loss of value because, for example, a road is built that divides what was previously one large tract. The separation of the tract may lower the total value of the land remaining after the road is built. If so, the owner is allowed compensation for this loss of value.

Another example of special damages occurs when the construction of a road or bridge interferes with drainage and causes flooding of river bottom lands. The inability to make use of this land lowers its value, thus increasing the amount of compensation to which the landowner is legally entitled.

As a general rule, eminent domain special damages are broken down into two categories. The first is referred to as *severance damages.* These result from dividing land into two or more tracts. The other category is *consequential damages.* Consequential damages occur when only a part of the property is taken, but the remainder of the property is of lower value because the proposed public improvement will destroy or impair a property right.

For example, one "property right" is lateral support for property from adjacent landowners (i.e., if someone digs a basement near his boundary, he must not negligently permit his neighbor's land to fall or slide into the excavation). If such support is impaired or destroyed because of a public taking, then a consequential damage has occurred that should be compensated.

The final element that is considered in determining net damages to the landowner is *special benefits.* Special benefits are increases in value of land remaining after a partial taking because of the improvement being made. If the state takes land for the purpose of improving drainage in an area, it must pay for the property used in digging drainage ditches. But if the property remaining is more valuable due to the better drainage, the owner experiences a special benefit. The value of this special benefit generally may be deducted from the value of the land being taken for construction of the ditches.

Compensation usually need not be paid for general damages. When used in regard to condemnation, the term *general damages* refers to conditions that the taking may impose on the people of the community. Increases in traffic, dust, or noise are examples of general damages. For example, if a new road is to be built near a landowner's property, the simple fact that traffic in the area will increase will not alone result in compensable damages. Of course, if such traffic does in fact lower the value of the remaining land, the owner thereof must be compensated. Eminent domain general damages are also sometimes referred to as *inconsequential damages*.

Nonjudicial Determination of Damages. When property is taken by condemnation, specific procedures set down by state or federal law must be followed. The whole process usually begins when a representative of the condemning authority approaches a landowner concerning sale of the property. The landowner and the agent then bargain, each trying to reach a fair value for what he is giving up. In the vast majority of cases, the process ends at this point. An agreeable price is found by both the landowner and the agency, and nothing remains but the conveyance of the property in exchange for the agreed price.

Before a landowner makes a final agreement to sell the property, even though he feels a fair value is offered, it is wise for him to seek competent legal counsel so that he may be fully informed concerning his rights. An attorney knows the peculiarities of both real estate law and eminent domain law, and can guide the landowner in reaching his decision. His advice in such matters may prove invaluable in determining how much compensation must be paid. Occasionally it may even be that his aid will result in the land not being taken at all.

Judicial Determination of Damages. If no agreement can be reached, the court procedure begins. Generally, the first step occurs when the condemning agency files a lawsuit in the basic trial court. This is the same method by which any suit at law is begun, since this proceeding ordinarily carries a guarantee of trial by jury of all factual issues. The proceeding differs, however, in the intermediate steps present.

The petition (written claim filed in the basic trial court) names the condemning agency as plaintiff and those having a compensable interest in the property as defendants. Usually the petition also contains a statement setting out the statute that enables the agency to take land.

The precise procedure to be followed from this point may differ, depending on the statute under which the condemning authority is acting and whether such authority is acting under the auspices of state or federal law. In addition to determining the issue of damages, the parties may also litigate such factors as whether a public use is involved and whether the land being taken is adaptable to another more valuable use.

Only a small percentage of condemnation proceedings initiated actually result in a trial being held. Quite often the parties reach an agreement or out-of-court settlement prior to the trial stage.

Adverse Possession

Adverse possession is a legal concept often referred to as *squatters' rights*. This concept permits a person to acquire title by being in possession if certain requirements are met. The doctrine is basically an application of the statue of limitations, and normally possession will ripen into title if two requirements are met: (1) that the occupancy be open, notorious, and visible, and (2) that the occupancy be continuous for the requisite number of years.

Additional requirements may exist in some states, including (1) that the adverse possessor must have some claim of an ownership right, (2) that the claim of right must be in writing, and (3) that the claim of right in some instances must be combined with additional overt conduct, such as cultivating, using, and enjoying the property, or adding improvements for occupation of the premises.

The requirement of open, notorious, and visible possession primarily means that the possession must be obvious and adverse to the interest of the true owner. In turn, this should provide adequate notice to the true owner that his interests are being interfered with.

The doctrine of adverse possession does not apply if the possessor has the owner's consent to be there because in that case the possession is not legally *adverse*. Similarly, if a life tenant is in possession of the land in which he has a life estate, he cannot thereby receive a full fee simple absolute title under the doctrine of adverse possession because he has a legal right to be in possession. Stated alternatively, since the remainderman has no legal right to be in possession until *after* the life tenant's death, the fact that the life tenant is in possession is not adverse to the rights of the remainderman.

In some jurisdictions, if a party in adverse possession transfers his interest to a third party, the period that each was in possession is added together to determine if adverse possession has existed for the necessary period of time. This is sometimes referred to as the *doctrine of tacking* because the two time periods are "tacked" together. However, other jurisdictions may limit this "tacking" to heirs (Alabama, Arkansas, and Oklahoma), devisees (Indiana, Georgia), spouses (Kentucky, Wisconsin), or blood relatives (Colorado, Montana, and Wyoming).

Furthermore, tacking does not apply if one adverse possessor simply moves out and another moves in. There must be a *transfer* of possession. Otherwise, the *continuous* use requirement is violated, and the adverse possession time reverts to zero and counting begins all over again.

The doctrine of adverse possession can be effective in some cases to create fee simple absolute ownership where none previously existed. To illustrate, suppose that Baker holds title to land in fee simple determinable, and that the event occurs on which his ownership is contingent. Since the original grantor (Able) retained a possibility of reverter, title automatically reverted to him when the stated contingency occurred. Moreover, as the full fee simple absolute owner, Able had the legal right of possession. If Baker thereafter continuously remains in possession for the requisite statutory period, he will receive fee simple absolute title under the doctrine of adverse possession.

There are a number of rather detailed adverse possession rules that can vary from state to state. These may include such factors as (1) a change in the time period because of an inability on the part of the adverse claimant to initiate a lawsuit against the adverse possessor (e.g., the true owner is a minor or insane), (2) possession begun as a tenant but wrongfully continued, (3) maximum amount of property that may be acquired by adverse possession, and (4) certain procedural problems as to how the adverse possession is ultimately to be effected. It is in an attempt to fairly apply these various additional requirements that the time period of adverse possession often differs among states. For instance, the required time periods may be quite short, such as three to five years if certain conditions are met (Texas, Idaho, California), or quite long under other circumstances (30 years or more in Louisiana). Ten years is a common time requirement.

There is one major exception to the doctrine of adverse possession. That is, it cannot be used against a governmental entity to acquire title to public lands (by either private claimants or another governmental agency), *People of the State of California* v. *United States*, 132 F. Supp. 208. Likewise, it cannot be used to acquire title to lands owned by charitable organizations such as churches and hospitals.

If an owner finds "squatters" occupying his real estate, he should take legal steps to have their possession terminated. Typically this involves filing a lawsuit to have the squatters ejected.

Intestate Succession   When a person dies leaving no will, he is said to have died *intestate*. All states have a statute of intestate descent, which specifies who will inherit title to property owned by anyone who dies without leaving a will. Since the intestate descent distribution may differ from that which the decedent would have preferred, in this sense intestate descent represents an involuntary conveyance. A court-appointed administrator oversees the proper administration and distribution of an intestate decedent's estate.

Generally, state law divides an intestate person's estate equally among those who are within the closest living degree of blood relationship. This distribution occurs after the proper probate proceedings. These proceedings are a matter of public record, and are utilized to show which heirs inherit real property and that they have good title to it. A basic function of probate is, of course, to keep real estate title clear of any clouds or discrepancies.

Foreclosure   A foreclosure proceeding involves the forced sale of real estate to pay a defaulted debt owed a secured lender. Where a true mortgage is used, foreclosure proceedings are judicial in nature. A deed of trust, on the other hand, typically involves a nonjudicial foreclosure proceeding. The important point to remember is that in either case the proper legal foreclosure procedure must be followed in order for the foreclosure deed to effectively convey title. Even then, in some states the borrower has a certain period of time in which to *redeem* his property by reimbursing the foreclosure sale purchaser for the amount he has laid out for it.

Absent an irregularity in the sale, the foreclosure sale generally will not be set aside merely because of inadequacy of price. Usually, the mortgagee can purchase the property at its own sale, so long as the sale is conducted fairly and in accordance with the terms of the mortgage or deed of trust.

If there are any excess funds (i.e., funds not needed to satisfy the mortgage debt), they are forwarded to the borrower after the expenses of sale have been paid. If the sale does not bring sufficient funds to satisfy the outstanding debt, the lender may obtain a deficiency judgment against the borrower for the balance in some states. This subject is covered in greater detail in Chapter 10, "Mortgages."

Tax Sales

Real property may be attached and sold to satisfy a federal income tax lien. However, most tax sales occur under state law and are the result of a failure to pay *ad valorem* (real property) taxes.

Generally, all property, whether real or personal, may be levied against to satisfy delinquent taxes. Sales of real property to pay delinquent taxes are usually specifically provided for by statute. In rare cases, there may be certain kinds of property exempt from a forced sale to collect taxes. Such exemptions may include homestead property, property in which marital rights are held, and perhaps special treatment for the elderly.

Tax sales of real property must be properly advertised and generally must be sold at public auction (usually at the courthouse door).

A tax deed is used to effect the proper sale. It conveys all the rights and interests that the former owner had when the taxes were assessed. Often it also provides for the redemption period, as well as for any penalties and payments due upon redemption.

Escheat

One of the basic property rights retained by the government when lands were initially parceled out to its citizens was that of *escheat.* This simply provides that should a person fail to dispose of his real property by will, in a situation in which he has no surviving heirs the real estate title shall revert or "escheat" to the government. Most statutes provide that the land revert to the state, and in one case (Illinois) the statute provides that the property revert to the county.

Escheat is a tool to effect a valid conveyance of real estate when there are no other possible means of conveyance, and generally it is controlled very strictly by statute. In many cases escheat proceedings are a last resort. It usually requires a lengthy court proceeding, and a foreclosure for tax sale is quicker.

SUMMARY

The term *conveyancing* refers to the various means of transferring real estate title. Such transfers may be either voluntary or involuntary. The principal voluntary conveyances involve execution of either a deed or a will. Involuntary conveyances, on the other hand, typically involve eminent domain, adverse possession, foreclosure or tax sales, transfers by intestacy, and escheat.

Deeds are the principal legal instruments used to make voluntary lifetime transfers of title to real property. Although there is some variation from state to state, the types of deeds available for this purpose usually include general warranty, special warranty, bargain and sale, and quitclaim deeds. The general warranty deed provides the greatest possible assurances that the grantor will "warrant and defend" the title being transferred against "all persons whomsoever." It warrants both that the title being conveyed is free of encumbrances and that all covenants cover the entire chain of title. A special warranty, on the other hand, warrants title only through the grantor. In most states a bargain and sale deed contains no warranties about the quality or extent of title. However, it does convey the grantor's interest and thus activates the after acquired title doctrine. The quitclaim deed does not activate this doctrine and technically is not even a conveyance; rather the grantor just "quits" whatever ownership interest he has in favor of the grantee.

There are several legal requirements for a valid deed. Generally, it must be in writing, be signed by the grantor, contain an adequate description of the property being conveyed, and be properly delivered to the grantee. In addition it must contain an identifiable grantor and grantee and show an intent to convey title. It need not be acknowledged by a notary public in order to be valid, but such acknowledgment is required to make a deed recordable in most states.

The after acquired title doctrine helps avoid fraudulent conveyances and unfair results. This doctrine provides that if a grantor transfers title to property that he has not yet acquired, such title automatically will be transferred to his grantee upon acquisition by the grantor. Deeds may contain exceptions and/or reservations. Exceptions are existing deficiencies in the grantor's title. Reservations refer to property rights retained by the seller in the same deed in which he transfers the balance of his ownership interests in a given tract of real estate.

Wills may also be used to transfer title to real property. Many contracts are drafted with this in mind, and they explicitly bind one's "heirs and assigns."

Dedication is another form of voluntary conveyancing and involves giving privately owned property for public use. Most states provide a statutory method for accomplishing this, which involves the execution of a deed. A dedicatory transfer may also be accomplished under the common law. It generally requires an intent to transfer on the part of the grantor and some use of the property by the public.

A major involuntary conveyancing method involves property taken under the rules of eminent domain. The right to take private property for public use is reserved to the U.S. Congress and state legislatures, but they, in turn, have delegated this power to many units of government, administrative agencies, and public utilities. Although these groups can take private property without an owner's consent, the law provides that the owner must receive "just compensation." Generally, this is measured by "fair market value," or the price a willing buyer would pay a willing seller in a free market.

Adverse possession, or "squatters' rights," also involve the involuntary transfer of real estate title. It occurs when one is openly and continuously in possession of another's real property for a specified time period, often ten years but varying from three to more than 30 years. Such possession must be adverse to the landowner's interest, and involuntary title transfers can be avoided if the owner has the "squatters" ejected before the required time limit expires.

Title to real property may also be transferred under state statues of intestate succession. Such statutes determine who inherits property when a decedent does not execute a valid will disposing of it. This is an involuntary conveyance in the sense that the legal distribution may differ from what the decedent would have preferred.

Other important involuntary conveyancing methods include foreclosure and tax sales. Both are the end result of a failure to meet one's financial obligations relating to real estate. A final involuntary conveyancing method is escheat. It gives real estate title to the state when the owner dies without heirs and without leaving a will directing its distribution.

1. Name the types of deeds existing in your state. Outline the advantages of each to (1) the seller and (2) the buyer.

2. What are the legal requirements of a valid deed?

3. Where should deeds be recorded in your state?

4. Explain the concept of just compensation under eminent domain for (1) a complete taking and (2) a partial taking.

DISCUSSION
QUESTIONS

9

Recording Interests in Real Estate

Each state has one or more laws collectively referred to as its *recording act*. This act outlines the legal consequences of recording, or failing to record, in the appropriate public land records office (in the county where the land is located) any and all legal instruments affecting title to real estate. Indirectly, this act also helps resolve disputes among two or more parties, each of whom claims a priority interest in a particular tract of real estate.

Before examining the specific types of recording acts that exist, it is important to recognize that their basic function is to resolve disputes when two basic principles of law conflict. These principles are:

1. A person can transfer no better title than he has.
2. A bona fide purchaser should be protected and should receive title free and clear of any "secret" (unknown) interests.

It makes sense that a person can convey no more or better title than he has. If the rules were otherwise, a life tenant could convey a fee simple absolute. This would be completely contrary to the intention of the individual who had originally created the life estate. At the same time, it is somewhat unfair to penalize those who purchase title in good faith and for valuable consideration, especially when they suffer substantial out-of-pocket losses by virtue of the fact that their seller did not have good title. Thus, although both legal principles have a sound basis, on occasion they may conflict with each other. When this happens, which principle should prevail? Where land is involved, it is the state recording act that answers this question.

Bona Fide Purchaser   Before looking at the basic idea behind recording acts and their
Requirements   requirements, it is essential to determine when a buyer is legally considered to be a *bona fide purchaser.* There are two basic requirements for being a bona fide purchaser. First, one must *give value* for the land. This simply means that land must be acquired by purchase, rather than be received as a gift. Second, to be a bona fide purchaser a buyer must be *without notice* that persons other than his seller have some interest in the land being conveyed.

There are legally two kinds of notice, actual notice and constructive notice. *Actual notice* exists when the subsequent purchaser or creditor has actual knowledge or express information about possible deficiencies in the seller's title—something that reasonable, diligent inquiry into all logically relevant sources of information would disclose, *O'Farrel* v. *Coolidge,* 225 S.W.2d 582. A method of receiving actual notice may occur when the grantor offers to sell his land for an abnormally low purchase price. This may be enough to arouse a reasonable person's suspicion, creating the legal responsibility to ask questions about the quality of title, and thereby giving him actual notice and preventing him from being a bona fide purchaser. Actual notice, then, also includes what the purchaser *should have known,* upon diligent inquiry.

Constructive notice is information or knowledge of a fact which the law imputes to a person even though he has no actual knowledge about it. Knowledge that someone other than the seller is in *actual possession* of the property, as well as knowledge of the content of public *real property records,* constitutes constructive notice, *Southwestern Petroleum Corp.* v. *Udall,* 361 F.2d 650 (1966) and *Rutherford* v. *John Hancock Mut. Life Ins. Co.,* 562 F.2d 290 (1977).

If someone other than the grantor is living on the land, this may be enough to arouse suspicion. This is referred to as the *doctrine of conspicuous occupancy.* If occupancy by a third party "looks suspicious," the general rule is that a purchaser always takes title subject to the rights of the party in possession. If the party in possession is a tenant, this simply means he has a right to continue living on the land under the terms (and until termination) of the lease he had with the previous owner. However, if the party in possession has an ownership interest in the land, regardless of whether it is a fee simple absolute or some lesser interest, the title that the grantee receives when purchasing this land is subject to such previous ownership interest. This is because, legally, if someone is in *possession,* this gives constructive notice as well as actual notice of a potential ownership interest. Therefore, the law would not consider the subsequent purchaser to be a bona fide purchaser.

However, the usual and most important method by which one receives constructive notice (and thereby fails to achieve the status of a bona fide purchaser) is by a previous purchaser *recording* his deed in the county land records office. Once a deed is recorded it is legally considered to give constructive notice to the entire world. Therefore, for economic protection against deficiencies in title, it is highly advisable that a purchaser either (1) secure an abstract of title and have it examined by his attorney, (2) obtain an owner's title insurance policy on the property, or (3) receive a certificate of registered title under the Torrens system (see discussion in Chapter 12). In the first two cases, the attorney or a representative of the title insurance company will be making a "title search." This search will disclose whether parties other than the grantor have an interest in the land. If there are no other ownership interests recorded, the buyer will be a bona fide purchaser (assuming that conspicuous occupancy or actual notice are not present). On the other hand, if they find others have an interest in the land, the title is not "marketable." Under the usual earnest money sales contract, the buyer would subsequently be relieved of his obligations to purchase the property.

TYPES OF RECORDING ACTS

As will be seen from the following discussion, whether one is classified as a bona fide purchaser is very important in determining the outcome of some disputes involving the title to land. As previously noted, the type of recording act in effect in a given state furnishes the basic rules for resolving such disputes. The land recording acts in the United States may be classified into three general types. The first is the race type, the second is the notice type, and the third is the race-notice type.

Race Type Recording Act

In order to win certain types of disputes involving land titles, it is often said that one must have the "protection of the recording act" in order to prevail. In those states that have a race type recording act, the sole test of priorities is the priority of recording. According to this type act, among two competing claimants the person winning the race to the courthouse will receive the superior title, even if he was aware of a competing claimant's prior interest. The only state that still utilizes this system for both deeds and mortgages is North Carolina. It also is used to a limited extent in Arkansas (mortgages), Ohio (mortgages, oil and gas leases), and Pennsylvania (nonpurchase money mortgages).

Notice Type Recording Act

Half of the states follow the notice type act in some form.[1] In order to win a title dispute with a competing claimant in states following a notice type recording act, a person must be a bona fide purchaser. If the first party to acquire his interest has not yet recorded it at the time the second party acquires his interest, the second party will prevail. A logical reason for this result is that the first party could have prevented the dispute from arising by recording sooner, because an alert second party would have discovered the first party's interest in the property and the second party would have decided not to acquire an interest in the property. Clearly this result serves as an incentive for all purchasers to record their deeds as soon after title acquisition as possible.

Race-Notice Type Recording Act

Twenty-four states[2] and the District of Columbia follow some form of the race-notice type recording act. It also requires a successful competing claimant to be a bona fide purchaser, and also to be the first competing claimant to record his interest. The race-notice act requirements are a combination of the race type and notice type acts.

Examples Applying the Recording Act

The examples that follow are designed to show how recording acts are used to resolve land title disputes. Let us first suppose that Sam Seller conveys his 160-acre farm, Blackacre, to Billy Buyer, by warranty deed. This transaction occurred on June 2, 1979, at which time Bill paid Sam the agreed purchase price of $50,000. Bill recorded his deed in the county land records office on June 3, 1979.

Let us further assume that Sam executes another warranty deed purporting to convey Blackacre to Paul Purchaser on June 20, 1979. Paul paid Sam the agreed price on that date, and recorded his

---

[1] These are Alabama, Arizona, Arkansas (deeds only), Colorado, Connecticut, Delaware, Florida, Illinois, Iowa, Kansas, Kentucky, Maine, Massachusetts, Missouri, New Hampshire, New Mexico, Ohio (deed only), Oklahoma, Rhode Island, South Carolina, Tennessee, Vermont, Virginia, and West Virginia.

[2] These states are Alaska, California, Georgia, Hawaii, Idaho, Indiana, Maryland, Michigan, Minnesota, Mississippi, Montana, Nebraska, Nevada, New Jersey, New York, North Dakota, Oregon, Pennsylvania (deeds and purchase money mortgages), South Dakota, Texas, Utah, Washington, Wisconsin, and Wyoming.

deed on the day he received it. Sam immediately "left the country" and his present residence is unknown.

Now Bill and Paul both claim to be the sole fee simple absolute owner of Blackacre. Who does own Blackacre? We must look at the recording act in effect in the state where these transactions occurred in order to answer this question.

In the state with the race type recording act, in order to receive the protection of the recording act, one must be the first to record his deed. Bill recorded first. He consequently meets the requirements of the race type recording act, and will be declared to be the owner of Blackacre in those states that have this type statute.

In states that follow either the notice or race-notice type recording act, Bill will again prevail over Paul under the circumstances assumed. Here, both parties have met one requirement of both of these type recording acts. They have both recorded their deed. However, Paul is *not* a bona fide purchaser because at the time Paul received his deed, Bill had already recorded his deed in the local land records office. Legally this gave Paul constructive notice that Bill had an ownership interest in Blackacre. For this reason Paul is not entitled to the protection of these recording acts because he has not met both of the requirements. He is not a bona fide purchaser since he had notice of a previous owner's interest.

The loser in a dispute over title may sue Sam to get his money back. However, this right to sue Sam may not be worth much if Sam cannot be found or has already spent the money. If Paul had insisted that Sam provide him with an abstract, subsequent examination by his attorney would have disclosed Bill's prior interest (title insurance would also have provided effective protection). Then Paul would not have purchased the land, and he would thereby have avoided this problem. This possibility of loss serves as an incentive to get a professional opinion regarding the status of the seller's title (or title insurance) before real estate is purchased.

From these examples it is obvious that when purchasing land, one should always record his deed as soon as possible. This gives constructive notice to everyone that a previous ownership interest has been recorded. This is often of critical importance to mortgagees. If two mortgagees have loaned money and taken the same land as security, the recording act determines which of the mortgagees has "priority" or the right to be paid first. It is in this context that a recording act is most often used to resolve disputes.

Remember that unrecorded deeds are still effective between the grantor and grantee. They do not, however, prevent a subsequent buyer from becoming a bona fide purchaser (except when he has actual knowledge of their existence).

THE PROCESS OF   Generally, the county land records offices in each state provide spe-
RECORDING   cial books in which deeds are recorded, although the process may
involve microfilming in some areas. Recordation is usually by the
volume and page number of the deed records of the county in
which the land is located. The entries are often made by hand in
separate volumes. One volume is kept for deed records, one for
mortgage records, and so forth. One usually finds instruments
recorded in this manner legally referred to as follows.

> ... recorded in Volume _____, Page
> _____ of the _____ Records of
> _____ County, Missouri.

Where the method of recording involves microfilming, a
recorded deed might be legally referred to as follows.

> Filed for record in the Official Public Records of
> _____ County, Texas, under Clerk's File
> No. _____ and recorded under Film Code
> No. _____.

The county land records office maintains a record of grantors
and grantees of each deed filed for record, called a *grantor–grantee
index*. This index can be used to create a "chain of title." That is, it
sets out a complete line of fee title from the original grant from the
sovereign (state or federal government) down to the current property owner. When a summarized history of all the recorded instruments relating to a parcel of real estate is arranged in chronological
order, it is called an *abstract of title.*

Since legal instruments filed in the county land records office
are a matter of public record, in most states individuals who wish
to search the title records of the county are allowed to do so
(Delaware is apparently an exception). They may use the
grantor–grantee index to trace the chain of title of any tract in
which they are interested. However, this is a laborious task as it
involves searching through the recording of many deeds and going
back and forth from the grantor to grantee indices. For this reason,
many prefer to hire private abstract companies to prepare an
abstract of title. Abstract companies also keep a list of all legal
instruments filed for public record, but they keep separate records
for each tract. This tract-indexing system permits them to trace the

chain of title and prepare an abstract of title quickly and conveniently.

One should keep in mind that an abstract of title alone does not assure that the title is good. Only an attorney or title examiner can determine this after examining the material in the abstract.

The county land records office contains records of many legal instruments other than deeds. These include subdivision Plats, condominium records, and *lis pendens* notices. The former two are self-explanatory, but the latter is unique and needs further explanation.

Lis Pendens

Literally translated, *lis pendens* means that the "law is pending." It consists of a record of lawsuits filed, but not yet decided, which could affect title to specific tracts of real estate.

Public filing of a *lis pendens* notice establishes constructive notice to subsequent creditors, purchasers, and other third parties that there is a lawsuit pending that involves an interest in that property. For this reason a subsequent purchaser will take title to that tract subject to the outcome of the lawsuit affecting the property. In some instances, this could mean that one of the parties of the pending lawsuit will receive full title to the property, so purchasers are reluctant to purchase property on which a *lis pendens* notice has been filed.

Filing a *lis pendens* notice is an effective method of protecting parties in litigation, because it helps assure that assets exist from which a favorable judgment can be collected. In this manner it discourages litigants from attempting to protect their assets by transferring title to others before the lawsuit is finally decided.

On the other hand, the *lis pendens* process can be abused, as when one party files a lawsuit and a notice when he has no realistic claim against the landowner. The effect of these notices is to place a cloud on the real estate title, making it difficult to sell until the cloud (notice of *lis pendens)* is removed from the public record.

Logically, it would seem that a libel action should be available when someone files a *lis pendens* notice when there is no reasonable basis for the underlying lawsuit. However, any information disclosed in the pleading to a lawsuit or in the courtroom generally is "privileged" (exempted from libel and slander action), and an individual is not liable for libel or slander if his allegations were made in good faith. (This use of "privilege" encourages free exchange of ideas and attitudes in the courtroom and helps solicit certain facts that otherwise might not be brought into the legal proceeding.) As a part of a lawsuit, *lis pendens* notice is given privileged status unless filed maliciously or in bad faith. See *Kropp* v. *Prather*, 526 S.W.2d 283 and *Scott-Kinnear, Inc.* v. *Eberly & Meade, Inc.*, 879 P.2d 838 (Okla. App.—1994).

Acknowledgments As previously discussed, an acknowledgment is required in most states to make instruments recordable. This may be, depending on the state, the only function of an acknowledgment. It usually does not make the instrument "official" or "legal"; it simply makes it recordable.

Acknowledgments are not the only method of making an instrument recordable. This can also be accomplished by the signatures of one or more subscribing witnesses, or by the sworn testimony of a person as to the authenticity of the handwriting of the signatory party and witnesses.

The usual requirements to make an effective acknowledgment are as follows:

1. The person who executed the instrument must appear before the person authorized to take the acknowledgment.

2. The officer taking the acknowledgment must know or have satisfactory evidence that the person making such acknowledgment is the individual who executed the instrument.

3. The signer must acknowledge to the officer taking the acknowledgment that he executed the instrument for the purposes of consideration therein expressed, and in the capacity therein stated.

4. The acknowledgment must be signed by the authorized officer, and sealed with his seal of office.

An example of an acknowledgment is shown in Figure 9-1.

Acknowledgments must be made before someone who has the legal authority to acknowledge a legal instrument. Usually acknowledgments are made by a notary public, but specifically named public officials may have this power in most states. Authority even exists for certain United States officials stationed abroad to notarize instruments with the same legal effect as if these instruments had been acknowledged in this country. With this exception, a notary public's authority is usually limited to his state or county of residence.

To help assure fairness and honesty of dealings, a person generally cannot acknowledge a deed in which he has a personal or financial interest.

The State of _____
County of _____

Before me _____ (here insert the name
and character of the notarizing officer) on this day
personally appeared _____ known to me (or
proved to me on the oath of _____) to be the
person whose name is subscribed to the foregoing
instrument and acknowledged to me that he executed the same for the purposes and consideration
therein expressed.

(Seal) Given under my hand and seal of office this
_____ day of _____ A.D.,
19 _____.

FIGURE 9-1   Sample Acknowledgment

The courts have rather liberally construed the requirements of
an effective acknowledgment. For instance, the failure of a notary
to show the date his commission (authority) expires does not invalidate an acknowledgment, but the acknowledgment is invalid
without his official seal. In at least one recent case, omitting the
name of the person making the acknowledgment (signer of the
instrument) did not render it fatally defective, *Sheldon v. Farinacci*,
535 S.W.2d 938. It appears that as long as the acknowledgment is
signed, sealed, and in substantially the same form as prescribed by
statute, it will be considered effective and valid.

Other Methods of Establishing Recordability

The legitimacy of an instrument offered for recording may also be
proved by one or more subscribing witness personally appearing
before some authorized officer. Such witness(es) generally must
state under oath that he (they) saw the person sign and/or execute
the instrument and that he executed it for the purposes and consideration therein stated.

Another frequent requirement is that the witnesses must be
personally known to the officer taking the proof, or must prove by
their oath that they are the witnesses testifying to the instrument's
execution. A sample form of a certificate where the execution of the
instrument is proved by a witness is shown in Figure 9-2.

Recordabililty may also be established by submitting proof of
the handwriting of the grantor and the testimony of one or more of
the subscribing witnesses. Circumstances under which this
method might be used include when the signatory party and/or

The State of _____
County of _____

Before me, _____ (here insert the name and character of the officer), on this day personally appeared _____, known to me (or proved to me on the oath of _____), to be the person whose name is subscribed as a witness to the foregoing instrument of writing, and after being duly sworn by me stated on oath that he saw _____, the grantor or person who executed the foregoing instrument, subscribe the same (or that the grantor or person who executed such instrument of writing acknowledged in his presence that he had executed the same for the purpose and consideration therein expressed), and that he had signed as a witness at the request of the grantor (or person who executed the same).

(Seal) Given under my hand and seal of office this _____ day of _____, A.D., 19_____.

FIGURE 9-2   Sample Acknowledgment Involving Proof by Witness

witnesses are dead, nonresidents, or of unknown residence, or where the signatory parties and witnesses are legally incompetent to testify.

The same general rules apply if there is a signatory party who has made his mark rather than signed his name.

Records of Acknowledgments

State laws usually require that all officers authorized or permitted by law to take acknowledgments shall keep a record of each acknowledgment or proof taken by them. The record usually recites the date on which the acknowledgment was taken, the name of the grantor and grantee of the instrument, its date, the name of the witness (if proved by the subscribing witness), and the residence of the witness.

If any person is injured by the failure, refusal, or neglect of any officer in complying with legal requirements or acknowledgments made before him, such person may generally sue the officer in court and recover upon proof of damages.

A *jurat* is a certificate of an officer or a person before whom a writing was sworn to. Basically, it is executed by the same people who have the authority to take acknowledgments. However, it is not an acknowledgment and should not be confused with it. An example of a jurat is shown in Figure 9-3. In a jurat, the signatory party is swearing that the facts contained in the instrument are true and not simply that he signed same for the purposes and consideration therein expressed.

The acknowledgment and the jurat are entirely different certificates used for entirely different purposes. The acknowledgment makes the instrument recordable. The jurat does not affect recordability, but rather verifies the facts contained in the instrument. A jurat is typically used in affidavits, when testimony is taken for court proceedings, or other evidentiary use.

Jurat

There are substantial reasons to promptly record in the local county land records office *all* legal instruments affecting or transferring title to real estate. In short, recording provides a large degree of protection against competing claimants to the same ownership interest.

Disputes among competing claimants are resolved by state recording acts. These acts determine both ownership interests and priority among mortgagees when two basic principles of law come into conflict. The first principle is that one can transfer no better title than he has. The second basic principle is that a bona fide purchaser should be protected and take title free and clear of any claims that were unknown at the time he bought the land.

By definition, a bona fide purchaser is one who acquires his ownership interest by purchase (rather than as a gift), and who has no actual or constructive notice that some person other than his grantor has an ownership interest in the land he is buying. Actual notice refers to express information known about third-party claims. Constructive notice refers to notice imputed by the law by circumstances that should have aroused the suspicions of a reasonable and diligent person. Constructive notice might arise from

SUMMARY

Subscribed and sworn to before me on this _____ day of _____, 19_____.

_____
Notary Public in and for
_____ County, Illinois

FIGURE 9-3   Sample Jurat

the conspicuous occupancy of the property by someone other than the grantor, or by recording. The latter is the main reason that all instruments affecting title to real estate should be promptly recorded.

There are three types of recording acts employed by the various states. The race type requires one to be the first to record his deed if he is to prevail against a competing claimant. If he wins the race to the courthouse, he will prevail even though he had knowledge of the competing claimant's interest at the time he acquired his interest. The notice type act requires one to be a bona fide purchaser, but he need not record his own deed. The race-notice type recording act requires the winning claimant to be a bona fide purchaser and the first claimant to record his deed. Both the notice and race-notice type acts encourage prompt recording in order to give subsequent purchasers constructive notice of previous ownership interests. Most conflicting claims resolved by recording acts involve competing mortgagees.

Historically, all deeds were recorded in large volumes in the county land records office and referred to by book and page. Today, microfilming is also used in many locales. In either case, records are essentially compiled in a grantor–grantee indexing system.

Abstract and title companies, on the other hand, keep up-to-date records of publicly filed instruments using a tract-indexing system. Thus, they can offer a quick and convenient title search and abstract preparation as compared to the time required to construct a chain of title in the public land records office.

Another public record providing protection to prospective real property purchasers is the record of *lis pendens* notices. It discloses the existence of lawsuits that have been filed but are not yet decided, that could affect title to specific tracts of real estate.

Acknowledgments, usually before a notary public, are the most common way of making a legal instrument eligible for recording in the county land records office. Contrary to popular opinion, an unacknowledged deed is still valid as far as the named grantor and grantee are concerned.

Depending on the state, eligibility for recording may also be established by the appearance of one or more subscribing witnesses, or by proof of handwriting of the grantor together with the testimony of one or more subscribing witnesses.

Persons eligible to take acknowledgments are required to keep a record of same in most states. Furthermore, they may be liable if their failure, refusal, or neglect in meeting legal requirements regarding acknowledgments causes financial loss to someone.

Acknowledgments should not be confused with jurats. Jurats are used to swear that facts contained in a legal instrument are true. They do not affect recordability.

1. Recording acts resolve conflicts between two basic principles of law. What are they? Logically, do both principles make sense?

2. What differences exist between actual notice and constructive notice?

3. Why should certain conditions be met before permitting a legal instrument to be recorded?

4. Where are deeds recorded in your state?

10

Mortgages

Arranging acceptable financing is often the key factor in being able to consummate a real estate sale. The real estate agent who understands the key details of various methods of financing has a clear advantage over his competitors because he can advise his clients and potential purchasers on much more than fair market value and comparable sales prices.

This chapter will discuss various types of mortgages and financing arrangements. The two most common types—the regular mortgage and the deed of trust—will be discussed first. Other types of mortgages—the deed absolute, sale and lease-back, and installment land contract—will also be discussed, as well as various mortgaging techniques that have become popular in recent years.

As these various types of mortgages are discussed, it should be remembered that states may generally be classified as lien theory states or title theory states, depending on their interpretation of what is being transferred by the mortgage instrument. Under a lien theory state, the borrower (mortgagor) retains title to the mortgaged property and the lender (mortgagee) receives a lien against that same property. In a title theory state, the borrower actually transfers title of the property to the lender. Some states, such as Illinois, adopt a mortgaging theory which has the elements of both theories. These states are called *intermediate theory* states.

Most common mortgage procedures require the execution of two instruments: the *promissory note* and, depending on the state, either a *mortgage* or a *deed of trust*. When financing real estate, the promissory note used is generally referred to as a *real estate lien note* or a

INSTRUMENTS REQUIRED TO CREATE A MORTGAGE

mortgage note. This note is the actual promise to pay. The only difference between a real estate lien note and other forms of promissory notes is the reference to the real estate serving as security for its payment.

Real Estate Lien Note   Figure 10-1 shows a sample real estate lien note. Several provisions are shown which must be present in every real estate lien note. These include:

1. The mortgagor's promise to pay the mortgagee.
2. The amount of the debt (principal).
3. The interest rate charged on the outstanding principal.
4. The time and amount of principal and interest payments.
5. A reference to the note's security.
6. The mortgagor's signature.

Other clauses not essential to the creation of the note but which may be inserted for business and economic reasons include:

1. Overdue (matured) principal and interest shall also earn interest at a specified rate;
2. Penalty charge for prepayment (arguably, these are to help assure the mortgagee of an acceptable rate of return on his loan, and they clearly have this effect during deflationary economic periods);
3. Whether amounts prepaid should be credited against the principal or future interest payments;
4. Default provisions, which often call for the note to accelerate and the entire debt to become due and payable in case of default (this permits a lender to initiate only one lawsuit to collect the entire debt, rather than being forced to sue in separate lawsuits for the amount due under each successive mortgage payment that is missed);
5. A requirement that the mortgagor pay the mortgagee's attorney's fees necessitated by the mortgagor's default (otherwise, a lender could never fully recoup losses caused by default);
6. A provision waiving any legal requirement that a mortgagor must be given notice when each successive payment becomes due (the mortgagor is aware of the payment schedule anyway from his copy of the note); and

TRUTH IN LENDING DISCLOSURES
MORTGAGE LOAN

┌─ LENDER ─────────────────────────────┐ ┌─ BORROWER ──────────────────────────┐
│   │ │   │
│   │ │   │
│   │ │   │
│   │ │   │
└──────────────────────────────────────┘ └─────────────────────────────────────┘

ANNUAL PERCENTAGE RATE	FINANCE CHARGE	AMOUNT FINANCED	TOTAL OF PAYMENTS
The cost of your credit as a yearly rate.	The dollar amount the credit will cost you.	The amount of credit provided to you or on your behalf.	The amount you will have paid after you have made all payments as scheduled.
%	$	$	$

ITEMIZATION (Check box if applicable)

☐ You will receive a good faith estimate of closing costs.　　☐ You will receive an itemization of the amount financed.

☐ You have the right to receive at this time an itemization of the amount financed.

　☐ I want an itemization.　　　☐ I do not want an itemization.

PAYMENT SCHEDULE

Your payment schedule will be:

Number of Payments	Amount of Payments	When Payments Are Due

Abbreviated payment schedule for loans with mortgage guarantee insurance:

Number of Payments	Amount of Payments Vary		When Payments Are Due
	Highest	Lowest	

VARIABLE RATE (Check one of the following boxes if applicable)

☐ Your loan contains a variable rate feature. Disclosures about the variable rate feature have been provided to you earlier.

☐ The annual percentage rate may increase during the loan term. The circumstances, limitations, effect and example of the payment terms are described in the Variable Rate Disclosure Addendum attached as part of this Truth in Lending Disclosure.

SECURITY

You are giving a security interest in:

☐ the goods or property being purchased.

☐ _____
　(brief description of other property)

☐ Collateral securing other loans with us may also secure this loan.

ASSUMPTION POLICY (Check box if applicable)

Someone buying your house

☐ may, subject to conditions, be allowed to

☐ cannot

assume the remainder of the mortgage on the original terms.

FILING FEES

$

LATE CHARGE

If a payment is late _____ days or more,

you will be charged _____% of the payment.

PREPAYMENT

If you pay off early

you ☐ may ☐ will not have to pay a penalty.

you ☐ may ☐ will not be entitled to a refund of part of the finance charge.

ADDITIONAL DISCLOSURES

SEE CONTRACT DOCUMENTS

See your contract documents for any additional information about nonpayment, default, any required repayment in full before the scheduled date, prepayment refunds and penalties, security interests and assumption policy.

INSURANCE

REQUIRED PROPERTY INSURANCE: You may obtain property insurance from anyone you want that is acceptable to us. If you get the insurance from us, you will pay $_____ for a term of _____ months.

CREDIT INSURANCE

REQUIRED ☐ Credit Life ☐ Credit disability insurance on _____ is required to obtain credit
　　　　　　　　　　　　　　　　　　　　　　　　　　　　　　(insured)

and the cost is included in the finance charge.

VOLUNTARY ☐ Credit life and credit disability insurance are not required to obtain credit, and will not be provided unless you sign and agree to pay the additional cost.

By signing below you will be indicating you wish to voluntarily purchase ☐ credit life ☐ credit disability insurance on

_____ for a term of _____ months and initial premium of $_____
　　　(insured)

_____　　　　　　　　_____
　　　　(Signature)　　　　　　　　　　　　　　　　　　　　　(Signature)

COPY RECEIVED

I have received a copy of this statement.

_____	_____	_____	_____
Signature	Date	Signature	Date

"e" means an estimate

11-4144 (7/88) T.I.L.(S.) Mortgage Loan Form　　　　To Reorder Call 1-800-252-9643 TX/1-800-531-5471 U.S.　　　　© 1988 Hart Graphics—Austin

FIGURE 10-1　Real Estate Lien Note

7. Acknowledgment of the existence of a vendor's lien in those states that permit them.

The real estate lien note is normally not a recorded instrument, since it does not create the lien interest in the real estate. For this reason it does not usually contain an acknowledgment. The lien interest in the real estate is created by the mortgage instrument.

The Regular Mortgage

Nature and Requirements.   The basic mortgage is a two-party instrument and is similar to a deed; it has the same general requirements for validity. It contains a *mortgagor* (person executing the mortgage), a *mortgagee* (lender making the loan), *words of grant,* and a *description* of the mortgaged land. It must be signed by the mortgagor, sealed or witnessed (if required by state law), and delivered. The mortgage is normally considered to be delivered when the mortgagor (signatory party) releases control over it with the intent of making it operative. Since most lenders require that the mortgage be recorded to perfect their lien and to protect their interest from subsequent creditors and purchasers, it should also be acknowledged. It is usually recorded as soon after execution as possible. A commonly used mortgage form is shown in Figure 10-2.

Release.   When the mortgage debt has been paid in full, the mortgagee must execute a *release of lien* (also called a *release deed, satisfaction, or discharge* of a mortgage debt), which is filed in the real property records to remove the existing mortgage lien of record.

Foreclosure.   Foreclosure under a regular mortgage requires *judicial due process,* similar to any other breach of contract. Therefore, all of the properties and defenses of any proceeding in litigation must be followed, which can be time consuming and costly. The signatory mortgagors are necessary parties, as well as the lender, *Mennonite Board of Missions* v. *Adams,* 103 S.Ct. 2706 (1983), and all must be served with notice of the pending litigation as provided by state law for all judicial proceedings. Upon receiving final judgment, the court will order a public foreclosure sale, typically for cash. There is seldom any competitive bidding (particularly if the mortgagor has a right of redemption), because the real estate purchased does not usually lend itself to quick, speculative profits. When the sale has taken place, the mortgagor's interest and all those interests acquired after the date of the initial recording of the foreclosed mortgage are extinguished. When the sale price is accepted and confirmed by the court, a deed is issued. Although

OMB No 2502-0265

M/S (1094)

A. U.S. DEPARTMENT OF HOUSING AND URBAN DEVELOPMENT	B. TYPE OF LOAN

	B. TYPE OF LOAN
	1. ☐ FHA 2. ☐ FMHA 3. ☐ CONV. UNINS. 4. ☐ VA 5. ☐ CONV. INS.
SETTLEMENT STATEMENT	6. FILE NUMBER 7. LOAN NUMBER
	8 MORTG INS CASE NO

C. NOTE: This form is furnished to give you a statement of actual settlement costs. Amounts paid to and by the settlement agent are shown. Items marked ("p.o.c.") were paid outside the closing; they are shown here for information purposes and are not included in the totals.

D. NAME OF BORROWER:

    ADDRESS:

E. NAME OF SELLER:

    ADDRESS: SELLER TIN:

F. NAME OF LENDER:

    ADDRESS:

G. PROPERTY LOCATION:

H. SETTLEMENT AGENT: SETTLEMENT AGENT TIN:

    ADDRESS:

PLACE OF SETTLEMENT: **I. SETTLEMENT DATE:**

    ADDRESS:

J. SUMMARY OF BORROWER'S TRANSACTION		K. SUMMARY OF SELLER'S TRANSACTION	
100 GROSS AMOUNT DUE FROM BORROWER:		**400 GROSS AMOUNT DUE TO SELLER.**	
101 Contract sales price		401 Contract sales price	
102 Personal property		402 Personal property	
103 Settlement charges to borrow (*line 1400*)		403	
104		404	
105		405	
ADJUSTMENTS FOR ITEMS PAID BY SELLER IN ADVANCE:		**ADJUSTMENTS FOR ITEMS PAID FOR SELLER IN ADVANCE:**	
106 City/town taxes to		406 City/town taxes to	
107 County taxes to		407 County taxes to	
108 Assessments to		408 Assessments to	
109 Maintenance to		409 Maintenance to	
110 School Taxes to		410 School Taxes to	
111 Water Taxes to		411 Water Taxes to	
112		412	

FIGURE 10-2   Mortgage Form

120 GROSS AMOUNT DUE FROM BORROWER:		420 GROSS AMOUNT DUE TO SELLER::	
200 AMOUNTS PAID BY OR IN BEHALF OF BORROWER:		**500 REDUCTIONS IN AMOUNT DUE TO SELLER:**	
201 Deposit or earnest money		501 Excess deposit (see instructions)	
202 Principal amount of new loan(s)		502 Settlement charges to seller (line 1400)	
203 Existing loan(s) taken subject to		503 Existing loan(s) taken subject to	
204		504 Payoff of first mortgage loan	
205		505 Payoff of second mortgage loan	
206		506	
207		507	
208		508	
209		509	
ADJUSTMENTS FOR ITEMS UNPAID BY SELLER:		**ADJUSTMENTS FOR ITEMS UNPAID BY SELLER:**	
210 City/town taxes to		510 City/town taxes to	
211 County taxes to		511 County taxes to	
212 Assessments to		512 Assessments to	
213 School Taxes to		513 School Taxes to	
214 Maintenance to		514 Maintenance to	
215 Water Taxes to		515 Water Taxes to	
216		516	
217		517	
218		518	
219		519	
220 TOTAL PAID BY/FOR BORROWER:		**520 TOTAL REDUCTION IN AMOUNT DUE SELLER:**	
300 CASH AT SETTLEMENT FROM/TO BORROWER:		**600 CASH AT SETTLEMENT TO/FROM SELLER:**	
301 Gross amount due from borrower (line 120)		601 Gross amount due to seller (line 420)	
302 Less amounts paid by/for borrower (line 220)		602 Less total reductions in amount due seller (line 520)	
303 **CASH (☐ FROM) (☐ TO) BORROWER:**		603 **CASH (☐ TO) (☐ FROM) SELLER:**	

SUBSTITUTE FORM 1099 SELLER STATEMENT-The information contained in Blocks E, G, H and I and on line 401 (or, if line 401 is asterisked, lines 403 and 404) is important tax information and is being furnished to the Internal Revenue Service. If you are required to file a return, a negligence penalty or other sanction will be imposed on you if this item is required to be reported and the IRS determines that it has not been reported.
SELLER INSTRUCTION-If this real estate was your principal residence, file form 2119, Sale or Exchange of Principal Residence, for any gain, with your income tax return; for other transactions, complete the applicable parts of form 4797, Form 6252 and/or Schedule D (Form 1040).

You are required by law to provide _____ with your correct taxpayer identification number.

If you do not provide _____ with your correct taxpayer identification number, you may be subject to civil or criminal penalties.

Under penalties of perjury, I certify that the number shown on this statement is my correct taxpayer identification number.

FIGURE 10-2   Continued

XAS LDI

L. SETTLEMENT CHARGES			PAID FROM BORROWER'S FUNDS AT SETTLEMENT	PAID FROM SELLER'S FUNDS AT SETTLEMENT
700. TOTAL SALES/BROKER'S COMMISSION Based on price $	@	%=		
Division of commission (line 700) as follows:				
701. $	to			
702. $	to			
703. Commission paid at settlement				
704.				
800. ITEMS PAYABLE IN CONNECTION WITH LOAN.				
801. Loan Origination fee	%			
802. Loan Discount	%			
803. Appraisal Fee	to			
804. Credit Report	to			
805. Lender's inspection fee				
806. Mortgage Insurance application fee	to			
807. Assumption Fee				
808. Commitment Fee				
809. FNMA Processing Fee				
810. Pictures				
811.				
900. ITEMS REQUIRED BY LENDER TO BE PAID IN ADVANCE.				
901. Interest from	to @ $	/day		
902. Mortgage insurance premium for	mo. to			
903. Hazard insurance premium for	yrs. to			
904. Flood Insurance	yrs. to			
905.				
1000. RESERVES DEPOSITED WITH LENDER				
1001. Hazard insurance	mo. @ $	per mo.		
1002. Mortgage insurance	mo. @ $	per mo.		
1003. City property taxes	mo. @ $	per mo.		
1004. County property taxes	mo. @ $	per mo.		
1005. Annual assessments (Maint.)	mo. @ $	per mo.		
1006. School Property Taxes	mo. @ $	per mo.		
1007. Water Dist. Prop. Tax	mo. @ $	per mo.		
1008. Flood Insurance	mo. @ $	per mo.		

FIGURE 10-2   Continued

1100. TITLE CHARGES:				
1101. Settlement or closing fee	to			
1102. Abstract or title search	to			
1103. Title examination	to			
1104. Title insurance binder	to			
1105. Document preparation	to			
1106. Notary fees	to			
1107. Attorney's fees to	to			
(includes above items No.				
1108. Title insurance	to			
(includes above items No.				
1109. Lender's coverage	$			
1110. Owner's coverage	$			
1111. Escrow Fee				
1112. Restrictions				
1113. Messenger Service				
1114. State of Texas Policy Guaranty Fee				
1200. GOVERNMENT RECORDING AND TRANSFER CHARGES				
1201. Recording fees: Deed $	Mortgage $	Releases $		
1202. City/county tax/stamps: Deed $	Mortgage $			
1203. State tax/stamps: Deed $	Mortgage $			
1204. Tax Certificates				
1205.				
1300. ADDITIONAL SETTLEMENT CHARGES				
1301. Survey	to			
1302. Pest inspection	to			
1303.				
1304.				
1305.				
1400. TOTAL SETTLEMENT CHARGES (entered on lines 103, Section J and 502, Section K)				

ERTIFICATION: I have carefully reviewed the HUD-1 Settlement Statement and to the best of my knowledge and belief, it is a true and accurate statement of all receipts and disbursements made on my account or by me in this transaction. I further certify -at I have received a copy of HUD-1 Settlement Statement.

Borrowers _____   Sellers _____

To the best of my knowledge, the HUD-1 Settlement Statement which I have prepared is a true and accurate account of the funds which were received and have been or will be disbursed by the undersigned as part of the settlement of this transaction

Settlement Agent _____   Date _____

ELLER'S AND/OR PURCHASER'S STATEMENT Seller's and Purchaser's signature hereon acknowledges his/their approval of tax prorations and signifies their understanding that prorations were based on taxes for the preceding year, or estimates ir the current year, and in the event of any change for the current year, all necessary adjustments must be made between Seller and Purchaser; likewise any default in delinquent taxes will be reimbursed to Title Company by the Seller. Title Company, in its capacity as Escrow Agent, is and has been authorized to deposit all funds it receives in this transaction in any financial institution, whether affiliated or not. Such financial institution may provide Title Company computer ccounting and audit services directly or through a separate entity which, if affiliated with Title Company, may charge the financial institution reasonable and proper compensation therefore and retain any profits therefrom. Any escrow fees paid by any arty involved in this transaction shall only be for checkwriting and input to the computers, but not for aforesaid accounting and audit services. Title Company shall not be liable for any interest or other charges on the earnest money and shall be under no ity to invest or reinvest funds held by it at any time. Sellers and Purchasers hereby acknowledge and consent to the deposit of the escrow money in financial institutions with which Title Company has or may have other banking relationships and further onsent to the retention by Title Company and/or its affiliates of any and all benefits (including advantageous interest rates on loans) Title Company and/or its affiliates may receive from such financial institutions by reason of their maintenance of said scrow accounts.

The parties have read the above sentences, recognize that the recitations herein are material, agree to same, and recognize Title Company is relying on the same.

urchasers/Borrowers _____   Sellers _____

RNING: It is a crime to knowingly make false statements to the United States on this or any other similar form. Penalties upon conviction can include a fine and imprisonment. For details see: Title 18: U.S. Code Section 1001 and Section 1010.

FIGURE 10-2   *Continued*

variations exist in state laws, it is difficult for the mortgagor to legally have the sale set aside once the deed has been issued.

All foreclosure judgments may be collaterally attacked or appealed. When coupled with the statutory redemption rights existing in many states, the foreclosure procedures can be quite complicated. Statutory redemption rights generally set out specific time periods following the foreclosure sale during which the mortgagor can "redeem" the real estate by reimbursing the foreclosure sale purchaser for all of his expenses. Statutory redemption periods are set out in Table 10-1, and are discussed more fully in a subsequent section. The type of foreclosure followed in each state is also listed in Table 10-1.

Nature and Requirements.   The deed of trust is a three-party instrument that can have one of two legal effects. It is considered to be (1) a *mortgage* in some states and (2) *in the nature of* a mortgage in others, *National Acceptance Co.* v. *Exchange National Bank*, 101 Ill. App. 2d 396, 243 N.E.2d 264 and *Lucky Homes, Inc.* v. *Tarrant Savings Association*, 390 S.W.2d 473.

    The three parties to a deed of trust are the *grantor* (mortgagor), the *trustee* (the party to whom the conveyance is made), and the *beneficiary* (the lending institution, also called the *mortgagee).* (See Figure 10-3.)

    The deed of trust is often characterized as a *mortgage with a power of sale.* It creates a conveyance in trust to the trustee, who holds the right to foreclosure pursuant to the terms of the deed of trust, often without pursuing any court action (see following discussion). Therefore, in addition to the requirements of the regular mortgage, a deed of trust instrument must also contain an appointed trustee (who may be the lender's agent, although an impartial third party is often required and/or preferable), a trust clause, and a power of sale clause. A typical form of a deed of trust is shown in Figure 10-4.

Release.   If a deed of trust is used in the nature of a mortgage, and the note is paid in full, the trustee generally executes a *deed of reconveyance* or *release deed*, which reconveys whatever title the trustee may have had back to the grantor/mortgagor. If a deed of trust is used as a mortgage, it normally contains a *defeasance clause*, which operates to render the deed of trust void upon payment of the debt. Since the record title still needs to be cleared, however, the beneficiary usually executes a *release of lien* to effectively eliminate the deed of trust lien.

Foreclosure.   The foreclosure provision in a deed of trust is of great importance. It typically provides that upon default, the beneficiary requests that the trustee sell the property at a foreclosure sale. There is no requirement for a judicial proceeding (although that method of foreclosure is still available), and therefore a deed of trust foreclosure sale is less expensive and less time-consuming

The Deed of Trust

TABLE 10-1
Mortgage Instruments, Type of Foreclosure, and Redemption Period by State

State	Normal Instrument	Foreclosure Action	Number Months of Redemption Period[1]
Alabama	Note & Mortgage	Power of sale	12
Alaska	Note, Mortgage & Trust Deed	Judicial & Power of Sale	12
Arizona	Note & Mortgage	Judicial & Power of Sale	6
Arkansas	Note & Mortgage	Judicial & Power of Sale	12/None for Power of Sale
California	Note & Trust Deed	Power of Sale or Equity Suit	None
Colorado	Note & Trust Deed	Judicial & Power of Sale	6/None
Connecticut	Note & Trust Deed	Strict Foreclosure	None
Delaware	Bond & Warrant, Mortgage or Trust Deed	Judicial	None
District of Columbia	Note & Trust Deed	Power of Sale	None
Florida	Note & Mortgage	Judicial	None
Georgia	Note Secured on Loan Deed	Judicial & Power of Sale	None
Hawaii	Note & Mortgage	Judicial & Power of Sale	None
Idaho	Note, Mortgage & Trust Deed	Judicial or Power of Sale	1/2 yr less than 20 1 yr 20 Acres/None for Power of Sale
Illinois	Note & Mortgage	Judicial	6–7
Indiana	Note & Mortgage	Judicial	None
Iowa	Note & Mortgage	Equity	0–12
Kansas	Note, Mortgage & Trust Deed	Judicial	0–12
Kentucky	Note, Mortgage & Trust Deed	Judicial Foreclosure	12
Louisiana	Note & Mortgage	Judicial	None
Maine	Note & Mortgage	Judicial & Power of Sale	3/0
Maryland	Note & Mortgage	Judicial	None
Massachusetts	Note & Mortgage	Entry, Publication & Sale	None
Michigan	Note & Mortgage	Judicial or Ad & Sale	6/1–6
Minnesota	Note & Mortgage	Judicial or Ad & Sale	6–12
Mississippi	Note & Trust Deed	Ad & Sale	None
Missouri	Note & Trust Deed	Ad & Sale	12
Montana	Note & Mortgage	Judicial or Ad & Sale	12
Nebraska	Note & Mortgage	Judicial	None
Nevada	Note, Mortgage & Trust Deed	Judicial Power of Sale for Trust Deed or Mortgage	12/None with Power of Sale
New Hampshire	Note & Mortgage	Ad & Sale	None

TABLE 10-1 Continued

State	Normal Instrument	Foreclosure Action	Number Months of Redemption Period[1]
New Jersey	Note or Bond & Mortgage	Judicial	6
New Mexico	Note & Mortgage	Judicial & Power of Sale	9/None
New York	Note or Bond & Mortgage	Judicial Ad & Sale	None
North Carolina	Note & Mortgage	Judicial & Ad & Sale	None
North Dakota	Mortgage	Judicial	6–12
Ohio	Note & Mortgage	Judicial	None
Oklahoma	Special State Form of Note & Mortgage	Judicial & Power of Sale	None
Oregon	Note & Trust Deed	Judicial & Ad & Sale	6/None
Pennsylvania	Bond, Warrant & Mortgage	Judicial	None
Rhode Island	Note & Mortgage	Ad & Sale	None
South Carolina	Note, Mortgage & Trust Deed	Judicial	None
South Dakota	Note	Judicial & Ad & Sale	6–12
Tennessee	Note & Trust Deed	Ad & Sale	24 may be waived for Trust Deed
Texas	Note & Trust Deed	Court Action or Power of Sale	None
Utah	Note & Mortgage	Judicial & Power of Sale	6/None
Vermont	Note & Mortgage	Judicial	6
Virginia	Note & Trust Deed	Ad & Sale	None
Washington	Note & Mortgage	Judicial & Power of Sale	12/None
West Virginia	Note & Trust Deed	Publication & Sale	None
Wisconsin	Special State Note & Mortgage	Judicial	2–12
Wyoming	Note & Mortgage	Judicial & Power of Sale in Mortgage	3

[1] Period usually measured from date of foreclosure sale. Exceptions exist in some states.
SOURCE: *Foreclosure Law & Related Remedies,* Edited by Sidney A. Keyles, published by the ABA Section of Real Property, Probate and Trust Law. Because of various state laws, the interpretation of this table should be supplemented by legal counsel.

than a judicial foreclosure sale. The foreclosure sale procedure is usually set out in the power of sale clause and is enforced as a contractual agreement between the parties. There is usually a provision requiring notification of the mortgagor/owner of the impending sale. Any party can bid at the foreclosure sale, although the

——————————————— [Space Above This Line For Recording Data] ———————————————

DEED OF TRUST

THIS DEED OF TRUST ("Security Instrument") is made on
The grantor is

("Borrower").
, whose address is

The trustee is

("Trustee").

The beneficiary is

, which is organized and existing
under the laws of   , and whose address is

("Lender").

Borrower owes Lender the principal sum of

Dollars (U.S. $). This debt is evidenced by Borrower's note dated the same date as this Security Instrument ("Note"), which provides for monthly payments, with the full debt, if not paid earlier, due and payable on   . This Security Instrument secures to Lender: (a) the repayment of the debt evidenced by the Note, with interest, and all renewals, extensions and modifications of the Note; (b) the payment of all other sums, with interest, advanced under paragraph 7 to protect the security of this Security Instrument; and (c) the performance of Borrower's covenants and agreements under this Security Instrument and the Note. For this purpose, Borrower irrevocably grants and conveys to Trustee, in trust, with power of sale, the following described property located in County, Oregon:

which has the address of
                                             [Street]   [City]

Oregon   ("Property Address");
           [Zip Code]

TOGETHER WITH all the improvements now or hereafter erected on the property, and all easements, appurtenances, and fixtures now or hereafter a part of the property. All replacements and additions shall also be covered by this Security Instrument. All of the foregoing is referred to in this Security Instrument as the "Property."

BORROWER COVENANTS that Borrower is lawfully seised of the estate hereby conveyed and has the right to grant and convey the Property and that the Property is unencumbered, except for encumbrances of record. Borrower warrants and will defend generally the title to the Property against all claims and demands, subject to any encumbrances of record.

THIS SECURITY INSTRUMENT combines uniform covenants for national use and non-uniform covenants with limited variations by jurisdiction to constitute a uniform security instrument covering real property.

OREGON - Single Family - Fannie Mae/Freddie Mac UNIFORM INSTRUMENT   Form 3038 9/90
                                                                                     SIORC1 12/95

FIGURE 10-3   Deed of Trust Instrument

UNIFORM COVENANTS. Borrower and Lender covenant and agree as follows:

1. Payment of Principal and Interest; Prepayment and Late Charges. Borrower shall promptly pay when due the principal of and interest on the debt evidenced by the Note and any prepayment and late charges due under the Note.

2. Funds for Taxes and Insurance. Subject to applicable law or to a written waiver by Lender, Borrower shall pay to Lender on the day monthly payment are due under the Note, until the Note is paid in full, a sum ("Funds") for: (a) yearly taxes and assessments which may attain priority over this Security Instrument as a lien on the Property; (b) yearly leasehold payments or ground rents on the Property, if any; (c) yearly hazard or property insurance premiums; (d) yearly flood insurance premiums, if any; (e) yearly mortgage insurance premiums, if any; and (f) any sums payable by Borrower to Lender, in accordance with the provisions of paragraph 8, in lieu of the payment of mortgage insurance premiums. These items are called "Escrow Items." Lender may, at any time, collect and hold Funds in an amount not to exceed the maximum amount a lender for a federally related mortgage loan may require for Borrower's escrow account under the federal Real Estate Settlement Procedures Act of 1974 as amended from time to time, 12 U.S.C. Section 2601 et seq. ("RESPA"), unless another law that applies to the Funds sets a lesser amount. If so, Lender may, at any time, collect and hold Funds in an amount not to exceed the lesser amount. Lender may estimate the amount of Funds due on the basis of current data and reasonable estimates of expenditures of future Escrow Items or otherwise in accordance with applicable law.

The Funds shall be held in an institution whose deposits are insured by a federal agency, instrumentality, or entity (including Lender, if Lender is such an institution) or in any Federal Home Loan Bank. Lender shall apply the Funds to pay the Escrow Items. Lender may not charge Borrower for holding and applying the Funds, annually analyzing the escrow account, or verifying the Escrow Items, unless Lender pays Borrower interest on the Funds and applicable law permits Lender to make such a charge. However, Lender may require Borrower to pay a one-time charge for an independent real estate tax reporting service used by Lender in connection with this loan, unless applicable law provides otherwise. Unless an agreement is made or applicable law requires interest to be paid, Lender shall not be required to pay Borrower any interest or earnings on the Funds. Borrower and Lender may agree in writing, however, that interest shall be paid on the Funds. Lender shall give to Borrower, without charge, an annual accounting of the Funds, showing credits and debits to the Funds and the purpose for which each debit to the Funds was made. The Funds are pledged as additional security for all sums secured by this Security Instrument.

If the Funds held by Lender exceed the amounts permitted to be held by applicable law, Lender shall account to Borrower for the excess Funds in accordance with the requirements of applicable law. If the amount of the Funds held by Lender at any time is not sufficient to pay the Escrow Items when due, Lender may so notify Borrower in writing, and, in such case Borrower shall pay to Lender the amount necessary to make up the deficiency. Borrower shall make up the deficiency in no more than twelve monthly payments, at Lender's sole discretion.

Upon payment in full of all sums secured by this Security instrument, Lender shall promptly refund to Borrower any Funds held by Lender. If, under paragraph 21, Lender shall acquire or sell the Property, Lender, prior to the acquisition or sale of the Property, shall apply any Funds held by Lender at the time of acquisition or sale as a credit against the sums secured by this Security Instrument.

3. Application of Payments. Unless applicable law provides otherwise, all payments received by Lender under paragraphs 1 and 2 shall be applied: first, to any prepayment charges due under the Note; second, to amounts payable under paragraph 2; third, to interest due; fourth, to principal due; and last, to any late charges due under the Note.

4. Charges; Liens. Borrower shall pay all taxes, assessments, charges, fines and impositions attributable to the Property which may attain priority over this Security Instrument, and leasehold payments or ground rents, if any. Borrower shall pay these obligations in the manner provided in paragraph 2, or if not paid in that manner, Borrower shall pay them on time directly to the person owed payment. Borrower shall promptly furnish to Lender all notices of amounts to be paid under this paragraph. If Borrower makes these payments directly, Borrower shall promptly furnish to Lender receipts evidencing the payments.

Borrower shall promptly discharge any lien which has priority over this Security Instrument unless Borrower: (a) agrees in writing to the payment of the obligation secured by the lien in a manner acceptable to Lender; (b) contests in good faith the lien by, or defends against enforcement of the lien in, legal proceedings which in the Lender's opinion operate to prevent the enforcement of the lien; or (c) secures from the holder of the lien an agreement satisfactory to Lender subordinating the lien to this Security Instrument. If Lender determines that any part of the Property is subject to a lien which may attain priority over this Security Instrument, Lender may give Borrower a notice identifying the lien. Borrower shall satisfy the lien or take one or more of the actions set forth above within 10 days of the giving of notice.

5. Hazard or Property Insurance. Borrower shall keep the improvements now existing or hereafter erected on the Property insured against loss by fire, hazards included within the term "extended coverage" and any other hazards, including floods or flooding, for which Lender requires insurance. This insurance shall be maintained in the amounts and for the periods that Lender requires. The insurance carrier providing the insurance shall be chosen by Borrower subject to Lender's approval which shall not be unreasonably withheld. If Borrower fails to maintain coverage described above, Lender may, at Lender's option, obtain coverage to protect Lender's rights in the Property in accordance with paragraph 7.

All insurance policies and renewals shall be acceptable to Lender and shall include a standard mortgage clause. Lender shall have the right to hold the policies and renewals. If Lender requires, Borrower shall promptly give to Lender all receipts of paid premiums and renewal notices. In the event of loss, Borrower shall give prompt notice to the insurance carrier and Lender. Lender may make proof of loss if not made promptly by Borrower.

Unless Lender and Borrower otherwise agree in writing, insurance proceeds shall be applied to restoration or repair of the Property damaged, if the restoration or repair is economically feasible and Lender's security is not lessened. If the restoration or repair is not economically feasible or Lender's security would be lessened, the insurance proceeds shall be applied to the sums secured by this Security Instrument, whether or not then due, with any excess paid to Borrower. If Borrower abandons the Property, or does not answer within 30 days a notice from Lender that the insurance carrier has offered to settle a claim, then Lender may collect the insurance proceeds. Lender may use the proceeds to repair or restore the Property or to pay sums secured by this Security instrument, whether or not then due. The 30-day period will begin when the notice is given.

Unless Lender and Borrower otherwise agree in writing, any application of proceeds to principal shall not extend or postpone the due date of the monthly payments referred to in paragraphs 1 and 2 or change the amount of the payments. If under paragraph 21 the Property is acquired by Lender, Borrower's right to any insurance policies and proceeds resulting from damage to the Property prior to the acquisition shall pass to Lender to the extent of the sums secured by this Security Instrument immediately prior to the acquisition.

6. Occupancy, Preservation, Maintenance and Protection of the Property; Borrower's Loan Application; Leaseholds. Borrower shall occupy, establish, and use the Property as Borrower's principal residence within sixty days after the execution of this Security Instrument and shall continue to occupy the Property as Borrower's principal residence for at least one year after the date of occupancy, unless Lender otherwise agrees in writing, which consent shall not be unreasonably withheld, or unless extenuating circumstances exist which are beyond Borrower's control. Borrower shall not destroy, damage or impair the Property, allow the Property to deteriorate, or commit waste on the Property. Borrower shall be in default if any forfeiture action or proceedings, whether civil or criminal, is begun that in Lender's good faith judgment could result in forfeiture of the Property or otherwise materially impair the lien created by this Security Instrument or Lender's security interest. Borrower may cure such a default and reinstate as provided in paragraph 18, by causing the action or proceeding to be dismissed with a ruling that, in Lender's good faith determination, precludes forfeiture of the Borrower's interest in the Property or other material impairment of the lien created by this Security Instrument or Lender's security interest. Borrower shall also be in default if Borrower, during the loan application process, gave materially false or inaccurate information or statements to Lender (or failed to provide Lender with any material information) in connection with the loan evidenced by the Note, including, but not limited to, representations concerning Borrower's occupancy of the Property as a principal residence. If this Security Instrument is on a leasehold, Borrower shall comply with all the provisions of the lease. If Borrower acquires fee title to the Property, the leasehold and the fee title shall not merge unless Lender agrees to the merger in writing.

7. Protection of Lender's Rights in the Property. If Borrower fails to perform the covenants and agreements contained in this Security Instrument, or there is a legal proceeding that may significantly affect Lender's rights in the Property (such as a proceeding in bankruptcy, probate, for condemnation or forfeiture or to enforce laws or regulations), then Lender may do and pay for whatever is necessary to protect the value of the Property and Lender's rights in the Property. Lender's actions may include paying any sums secured by a lien which has priority over this Security Instrument, appearing in court, paying reasonable attorneys' fees and entering on the Property to make repairs. Although Lender may take action under this paragraph 7, Lender does not have to do so.

Any amounts disbursed by Lender under this paragraph 7 shall become additional debt of Borrower secured by this Security Instrument. Unless Borrower and Lender agree to other terms of payment, these amounts shall bear interest from the date of disbursement at the Note rate and shall be payable, with interest, upon notice from Lender to Borrower requesting payment.

8. Mortgage Insurance. If Lender required mortgage insurance as a condition of making the loan secured by this Security Instrument, Borrower shall pay the premiums required to maintain the mortgage insurance in effect. If, for any reason, the mortgage insurance coverage required by Lender lapses or ceases to be in effect, Borrower shall pay the premiums required to obtain coverage substantially equivalent to the mortgage insurance previously in effect, at a cost substantially equivalent to the cost to Borrower of the mortgage insurance previously in effect, from an alternate mortgage insurer approved by Lender. If substantially equivalent mortgage insurance coverage is not available, Borrower shall pay to Lender each month a sum equal to

SIORC2 01/96

FIGURE 10-3   Continued

one-twelfth of the yearly mortgage insurance premium being paid by Borrower when the insurance coverage lapsed or ceased to be in effect. Lender will accept, use and retain these payments as a loss reserve in lieu of mortgage insurance. Loss reserve payments may no longer be required, at the option of Lender, if mortgage insurance coverage (in the amount and for the period that Lender requires) provided by an insurer approved by Lender again becomes available and is obtained. Borrower shall pay the premiums required to maintain mortgage insurance in effect, or to provide a loss reserve, until the requirement for mortgage insurance ends in accordance with any written agreement between Borrower and Lender or applicable law.

9. Inspection. Lender or its agent may make reasonable entries upon and inspections of the Property. Lender shall give Borrower notice at the time of or prior to an inspection specifying reasonable cause for the inspection.

10. Condemnation. The proceeds of any award or claim for damages, direct or consequential, in connection with any condemnation or other taking of any part of the Property, or for conveyance in lieu of condemnation, are hereby assigned and shall be paid to Lender.

In the event of a total taking of the Property, the proceeds shall be applied to the sums secured by this Security Instrument, whether or not then due, with any excess paid to Borrower. In the event of a partial taking of the Property in which the fair market value of the Property immediately before the taking is equal to or greater than the amount of the sums secured by this Security instrument immediately before the taking, unless Borrower and Lender otherwise agree in writing, the sums secured by this Security Instrument shall be reduced by the amount of the proceeds multiplied by the following fraction: (a) the total amount of the sums secured immediately before the taking, divided by (b) the fair market value of the Property immediately before the taking. Any balance shall be paid to Borrower. In the event of a partial taking of the Property in which the fair market value of the Property immediately before the taking is less than the amount of the sums secured immediately before the taking, unless Borrower and Lender otherwise agree in writing or unless applicable law otherwise provides, the proceeds shall be applied to the sums secured by this Security instrument whether or not the sums are then due.

If the Property is abandoned by Borrower, or if, after notice by Lender to Borrower that the condemnor offers to make an award or settle a claim for damages, Borrower fails to respond to Lender within 30 days after the date the notice is given, Lender is authorized to collect and apply the proceeds, at its option, either to restoration or repair of the Property or to the sums secured by this Security Instrument, whether or not then due.

Unless Lender and Borrower otherwise agree in writing, any application of proceeds to principal shall not extend or postpone the due date of the monthly payments referred to in paragraphs 1 and 2 or change the amount of such payments.

11. Borrower Not Released; Forbearance by Lender Not a Waiver. Extension of the time for payment or modification of amortization of the sums secured by this Security Instrument granted by Lender to any successor in interest of Borrower shall not operate to release the liability of the original Borrower or Borrower's successors in interest. Lender shall not be required to commence proceedings against any successor in interest or refuse to extend time for payment or otherwise modify amortization of the sums secured by this Security Instrument by reason of any demand made by the original Borrower or Borrower's successors in interest. Any forbearance by Lender in exercising any right or remedy shall not be a waiver of or preclude the exercise of any right or remedy.

12. Successors and Assigns Bound; Joint and Several Liability; Co-signers. The covenants and agreements of this Security Instrument shall bind and benefit the successors and assigns of Lender and Borrower, subject to the provisions of paragraph 17. Borrower's covenants and agreements shall be joint and several. Any Borrower who co-signs this Security Instrument but does not execute the Note: (a) is co-signing this Security Instrument only to mortgage, grant and convey that Borrower's interest in the Property under the terms of this Security Instrument; (b) is not personally obligated to pay the sums secured by this Security Instrument; and (c) agrees that Lender and any other Borrower may agree to extend, modify, forbear or make any accommodations with regard to the terms of this Security Instrument or the Note without that Borrower's consent.

13. Loan Charges. If the loan secured by this Security Instrument is subject to a law which sets maximum loan charges, and that law is finally interpreted so that the interest or other loan charges collected or to be collected in connection with the loan exceed the permitted limits, then: (a) any such loan charge shall be reduced by the amount necessary to reduce the charge to the permitted limit; and (b) any sums already collected from Borrower which exceeded permitted limits will be refunded to Borrower. Lender may choose to make this refund by reducing the principal owed under the Note or by making a direct payment to Borrower. If a refund reduces principal, the reduction will be treated as a partial prepayment without any prepayment charge under the Note.

14. Notices. Any notice to Borrower provided for in this Security Instrument shall be given by delivering it or by mailing it by first class mail unless applicable law requires use of another method. The notice shall be directed to the Property Address or any other address Borrower designates by notice to Lender. Any notice to Lender shall be given by first class mail to Lender's address stated herein or any other address Lender designates by notice to Borrower. Any notice provided for in this Security Instrument shall be deemed to have been given to Borrower or Lender when given as provided in this paragraph.

15. Governing Law; Severability. This Security Instrument shall be governed by federal law and the law of the jurisdiction in which the Property is located. In the event that any provision or clause of this Security Instrument or the Note conflicts with applicable law, such conflict shall not affect other provisions of this Security Instrument or the Note which can be given effect without the conflicting provision. To this end the provisions of this Security Instrument and the Note are declared to be severable.

16. Borrower's Copy. Borrower shall be given one conformed copy of the Note and of this Security Instrument.

17. Transfer of the Property or a Beneficial Interest in Borrower. If all or any part of the Property or any interest in it is sold or transferred (or if a beneficial interest in Borrower is sold or transferred and Borrower is not a natural person) without Lender's prior written consent, Lender may, at its option, require immediate payment in full of all sums secured by this Security Instrument. However, this option shall not be exercised by Lender if exercise is prohibited by federal law as of the date of this Security Instrument.

If Lender exercises this option, Lender shall give Borrower notice of acceleration. The notice shall provide a period of not less than 30 days from the date the notice is delivered or mailed within which Borrower must pay all sums secured by this Security Instrument. If Borrower fails to pay these sums prior to the expiration of this period, Lender may invoke any remedies permitted by this Security Instrument without further notice or demand on Borrower.

18. Borrower's Right to Reinstate. If Borrower meets certain conditions, Borrower shall have the right to have enforcement of this Security Instrument discontinued at any time prior to the earlier of: (a) 5 days (or such other period as applicable law may specify for reinstatement) before sale of the Property pursuant to any power of sale contained in this Security Instrument; or (b) entry of a judgment enforcing this Security Instrument. Those conditions are that Borrower: (a) pays Lender all sums which then would be due under this Security Instrument and the Note as if no acceleration had occurred; (b) cures any default of any other covenants or agreements; (c) pays all expenses incurred in enforcing this Security Instrument, including, but not limited to, reasonable attorneys' fees; and (d) takes such action as Lender may reasonably require to assure that the lien of this Security Instrument, Lender's rights in the Property and Borrower's obligation to pay the sums secured by this Security Instrument shall continue unchanged. Upon reinstatement by Borrower, this Security Instrument and the obligations secured hereby shall remain fully effective as if no acceleration had occurred. However, this right to reinstate shall not apply in the case of acceleration under paragraph 17.

19. Sale of Note; Change of Loan Servicer. The Note or a partial interest in the Note (together with this Security Instrument) may be sold one or more times without prior notice to Borrower. A sale may result in a change in the entity (known as the "Loan Servicer") that collects monthly payments due under the Note and this Security Instrument. There also may be one or more changes of the Loan Servicer unrelated to a sale of the Note. If there is a change of the Loan Servicer, Borrower will be given written notice of the change in accordance with paragraph 14 above and applicable law. The notice will state the name and address of the new Loan Servicer and the address to which payments should be made. The notice will also contain any other information required by applicable law.

20. Hazardous Substances. Borrower shall not cause or permit the presence, use, disposal, storage, or release of any Hazardous Substances on or in the Property. Borrower shall not do, nor allow anyone else to do, anything affecting the Property that is in violation of any Environmental Law. The preceding two sentences shall not apply to the presence, use, or storage on the Property of small quantities of Hazardous Substances that are generally recognized to be appropriate to normal residential uses and to maintenance of the Property.

Borrower shall promptly give Lender written notice of any investigation, claim, demand, lawsuit or other action by any governmental or regulatory agency or private party involving the Property and any Hazardous Substance or Environmental Law of which Borrower has actual knowledge. If Borrower learns, or is notified by any governmental or regulatory authority, that any removal or other remediation of any Hazardous Substance affecting the Property is necessary, Borrower shall promptly take all necessary remedial actions in accordance with Environmental Law.

As used in this paragraph 20, "Hazardous Substances" are those substances defined as toxic or hazardous substances by Environmental Law and the following substances: gasoline, kerosene, other flammable or toxic petroleum products, toxic pesticides and herbicides, volatile solvents, materials containing asbestos or formaldehyde, and radioactive materials. As used in this paragraph 20, "Environmental Law" means federal laws and laws of the jurisdiction where the Property is located that relate to health, safety or environmental protection.

SIORC3 01/96

FIGURE 10-3   Continued

21. **Acceleration; Remedies.** Lender shall give notice to Borrower prior to acceleration following Borrower's breach of any covenant or agreement in this Security Instrument (but not prior to acceleration under paragraph 17 unless applicable law provides otherwise). The notice shall specify: (a) the default; (b) the action required to cure the default; (c) a date, not less than 30 days from the date the notice is given to Borrower, by which the default must be cured; and (d) that failure to cure the default on or before the date specified in the notice may result in acceleration of the sums secured by this Security Instrument and sale of the Property. The notice shall further inform Borrower of the right to reinstate after acceleration and the right to bring a court action to assert the non-existence of a default or any other defense of Borrower to acceleration and sale. If the default is not cured on or before the date specified in the notice, Lender at its option may require immediate payment in full of all sums secured by this Security Instrument without further demand and may invoke the power of sale and any other remedies permitted by applicable law. Lender shall be entitled to collect all expenses incurred in pursuing the remedies provided in this paragraph 21, including, but not limited to, reasonable attorneys' fees and costs of title evidence.

If Lender invokes the power of sale, Lender shall execute or cause Trustee to execute a written notice of the occurrence of an event of default and of Lender's election to cause the Property to be sold and shall cause such notice to be recorded in each county in which any part of the Property is located. Lender or Trustee shall give notice of sale in the manner prescribed by applicable law to Borrower and to other persons prescribed by applicable law. After the time required by applicable law, Trustee, without demand on Borrower, shall sell the Property at public auction to the highest bidder at the time and place and under the terms designated in the notice of sale in one or more parcels and in any order Trustee determines. Trustee may postpone sale of all or any parcel of the Property by public announcement at the time and place of any previously scheduled sale. Lender or its designee may purchase the Property at any sale.

Trustee shall deliver to the purchaser Trustee's deed conveying the Property without any covenant or warranty, expressed or implied. The recitals in the Trustee's deed shall be prima facie evidence of the truth of the statements made therein. Trustee shall apply the proceeds of the sale in the following order: (a) to all expenses of the sale, including, but not limited to, reasonable Trustee's and attorneys' fees; (b) to all sums secured by this Security Instrument; and (c) any excess to the person or persons legally entitled to it.

22. **Reconveyance.** Upon payment of all sums secured by this Security Instrument, Lender shall request Trustee to reconvey the Property and shall surrender this Security Instrument and all notes evidencing debt secured by this Security Instrument to Trustee. Trustee shall reconvey the Property without warranty to the person or persons legally entitled to it. Such person or persons shall pay any recordation costs. Lender may charge such person or persons a fee for reconveying the Property, but only if the fee is paid to a third party (such as the Trustee) for services rendered and the charging of the fee is permitted under applicable law.

23. **Substitute Trustee.** Lender may from time to time remove Trustee and appoint a successor trustee to any Trustee appointed hereunder. Without conveyance of the Property, the successor trustee shall succeed to all the title, power and duties conferred upon Trustee herein and by applicable law.

24. **Attorneys' Fees.** As used in this Security Instrument and in the Note, "attorneys' fees" shall include any attorneys' fees awarded by an appellate court.

25. **Riders to this Security Instrument.** If one or more riders are executed by Borrower and recorded together with this Security Instrument, the covenants and agreements of each such rider shall be incorporated into and shall amend and supplement the covenants and agreements of this Security Instrument as if the rider(s) were a part of this Security Instrument. [Check applicable box(es)].

☐ Adjustable Rate Rider	☐ Condominium Rider	☐ 1-4 Family Rider
☐ Graduated Payment Rider	☐ Planned Unit Development Rider	☐ Biweekly Payment Rider
☐ Balloon Rider	☐ Rate Improvement Rider	☐ Second Home Rider
☐ Other(s) [specify]		

BY SIGNING BELOW, Borrower accepts and agrees to the terms and covenants contained in this Security Instrument and in any rider(s) executed by Borrower and recorded with it.

Witnesses:

_____   _____(Seal)
                                                                    -(Borrower)

_____   _____(Seal)
                                                                    -(Borrower)

                                      _____(Seal)
                                                                    -(Borrower)

                                      _____(Seal)
                                                                    -(Borrower)

_____ [Space Below This Line For Acknowledgment] _____

STATE OF OREGON,   **County ss:**

On this_____day of_____,_____, personally appeared the above named

                                                                    and acknowledged
the foregoing instrument to be _____voluntary act and deed.

My Commission Expires: Before me:
(Official Seal)   _____
                                              Notary Public for Oregon

FIGURE 10-3   Continued

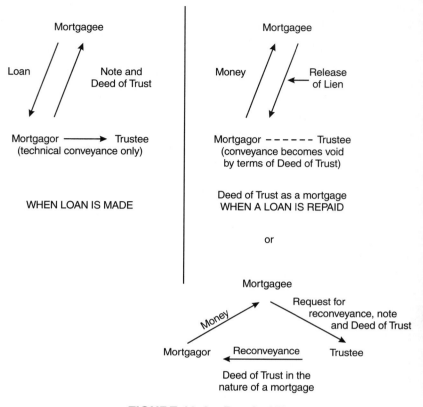

FIGURE 10-4   Deed of Trust

mortgagee is typically the only bidder. When the nonjudicial foreclosure sale is properly conducted, it has the same effect as a judicial foreclosure. Therefore, all persons claiming an interest under or through the mortgagor lose their interest when the foreclosure sale is completed. Title acquired by a foreclosure sale relates back to the date the deed of trust was recorded, extinguishing all subsequent liens and ownership interests, subject to the various rights of redemption, *L. M. Sullivan Co., Inc.* v. *Essex Broadway Sav. Bank*, 380 A.2d 1087 (N.H. 1977).

Since the foreclosure sale under a deed of trust is usually a nonjudicial proceeding, the mortgagor cannot appeal it directly. On the other hand, he can initiate a lawsuit to enjoin the sale prior to its taking place, or to set aside the sale after it has taken place upon proof of irregularities (e.g., violations of contractual rights). However, if the mortgagor was properly notified and the foreclosure sale was properly executed, it will seldom be set aside. Although this may seem somewhat harsh to the mortgagor, he still may be able to regain title under the statutory right of redemption existing in some states (see following discussion and Table 10-1).

AFTER FORECLOSURE

If the foreclosure sale proceeds exceed the sum of the existing mortgage debt and the foreclosure sale expenses, such excess will be paid to the mortgagor. The mortgagee is never entitled to more money than the principal and interest due, plus the expenses incurred to collect the overdue debt. On the other hand, if the proceeds are insufficient to satisfy the outstanding debt, in most states the mortgagee may obtain a *deficiency judgment* against the mortgagor. This means that the mortgagor still has the legal obligation to pay the unpaid balance of the loan. However, as a practical matter, this debt may be difficult to collect, since the mortgagee has lost his security (the real estate sold at foreclosure) and the mortgagee no longer has a "lien" on any of the mortgagor's specific assets. This places the mortgagee in a similar position to the mortgagor's other *general,* or *unsecured,* creditors.

Equity of Redemption and Statutory Redemption

At one time in history, any failure to meet a mortgage payment in a timely fashion automatically caused the mortgagor to lose his entire interest in the land. Because of the severity of this penalty, the law gradually moved toward legal solutions that were less financially devastating to borrowers. These solutions that evolved included an *equitable redemption* and a *statutory redemption* for the mortgagor.

The *equitable redemption* is available in all states to prevent foreclosure. It permits a mortgagor to prevent foreclosure from occurring by paying the mortgagee the principal and interest due, plus any expenses the mortgagee has incurred in attempting to collect the debt and in initiating foreclosure proceedings. Equitable redemption may be exercised by mortgagors, junior mortgagees, the mortgagor's heir and devisees, any other party potentially adversely affected by foreclosure, and by anyone who buys the *equity of redemption (right to redeem)* from the mortgagor.

Most courts have generally ruled that an equitable right of redemption may not be waived, and that waiver clauses in a mortgage are null and void, although this is not always the case, *U.S.* v. *Stadium Apartments,* 425 F.2d 358. Legally, these courts hold that an equitable right of redemption is automatically a part of every mortgage and cannot be contractually modified by the parties. To decide otherwise would be somewhat unfair to mortgagors, as some lenders might otherwise refuse to lend unless the equity of redemption was waived.

Statutory redemption rights, on the other hand, permit a mortgagor to redeem (retrieve) mortgaged property after the foreclosure sale. Not all states permit statutory redemption, and in those that do permit it, the maximum permissible redemption time period varies from six months to two years (see Table 10-1).

Lien Priority   A foreclosure sale generally extinguishes all inferior lien interests and real property interests (including leases!), *R-Ranch Markets No. 2* v. *Old Stone Bank,* 21 Cal Rptr. 21 (Cal. App.—1993)). For this reason, the holders of inferior liens often bid on and/or buy property at foreclosure sales to make sure the sale price is sufficient to cover the outstanding loan balance owed them. Alternatively, as previously suggested, inferior lien holders may exercise the equity of redemption to protect their lien interest.

If the foreclosure sale covers only a defaulted inferior lien holder's interest (rather than the interest of the first lien holder), the property is sold subject to the superior security interests. In that situation, the purchaser must make the payments on the prior existing indebtedness. He is considered to be *subrogated,* or placed in the position of the original mortgagor on the inferior lien. Thus, in the foreclosure process the purchaser at a foreclosure sale is said to have acquired the right to "redeem up," and the trustee or court "forecloses down." This simply means that foreclosure dissolves all inferior interests, and the foreclosure sale purchaser acquires the right to pay off the superior interests.

Lien priorities generally follow the so-called "barber shop rule," meaning that the first in time gets priority. Priority is established by compliance with recording acts (see discussion in Chapter 9), however, so both lack of knowledge of previous mortgages and the date that competing mortgages are recorded are important factors in determining priority of mortgage payment in case of foreclosure.

ADDITIONAL   It is often said that lenders operate under the "golden rule"; that is,
MORTGAGE OR   "They have the gold, so they make the rules!" Therefore, one often
DEED OF TRUST   finds that, in addition to the basic legal requirements, there are
PROVISIONS   other provisions in mortgages or deeds of trust that are added to protect the lender's interest. The lender needs to be sure that no additional conflicting claims may arise in his security, and that the real estate is kept in good enough condition so that the value of his security in the real estate is not impaired. Provisions included in the deed of trust instrument in Figure 10-3 include the requirements for payment of all taxes and assessments, requirements to

keep the property adequately insured, provisions for a substitute trustee, and provisions for bankruptcy. Other common provisions that one may encounter when reading various deed of trust instruments are shown in the example in Figure 10-3 and include the assignment of rentals, condemnation, partial releases, due-on clause, and no personal liability provision. All of these will be discussed below.

Assignment of Rentals

Assignment of rentals normally assures the lender that in the event that the subject property is leased or rented, he is entitled to the rentals obtained from that property if he so requests. This helps ensure that periodic mortgage payments will be received in a timely fashion.

Condemnation

The proceeds from a condemnation sale usually are paid directly to the lender and applied against the unpaid balance of the note. This helps assure that the property remaining after condemnation will be of sufficient value to adequately secure the now smaller balance on the note.

Partial Releases

Partial releases are used to provide clear title to someone who purchases part of the property secured by a mortgage. Partial releases are given by lenders under conditions carefully set out in the mortgage instrument (or deed of trust). The lender's main concern is that the remaining land still subject to the mortgage is of sufficient value to provide adequate security for the payment of the remaining debt. Partial release clauses are commonly utilized in loans to subdivision developers. Certain areas of a subdivision may be more valuable than others, and such differences in value must be taken into consideration in specifying the loan payments and conditions required for the granting of partial releases. Otherwise it is possible for a lender to find himself with a loan balance exceeding the value of the remaining secured property.

Due-On Clause

A "due-on" or "due-on-sale" clause, often called a *call* clause, provides that the mortgagor may not convey the property to another party without first paying off the note or renegotiating the interest rate. In essence, this precludes a purchaser from assuming an existing mortgage. Due-on-sale clauses may eliminate an important incentive for buyers to purchase property that has a mortgage on it, particularly when the interest rate on the current mortgage is substantially lower than that available on new mortgage loans. On the other hand, due-on-sale clauses protect lenders by giving them an opportunity to make a new loan on terms that are more favorable to them.

There are two main items of contention regarding "due-on-sale" clauses: (1) in inflationary times, lenders view due-on-sale clauses as necessary for their economic security, if not economic survival, but (2) borrowers see due-on-sale clauses as unfair, as an unreasonable restraint on title transfer opportunities, and as an attempt to "gouge" the public for purely economic reasons. The basic difference of opinion (between lenders and borrowers) has resulted in extensive litigation. There are some states that tend to favor automatic enforcement of the "due-on-sale" clause, including Colorado, Illinois, Nevada, New Hampshire, New Jersey, New York, North Carolina, Ohio, Texas, and Tennessee. Those states that tend not to approve this clause, unless a mortgage assumption results in a material detriment to the security interest, are Alabama, Arizona, Arkansas, Florida, Michigan, Mississippi, Oklahoma, and California. However, all states tend to look for equitable and just results when the case merits it. There are so many exceptions and extreme fact situations that a lot of the due-on-sale litigations are determined on a case-by-case basis.

Some states have attempted to define their position statutorily, but this also created conflicts. In an effort to remedy these inconsistencies between states, Congress passed the Garn-St. Germain Depository Institutions Act of 1982. A part of this statute is the federal government's preemption of state laws prohibiting enforcement of due-on-sale clauses "notwithstanding any provision of the Constitution or laws (including the judicial decisions) of any State to the contrary" [§341(b)l]. This preemption was reinforced in one case wherein it was held that the preemption can override state laws because it is enabled by the supremacy clause of the United States Constitution [Article VI, Clause 2], *Fidelity Federal Savings and Loan Association* v. *de la Cuesta,* 102 S.Ct. 3014 (1982). Therefore, federal law will control over any contravening state law.

If there is a loan secured by a lien on residential real property of one to four dwelling units, under Garn-St. Germain, a lender may not exercise his option pursuant to a due-on-sale clause upon the following items:

1. The creation of a lien or other encumbrance subordinate to the lender's security instrument which does not relate to the transfer of rights of occupancy in the property.
2. The creation of a purchase money security interest for household appliances.

3. A transfer by devise, dissent, or operation of law on the death of a joint tenant or a tenant by the entirety.

4. A leasehold interest of three years or less, not containing an option to purchase.

5. A transfer to a relative resulting from the death of the borrower.

6. A transfer when the spouse or the children of the borrower become owner(s) of the property.

7. A transfer resulting from a decree of dissolution of a marriage, legal separation agreement, or from an incidental property settlement agreement, by which the spouse of the borrower becomes an owner of the property.

8. A transfer into an *inter vivos* trust in which the borrower is and remains a beneficiary and which does not relate to a transfer of rights of occupancy in the property, or any other transfer of disposition described in regulations prescribed by the Federal Home Loan Bank Board.

The Act also provides an encouragement clause that requires national banks to blend the previous rate with the current rate. Prepayment penalties may not be imposed by the lenders when exercising their due-on-transfer clauses. The acceleration of the indebtedness eliminates prepayment, *American Federal Savings and Loan Association of Madison* v. *Mid-America Service Corp.*, 329 N.W.2d 124 (S.D. 1983).

Many practitioners and brokers have attempted to get around due-on-sale clauses by redefining the "transfer" of the property so it would not constitute a sale. According to the Federal Home Loan Bank Board rules, however, these attempts to get around the due-on-sale clauses will probably not be effective. A "sale or transfer" by their rules includes the "conveyance of real property or any right, title, or interest therein, whether legal or equitable, whether voluntary or involuntary, by outright sale, deed, installment sale contract, land contract, contract for deed, leasehold interest with a term greater than three years, lease option contract, or any other method of conveyance of real property interest."

Apparently, unless state statute declares otherwise, the due-on-sale provisions are facts of life now, unless you are within a state "window period." They are enforceable and must be complied with.

On occasion, a borrower is fortunate enough to have a lender who is so confident as to the value of the real estate that he will provide   *No Personal Liability* that, in the event of default, he will not seek a money judgment against the purchaser but will limit his remedies to foreclosing and retaking possession of the real estate. This is one form of nonrecourse financing.

Why Have Two Instruments?

A question that is anticipated when discussing mortgages is, Why are there two separate instruments, the promissory note and the mortgage? The reason for this is fairly simple but is often overlooked. The promissory note, being the actual promise to pay, is considered a *negotiable instrument* (the mortgage is not). This means that the promissory note, similar to a bank draft, can be endorsed on the back and sold to an investor. This is a very common practice in the mortgage business, in which mortgage companies will often sell millions of dollars in loans using the promissory note as the primary instrument of transfer. The new note holder, then, becomes *subrogated* to (stands in the same place as) the rights of the previous note holder, giving him the right to enforce payment. The purchaser of the promissory note becomes a *holder in due course*, which means he takes the note free and clear of all defenses that the maker may have, except for fraud in the inducement. This gives the purchaser of the note a very privileged status, since all the endorsers of this note, including the primary lender, have guaranteed that the payments will be made on the note.

Legally, since a promissory note is a negotiable instrument, it is considered to be an unconditional promise to pay by the maker of the note. There should be no other conditions to payment, and most cases have held that the obligation of the maker to pay the note is absolute. There can be exceptions when a note holder consistently accepts late payments, but the general rule is that the holder of the note has the absolute right to accelerate all the payments (call the total amount of the note due) when one payment is a day late. This, in turn, gives him the right to foreclose under the deed of trust which secures the payment of that note. This is true even if the mortgage hasn't been assigned to the new note holder, as the right to foreclose under the old mortgage also passes to the new note holder.

The separate promissory note also creates other misconceptions. For instance, when a person refinances his house, he often merely renegotiates his note to reflect different payments, a different interest rate, different term, or other method of payment. The note may still be secured by the same mortgage that was originally in existence, but that might be extended (or renewed) to include the payments on the new note in place of the previous note.

The mortgage, on the other hand, is the document that evidences a lien interest against the real estate. This is normally recorded to reflect the lender's interest in the real estate. It then becomes part of the official public records of the county in which the property is located.

Both instruments serve entirely different functions, but are dependent on each other to effect a sufficient promise to pay and perfect a lien interest in real estate.

Although true mortgages and deeds of trust are by far the most commonly used mortgage instruments, there are a number of other types of mortgages and mortgaging techniques. Some are different mortgage instruments altogether, and others may be mortgages or deeds of trust with special provisions to achieve a particular purpose.

OTHER TYPES OF MORTGAGES

In lien theory states there are times when a lender will request that the mortgagor (borrower/purchaser) give the lender a deed to the property as a method of mortgaging. This may be preferable to taking a lower lien status of property that is already encumbered. Although a transfer of legal title does take effect, the parties intend this transfer to assure the lender's security rather than being a complete sale of the property. When this occurs, one normally finds that the grantor retains possession of the premises and that the market value of the property is in excess of the consideration given for the transfer. This technique is similar to true mortgages in title theory states (where the lender is determined to have legal title and the mortgagor merely a lien on the real estate). When the property is fully paid for, the mortgagee executes another deed (sometimes called a *release deed)* or reconveys the property to the mortgagor. When an absolute deed is used as a mortgage, it is necessary that parol evidence be allowed to show the clear import of the deed, even though the deed itself may be clear and unambiguous on its face. This is one of the few exceptions to a strict application of the parol evidence rule. (See parol evidence rule discussion in Chapter 7.)

Absolute Deed as a Mortgage

The instruments used for a mortgage pursuant to the sale and lease-back method normally include a deed and a lease; and, if the sale is not for cash, a mortgage or deed of trust may also be used. In a typical sale and lease-back situation, an owner will sell his property for cash to an investor. He will then lease the property

Sale and Lease-Back

back from him. This has the effect of guaranteeing a definite rate of return on the purchaser's investment.

To illustrate, Acme Manufacturing Company may sell its plant, improvements, and other facilities to B. T. Operator for a cash payment of $100,000. At the same time the deed is signed, Acme Manufacturing Company executes a lease, as tenant, with B. T. Operator as landlord, at a rate of $11,000 per year. This essentially guarantees an 11% return cash-on-cash investment for B. T. Operator. Figure 10-5 graphically illustrates this transaction.

Advantages. In the transaction in Figure 10-5, the Acme Manufacturing Company obtains a free and clear $100,000 in working capital, which it can use to expand, make capital improvements, and streamline its manufacturing efficiency, instead of having it tied up in real estate. Most companies would like to utilize their money in income-producing manufacturing methods rather than as a capital investment in non-income-producing real estate. To make the transaction more attractive, there may be a provision in the lease for an option to buy the property back for a relatively low price at the end of 30 years (the regular amortization period of a loan).

The sale and lease-back transaction benefits the purchaser because he is assured of a definite return on his investment. He can also deduct the depreciation for the improvements on the proper-

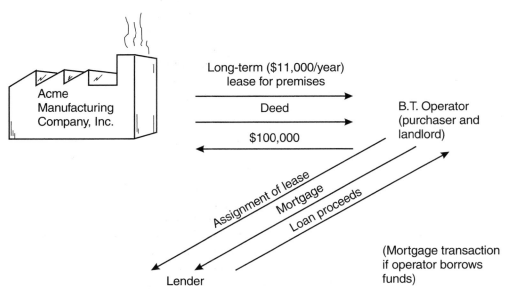

FIGURE 10-5   Illustration of a Sale and Lease-Back Transaction

ty. If he has borrowed the money to finance the transaction, he can further deduct the interest paid on his loan. This may provide substantial income tax advantages for the purchaser.

The advantages for the seller, the Acme Manufacturing Company, are that it can pay a tax-deductible lease payment every month, and it receives a large influx of working capital (which is normally utilized to improve its monthly cash flow). It may also get a capital gain tax treatment upon the sale of the property (the tax on which might be thought of as part of the cost of acquiring capital), and it has the option to repurchase the property if a repurchase option is included in the lease.

If multiple sites are concerned (e.g., Pizza Hut, Dunkin' Donuts), the company can effectively get long-term financing at very favorable rates (below prime) by seeking private investors looking for tax benefits and higher returns than from savings deposits.

Disadvantages.   Although the sale and lease-back example may suggest a perfect relationship in which everyone appears to come out ahead, there also may be disadvantages. The primary disadvantage is the possible adverse position of the Internal Revenue Service (IRS). If the transaction is not carefully done, or if there is too close a relationship between the buyer and the seller, the IRS may choose to treat the transaction as a loan rather than as a true sale. If such is the case, the tax ramifications are dramatically different. In determining how to treat the sale and lease-back transaction, the IRS normally looks to the intention of the parties surrounding the circumstances of the lease agreement itself, whether or not the option to repurchase is legitimate or appears to be a sham, whether or not the price of the sale is related to fair market value, and the appropriateness and size of the rental payments.

If done properly, the sale and lease-back can be a tremendous benefit as a mortgage instrument, both for the purchaser and the seller, if they can avoid the pitfalls of the Internal Revenue Code, and if the transaction is done in good faith and is not a sham.

Installment Land Contracts

An *installment land contract* (frequently known as a *contract for deed*) is a very effective means of providing a mortgage, particularly for low-income transactions or for transactions for which financing isn't readily available (e.g., farms and high-risk property). An installment land contract provides for seller financing pursuant to the terms set out in it. Since the seller is financing the sale himself, he can establish his own criteria as to the creditworthiness and risks involved in evaluating the purchaser. The purchaser buys the realty in accordance with the installment land contract, usually for a small down payment, and when he has completed the full number of monthly payments, normally for a term of years, the seller will convey the property to the purchaser by execution of a deed.

As discussed in Chapter 7, there is no concern for foreclosure. The contract is simply forfeited and rescinded in the event of default. There are obviously risks involved for the purchaser, because the seller may not have clear title at the time the purchase price is fully paid (see discussion in Chapter 7). However, if the seller operates in good faith, this technique provides a very efficient means by which low-income families can buy housing without having to qualify for a loan or go through the red tape of mortgage insurance and financial statements, and having to sit across from the glare of a suspicious lender's interrogation. The contract document itself is the mortgage instrument, and it may contain many onerous provisions. Again, the "golden rule" applies.

For the seller who is not a "dealer," there are additional tax benefits in that he can report his income from the installment land contract over a period of years, rather than taking all of his profit on the sale of the house in his first year. However, there are pitfalls in that the Internal Revenue Service may consider the installment land contract to be a lease rather than an actual sale. The seller may then have to declare the income as ordinary income rather than as capital gains. As in the sale and lease-back situation, great care should be taken to be sure that the transaction is truly bona fide and not a sham.

Installment land contracts may be harsh to buyers, such as when 90% of the purchase price has been paid when default occurs. For this reason, in some jurisdictions forfeiture protection is provided for buyers and in others the use of installment land contract provisions is looked on with judicial disfavor.

Construction Mortgages   A construction mortgage normally utilizes the standard deed of trust or mortgage form, but it contains special provisions because of (1) the short-term nature of this type of mortgage, (2) the requirements of partial advances while construction is in progress, and (3) the incorporation of certain items of personalty into the real estate in which the lender wants to maintain a prior security interest.

Mortgages of this type are often set up as tri-party agreements in which the permanent lender (mortgagee), the construction lender (usually a local bank), and the mortgagor enter into an agreement by which the permanent lender promises to pay off the construction lender's mortgage upon completion of the construction to the permanent mortgagee's satisfaction. When the construction lender is paid by the permanent lender, the mortgagor then begins making his monthly payments to the permanent lender. The interest rate on construction loans is generally somewhat higher than that on permanent loans, and the construction lender is normally a local financing institution that can personally inspect the construction on a daily basis. The permanent lender is often located in another state and is not staffed to maintain this type of inspection policy on a routine day-to-day basis.

Special provisions that one may find in a construction loan mortgage normally include what is called a *dragnet* clause or *future advance* clause, which secures all sums loaned or advanced by the construction lender to the account of the mortgagor. The mortgage may also include an *additional property* clause, which provides for any property attached at a later date to the premises to also be secured by the deed of trust. However, even if there are additional property clauses contained in the construction deed of trust (mortgage), a mechanics' and materialmen's lien is superior to that deed of trust (mortgage) if the additional property placed there by the mechanic or materialman can be removed without material injury to the property, *First National Bank of Dallas* v. *Whirlpool Corporation*, 502 S.W.2d 185 and *Ault* v. *Harris* 317 F. Supp. 373.

If an owner's mortgage does not contain a due-on clause, there are two methods by which property can be conveyed without having to change the terms of, or pay off, the original mortgage note. One method involves an *assumption* of the mortgagor's existing indebtedness; the second involves buying the property *subject* to the existing indebtedness.

TRANSFER OF THE MORTGAGOR'S INTEREST

In the assumption loan situation, the grantee of the property becomes primarily liable on the note and mortgage, whereas the grantor operates as a surety in the event the note is not paid in full. If there is a default on the note, the lender must pursue his remedy against the grantee first; but if the grantee cannot satisfy the indebtedness, the lender then may sue the original grantor as the original signatory party on the note and mortgage. It is sometimes a surprise to the grantor (when he sells his house on an assumption basis) that if there is a subsequent default, he may still be liable on that note at some later date. Figure 10-6 graphically shows how the assumption procedure takes effect.

Assumption

When property is sold *subject to* an existing mortgage, the grantee does not become personally obligated to pay off the mortgage but

Subject To

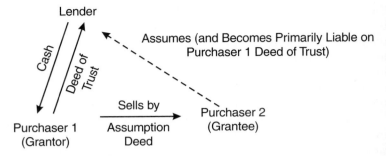

FIGURE 10-6   *Illustration of an Assumption of an Existing Mortgage*

merely has the option of paying the mortgage if he so chooses. The grantor remains primarily liable on the note, and the grantee has no obligation at all to the original lender. Figure 10-7 illustrates how the "subject to" mortgage situation takes effect. It represents another type of nonrecourse financing, because it does not personally obligate the purchaser to pay the existing mortgage.

If there is a *call clause* in the original mortgage, the assumption situation normally cannot take effect until the subsequent grantee has been approved by the lender. In the subject to situation, however, since the original mortgagor remains primarily liable on the note, there is some question as to whether it requires the approval of the lender before such a conveyance can take place. After all, the lender's security is not impaired because the original mortgagor is

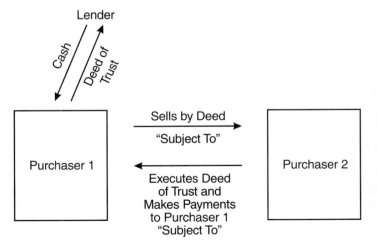

FIGURE 10-7   *Illustration of Purchasing Property Subject to an Existing Mortgage*

still personally liable on the note, whereas this fact does not exist in the assumption situation.

Commercial transactions and land syndication schemes have made widespread use of the subject to mortgage, particularly in a form commonly called a *wrap-around mortgage.* The property is conveyed by a deed subject to the existing mortgage, and a second mortgage between the grantor and grantee is signed by the grantee subject to, but not promising to pay, the prior existing mortgage. The payments made on the mortgage to the grantor include amounts to be paid to the first lien holder. The wrap-around mortgage has basically the same effect as creating a large second lien deed of trust, except that the obligation of the grantee is to pay the entire mortgage amount to the grantor, and the grantor, in turn, has the obligation to pay the lender (first lien holder) the lesser mortgage amount owed by the grantor.

Wrap-Around Mortgage

This type of financing became so common during the rampant real estate syndication craze in the early 1970s that it is not uncommon to see extended chains of wrap-around mortgages, similar to the illustration in Figure 10-8.

Advantages. The wrap-around mortgage provides advantages to both the buyer and the seller similar to those of installment land sale contracts. Since the grantor is selling to the grantee *subject to* the existing mortgage, normally no outside financing has to be obtained by the grantee, and this results in the basic seller-financing situation. Since the grantee pays the grantor, this method also avoids the risks of the more typical second lien situation, since the

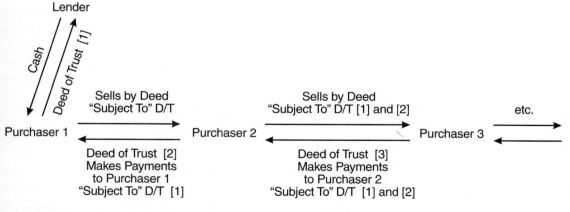

FIGURE 10-8   Illustration of a Wrap-Around Mortgage

grantee must pay the grantor directly. The grantor, then, is always sure that the first lien mortgage payments are being made. If there is a default in the initial payment, the grantor is immediately on notice and can exercise his right of foreclosure to reinstate his interest in the property before there is a default to the primary lender.

The terms of a sale of this kind are usually more attractive to a seller than sales utilizing more conventional financing techniques. For example, the sale price is normally higher, there is a higher interest yield, and the seller can normally take an installment sale advantage as a tax benefit (see income tax discussion in Chapter 18). The buyer's advantage generally centers on the fact that he deals with the seller and lender directly, so he can get more attractive terms (interest only, or perhaps longer terms), and there are no credit requirements or loans to apply for.

Disadvantages. A major disadvantage to a wrap-around note and mortgage is that the buyer runs the risk that the seller may not pay off the prior lien note(s). In that event, even though the purchaser has paid his note, he may lose his ownership interest when the prior lender forecloses. This problem can sometimes be overcome by the use of a third-party escrow agent. In that case, the grantee pays the escrow agent, and the escrow agent pays the required payment to the lender and the remainder to the grantor. This assures the subsequent grantee that all obligations pursuant to the prior existing mortgages have been met.

There has been little case law to date and little information as to the effect that the court will give these mortgages. Each grantee may also find additional liability as he changes his status from grantee to grantor, because he may undertake the additional obligation to assure his grantee that the prior mortgage payments are made, *Newson* v. *Starkey*, 541 S.W.2d 468.

The wrap-around mortgage has proved to be an effective tool for creating installment sales and for obtaining easy financing. For investment groups, it has not been at all uncommon for the property to be conveyed using the wrap-around mortgage several times without the primary lien holder ever being paid in full. The more this type of mortgage is used in a sequencing chain of sales and purchases, however, the bigger the risks the subsequent grantees are forced to take.

SUMMARY   Arranging acceptable financing is a key factor leading to the consummation of many real estate transactions. Interest rates, proportion of sale price that can be borrowed, length of debt repayment period, and the rights and liabilities associated with alternative mortgage instruments are all important considerations.

The two most common instruments used to protect lenders making real estate loans are the mortgage and deed of trust. Both of these instruments are used in conjunction with a promissory note, which is the actual promise to pay.

The rights created when these instruments are executed vary, depending on whether a particular state follows title theory or lien theory. With the former, the lender receives title to the mortgaged real estate. With the latter, he only receives a security interest or lien against the land.

There are two parties to a mortgage. The borrower is called the *mortgagor,* and the lender is the *mortgagee.*

At one time a mortgagor lost his entire interest in the land and forfeited all monies paid toward purchase if he defaulted on the terms of the note. To avoid this harsh and unfair result, both the "equity of redemption" and the right of statutory redemption exist in some states. Both permit the mortgagor to get the property back upon paying foreclosure expenses. The equity of redemption may be exercised prior to foreclosure, while statutory redemption rights exist after foreclosure in some states. Generally, it is not possible to waive an equity of redemption; so clauses placed in mortgages and deeds of trust that purport to do so are simply null, void, and of no legal effect.

Foreclosure refers to the process required for terminating a defaulting mortgagor's right to the property, and includes selling the land to pay the outstanding debt due the mortgagee. Court action is required to foreclose a regular mortgage, but the deed of trust authorizes a nonjudicial foreclosure proceeding. The latter is generally a much quicker and less expensive procedure.

Foreclosure is voided altogether under a conditional land sales contract. Since the seller holds title under it until the debt is fully paid, he need do nothing to protect his interests if the mortgagor should default.

Unlike a true mortgage and a conditional land sales contract, a deed of trust involves three parties: mortgagor, trustee, and mortgagee. The trustee simply holds a power of sale in case of default, which generally permits him to sell the property at the courthouse door after giving proper public notice of the impending public sale.

Depending on the state, there may be several requirements for making mortgages and deeds of trust enforceable. There must be a granting clause naming the grantor and grantee, describing the real property involved, and outlining the interest being conveyed. A warranty clause also exists stating that the grantor's title is good and sufficient. In a deed of trust, the trust relationship must be clearly set out and the power of sale specified.

The amount of the promissory note being received is usually set out, although the terms of the note may be incorporated by reference.

If and when foreclosure occurs, all inferior liens are dissolved, so inferior lien holders generally attend foreclosure sales and bid on the property to protect their interests. If the foreclosure is of an inferior lien, the purchaser acquires the right to pay off all superior lien interests.

Other common provisions found in many mortgages and deeds of trust include requirements for the payment of property taxes and special assessments, adequate insurance coverage, substitute trustee(s), rights existing in case of bankruptcy, assignment of rentals, distribution of condemnation proceeds, rights to and procedure for obtaining partial releases, due-on transfer clauses, and nonrecourse financing.

The creation of a mortgage requires two legal instruments: a mortgage or deed of trust, and a promissory note. The latter is the actual promise to pay. It is a negotiable instrument and may be sold to investors. This fact has led to the development of mortgage companies that market large numbers of notes and mortgages.

Important features found in promissory notes include:

- The actual promise to pay.
- The principal amount.
- The interest rate, additional interest provisions for past due principal and interest.
- Due dates for payments.
- Prepayment privileges and penalties.
- Acceleration of the entire debt to become due upon default.
- Mortgagor's responsibility to pay mortgagee's attorney fees if legal proceedings are required to collect the debt.
- Waiver of notice as to when payments are due.
- Creation of any vendor's, mortgage, or deed of trust liens.
- The legal description of the secured property.
- The mortgagor(s)' signatures.

There are other types of mortgages and mortgaging techniques. An absolute deed conveying title to a lender may be construed as a mortgage if the intent to create a mortgage can be proven by parol evidence. An exception to the parol evidence rule permits the use of parol evidence for this limited purpose.

The sale and lease-back technique is a method of acquiring funds in which real property is sold and then leased back from the purchaser. Buy-back privileges are often provided for, after a specified time period. If structured correctly, this technique can be attractive to both parties.

Installment land contracts are often used to provide seller financing. They may be the only source of financing available to certain parties who have been judged poor credit risks by commercial lending institutions. These contracts are somewhat risky to buyers, because the seller may have clear title at the time the contract is entered into, but not at the time he is to convey title. For this reason, title insurance companies generally will not insure a title to be transferred under an installment land sale contract.

Construction mortgages are short-term in nature and are created to provide funds needed for construction. Generally, such funds are distributed at the completion of major project phases rather than in one lump sum prior to construction. When combined with visual inspection of the property, this helps assure the lender that sufficient security exists to recover his money if default occurs. When construction is completed, the construction mortgagee is generally paid in full, and long-term financing is taken out with a permanent lender.

When purchasing property on which a mortgage currently exists, the parties have three options. One is to pay off the current mortgage and execute a new one. A second is for the purchaser to assume the existing mortgage. The final option is to purchase the property subject to the existing mortgage.

The major distinction between "assuming" and purchasing "subject to" an existing mortgage is in the liabilities facing the new owner. He is primarily liable to pay off the mortgage when he assumes it, but he has no legal responsibility to pay it off when he buys under a subject to arrangement. The latter is a variation of nonrecourse financing and gives the purchaser the option of walking away from a deal without the fear of further liability on the promissory note.

Wrap-around mortgages involve purchasing property subject to an existing mortgage, but also involve a second mortgage that is "wrapped around" the first. The buyer generally provides all funds for the payment of both mortgages, but the seller or an escrow agent has the responsibility to make the required payments on the first mortgage. Wrap-arounds are often used by syndications and others when the existing mortgage's interest rate is lower than the rate currently available, or perhaps where a substantial prepayment penalty will be required if it is paid off.

DISCUSSION QUESTIONS

1. What mortgage instruments, types of foreclosure, and statutory redemption period exist in your state?

2. What is the difference between title theory states and lien theory states?

3. What are the advantages and disadvantages of a sale and leaseback arrangement?

4. What are the differences between assuming an existing mortgage and purchasing property subject to an existing mortgage?

5. What is the effect of foreclosure on junior lien holders?

11

Regulations Affecting Real Estate Lending

The mortgagor–mortgagee relationship is one of the last vestiges of true free enterprise. The lender (mortgagee) makes an effort to maximize the return on investment, and the borrower (mortgagor) "shops around" at various savings and loan associations, mortgage companies, and other primary lending sources in an effort to find the best rates for his loan. There has been serious effort, however, on the part of state and federal governments to protect borrowers and consumers from loan sharks, "sharpies," and con artists who abuse their expertise in the mortgage and lending business. The tongue-in-cheek "golden rule" that was referred to in the previous chapter cannot extend itself to violate public policy, to discriminate, or to promote unconstitutional objectives. In addition, the legislatures (both state and federal) have made a concerted effort to effect disclosure of loan costs (finance charges), provide equal credit opportunity, and limit the amount of interest that can be charged. There are few areas of lending that more directly affect the consumer than these areas of federal and state regulation of real estate lending.

To begin with, two distinctly separate areas of the law deal with the cost of obtaining money: a state law and a federal law.

TRUTH-IN-LENDING ACT

Originally passed in 1968, the Federal Consumer Credit Protection Act, under Title I of the Truth-in-Lending Act (T-i-L Act), required extensive disclosure by creditors when making loans to consumers. The T-i-L Act placed the job of implementing the act on the Board of Governors of the Federal Reserve System. This was accomplished by the board's promulgation of Regulation Z (Reg. Z), an exhaustive publication dealing with almost every imaginable area of extension of credit. There are entire sets of books written on these regulations alone (not to mention the interpretative rulings, public information letters, staff opinions, or published forms), and there will be little attempt made here to explain anything but the most general applications of the T-i-L Act.

The purpose of the T-i-L Act is to assure that everyone being extended commercial credit by a creditor covered by the act is given meaningful disclosures with respect to the cost of the credit being extended. The disclosures must be clear and according to the statutory forms published pursuant to the T-i-L Act and Reg. Z.

Creditors covered by the T-i-L Act must comply fully with all Reg. Z requirements if four conditions are met:

1. The credit is offered or extended to consumers (must be natural persons).
2. The credit is offered and extended regularly (for transactions secured by dwellings, more than five times in a preceding year).
3. The credit is subject to "finance charge" *or* payable by written agreement in more than four installments.
4. The credit is extended primarily for personal, family, or household purposes.

The disclosures must be made in terms of deferred *finance charge* and *annual percentage rate* (APR), so that the consumer will clearly understand what is being disclosed to him.

Finance charge is defined as:

> ... the sum of all charges, payable directly or indirectly by the creditor as an incident to or as a condition of the extension of credit, whether paid or payable by the customer, the seller, or any other person on behalf of the customer to the creditor or a third party ... [Reg. Z, Section 226.4(a)].

The APR is the rate charged (expressed as a percentage) as determined by applying the federal government's definition of *finance charge* to the federal government's definition of *consumer credit*. The finance charge is not necessarily *interest* as defined by state statute. A Reg. Z disclosure form is shown in Figure 11-1. It is important to note that there are exemptions and exclusions from the determination of finance charges as they apply to certain real

	BORROWER			**FIXED RATE**

FIXED RATE
TRUTH-IN-LENDING
DISCLOSURE
STATEMENT

BORROWER

ADDRESS

TELEPHONE NO.   IDENTIFICATION NO.

OFFICER INITIALS	INTEREST RATE	PRINCIPAL AMOUNT	FUNDING DATE	MATURITY DATE	CUSTOMER NUMBER	LOAN NUMBER

TRUTH-IN-LENDING DISCLOSURE STATEMENT

ANNUAL ****PERCENTAGE RATE****	FINANCE **** CHARGE ****	AMOUNT FINANCED	TOTAL OF PAYMENTS
THE COST OF THE CREDIT AS A YEARLY RATE.	THE DOLLAR AMOUNT THE CREDIT WILL COST.	THE AMOUNT OF CREDIT PROVIDED TO THE BORROWER OR ON BORROWER'S BEHALF.	THE AMOUNT BORROWER WILL HAVE PAID AFTER ALL PAYMENTS HAVE BEEN MADE AS SCHEDULED.

PAYMENT SCHEDULE

NUMBER OF PAYMENTS	AMOUNT OF PAYMENTS	WHEN PAYMENTS ARE DUE

DEMAND FEATURE: ☐ This Note has a demand feature.

REQUIRED DEPOSIT ACCOUNT: ☐ The Annual Percentage Rate does not take into account required deposits.

SECURITY: A security interest has been granted in: ☐ Collateral securing other loans with Lender may also secure this loan; ☐ Any deposit account maintained with Lender; ☐ The goods or property being purchased; ☐ Other (describe):

FILING FEES: $ _____ in fees are being paid to public officials in order to research, perfect or release a security interest in the Collateral.

PREPAYMENT CHARGE: If Borrower pays off early, Borrower ☐ may ☐ will not have to pay a penalty.
☐ may ☐ will not be entitled to a refund of part of the finance charge.

ITEMIZATION: ☐ Borrower has the right to receive at this time an itemization of Amount Financed. Borrower ☐ does ☐ does not want an itemization.

LATE PAYMENT CHARGES: If an installment payment is more than _____ days late, ☐ Borrower will be charged a late payment charge of _____ % of the late installment; ☐ Lender will increase the interest rate on the installment that is past due, to _____ percent per annum, until paid.

ASSUMPTION: ☐ This loan may not be assumed on its original terms, ☐ This loan may be assumed on its original terms, subject to certain conditions.

See your contract documents for additional information about nonpayment, default, prepayment penalties, refunds, and acceleration.

e means an estimate

ACKNOWLEDGMENT

Borrower acknowledges that Borrower has read and received a completed copy of this disclosure statement prior to executing this acknowledgment and before entering into any agreement with Lender concerning this credit transaction.

DATED:

BORROWER: _____   BORROWER: _____

BORROWER: _____   BORROWER: _____

LP-TX104 © FormAtion Technologies, Inc. (3/11/94) (800) 937-3799

FIGURE 11-1 Reg. Z Disclosure Form

estate transactions (primarily in buying homes). However, good practice favors disclosure of the items to assure compliance. One should also note that there is no ceiling (limitations) to finance charges; the requirements specify only that the charges be disclosed.

The Federal Truth-in-Lending Act and Regulation Z were both changed in 1980 by the Truth-in-Lending Simplification and Reform Act. This new statute became effective on April 1, 1982. It was changed again in 1983 to comply with the Depository Institutions Act of 1982. The most significant changes affecting real estate, however, are the definitions of creditor and arrangers of credit. A *creditor* is basically a person who extends credit more than five times in a preceding calendar year or in a current calendar year for a transaction secured by a dwelling [Reg. Z, Section 226.2(a) (17)]. An *arranger* of credit could easily include real estate brokers who arrange for sellers to take secondary loans. This is discussed in greater detail in Chapter 5, "Real Estate Brokerage and Management."

In 1995, special disclosures were mandated by federal law for certain types of mortgages: (1) reverse mortgages and (2) high-rate loans.

A *reverse mortgage loan* is defined under the Truth-in-Lending Act as:

1. A nonrecourse loan.
2. Secured by a mortgage or its equivalent on the borrower's principal dwelling.
3. Securing one or more advances.
4. Where repayment of principal, interest, and shared appreciation or equity is due only after the dwelling ceases to be the borrower's principal dwelling.

The additional disclosures are that (1) the borrower is not obligated to complete the reverse-mortgage transaction, (2) that the good-faith projection and explanation of the total cost of the credit, expressed as a table, must be labeled "total annual loan cost rate," and (3) that an itemization of certain, specified loan terms must be set out in the statute.

A *high-rate loan* is a loan secured by a borrower's principal dwelling that is not a purchase loan, a reverse mortgage loan, or an open end line of credit, where the rate of the loan is at least ten points higher than the yield on Treasury securities with a comparable maturity or where the total points in fees paid by the borrower exceeds the greater of $400 or 8% of the total loan amount. The additional disclosures required under high-rate loans include:

1. A statement that the borrower need not complete the transaction simply because the borrower has completed the loan application, or received the disclosure.

2. A statement that, if there is a default, the borrower could lose his or her home.

3. The annual percentage rate, the regular monthly payment, and, in the case of a variable mortgage, a statement that the interest rate and monthly payment may increase, and the payment that will be required at the maximum possible rate.

One of the most effective parts of the T-i-L Act is the *right of rescission*. When a consumer enters into a credit transaction, he is given the right to rescind (back out of) the transaction by midnight of the third business day after (1) he has signed the documents to secure the credit, or (2) delivery of the notice of right to rescind, or (3) delivery of all material disclosures. If the consumer exercises this right, the documents are void, and any money advanced by the consumer (other than for lender's actual expenses) must be returned to the consumer. The consumer can waive this right to rescind for a bona fide financial emergency.

Right of Rescission

The Equal Credit Opportunity Act (hereinafter called *ECOA*) and Federal Reserve Regulation B (the ECOA interpretive regulation) have been in effect since 1975. ECOA initially prohibited the use of sex or marital status as factors in credit-granting decisions. Since 1977, seven other factors have been outlawed as causes for discrimination in lending. These are race, color, religion, country of national origin, age, receipt of public assistance benefits, and the good faith exercising of rights held under the Consumer Credit Protection Act. In short, the ECOA is an attempt to assure that credit-granting decisions are based solely on business judgment and repayment capacity.

EQUAL CREDIT OPPORTUNITY ACT

The ECOA requires lenders to notify credit applicants of the decision made on their application. In the case of credit denial, applicants must be notified of the reason why they were refused credit and of their right to be told those reasons. An explanation must be made in writing within 30 days any time "adverse action" is taken on a credit application. Offering different terms or a lesser amount is not considered adverse action, but rather is interpreted as a counteroffer. Action taken as a result of a borrower's default is not considered adverse action.

The required ECOA notice contains a statement that discrimination is illegal, as well as a list of factors considered discriminatory. It also names the federal agency responsible for enforcing the ECOA (which varies, depending on the type of lender involved).

Credit is often denied for a combination of factors rather than for one specific factor. For this reason in the past some creditors had developed a scoresheet containing several factors, and they denied credit when a certain aggregate score was not obtained. Under the ECOA, failure to attain the required score is not a sufficient reason for denying credit. Rather, specific reasons must be listed. Also, the ECOA tries to eliminate the illegal practice of "redlining" certain classes of borrowers or borrowers from certain geographical areas.[1]

In order to monitor and enforce ECOA compliance, residential mortgage credit application forms are required to ask questions that establish sex, age, marital status, and so forth.

Courts generally use what is called an "effects" test to determine when discrimination has occurred, *Griggs* v. *Duke Power Company*, 401 U.S. 424 (1971). The courts have been specifically directed by Congress to do so, *Senate Report No. 94-589*, 94th Congress, Sec. Sess. (1976), pp. 4 and 5. The Griggs case seems to eliminate the necessity of proving an intent to discriminate. A companion case included in the congressional directive was *Albermarle Paper Company* v. *Moody*, 422 U.S. 405 (1975), which suggests that showing a disproportionate (racial) impact creates a prima facie discrimination case and shifts the burden of proof to the defendant to prove nondiscrimination.

The effects test has been undergoing continual judicial interpretation, *General Electric* v. *Gilbert*, 45 U.S.L.W. 4031, which may have some impact on the way the ECOA is applied.

FAIR CREDIT REPORTING ACT

The Fair Credit Reporting Act (FCRA) is designed to help a person determine whether he has a good or bad credit rating, and primarily applies to credit bureaus. Prior to its passage it was not possible to learn of the source of one's bad credit rating, let alone to be in a position to have it corrected. The FCRA is important to the real estate industry because lending decisions often are based on credit ratings.

Furthermore, real estate lenders may be considered "credit reporting agencies" and, thus, be subject to the act if they give

---

[1] "Redlining" refers to the alleged policies of lenders to refuse to make any loans to certain classes of people or, more usually, to all applicants from a certain geographical area.

opinions over and above factual information about credit-worthiness. If real estate lenders use information from a "consumer reporting agency" (credit bureau) to deny credit or to increase the interest rates, they must disclose to the prospective borrower the nature of the information and the name of the agency from which it was obtained. A provision exists for the consumer to have corrected any false, unsubstantiated, or out-of-date facts adversely affecting his credit rating.

New rules now provide that the credit reporting agency must include any information that it has concerning the consumer's failure to pay overdue child support. There are certain limitations on the credit reporting agency with respect to such information, and the information provided may not predate the credit report by more than seven years.

HOME MORTGAGE DISCLOSURE ACT

The Home Mortgage Disclosure Act (HMDA) is an attempt to eliminate the practice of "redlining" or refusing to make loans in certain geographical areas. It requires certain lenders to disclose the magnitude of mortgage loans made in each census tract or zip code area in the Standard Metropolitan Statistical Area (SMSA) that they serve. This act applies to lending institutions whose net worth exceeds $10 million and who make "federally related mortgages." With respect to the latter, the act applies to any lender who is federally insured or regulated. In this way, the HMDA reporting requirements may serve to encourage lenders to make loans in all areas.

STATE USURY LAWS

Usury rates are the highest possible interest rates that can be charged by law. Not all states have usury laws, and recent market increases in interest rates have caused many states to consider raising or eliminating their usury rates.

To better understand the usury law and its impact, it is helpful to briefly review usury in a historical context. Most usury ceilings were established many years ago at a time when many communities had only one lender. Furthermore, the society of that era was relatively immobile. This combination of circumstances resulted in many banks being in the position of a business monopoly. A few banks took advantage of this situation and charged interest rates that exceeded those that would have been present in a competitive lending market. Thus, usury legislation which set maximum interest rates was an attempt to prevent a few lenders from taking unfair advantage of the borrowers' weak bargaining position.

Today, of course, our society is much more mobile, and lenders usually are quite competitive in both interest rates and customer services. Furthermore, substantial competition for loanable funds exists among lenders from different states. Putting a lower than competitive market usury ceiling on interest rates in one state may limit its lender profit opportunities, and may cause funds to flow into other states with higher or no usury limits. This can stifle real estate development activities in the former state and contribute to a development boom in another. This "other" state will not experience a boom, of course, unless the market interest rates are rates at which borrowers are willing to lock themselves in on long-term loans.

Usury rates, kinds of loans, and transactions that are exempt from usury laws all vary from state to state. The exempt transactions are extremely important because, like interest rates, they impact directly on the flow of funds between states. For example, if residential loans are exempt from usury penalties and if the major local demand for loanable funds is for residential purchase and construction, a 6% usury rate probably would cause large amounts of loanable funds to flow out of the community to other states.

Federal Intervention of State Usury Laws. In 1980 federal laws were passed that declared that the constitutional laws of any state expressly limiting the rate or amount of interest shall not apply to any loan which is:

1. Secured by a first lien on residential property, by a first lien on stock in residential cooperative housing corporations, or by a first lien on a residential manufactured home.
2. Made after March 31, 1980.
3. Described in Section 527(b) of the National Housing Act, where an individual finances the sale or exchange of residential real property which the individual owns and which the individual has occupied as his principal residence.

There is an exception that provides that the statute does not apply to any loan made in any state on or after April 1, 1980, and before April 1, 1983, if the state adopts a law or certifies that the voters of the state have voted in favor of any provision, constitutional or otherwise, which states explicitly and by its terms that the state does not want the provisions of the new federal statute to apply with respect to the loans and advances made in the state.

Another provision of the federal statute that is applicable to business or agricultural loans provides a new ceiling for loans made for business or agricultural purposes in the amount of $1,000 or more. These loans may carry a rate of interest of not more than 5% per annum in excess of the discount rate, including any surcharge thereon, on 90-day commercial paper in effect at the Federal Reserve Bank in the federal reserve district where the person is located. There are provisions for the state to preempt this provision also, under conditions similar to that of the prior provision.

In interpreting the statute, the Federal Home Loan Bank Board has taken the position that residential real property means real estate improved or to be improved by structures or a structure designed for dwelling, as opposed to primarily commercial use. There has even been some further discussion that a wrap-around mortgage may be included as a first lien loan because of the "all-inclusive" nature of such mortgages.

Determination of Interest

The most difficult question to date has been, What constitutes interest as a charge for the "forbearance or detention" of money? There are an almost indeterminable number of fees that have been tacked on, added to, credited to, paid collaterally with, and given in exchange for, all kinds of loan transactions. Most of these charges incurred when obtaining a loan are clearly established and understood. The lender must be very careful in requiring these charges, so that the interest charged will not be considered to be usurious. Therefore, the determination of these charges as "interest" is very important to the lender's business practice. Some of the more common charges for obtaining a loan may constitute interest and deserve more detailed discussion.

Points, Commitment Fees, and Loan Brokerage Fees. Points, commitment fees, and loan brokerage fees may be paid to a lender when obtaining a loan. A *point* is a charge for making the loan that is payable at the time of the loan. Each point represents 1% of the loan. For instance, a $100,000 loan requiring three "points" would require a fee of $3,000 to be paid when the loan is granted.

In some states and for some purposes, points are not considered to be interest. One test used to determine if points are interest is whether they are directly attributable to expenses incurred by the lender in making the loan, *Terry* v. *Teachworth*, 431 S.W.2d 918, and *Gonzales County Savings and Loan Association* v. *Freeman*, 534 S.W.2d 903. If points are charged to offset a lender expense incurred in making the loan, they do not constitute interest, *Lederman Enterprises Inc.* v. *Westinghouse Credit Corp.*, 347 F. Supp. 1291.

In contrast to points, a *commitment fee* is normally a fee charged for the promise of securing loan funds at some future date. It can be characterized as an option to enter into a future loan. As long as the fee is reasonably related to the risks taken by the lender, it will not be construed to be interest, *Gonzales County Savings and Loan Association, supra.*

Brokerage fees are charges made by mortgage brokers for "placing" a loan with a lender. Brokerage fees are not normally considered to be interest, as long as the fee does not go to the lender. This holds true as long as there is no joint control or agreement to split brokerage fees between the lender and the broker.

In some states and areas it is common for a mortgage company or savings and loan association to operate as a mortgage broker, charging one to five points as a fee for finding another lender to make the loan. In this capacity the mortgage company or savings and loan association is serving only as a mortgage broker. Thus, a broker's fee for finding a lender is not interest, *Crow* v. *Home Savings Association,* 522 S.W.2d 457 and *Greever* v. *Persky,* 165 S.W.2d 709. However, fees charged by a broker who is working as a lender's agent may be considered interest, *Investment Fund Corp.* v. *Bomar,* 303 F.2d 592.

Prepayment Penalties and Partial Release Fees. *Prepayment penalties* are fees that a lender charges the borrower for prematurely paying off a loan. Arguably, these fees may be justified as constituting lost lender profits suffered as a result of premature payment. Conceivably, such damages could consist of additional costs incurred and/or interest payments lost.

Some courts may not construe prepayment penalties as interest, but rather as consideration for the termination of the loan contract, *Boyd* v. *Life Insurance Company,* 546 S.W.2d 132 and *Gulf Coast Investment Corp.* v. *Prichard,* 438 S.W.2d 658. Others may call them interest if they are not reasonable expenses in light of the actual amount of work done, and/or do not bear some reasonable relationship to the amount of loss or inconvenience suffered by the lender due to prepayment, *Gonzales County Savings and Loan Association, supra.*

Partial release fees may be charged when the borrower pays off part of the loan and receives clear title to a part of the mortgaged tract. These fees are normally attributable to the preparation of legal instruments, bookkeeping, and clerical costs for releasing the security and resulting adjustments of the principal balance due under the terms of the loan. Partial release fees of this type are generally not considered interest.

Compensating Balances.   Banks and other lenders make a profit by taking funds deposited with them and loaning them to others. To acquire additional funds for lending, they sometimes will require borrowers to keep a certain amount of money on deposit throughout the loan period. These required deposits are called *compensating balances.*

Compensating balances may be part of an oral agreement and may not be mentioned in the loan documents themselves. One theory sees compensating balances as creating separate and independent obligations (on which interest is paid by the lender, at least when the deposit is in a savings rather than a checking account) and are not deemed interest. On the other hand, if the lender freezes the loan proceeds or requires the compensating balance on the loan document, it *may* be considered interest.

Matured Interest.   As illustrated in Figure 10-1 of the preceding chapter, many promissory notes have penalty provisions that apply in the event of default. These provisions usually state that default causes the entire principal amount to become due (matured) and that matured unpaid principal and interest will both bear interest at some specified rate until paid. The latter is sometimes referred to as *interest on interest.*

Generally, however, this penalty is not considered interest on the loan for usury purposes, *Crider* v. *San Antonio Real Estate Building and Loan Association*, 35 S.W. 1047, and *Madison Personnel Loan* v. *Parker*, 124 F.2d 143. Rather, default creates a new obligation, and the interest on the note and past due principal do not, taken together, constitute a new higher rate of interest.

Compulsory Loan Retirement.   In some areas it is common practice for lenders to require a borrower to pay off all of his preexisting indebtedness in order to obtain a new loan. This normally is not considered interest. However, such a requirement may be considered interest if there is also a prepayment penalty on the loans to be paid off.

Turn-Around Sales.   *Turn-around sales* involve a sale from a borrower to a lender, followed by a sale at a higher price from the lender back to the borrower. In at least one case this technique was determined to be interest for purposes of the usury statute, *Commerce Savings Association* v. *GGE Management Co.*, 543 S.W.2d 862.

Equity Participation.   Lenders have become increasingly aware of their ability to participate in real estate development projects as an equity investor. The profits realized from equity participation do not constitute interest, as long as the lender is taking risks similar to that of the borrower. However, if the lender gets a preferred return on his investment, this may be determined to be interest and, if high enough, may be usurious, *Johns v. Jabe*, 518 S.W.2d 857. On the other hand, generally if the lender shares in the risks, and the return on his investment is not readily ascertainable, he is considered to be a true equity participant.

Required Incorporation   In most states, corporate loans are not subject to the usury law. Thus, as usury ceilings are raised, lenders may require businesses to incorporate so that higher rates of interest may be charged on loans to them. There is case law that holds that the practice of requiring the borrower to form a corporation as a condition of the loan does not *by itself* indicate that the corporation was created to cover up for a fraudulent transaction, or to evade usury statutes, *Skeen* v. *Glenn Justice Mortgage Company*, 526 S.W.2d 252, and *Sage Trading Corp.* v. *Seventh Operating Corp.*, 270 N.Y.S.2d 642.

Another important legal question is whether a lender's requirement that an individual guarantee a corporation's indebtedness constitutes usury. Two recent cases suggest that since the loan was made to the corporation and not to the individual, the transaction did not constitute usury, *Loomis Land and Cattle Company* v. *Diversified Mortgage*, 533 S.W.2d 420, *Buoninfante* v. *Hoffman*, 367 N.Y.S.2d 984, and *Nation Wide Inc.* v. *Scullin*, 256 F. Supp. 929.

Another interesting legal question is whether two corporations that have formed a partnership are subject to usury limits. Although the answer could vary among states, generally such partnerships are subject to the usury ceiling for noncorporate borrowers.

Spreading   Once it has been determined whether the previously discussed extra loan-connected charges, such as points, turn-around sales, and so forth, legally constitute interest, there still remains the question as to how interest is calculated in determining whether it is usurious. To do this, some states have adopted the concept of *spreading*. The spreading doctrine permits various loan-connected charges to be "spread" over the life of the loan in computing the interest rate charged. In some instances, spreading permits substantial "front-end" charges to be made without violating the usury law.

The penalties for usury are substantial in most states. Furthermore, the law of usury generally is strictly construed against the lender. Most lenders find that the risks of charging usurious interest far outweigh the small extra profit that might be earned from higher rates.

Penalty for Usurious Transactions

The credit industry has been the target of a good deal of consumer protection legislation at both federal and state levels. One of the best known federal laws in this area is the Truth-in-Lending (T-i-L) Act. Its basic purpose is to assure that creditors subject to it give meaningful disclosures to their borrowers about actual credit costs. Many real estate loans are covered by T-i-L requirements, but some purchases (primarily home purchases) are exempt from finance charge determination requirements.

SUMMARY

The Equal Credit Opportunity Act (ECOA) prevents lending decision discrimination on the basis of sex, marital status, race, color, religion, country of national origin, age, receipt of public assistance benefits, and the good faith exercising of rights under the Consumer Credit Protection Act. ECOA is an attempt to assure that credit-granting decisions are based solely on business judgment and perceived repayment capacity. Congress has suggested that an effects test be used to enforce the ECOA, meaning that showing of a disproportionate impact creates a prima facie discrimination case and shifts the burden of proof to the defendant.

The Fair Credit Reporting Act makes it possible for borrowers with bad credit ratings to determine the source of their rating and, when errors have been involved, to correct their credit ratings.

The Home Mortgage Disclosure Act (HMDA) is a federal law enacted in an attempt to curb the illegal practice of "redlining." HMDA reporting requirements encourage lenders to make loans in all geographic areas within their customer service region.

State usury laws set upper limits on interest rates that may be charged borrowers. Most of these laws were adopted at a time when our population was relatively immobile, and when only one commercial lender served a local community. Initially, then, usury laws were enacted to prevent creditors from exploiting their monopoly position and taking unfair advantage of borrowers' weak bargaining positions.

As inflation occurs and interest rates creep up along with the general price level, states with relatively low usury rate ceilings begin to find loanable funds difficult to locate. This is because lenders' profits are constrained by usury ceilings, thereby encouraging them to shift loanable funds to other, more profitable investments (which are often located in states with no usury ceilings). Both the level of usury rates and the kinds of loans and borrowers that are exempt from the law may cause mortgage funds to flow from one state to another.

Not all states have usury laws, and the definition of what constitutes interest varies somewhat in different states. Points refer to a charge paid to the lender for making a loan. Each point represents 1% of the loan. In general, whether points constitute interest depends on whether they are charged to offset a lender's expense in making a loan.

Loan commitment fees are fees charged for the promise of securing loan funds at some later date. So long as these fees are reasonably related to lender risks, they usually are not considered interest for usury purposes.

Brokerage fees are charges made by mortgage brokers for placing a loan with a lender. As long as these fees are paid solely for finding the lender, they are not considered interest.

Prepayment penalties are fees that the lender charges the borrower for paying off the loan prior to maturity. Prepayment penalties are often construed as consideration for terminating the loan contract, and as such normally are not considered interest.

Partial release fees are charged the borrower when he pays off part of the mortgage and is given unencumbered title to part of the mortgaged real estate. So long as the fees are attributable to the preparation of legal instruments, extra bookkeeping, and clerical costs occasioned by the partial release, they normally are not considered interest.

Compensating balances are deposits required of borrowers as a condition of receiving a loan. Lenders often make a profit on such deposits by lending them to others. If compensating balances are required in the loan document, they may be considered interest.

Interest is sometimes charged on interest, as when a mortgage calls for a default to cause acceleration of the entire debt and interest to be earned on both unpaid principal and unpaid interest. Usually default is considered to have created a new obligation, so for usury purposes the interest on interest is not considered part of the interest charges on the original note.

On some occasions borrowers may be required to pay off all existing loans as a condition for receiving a new one (and the new loan is often at a higher interest rate than the old one). For usury purposes this practice of compulsory loan retirement is not normally considered interest, but it may be when prepayment penalties are charged for paying off the old loan.

Turn-around sales involve the sale of property from a borrower to a lender, followed by a sale of the same property at a higher price from the lender to the borrower. There is case law to suggest this will be interpreted as usurious if the net interest paid exceeds that which would have been paid on the amount of money in the "real" loan.

Lenders now participate with borrowers as equity investors in some ventures. As long as lenders do not get a preferred return on their investment, the income will not be considered interest.

In many states, loans to corporations are not subject to usury limits. For this reason, it is not unusual for lenders to require borrowers to incorporate so higher interest rates may be charged. Generally, such practices and loans are not considered usurious. The same is true when a shareholder is required to guarantee a loan to a corporation, because the important fact is that the loan was made to a corporation.

In many states, if one or more of the previously discussed lender charges are treated as interest, their cost may be spread throughout the loan period to determine whether a particular loan is usurious. Thus, the "spreading" doctrine permits avoidance of usury penalties in some instances, even though many of these expenses occurred as "front-end" charges.

Because usury penalties are often severe, most lenders make every effort to avoid them.

DISCUSSION QUESTIONS

1. Under T-i-L, what is the importance of the annual percentage rate computation?

2. What are the basic purposes, respectively, of the Equal Credit Opportunity Act and the Home Mortgage Disclosure Act?

3. Does your state have a usury law? What is your usury rate? What kinds of loans and/or lenders are exempt from your state usury laws?

4. What is the difference between a point and a loan commitment fee?

12

Methods of Title Assurance

All real estate purchasers want to receive a title that is "good." Although on occasion those who deal frequently in real estate may be willing to accept something less than a perfect title, they still want to be aware of the nature of the title defects, so that they can evaluate the business risks involved.

Most people, of course, purchase real estate only once or twice during their lifetime, and few people understand how to assure themselves that a title is acceptable. Therefore, they rely on sellers or third parties for that assurance. Depending on the state and the locality, the assurance of title might be obtained in a number of ways. The more common ones, to be discussed here, include the Torrens system of title registration, a personal warranty from the grantor, a lawyer's title opinion, an abstractor's certificate, and a title insurance policy. In comparing these various methods of title assurance, two factors must always be considered: (1) the solvency of the assurer of title facts and (2) the extent to which the title is guaranteed and the purchaser is protected.

TORRENS REGISTRATION SYSTEM

The Torrens system of title registration was developed in Australia, and is available by statute in several states (including Colorado, Georgia, Hawaii, Illinois, Massachusetts, Minnesota, New York, North Carolina, Ohio, Pennsylvania, Virginia, and Washington). The use of the Torrens system, though, is quite limited even in those states. It was originally enacted in eight other states, but those statutes were subsequently repealed.

The basic principle of the Torrens system is the registration of the title to the land, similar to that of registering title to an automobile. A transfer of title or a new lien on the property is shown by turning in the old registration certificates and obtaining a new registration certificate reflecting the change. The old registration certificate is destroyed. Therefore, only one registration certificate exists at any one time for any parcel of real estate.

When the certificate of title has been obtained, it is a conclusive evidence of title and a termination of all adverse claims. Title acquired by adverse possession cannot occur on real property registered under the Torrens system. Therefore, title is presumed to be good under a Torrens system, subject only to the encumbrances and exceptions reflected on the certificate. Frequently, however, it requires legal help to determine the true status of title if a Torrens certificate reflects a large number of encumbrances.

A Torrens title registration system appears to work well when a state or county adopts it initially. However, there are difficulties in introducing it into a state that is already following a different title transfer procedure. The primary difficulty is that the Torrens registration system initially requires a judicial determination of title quality for every single parcel of real estate. Since any judicial title determination is subject to the same legal procedures as any lawsuit, this can be a very lengthy and costly process. Unless a special judicial system is set up to make such determinations of title the burden on the existing court system is substantial and possibly insurmountable. Furthermore, changes would probably be required in recording acts, insurance codes (to the extent they involve title insurance), and methods of recordation in county courthouses. In total, these required changes constitute major roadblocks, making it unlikely that the Torrens system will be widely adopted in this country.

A particularly significant drawback to the Torrens registration system is the manner in which it guarantees the title to the property owner. Normally an assurance fund is set up for each county where the Torrens system is established. In the event there is a failure of title, the county would ultimately have to pay damages to the claimant. Claimants suing the county find recovery a tedious process. Although counties are usually solvent, California had a statewide assurance fund that was wiped out by a single judgment. As might be expected, California repealed its Torrens registration statute.

Another disadvantage of the Torrens system is the time required for registration. Under non-Torrens recording systems, items can be recorded and filed and originals returned to the owner within a reasonably short period of time. Under the Torrens system, the clerk must file the instrument, review it, compare it to the new Torrens certificate to be prepared and issued by the courthouse, destroy the old certificate, and mail the new instrument to the title holder. It is not uncommon for a Torrens registration procedure to require eight or nine months in more populated counties. If the subject property should change hands several times within an eight- or nine-month period, substantial backlog and confusion may result. In some of the larger Torrens jurisdictions, there has been discussion of eliminating the system because it is so time consuming and burdensome.

GRANTOR'S WARRANTIES

A second method of title assurance is the personal warranty of the grantor. As discussed in Chapter 8, the execution of different types of deeds results in different warranties being made by the grantor. If there is a defect in title, the purchaser has the right to sue the grantor on his warranty. Such warranties may be difficult to enforce for a number of reasons, however. The grantor may be dead, or no longer in existence (in the case of a corporation or other business entity). Even if he is available, he may not be financially solvent.

However, the personal warranty of the grantor, coupled with applicable adverse possession statutes, does provide some degree of title assurance. It is an effective method when the grantor exists and is large, solvent, and reputable. As will be explained later, in some instances solvent grantors probably provide better title assurance than some title companies.

ABSTRACTOR'S CERTIFICATE

An abstractor is a person employed to compile an abstract of title to a certain parcel of real estate. The abstract reflects a complete chain of title from the current date back to the original transfer from the "sovereign." It should contain all publicly recorded instruments affecting title to the real estate parcel under consideration.

The existence of an abstract does not, by itself, give any assurance about the quality of title. The abstractor's certificate accompanying the abstract just warrants that it contains all matters of public record that affect the title. For this reason, further assurance of title, either by an attorney's opinion or by title insurance, generally is and should be sought. An abstractor does not, of course, interpret any of the legal documents identified in an abstract. Since this would constitute the illegal practice of law without a license, such interpretations must be made by a lawyer.

Negligent errors by abstractors can, of course, lead to substantial losses. For this reason many states require abstractors to be bonded as a condition of doing business. Whether this is sufficient to cover losses they cause depends on the amount of the bond they carry and also on their financial resources.

LAWYER'S TITLE OPINION

The lawyer's title opinion was once the most common method of title assurance, and is still used extensively in many areas. Using this method, an attorney is asked to examine an abstract of title to a particular tract and to render his opinion as to the quality and extent of title that the grantor has.

The attorney must base his opinion on the type of title called for in the earnest money contract. The contract may require title *marketable of record* (as shown by public records) or *marketable in fact* (not shown in the public record but provable by adverse possession). Attorneys generally state their opinions as to whether the title is marketable of record. On the other hand, title insurance companies generally insure that a title is marketable in fact.

The disadvantages in using the attorney's opinion method of title assurance include the following factors.

1. Abstract examination is a slow, time-consuming process, which may make it difficult to meet contractual deadlines, particularly when the transaction is a complicated one.

2. There is always the risk that the abstract is incomplete or is missing some instruments in the chain of title.

3. Since an abstract does not contain original documents, a forgery would be impossible to detect. An attorney basically is liable only for negligent errors in rendering an *opinion,* and his opinion provides no protection against the possibility of a forged document or incapacity of parties.

4. Although a lawyer is liable for negligent errors, recovery is still limited by his financial solvency. Most lawyers carry malpractice insurance to cover errors and omissions, but the policy limits may be too low to cover all losses.

There has been considerable effort in recent years on the part of the legal community to reinstate lawyers in the business of assuring title to real property. As a result, some states have made provisions for an attorneys' title insurance company in their insurance codes. The attorney's title insurance company has regulations similar to those of title insurance companies generally. However, there has not been a shift toward utilizing these companies for title assurance to date.

TITLE INSURANCE

A title insurance policy is by far the most common method of title assurance, and incorporates several methods of title assurance that have already been mentioned.

Title companies originally came into being because of the need for an insurance policy for a lawyer's title opinion. Title insurance allows for spreading financial risk and offers an increased possibility of solvency to damaged purchasers. Most title companies have their own abstract plans and their own abstractors. They also have their own lawyers (either employed or with outside firms) for title opinions. In addition, they are insured by a state-authorized insurance company. So, for these combined reasons, many believe this is the most efficient method of title assurance, with the greatest probability of solvency sufficient to cover all losses.

Furthermore, since title insurance can be concentrated into a volume business, it normally provides a faster, more efficient service to the customer. It also relieves sellers of their direct liability on their warranties to the purchasers, because the title company agrees to indemnify the purchaser for any insured losses. (But note that the seller remains liable to the title company.) The buyer gets the absolute assurance that the title is good, subject to any coverage exceptions in the policy.

A title insurance policy is a contract of indemnity. For a one-time premium charge, it guarantees that the purchaser (or mortgagee) will be indemnified (protected) from any insured loss in the event his title fails for any defect that accrued prior to the effective date of the policy. The title company has no affirmative duty to clear the title, but only to defend it from adverse claims.

The rates for title policies are set by boards of insurance in many states. So in those states there is no advantage to "shopping around" for a better price on a title insurance policy.

Types of Title Insurance. There are normally two types of policies issued: one is issued for the benefit of the mortgagee (lender), and the other is issued for the benefit of the mortgagor (new owner). When issued simultaneously with the owner's policy, the mortgagee's title policy is generally issued at a nominal cost. It assures the mortgagees that their lien interest has the proper priority and provides coverage up to the current outstanding loan balance. Moreover, it generally has better warranties and somewhat better title coverage than does the more expensive owner's title policy. The maximum insured amount decreases as mortgage payments are made.

When the subject real estate is sold, the owner's policy usually converts to a warrantor's policy. Furthermore, if the mortgage is foreclosed, the mortgagee's title insurance policy usually is converted to an owner's policy.

Scope of Coverage   The basic duty of a title company is to indemnify the insured
against any loss caused by defects in title, *McLaughlin* v. *Attorney's
Title Guaranty Fund, Inc.*, 378 N.E.2d 355 (111. 1978) and *Diversified
Mortgage Investors* v. *U.S. Life Insurance Co. of New York*, 544 F.2d 571.
The duty to defend any causes of action against that title is gener-
ally set out in the terms of the title policy.

Although Texas, New York, and California have promulgated
their own title insurance forms, the vast majority of states use
forms of the American Land Title Association (ALTA). A copy of a
sample ALTA title insurance form in shown in Figure 12-1 for reference.

The standard form title insurance policy insures the title holder against loss or damage and covers attorney's fees and expenses
that the insured may become obligated to pay by reason of:

1. Title to the estate or interest described in Schedule A (of the
   ALTA Form) being vested otherwise than as stated therein,
   subject to the stated exclusions, that do not constitute title
   matters or that are not within the expertise of the title
   insured.

2. Any defect in, lien, or encumbrance on such title.

3. Unmarketability of such title.

4. Lack of right of access to and from the land.

Note that the standard form policy insures against both defects
disclosed by the public records and those that are not disclosed
(provided the latter are not known to the insured at the time the
policy takes effect). It also covers the cost of defending the title
against attack, as well as covering the mistakes of title examiners
and agents of the company.

Some other important points to note in the standard form policy are as follows. (All references are to paragraphs or schedules as
shown in Figure 12-1.)

1. The title insurance company is obligated to defend the
   insured in every action or proceeding adverse to the title or
   interest as set out in paragraph 7 of the policy.

2. The company is required to defend any claims except
   those entered in the policy under Schedule B.

3. The insured party must, within a reasonable time, give the
   company written notice that an action against title is pending, thus giving the company authority to defend the title
   (paragraph 3), *Houston Title Guaranty Co.* v. *Fontenot*, 339
   S.W.2d 347.

LTIC LTIC LTIC LTIC LTIC LTIC LTIC LTIC LTIC LTIC LTIC LTIC LTIC LTIC LTIC LTIC LTIC LTIC LTIC LTIC LTIC LTIC LTIC LTIC LTIC LTIC LTIC LTIC LTIC LTIC LTIC

Lawyers Title
Insurance Corporation

SPECIMEN COPY

NATIONAL HEADQUARTERS
RICHMOND, VIRGINIA

1992 ALTA
Owner's Policy

Owner's Policy Number
136 - 00 - 609856

SUBJECT TO THE EXCLUSIONS FROM COVERAGE, THE EXCEPTIONS FROM COVERAGE CONTAINED IN SCHEDULE B AND THE CONDITIONS AND STIPULATIONS, LAWYERS TITLE INSURANCE CORPORATION, a Virginia corporation, herein called the Company, insures, as of Date of Policy shown in Schedule A, against loss or damage, not exceeding the Amount of Insurance stated in Schedule A, sustained or incurred by the insured by reason of:

1. Title to the estate or interest described in Schedule A being vested other than as stated therein;
2. Any defect in or lien or encumbrance on the title;
3. Unmarketability of the title;
4. Lack of a right of access to and from the land.

The Company also will pay the costs, attorneys' fees and expenses incurred in defense of the title, as insured, but only to the extent provided in the Conditions and Stipulations.

EXCLUSIONS FROM COVERAGE

The following matters are expressly excluded from the coverage of this policy and the Company will not pay loss or damage, costs, attorneys' fees or expenses which arise by reason of:

1. (a) Any law, ordinance or governmental regulation (including but not limited to building and zoning laws, ordinances, or regulations) restricting, regulating, prohibiting or relating to (i) the occupancy, use, or enjoyment of the land; (ii) the character, dimensions or location of any improvement now or hereafter erected on the land; (iii) a separation in ownership or a change in the dimensions or area of the land or any parcel of which the land is or was a part; or (iv) environmental protection, or the effect of any violation of these laws, ordinances or governmental regulations, except to the extent that a notice of the enforcement thereof or a notice of a defect, lien or encumbrance resulting from a violation or alleged violation affecting the land has been recorded in the public records at Date of Policy.

   (b) Any governmental police power not excluded by (a) above, except to the extent that a notice of the exercise thereof or a notice of a defect, lien or encumbrance resulting from a violation or alleged violation affecting the land has been recorded in the public records at Date of Policy.

2. Rights of eminent domain unless notice of the exercise thereof has been recorded in the public records at Date of Policy, but not excluding from coverage any taking which has occurred prior to Date of Policy which would be binding on the rights of a purchaser for value without knowledge.

3. Defects, liens, encumbrances, adverse claims or other matters:
   (a) created, suffered, assumed or agreed to by the insured claimant;

   (b) not known to the Company, not recorded in the public records at Date of Policy, but known to the insured claimant and not disclosed in writing to the Company by the insured claimant prior to the date the insured claimant became an insured under this policy;

   (c) resulting in no loss or damage to the insured claimant;

   (d) attaching or created subsequent to Date of Policy; or

   (e) resulting in loss or damage which would not have been sustained if the insured claimant had paid value for the estate or interest insured by this policy.

4. Any claim, which arises out of the transaction vesting in the insured the estate or interest insured by this policy, by reason of the operation of federal bankruptcy, state insolvency, or similar creditors' rights laws that is based on:
   (a) the transaction creating the estate or interest insured by this policy being deemed a fraudulent conveyance or fraudulent transfer; or

   (b) the transaction creating the estate or interest insured by this policy being deemed a preferential transfer except where the preferential transfer results from the failure:
      (i) to timely record the instrument of transfer; or
      (ii) of such recordation to impart notice to a purchaser for value or a judgment or lien creditor.

LTIC LTIC LTIC LTIC LTIC LTIC LTIC LTIC LTIC LTIC LTIC LTIC LTIC LTIC LTIC LTIC LTIC LTIC LTIC LTIC LTIC LTIC LTIC LTIC LTIC LTIC LTIC LTIC LTIC LTIC LTIC

Policy 136 - Litho in U.S.A.
035-0-136-0006

Cover Sheet ALTA Owner's Policy (10-17-92)

FIGURE 12-1   Sample ALTA Title Insurance Form

CONDITIONS AND STIPULATIONS

1. DEFINITION OF TERMS.

The following terms when used in this policy mean:

(a) "insured": the insured named in Schedule A, and, subject to any rights or defenses the Company would have had against the named insured, those who succeed to the interest of the named insured by operation of law as distinguished from purchase including, but not limited to, heirs, distributees, devisees, survivors, personal representatives, next of kin, or corporate or fiduciary successors.

(b) "insured claimant": an insured claiming loss or damage.

(c) "knowledge" or "known": actual knowledge, not constructive knowledge or notice which may be imputed to an insured by reason of the public records as defined in this policy or any other records which impart constructive notice of matters affecting the land.

(d) "land": the land described or referred to in Schedule A, and improvements affixed thereto which by law constitute real property. The term "land" does not include any property beyond the lines of the area described or referred to in Schedule A, nor any right, title, interest, estate or easement in abutting streets, roads, avenues, alleys, lanes, ways or waterways, but nothing herein shall modify or limit the extent to which a right of access to and from the land is insured by this policy.

(e) "mortgage": mortgage, deed of trust, trust deed, or other security instrument.

(f) "public records": records established under state statutes at Date of Policy for the purpose of imparting constructive notice of matters relating to real property to purchasers for value and without knowledge. With respect to Section 1(a)(iv) of the Exclusions From Coverage, "public records" shall also include environmental protection liens filed in the records of the clerk of the United States district court for the district in which the land is located.

(g) "unmarketability of the title": an alleged or apparent matter affecting the title to the land, not excluded or excepted from coverage, which would entitle a purchaser of the estate or interest described in Schedule A to be released from the obligation to purchase by virtue of a contractual condition requiring the delivery of marketable title.

2. CONTINUATION OF INSURANCE AFTER CONVEYANCE OF TITLE.

The coverage of this policy shall continue in force as of Date of Policy in favor of an insured only so long as the insured retains an estate or interest in the land, or holds an indebtedness secured by a purchase money mortgage given by a purchaser from the insured, or only so long as the insured shall have liability by reason of covenants of warranty made by the insured in any transfer or conveyance of the estate or interest. This policy shall not continue in force in favor of any purchaser from the insured of either (i) an estate or interest in the land, or (ii) an indebtedness secured by a purchase money mortgage given to the insured.

3. NOTICE OF CLAIM TO BE GIVEN BY INSURED CLAIMANT.

The insured shall notify the Company promptly in writing (i) in case of any litigation as set forth in Section 4(a) below, (ii) in case knowledge shall come to an insured hereunder of any claim of title or interest which is adverse to the title to the estate or interest, as insured, and which might cause loss or damage for which the Company may be liable by virtue of this policy, or (iii) if title to the estate or interest, as insured, is rejected as unmarketable. If prompt notice shall not be given to the Company, then as to the insured all liability of the Company shall terminate with regard to the matter or matters for which prompt notice is required; provided, however, that failure to notify the Company shall in no case prejudice the rights of any insured under this policy unless the Company shall be prejudiced by the failure and then only to the extent of the prejudice.

4. DEFENSE AND PROSECUTION OF ACTIONS; DUTY OF INSURED CLAIMANT TO COOPERATE.

(a) Upon written request by the insured and subject to the options contained in Section 6 of these Conditions and Stipulations, the Company, at its own cost and without unreasonable delay, shall provide for the defense of an insured in litigation in which any third party asserts a claim adverse to the title or interest as insured, but only as to those stated causes of action alleging a defect, lien or encumbrance or other matter insured against by this policy. The Company shall have the right to select counsel of its choice (subject to the right of the insured to object for reasonable cause) to represent the insured as to those stated causes of action and shall not be liable for and will not pay the fees of any other counsel. The Company will not pay any fees, costs or expenses incurred by the insured in the defense of those causes of action which allege matters not insured against by this policy.

(b) The Company shall have the right, at its own cost, to institute and prosecute any action or proceeding or to do any other act which in its opinion may be necessary or desirable to establish the title to the estate or interest, as insured, or to prevent or reduce loss or damage to the insured. The Company may take any appropriate action under the terms of this policy, whether or not it shall be liable hereunder, and shall not thereby concede liability or waive any provision of this policy. If the Company shall exercise its rights under this paragraph, it shall do so diligently.

(c) Whenever the Company shall have brought an action or interposed a defense as required or permitted by the provisions of this policy, the Company may pursue any litigation to final determination by a court of competent jurisdiction and expressly reserves the right, in its sole discretion, to appeal from any adverse judgment or order.

(d) In all cases where this policy permits or requires the Company to prosecute or provide for the defense of any action or proceeding, the insured shall secure to the Company the right to so prosecute or provide defense in the action or proceeding, and all appeals therein, and permit the Company to use, at its option, the name of the insured for this purpose. Whenever requested by the Company, the insured, at the Company's expense, shall give the Company all reasonable aid (i) in any action or proceeding, securing evidence, obtaining witnesses, prosecuting or defending the action or proceeding, or effecting settlement, and (ii) in any other lawful act which in the opinion of the Company may be necessary or desirable to establish the title to the estate or interest as insured. If the Company is prejudiced by the failure of the insured to furnish the required cooperation, the Company's obligations to the insured under the policy shall terminate, including any liability or obligation to defend, prosecute, or continue any litigation, with regard to the matter or matters requiring such cooperation.

5. PROOF OF LOSS OR DAMAGE.

In addition to and after the notices required under Section 3 of these Conditions and Stipulations have been provided the Company, a proof of loss or damage signed and sworn to by the insured claimant shall be furnished to the Company within 90 days after the insured claimant shall ascertain the facts giving rise to the loss or damage. The proof of loss or damage shall describe the defect in, or lien or encumbrance on the title, or other matter insured against by this policy which constitutes the basis of loss or damage and shall state, to the extent possible, the basis of calculating the amount of the loss or damage. If the Company is prejudiced by the failure of the insured claimant to provide the required proof of loss or damage, the Company's obligations to the insured under the policy shall terminate, including any liability or obligation to defend, prosecute, or continue any litigation, with regard to the matter or matters requiring such proof of loss or damage.

In addition, the insured claimant may reasonably be required to submit to examination under oath by any authorized representative of the Company and shall produce for examination, inspection and copying, at such reasonable times and places as may be designated by any authorized representative of the Company, all records, books, ledgers, checks, correspondence and memoranda, whether bearing a date before or after Date of Policy, which reasonably pertain to the loss or damage. Further, if requested by any authorized representative of the Company, the insured claimant shall grant its permission, in writing, for any authorized representative of the Company to examine, inspect and copy all records, books, ledgers, checks, correspondence and memoranda in the custody or control of a third party, which reasonably pertain to the loss or damage. All information designated as confidential by the insured claimant provided to the Company pursuant to this Section shall not be disclosed to others unless, in the reasonable judgment of the Company, it is necessary in the administration of the claim. Failure of the insured claimant to submit for examination under oath, produce other reasonably requested information or grant permission to secure reasonably necessary information from third parties as required in this paragraph shall terminate any liability of the Company under this policy as to that claim.

6. OPTIONS TO PAY OR OTHERWISE SETTLE CLAIMS; TERMINATION OF LIABILITY.

In case of a claim under this policy, the Company shall have the following additional options:

(a) **To Pay or Tender Payment of the Amount of Insurance.**

To pay or tender payment of the amount of insurance under this policy together with any costs, attorneys' fees and expenses incurred by the insured claimant, which were authorized by the Company, up to the time of payment or tender of payment and which the Company is obligated to pay.

Upon the exercise by the Company of this option, all liability and obligations to the insured under this policy, other than to make the payment required, shall terminate, including any liability or obligation to defend, prosecute, or continue any litigation, and the policy shall be surrendered to the Company for cancellation.

(b) **To Pay or Otherwise Settle With Parties Other than the Insured or With the Insured Claimant.**

(i) to pay or otherwise settle with other parties for or in the name

continued on next page of cover sheet

FIGURE 12-1   Continued

CONDITIONS AND STIPULATIONS—CONTINUED

of an insured claimant any claim insured against under this policy, together with any costs, attorneys' fees and expenses incurred by the insured claimant which were authorized by the Company up to the time of payment and which the Company is obligated to pay; or

(ii) to pay or otherwise settle with the insured claimant the loss or damage provided for under this policy, together with any costs, attorneys' fees and expenses incurred by the insured claimant which were authorized by the Company up to the time of payment and which the Company is obligated to pay.

Upon the exercise by the Company of either of the options provided for in paragraphs (b)(i) or (ii), the Company's obligations to the insured under this policy for the claimed loss or damage, other than the payments required to be made, shall terminate, including any liability or obligation to defend, prosecute or continue any litigation.

7. DETERMINATION, EXTENT OF LIABILITY AND COINSURANCE.

This policy is a contract of indemnity against actual monetary loss or damage sustained or incurred by the insured claimant who has suffered loss or damage by reason of matters insured against by this policy and only to the extent herein described.

(a) The liability of the Company under this policy shall not exceed the least of:

(i) the Amount of Insurance stated in Schedule A; or,

(ii) the difference between the value of the insured estate or interest as insured and the value of the insured estate or interest subject to the defect, lien or encumbrance insured against by this policy.

(b) In the event the Amount of Insurance stated in Schedule A at the Date of Policy is less than 80 percent of the value of the insured estate or interest or the full consideration paid for the land, whichever is less, or if subsequent to the Date of Policy an improvement is erected on the land which increases the value of the insured estate or interest by at least 20 percent over the Amount of Insurance stated in Schedule A, then this Policy is subject to the following:

(i) where no subsequent improvement has been made, as to any partial loss, the Company shall only pay the loss pro rata in the proportion that the amount of insurance at Date of Policy bears to the total value of the insured estate or interest at Date of Policy; or

(ii) where a subsequent improvement has been made, as to any partial loss, the Company shall only pay the loss pro rata in the proportion that 120 percent of the Amount of Insurance stated in Schedule A bears to the sum of the Amount of Insurance stated in Schedule A and the amount expended for the improvement.

The provisions of this paragraph shall not apply to costs, attorneys' fees and expenses for which the Company is liable under this policy, and shall only apply to that portion of any loss which exceeds, in the aggregate, 10 percent of the Amount of Insurance stated in Schedule A.

(c) The Company will pay only those costs, attorneys' fees and expenses incurred in accordance with Section 4 of these Conditions and Stipulations.

8. APPORTIONMENT.

If the land described in Schedule A consists of two or more parcels which are not used as a single site, and a loss is established affecting one or more of the parcels but not all, the loss shall be computed and settled on a pro rata basis as if the amount of insurance under this policy was divided pro rata as to the value on Date of Policy of each separate parcel to the whole, exclusive of any improvements made subsequent to Date of Policy, unless a liability or value has otherwise been agreed upon as to each parcel by the Company and the insured at the time of the issuance of this policy and shown by an express statement or by an endorsement attached to this policy.

9. LIMITATION OF LIABILITY.

(a) If the Company establishes the title, or removes the alleged defect, lien or encumbrance, or cures the lack of a right of access to or from the land, or cures the claim of unmarketability of title, all as insured, in a reasonably diligent manner by any method, including litigation and the completion of any appeals therefrom, it shall have fully performed its obligations with respect to that matter and shall not be liable for any loss or damage caused thereby.

(b) In the event of any litigation, including litigation by the Company or with the Company's consent, the Company shall have no liability for loss or damage until there has been a final determination by a court of competent jurisdiction, and disposition of all appeals therefrom, adverse to the title as insured.

(c) The Company shall not be liable for loss or damage to any insured for liability voluntarily assumed by the insured in settling any claim or suit without the prior written consent of the Company.

10. REDUCTION OF INSURANCE; REDUCTION OR TERMINATION OF LIABILITY.

All payments under this policy, except payments made for costs, attorneys' fees and expenses, shall reduce the amount of the insurance pro tanto.

11. LIABILITY NONCUMULATIVE.

It is expressly understood that the amount of insurance under this policy shall be reduced by any amount the Company may pay under any policy insuring a mortgage to which exception is taken in Schedule B or to which the insured has agreed, assumed, or taken subject, or which is hereafter executed by an insured and which is a charge or lien on the estate or interest described or referred to in Schedule A, and the amount so paid shall be deemed a payment under this policy to the insured owner.

12. PAYMENT OF LOSS.

(a) No payment shall be made without producing this policy for endorsement of the payment unless the policy has been lost or destroyed, in which case proof of loss or destruction shall be furnished to the satisfaction of the Company.

(b) When liability and the extent of loss or damage has been definitely fixed in accordance with these Conditions and Stipulations, the loss or damage shall be payable within 30 days thereafter.

13. SUBROGATION UPON PAYMENT OR SETTLEMENT.

(a) **The Company's Right of Subrogation.**

Whenever the Company shall have settled and paid a claim under this policy, all right of subrogation shall vest in the Company unaffected by any act of the insured claimant.

The Company shall be subrogated to and be entitled to all rights and remedies which the insured claimant would have had against any person or property in respect to the claim had this policy not been issued. If requested by the Company, the insured claimant shall transfer to the Company all rights and remedies against any person or property necessary in order to perfect this right of subrogation. The insured claimant shall permit the Company to sue, compromise or settle in the name of the insured claimant and to use the name of the insured claimant in any transaction or litigation involving these rights or remedies.

If a payment on account of a claim does not fully cover the loss of the insured claimant, the Company shall be subrogated to these rights and remedies in the proportion which the Company's payment bears to the whole amount of the loss.

If loss should result from any act of the insured claimant, as stated above, that act shall not void this policy, but the Company, in that event, shall be required to pay only that part of any losses insured against by this policy which shall exceed the amount, if any, lost to the Company by reason of the impairment by the insured claimant of the Company's right of subrogation.

(b) **The Company's Rights Against Non-insured Obligors.**

The Company's right of subrogation against non-insured obligors shall exist and shall include, without limitation, the rights of the insured to indemnities, guaranties, other policies of insurance or bonds, notwithstanding any terms or conditions contained in those instruments which provide for subrogation rights by reason of this policy.

14. ARBITRATION.

Unless prohibited by applicable law, either the Company or the insured may demand arbitration pursuant to the Title Insurance Arbitration Rules of the American Arbitration Association. Arbitrable matters may include, but are not limited to, any controversy or claim between the Company and the insured arising out of or relating to this policy, any service of the Company in connection with its issuance or the breach of a policy provision or other obligation. All arbitrable matters when the Amount of Insurance is $1,000,000 or less shall be arbitrated at the option of either the Company or the insured. All arbitrable matters when the Amount of Insurance is in excess of $1,000,000 shall be arbitrated only when agreed to by both the Company and the insured. Arbitration pursuant to this policy and under the Rules in effect on the date the demand for arbitration is made or, at the option of the insured, the Rules in effect at Date of Policy shall be binding upon the parties. The award may include attorneys' fees only if the laws of the state in which the land is located permit a court to award attorneys' fees to a prevailing party. Judgment upon the award rendered by the Arbitrator(s) may be entered in any court having jurisdiction thereof.

The law of the situs of the land shall apply to an arbitration under the Title Insurance Arbitration Rules.

A copy of the Rules may be obtained from the Company upon request.

15. LIABILITY LIMITED TO THIS POLICY; POLICY ENTIRE CONTRACT.

(a) This policy together with all endorsements, if any, attached hereto

continued on remainder of cover sheet

FIGURE 12-1 Continued

CONDITIONS AND STIPULATIONS—CONTINUED

by the Company is the entire policy and contract between the insured and the Company. In interpreting any provision of this policy, this policy shall be construed as a whole.

(b) Any claim of loss or damage, whether or not based on negligence, and which arises out of the status of the title to the estate or interest covered hereby or by any action asserting such claim, shall be restricted to this policy.

(c) No amendment of or endorsement to this policy can be made except by a writing endorsed hereon or attached hereto signed by either the President, a Vice President, the Secretary, an Assistant Secretary, or validating officer or authorized signatory of the Company.

16. SEVERABILITY.

In the event any provision of the policy is held invalid or unenforceable under applicable law, the policy shall be deemed not to include that provision and all other provisions shall remain in full force and effect.

17. NOTICES, WHERE SENT.

All notices required to be given the Company and any statement in writing required to be furnished the Company shall include the number of this policy and shall be addressed to its Corporate Headquarters, 6630 West Broad Street, Richmond, Virginia 23230. Mailing address: P.O. Box 27567, Richmond, Virginia 23261.

IN WITNESS WHEREOF the Company has caused this policy to be signed and sealed, to be valid when Schedule A is countersigned by an authorized officer or agent of the Company, all in accordance with its By-Laws.

Lawyers Title Insurance Corporation

Attest:

Secretary

By:

President

POLICY OF TITLE INSURANCE

A WORD OF THANKS . . .

As we make your policy a part of our permanent records, we want to express our appreciation of this evidence of your faith in Lawyers Title Insurance Corporation.

There is no recurring premium.

This policy provides valuable title protection and we suggest you keep it in a safe place where it will be readily available for future reference.

If you have any questions about the protection provided by this policy, contact the office that issued your policy or you may write to:

Consumer Affairs Department
Lawyers Title Insurance Corporation
P.O. Box 27567
Richmond, Virginia 23261
TOLL FREE NUMBER: 1-800-446-7086

FIGURE 12-1   *Continued*

LTIC LTIC LTIC LTIC LTIC LTIC LTIC LTIC LTIC LTIC LTIC LTIC LTIC LTIC LTIC LTIC LTIC LTIC LTIC LTIC LTIC LTIC LTIC LTIC LTIC LTIC LTIC LTIC LTIC LTIC

Lawyers Title
Insurance Corporation

NATIONAL HEADQUARTERS
RICHMOND, VIRGINIA

SCHEDULE A   **OWNER'S POLICY**

CASE NUMBER	DATE OF POLICY	AMOUNT OF INSURANCE	ENDORSEMENTS	POLICY NUMBER

1. Name of insured:

2. The estate or interest in the land which is covered by this policy is:

3. Title to the estate or interest in the land is vested in:

4. The land referred to in this policy is described as follows:

SPECIMEN COPY

_____   _____
Countersignature Authorized Officer or Agent   Issued at (Location)

LTIC LTIC LTIC LTIC LTIC LTIC LTIC LTIC LTIC LTIC LTIC LTIC LTIC LTIC LTIC LTIC LTIC LTIC LTIC LTIC LTIC LTIC LTIC LTIC LTIC LTIC LTIC LTIC LTIC LTIC

Policy 136   This Policy is invalid unless the cover   035-0-136-0000
ALTA Owner's Policy (10-17-92)   sheet and Schedule B are attached.

ORIGINAL

FIGURE 12-1   Continued

Lawyers Title Insurance Corporation

OWNER'S POLICY

CASE NUMBER

POLICY NUMBER

SCHEDULE B

EXCEPTIONS FROM COVERAGE

This policy does not insure against loss or damage (and the Company will not pay costs, attorneys' fees or expenses) which arise by reason of:

SPECIMEN COPY

Policy 136 Litho in U.S.A.
ALTA Owner's Policy (10-17-92)

ORIGINAL

035-0-136-0001

FIGURE 12-1 Continued

4. The company is not liable for any damages until the adverse claim or interest has been established in the court of last resort (paragraph 9).

5. The policy is not transferable.

6. In the event title does fail and the title company settles the claim, the company is subrogated to the rights of the insured. This means that the title company is entitled to pursue all rights and remedies that the insured claimant would have had against any person or property claiming the adverse interest or creating the cloud on title. Furthermore, at this point the insured has no further rights against these adverse claimants. See paragraph 13.

Determination of Loss

The standard policy form provides that the company's liability shall not exceed the least of (1) the amount of insurance stated on the face of the policy; or, (2) the difference between the value of the insured estate or interest as insured and the value of the insured estate or interest subject to the defect, lien, or encumbrance insured against by this policy. The company is also obligated to pay all litigation costs and attorneys' fees of the insured, including those incurred by the insured if incurred *with the written authorization of the company.*

If it appears that a defect in the title is cured, only nominal damages are due, irrespective of what transpired between the time the title defect became apparent and the time the title company cured it, *Southern Title Guaranty Company v. Prendergast,* 494 S.W.2d 154, 158. See paragraph 9(a).

More difficult questions may arise if there is a partial failure of title. In all cases, the provisions of the policy will control, *Lawyers Title Insurance Corp. v. McKee,* 354 S.W.2d 401. (Note paragraph 8 of Conditions and Stipulations in Figure 12-1.) The extent of policy coverage may be difficult to determine, especially when the policy contains a number of encumbrances and when the damage any single deficiency may cause is in question. In some cases, the expenditure necessary to discharge the encumbrance has been held to be sufficient. In others, a proportional loss of value has been used as the measure of damages, *Hillsboro Cove, Inc. v. Archibald,* 322 So.2d 585. Recovery equal to the policy's face value seldom occurs, and many losses are not fully compensated. This is not because title insurance companies will not pay claims, but rather because policies are seldom written to cover appreciation in value.

Standard Exceptions   Certain standard exceptions are included in most title policies. Exceptions are potential title defects against which the policy does not insure. Insurance coverage against them generally is available only if an additional premium is paid and/or special riders are attached to the policy.

Some standard exceptions are listed under Schedule B of the sample standard owner policy of title insurance and could include the following:

1. *Rights or claims of parties in possession not shown by the public records.* It should be remembered that parties in possession may constitute constructive and/or actual notice to the lot purchaser. (This is discussed in greater detail in Chapter 9.) This exception may be eliminated and coverage made available if the title company is willing to make an on-site inspection of the property.

   The courts have been fairly consistent in holding that a purchaser has a duty to inspect the property to discover (1) any rights of parties in possession, *American Medical Intern, Inc.* v. *Feller,* 131 Cal Rptr. 270 (Cal. 1976), and (2) any easements or other obvious encumbrances. The courts hold that through personal inspection the purchaser should have known of any rights of the parties in possession, even though the title insurance company does not, *Halvorson* v. *National Title and Abstract Company,* 391 S.W.2d 112, and *Lawyers Title Insurance Corp.* v. *Research Loan and Investment Corp.* 361 F.2d 764.

2. *Easements, or claims of easements, not shown by public records.* This exception is particularly applicable for prescriptive easement rights.

3. *Encroachments, overlaps, boundary line disputes,* or other matters that would be disclosed by an accurate survey or inspection of the premises. Many of these exceptions can be deleted if requested, and if a current survey is provided. Some states require an additional charge. Before insuring these items, the title company normally would hire an approved surveyor to assist in determining whether the title is an insurable risk. The title company always has the option of not insuring title in the event it discovers encroachment or overlapping improvements.

   Courts have generally construed the title insurance policy against the insurer in the event there is a title defect due to a shortage or boundary conflict, *Brown* v. *St. Paul Title Ins. Corp.,* 634 F.2d 1103, *Dallas Title and Guaranty Company*

v. *Valdes*, 445 S.W.2d 26, and *McDaniel* v. *Lawyers Title Guaranty Fund*, 327 So.2d 852 (Fla. 1976).

4. *Any lien, or right to lien, for services, labor, or materials* heretofore or hereafter furnished, imposed by law and not shown by the public records. Title insurance does not cover any subsequent assessments or liens arising after the date of the policy.

5. *Taxes not yet due and payable.* Everyone is considered by law to be on notice of the existence of taxes and tax liens. They arise at the first of every year and remain with the property until paid. Most title policies insure that the only taxes that the purchaser will be liable for are those for the current year and subsequent years.

Clearly, excepting items such as these from coverage substantially limits the title insurance companies' exposure to liability. Those property owners desiring broad insurance coverage need to pay particular attention to the list of exceptions, and to consider paying additional fees to obtain such coverage when warranted by the circumstances.

Disadvantages and Limitations of Title Insurance

Title insurance does not provide complete coverage under all circumstances. One obvious instance is when a property is so valuable that it exceeds the value of the title insurance company's assets. This occurs more often than one might think, as in construction costing tens of millions of dollars. These problems are usually handled by obtaining coinsurance or reinsurance to spread the risk with other companies.

Title insurance may also not provide the desired protection when a large block of raw land is being purchased in a major metropolitan center. Title policies do not ordinarily cover the cost of the subsequent improvements erected on that property unless the title policy has specific provisions for renewal in the event certain improvements are constructed, although in some states a credit can be applied toward a policy that includes the improvements. Since the title policy is for a fixed amount, it also does not cover inflationary or other increases in real estate values.

Finally, there are circumstances under which the grantor may be more solvent than the title insurance company. In such instances, the grantor's personal warranty may be worth more than a title insurance policy. However, this possibility is offset somewhat by the purchaser's affirmative duty and expense of filing the lawsuit (whereas the title insurance company is required to provide indemnification with no legal fee expenses to the purchaser).

SUMMARY   To guard against major financial losses, all real estate purchasers desire some degree of assurance that they are receiving a good and sufficient title. Available methods of title assurance include Torrens registration, the grantor's warranties, an abstractor's certificate, an attorney's opinion of title, and title insurance.

Torrens registration is not widely available. It envisions a system similar to that used to transfer automobile titles. A new registration certificate is issued when the title is transferred, mortgaged, and so forth.

Grantor's warranties of title refer to warranties made in the deed transferring title; these were outlined in Chapter 8. They provide adequate protection when the grantor is still alive and has the financial capacity to pay a large judgment.

An abstractor's certificate actually provides little assurance of title. Rather, it only certifies that an abstract contains all matters of record affecting title to the subject tract of real estate. The abstract itself is then used as the basis for an attorney's opinion on title, or perhaps for a title search by a title insurance company. Clearly, an error in an abstract could affect the legal opinion or title search on the title. So abstractors are liable for damages caused by their errors. For these reasons they are required to be bonded in many states.

An attorney's examination of abstract with his subsequently delivered opinion on title is the oldest of the two major methods of title assurance. If the attorney is negligent in his assessment of title and this causes a purchaser to suffer financial losses, he is legally responsible for these damages. For this reason, many lawyers carry errors and omissions (malpractice) insurance coverage.

Increasingly, real estate purchasers are turning to title insurance as their chosen method of title assurance. For a one-time fee, two different kinds of policies are typically available: (1) A mortgagee title policy protects lenders against financial loss when the title proves defective. (2) An owner's title insurance policy provides protection for real estate purchasers/mortgagors. Since only the initial value or cost is insured, the coverage does not increase when inflation occurs. Additionally, proportional reduction clause formulas may limit recovery to the value of particular property rights held by others, and the title insurance company need not pay any damages if it corrects the title defect. On the other hand, it often is required to pay the insured's reasonable attorney's fees incurred in defending suits against adverse claimants.

Title insurance policies typically except several items from coverage unless an additional premium is paid. These exceptions may include discrepancies or conflicts in boundary lines, shortages in area, encroachments or overlapping of improvements, property taxes for current and subsequent years, liens, rights of parties in possession, and rights under leases or easements.

Title insurance does not provide adequate coverage under all circumstances. Examples of instances when it may be inadequate include when the property's value exceeds the title insurance company's assets, and when subsequent improvements are excluded from coverage.

---

1. What are the methods of title assurance most often used in your state? In your geographical area?

2. How does protection provided by title insurance differ from protection provided by an attorney's opinion on the quality of title?

3. What are the advantages and disadvantages of the Torrens title registration system?

4. Why is an abstractor's certificate, taken alone, usually considered to be an inadequate method of title assurance?

DISCUSSION
QUESTIONS

13

Closings

The final consummation of a real estate transaction is commonly termed the *settlement* or the *closing*. It is at the closing that the deeds and other documents are signed and delivered, and purchase money and mortgage funds are distributed. After closing, all legal obligations of and to the parties should have been fulfilled.

A closing is both a legal and a business function. In a well-planned closing, all papers are prepared by the attorneys and are reviewed by the clients prior to the actual closing.

    The vast majority of closings in the Midwest and Far West are held at title companies, where a third-party escrow agent serves as a depository for all legal instruments and funds. The escrow agent is normally a disinterested third party who holds and distributes the instruments and funds pursuant to the terms of the earnest money contract or formal escrow agreement.

    The widespread use of escrow closings generally makes it unnecessary for all the parties to attend the closing together, because they may execute all legal instruments in advance of closing and rely on the escrow agent to deliver them as called for by the earnest money contract. In fact, many attorneys, brokers, and lenders prefer all parties not attend the closing at the same time. Depending on the circumstances, and especially with residential sales, the presence of both the buyer and the seller may create an air of tension or emotionalism that actually hinders the closing process.

    Closings in the North, Northeast, and East Coast are generally held at the lender's place of business, at one of the parties' lawyer's offices, or at the Registry of Deeds. The services of an escrow agent may not be utilized. When there is no disinterested third-party escrow agent, it is important that both parties (buyer and seller) be represented by their legal counsel and their real estate agents to make sure they both are adequately represented and protected.

The typical residential transaction actually involves two closings rather than one. First, there is the closing of the sale from the seller to the purchaser. Second, there is the closing of the loan involving the mortgagee and the mortgagor. The mortgagee's only interest in the actual sale closing (between the seller and purchaser) is that the purchaser is getting a clear, unencumbered title, subject only to the mortgagee's new lien to be created at the loan closing. On the other hand, at the loan closing transaction the seller has no interest in the papers and documents to be signed between the purchaser and the lender.

On occasion, there are closings in which no sale transaction takes place. An example is a loan closing that involves the refinancing of real estate by the owner, or the borrowing of money that is to be secured by the owner's real estate. This type of closing is very common among real estate developers, contractors, and investors.

The diagram shown in Figure 13-1 indicates how the typical residential transaction closing is handled.

ESCROW CLOSINGS   The escrow function is often handled by a title company or by a disinterested attorney, and is one of the keys to a successful closing. An escrow officer who is trusted by both parties helps ease the air of suspicion or distrust that may exist when the parties think of themselves as adversaries.

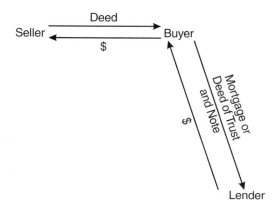

FIGURE 13-1   Illustration of Typical Residential Transaction Closing

Escrow closings often are created pursuant to an escrow agreement in which specific instructions are given to escrow officers. In some situations, the intent and specifications for the escrow may be contained in the earnest money contract, *Ferguson* v. *Caspar*, 359 A.2d 17 (D.C., 1976) and *Press* v. *Marvalan Industries, Inc.*, 422 F. Supp. 346 (1976).

Escrow agreements are generally considered to be irrevocable. Although this may at first seem harsh, it must be remembered that the escrow officer must be in a position to act impartially. It is difficult for him to function if he is expected to respond to the whims and capricious desires of either party.

The function of the escrow officer is to hold the instruments and funds in trust until the conditions and specific obligations required in the earnest money contract or escrow instructions are performed. At that time, he distributes the funds and signed instruments, and the transaction is considered complete.

Relation-Back Doctrine

The irrevocability of escrow agreements has led to the adoption of the relation-back doctrine. To illustrate it, suppose a deed is deposited with an escrow officer for delivery to the grantee upon compliance with specified conditions found in the escrow agreement. Under this doctrine, this delivery relates back to the time of escrow deposit so as to divest the grantor of title at the time the deed is delivered into escrow. However, title does not pass to the grantee until all the escrow conditions have been performed and the escrow agent delivers the deed to him. Thus, the relation-back doctrine supports the theory of irrevocability by divesting the grantor of title at the time of deposit into escrow. The doctrine is particularly useful in facilitating final consummation of a transaction when a grantor dies or becomes insane after delivering the deed into escrow.

Closing into Escrow

The escrow function also performs a very valuable accommodation to the parties by allowing different closing times for each of the parties. To illustrate, one party may be forced to leave town at an early date. If so, he may simply sign all instruments as required by the contract and leave them with the escrow agent. This is called *closing into escrow.*

The other party may perform the obligations required of him at some later date. As long as all contracting parties perform their obligations within the time specified, the escrow closing should proceed in a normal manner.

As stated previously, many knowledgeable professionals prefer that the parties close into escrow, so that potential tension may be avoided at closings. One only needs to leave one closing with all the parties crying (including the real estate agents and escrow officer) to realize how valuable closing into escrow can be!

Escrow Agent Liabilities and Duties

A person or business entity acting as an escrow agent is normally held to a duty of due care, honesty, and integrity. Usually, the full liability of the escrow officer in the event of a mistake or negligent error is to pay the expense of restoring the status quo, *Buhler* v. *Marrujo,* 524 P.2d 1015 (N.M. 1974).

One of the more perilous undertakings of the escrow officer at closing is when one party indicates that the other has breached the contract. When this occurs, the escrow agent normally waits for a judicial determination of whether the contract has been broken before returning any documents or earnest money to either party. That is, he does not take sides, but rather performs his function as ordered by a court. To do otherwise would involve a risk of breaching his duty of care as an escrow agent.

DOCUMENTS DISTRIBUTED AT CLOSINGS

To determine exactly which instruments need to be executed and delivered at the closing (irrespective of whether it is an escrow closing), it is good advice for brokers and lawyers to prepare a closing checklist. This is a very simple thing to do, and helps ensure a successful closing.

The closing checklist is very simply created by carefully reading the earnest money contract and making a list of all documents and funds each party should have in his possession upon leaving the closing. Furthermore, a checklist should be prepared naming those documents that will be transferred directly to the courthouse for recordation before being distributed to the proper parties.

A typical closing checklist for the seller might include the following items:

1. Cash (this may be delayed until funded by the purchaser's loan).
2. Mortgage or deed of trust, if the seller is financing the transaction.
3. A promissory note, if seller financing is involved.

In a similar fashion, a buyer's checklist might include these items:

1. The deed transferring title (which is normally forwarded to the courthouse for recording).
2. Warranties as requested or required (e.g., mechanical equipment inspection, termite inspection, slab inspection, or roof inspection).
3. The owner's title insurance policy.
4. A bill of sale (if any personal property is transferred).
5. Estoppel certificates to evidence the payoff figure for the underlying indebtedness, if any.
6. A receipt for the purchase price paid.

If the purchase involves income-producing property, the buyer may walk away with the following additional items:

1. Estoppel letter by tenants.
2. Landlord's estoppel certificates, signed by the prior landlord.
3. Assignments, which may include the following:
   a. Service contracts.
   b. Warranties on mechanical equipment.
   c. Rents and deposits.
   d. Escrow funds contained in the seller's mortgage account.
   e. Insurance policies.
4. A letter from the seller to the tenants indicating the new ownership.
5. A letter to the building manager indicating the change in ownership.
6. The rental rolls (normally certified).
7. Copies of leases.
8. Employment contracts.
9. Assignment of trade name.

If the property purchased is a condominium, the following additional items may be obtained:

1. The master deed or condominium declaration.
2. The bylaws of the condominium homeowners' association.
3. Copies of the builder's warranties.

The use of a closing checklist provides an easy method of assuring that the closing will go properly and that no documents are misplaced or funds misappropriated.

PARTIES AND THEIR ROLES AT THE CLOSING

To secure a smooth closing it is important that all parties understand the role of each party involved. The parties who may be present at the closing include the following:

1. The escrow officer.
2. The seller.
3. The purchaser.
4. The real estate agent(s).
5. The attorneys.

On occasion, lenders or their attorneys may also attend.

The escrow agent may perform two functions. He always performs the previously discussed duties of an escrow agent. Additionally, if the escrow agent represents a title company, he also functions as the agent of the title guarantor. Although commonly misunderstood, the escrow agent's duties do not include being a "gopher," negotiator, or soothsayer. It is not his job to make phone calls, check on loan proceeds, or talk to anyone's relatives or friends with respect to the closing. Rather, he simply distributes the instruments and funds as called for by the escrow agreement or earnest money contract.

The purchaser or seller is often represented by both a real estate agent and an attorney. The latter in particular is there to protect the interests of his client.

The real estate agent's role is primarily that of negotiator and arbiter between the parties. He may be invaluable in keeping the parties aware of what is happening at the closing and in avoiding conflicts that could lead to one party backing out of the deal. Most real estate transfers are very personal transactions that are people-oriented. Since the agent knows and understands the parties' personal objectives and business relationships, he is very helpful in performing these functions.

Although a closing is not technically a legal function, the buyer and seller should be represented by their attorneys. It is the attorney who is uniquely qualified to understand the legal ramifications of the escrow agent's function, the representations made by both parties, and the interpretations of the instruments used at the closing. He is the only individual present who is capable of explaining an individual's legal rights as these pertain to the transaction. Moreover, any nonlawyer who attempts to interpret the documents for another or to explain an individual's legal rights is practicing law without a license.

The separate roles and functions of all parties—escrow agent, buyer, seller, real estate agent, and attorney—overlap to a certain degree. At the same time, each has a unique role to perform. Although it is not absolutely essential that each be present at closing, care should be taken to make sure that the rights of both the buyer and the seller are fully protected.

RESPA

REAL ESTATE SETTLEMENT PROCEDURES ACT

Most closings are relatively simple and do not last very long, depending on the complications involved and the number of parties required to consummate the transaction. However, there have been a number of severe criticisms of closings generally because of the amount of fees and costs that are taken out of the purchaser's and seller's funds—expenses that were not disclosed prior to the closing. It was as a result of some of these imprudent practices across the country that Congress felt compelled to pass a new law called the *Real Estate Settlement Procedures Act,* which required certain disclosures to all parties prior to a closing and the use of certain forms during the closing. These requirements are of particular importance in residential transactions, and therefore will be discussed here in some detail.

The Real Estate Settlement Procedures Act (RESPA) was originally passed in 1974. Amendments to the act, as well as to the applicable regulations, were passed in 1975 and 1976. Most of the provisions of RESPA were passed to control practices of certain states that had a large number of fees going to the escrow officers, attorneys, and other various and sundry parties—fees that came as a surprise to the consumer when he attended the closing. As a federal statute, RESPA applies in all states.

Transactions Covered

Just as the federal Truth-in-Lending Act passed Regulation Z to establish guidelines for the enforcement of the Truth-in-Lending Act, so the Department of Housing and Urban Development passed what we call *Regulation X,* which establishes the guidelines for enforcement of the Real Estate Settlement Procedures Act (RESPA). There were significant changes to RESPA in 1992. Under Regulation X, RESPA is construed to apply to all federally related loans, which are loans that meet the following requirements:

1. The loan (other than temporary financing, such as a con-

struction loan) must be secured by a first or subordinate lien on residential real property.

2. The loan must be secured by a lien on property upon which there is located a one- to four-family residential structure, either presently existing or to be constructed from the loan proceeds, or a condominium or co-op unit.

3. The mortgaged property must be located in a state.

4. The loan must be made by a lender whose accounts are insured by, or the lender regulated by, an agency of the federal government. RESPA also requires that the lender, other than a state agency, invest in more than $1 million per year in residential real estate loans; or the loan must be insured, guaranteed, or assisted by the federal government; or the loan must be made in connection with the Housing and Urban Development program administered by the government; or the loan must be intended to be sold to FNMA, GNMA, FHLMC, or to a lender who intends to sell the mortgage to FHLMC.

Any installment sales contract, land contract, or other contract for otherwise qualifying residential property is a federally regulated mortgage loan if the contract is being funded in whole or in part by process of the loan made by any maker of mortgage loans specified under the Act.

It is not difficult to see that RESPA applies to all institutional lenders and to virtually all residential transactions.

Exemptions from RESPA   Originally, there were eight exemptions to the application of RESPA. The Housing and Community Development Act of 1992, however, limited those exceptions to:

1. Farms of 25 acres or more.

2. Home equity line of credit transactions.

3. Transactions involving only modification of existing obligations (excluding new obligations created to satisfy an existing obligation or loans for increased amounts).

4. Bridge loans.

5. Assumptions, if no lender approval is required.

6. Temporary financing such as a construction loan.

7. Secondary market transactions.

The general requirements of RESPA, similar to those of the Truth-in-Lending Act, simply involve disclosure of all costs and items applicable to a particular closing transaction. We will now discuss some of these disclosures that are important to the purchaser: disclosures that involve the lender, the escrow agent, and the title companies.

Lender Requirements

The requirements of RESPA imposed on the lender consist primarily of the lender giving a special information booklet in any RESPA-covered transaction to every person who submits a loan application in writing, Rev. Reg. X, §3500.6(a). The purpose of the booklet is to provide as much information as possible about the borrower's rights and obligations in connection with the closing of the loan transaction. The booklet must be provided to the borrower not later than the third business day after the lender receives the loan application, Rev. Reg. X, §3500.6(a). The book is basically in the format provided by HUD, although certain variations are allowed to be made by the lender as long as they are HUD-approved.

In addition to the special information booklet, the lender must also furnish the borrower with a good faith estimate of the settlement charges that the borrower is likely to incur in connection with the loan transaction, Rev. Reg. X, §3500.7(a). Although there is some discretion allowed for the good faith estimate, it is required that the form used must include the lender's name, must be clear and concise, and must inform the borrower that other charges may be incurred at the time of closing, Rev. Reg. X, §3500.7(d).

Regulations effective April 1, 1991 require lenders and servicers of loans to provide borrowers disclosure statements concerning the establishment and maintenance of escrow accounts. The lender must provide an initial escrow account statement within 45 days of closing, or show it on the HUD-1 statement at closing. The form to be used is promulgated by the federal government, and is required to be used, 12 U.S.C. 2609, §10(c)(1)(C).

Settlement Agent's Requirements

RESPA requires that the escrow agent must use the standard settlement or closing statement, often referred to as *HUD-1* (or *HUD-1A* for refinancings), Rev. Reg. X, §3500.8(a). There are exceptions provided when the borrower is not required to pay any closing costs, but, at least to date, this option has not been widely utilized. There have been some complaints about the use of HUD forms because they are confusing in parts and sometimes difficult to explain to prospective purchasers during the closing transaction.

There is a basic requirement to itemize all charges paid by the borrower and seller, except for those that are not imposed by the lender and are paid for outside of the closing. If there are any costs required by the lender, even if paid outside the closing, they must still be noted on the settlement form; these would be marked P.O.C. to indicate their payment outside of the closing. It is interesting to note that both the buyer's and seller's expenses are noted on the same form. There have been some complaints that the buyer and the seller preferred to keep their parts of the transaction confidential. Therefore, RESPA regulations provide that the seller's columns may be deleted from the buyer's copy and the buyer's columns may be deleted from the seller's copy, Rev. Reg. X, §3500.8(b). There is additionally a general requirement that the settlement agent must provide the lender with a copy of each settlement statement.

One of the more fundamental required disclosures is that, upon the buyer's request, the settlement agent must permit the borrower to inspect the HUD forms at any time during the business day before the scheduled closing. There is some limitation on this, however, in that the escrow officer need only complete the items known at the time, and has no obligation to furnish information not available prior to the closing date. With few exceptions, the final settlement statement is to be delivered to the borrower and seller, or to their agents, at or before the time of the settlement.

Controlled Business and Referral Fees

Prohibitions apply to controlled businesses wherein a lender or other person is in the position to refer business as part of a real estate settlement service. This simply prevents "kickbacks" and unearned fees from going to a party in a position of control who might take advantage of the other person's lack of bargaining power. These prohibitions are a particular concern for real estate agents because they may often find themselves in situations where somebody providing a settlement service (appraisal, inspection, title examination, preparation of documents, origination fees for loans) may be willing to pay the broker a referral fee for "networking" that business. These kinds of referral fees are strictly prohibited. The purpose of RESPA is to eliminate those kickbacks or referral fees that tend to unnecessarily increase the cost of settlement services to the consumer. The interpretations under the statute are very broad. A referral includes any oral or written action which has the effect of affirmatively influencing the selection by any person of a provider of a settlement service when such person will pay for such settlement service or business. It also refers to a person being required to pay for a settlement service to a particular provider of that settlement service, or business incident thereto.

There are specific exceptions to Section 8 that also affect a real estate licensee. With the advent of computerized loan origination services (which some brokers choose to utilize) the borrower may pay for those computer loan origination services as long as the required disclosure is provided. Controlled business arrangements are also exceptions, provided that:

1. At or prior to the time of the referral a disclosure is made of the existence of such an arrangement to the person being referred, and, in connection with such referral, such person is provided a written estimate of the charge or range of charges generally made by the provider to which the person is referred, except that when a lender makes a referral, this requirement may be satisfied at the time that the estimates of settlement charges are required.

2. That person is not required to use any particular provider of settlement services.

3. The only thing of value that is received from the arrangement, other than the permitted payments, is a return on the ownership interest or franchise relationship.

A controlled business arrangement is defined by the statute as an arrangement in which a person who is in a position to refer business incident to or a part of a real estate settlement service involving a federally related mortgage loan, or an associate of such person, has either an affiliate relationship with or a direct or beneficial ownership interest of more than 1% in the provider or affirmatively influences the selection of that provider.

Any person who violates RESPA shall be fined not more than $10,000 or imprisoned for not more than one year, or both. Those who violate the prohibitions are also jointly and severally liable to the person or persons charged with the settlement service involved in the violation in an amount equal to three times the amount of any charge paid for such settlement service. (See RESPA §8(b).)

Anyone who violates this provision is liable to the buyer in an amount equal to three times the charge for such title insurance, or other damages received, RESPA §9(b).

Simple? Afraid not. Real estate brokers have recently expanded business opportunities to make additional income through computerized loan origination, providing settlement services, and other affiliated business relationships.

New Rules

HUD published a new "final rule," addressing control business arrangements, referral fees, computerized loan origination systems, and other related issues under RESPA. The final rule is accompanied by three "Statements of Policy"—1996-1, 1996-2, and 1996-3. The final rule became effective October 7, 1996. These are discussed in Chapter 6.

Escrow Accounts   There has been a common practice among lenders to require the borrower to maintain an escrow account for the payment of taxes and insurance during the term of the mortgage. There have been some complaints made by the borrowers that they are required to pay certain advanced amounts into the escrow account that exceed the amount that would be required to pay for the tax and insurance requirements. The RESPA rules provide that any amounts collected for escrow accounts for payments of taxes and insurance can only be as much as needed to pay the taxes, insurance premiums, and other charges attributable to the period between the closing and the time the amount is to be paid, plus one-sixth (two months) of the estimated annual amount to be paid. All future collections for payment into the escrow account are limited to one-twelfth of the charges to become due within the next year.

The foregoing is, of course, not even a slight attempt at explaining all the RESPA rules. As in the case of the Truth-in-Lending Act, there are many publications available that explain most of the provisions of the RESPA Act and Regulation X in much greater detail than can be given here.

This area of the law has also been greatly expanded by new rules, applicable to lender's escrow or improved account procedures.

SUMMARY   The consummation of a real estate transaction is referred to as the settlement or closing. It is here that all deeds, documents, and purchase money change hands, and the terms of the earnest money contract are fully carried out.

Technically, two closings are usually involved in the consummation of a real estate transaction. One closes the sale transaction. The other closes the loan transaction.

Disinterested third parties often serve as escrow agents to handle the closing. The use of escrow agents makes it possible for closings to occur without both the buyer and the seller being present at the same time. Deeds and other legal documents are executed and deposited in escrow for delivery at the closing. The escrow agent is

A. SETTLEMENT STATEMENT

U.S. DEPARTMENT OF HOUSING
AND URBAN DEVELOPMENT

OMB NO. 2502-0265

B. TYPE OF LOAN		
1. [ ] FHA 2. [ ] FmHA 3. [X] Conv. Unis.	6. FILE NUMBER DELONE	7. LOAN NUMBER
4. [ ] VA 5. [ ] Conv. Ins.		

8. MORTGAGE INS CASE NUMBER

C. NOTE:This form is furnished to give you a statement of actual settlement costs. Amounts paid to and by the settlement agent are shown. Items marked "[POC]" were paid outside the closing; they are shown here for informational purposes and are not included in the totals.   4.2   05-95   (4/DELONE)

D. NAME AND ADDRESS OF BORROWER	E. NAME AND ADDRESS OF SELLER	F. NAME AND ADDRESS OF LENDER
Heidi Delone 2424 Newpaige Lane City, State 00000	Homer Leavitt 1654 West 12th Street City, State 00000	Acme National Bank 1111 West 1st Street City, State 00000

G. PROPERTY LOCATION	H. SETTLEMENT AGENT 141777938	I. SETTLEMENT DATE
1654 West 12th Street City, NY 00000 Any County, New York	Honen & Wood, P.C. PLACE OF SETTLEMENT 126 State Street, 5th Floor City, State 00000	September 15, 1996

J. SUMMARY OF BORROWER'S TRANSACTION		K. SUMMARY OF SELLER'S TRANSACTION	
100. GROSS AMOUNT DUE FROM BORROWER		400. GROSS AMOUNT DUE TO SELLER	
101. Contract Sales Price	123,000.00	401. Contract Sales Price	123,000.00
102. Personal Property		402. Personal Property	
103. Settlement Charges to Borrower line 1400	4,036.89	403.	
104. Payoff Mortgage		404.	
105.		405.	
Adjustments for items paid by Seller in advance		Adjustments for items paid by Seller in advance	
106. Village Taxes to		406. Village Taxes to	
107. County taxes 09-16-96 to 01-01-97	233.88	407. County taxes 09-16-96 to 01-01-97	233.88
108. School Taxes 09-16-96 to 07-01-97	789.62	408. School Taxes 09-16-96 to 07-01-97	789.62
109. Fuel Oil Adjustment	130.00	409. Fuel Oil Adjustment	130.00
110.		410.	
111.		411.	
112.		412.	
120. GROSS AMOUNT DUE FROM BORROWER	128,190.39	420. GROSS AMOUNT DUE TO SELLER	124,153.50
200. AMOUNTS PAID BY OR IN BEHALF OF BORROWER		500. REDUCTIONS IN AMOUNT DUE TO SELLER	
201. Deposit or earnest money	3,000.00	501. Excess Deposit (see instructions)	
202. Principal Amount of New Loan(s)	90,000.00	502. Settlement Charges to Seller line 1400	8,510.50
203. Existing Loan(s) Taken Subject to		503. Existing Loans Taken Subject to	
204.		504. Payoff 1st Mtg to 1st National Bank	48,000.00
205.		505. Payoff of second mortgage loan	
206.		506. Deposit retained by seller	3,000.00
207.		507.	
208.		508.	
209.		509.	
Adjustments for items unpaid by Seller		Adjustments for items unpaid by Seller	
210. Village Taxes to		510. Village Taxes to	
211. County taxes to		511. County taxes to	
212. School Taxes to		512. School Taxes to	
213.		513.	
214.		514.	
215.		515.	
216.		516.	
217.		517.	
218.		518.	
219.		519.	
220. TOTAL PAID BY/FOR BORROWER	93,000.00	520. TOTAL REDUCTION AMOUNT DUE SELLER	59,510.50
300. CASH AT SETTLEMENT FROM/TO BORROWER		600. CASH AT SETTLEMENT TO/FROM SELLER	
301. Gross Amt Due from Borrower (line 120)	128,190.39	601. Gross Amount Due to Seller (line 420)	124,153.50
302. Less Amt Paid by/for Borrower (line 220) (	93,000.00)	602. Less Reductions Due Seller (line 520) (	59,510.50)
303. CASH [X] FROM [ ] TO BORROWER	35,190.39	603. CASH [X] TO [ ] FROM SELLER	64,643.00

The undersigned hereby acknowledge receipt of a completed copy of pages 1&2 of this statement & any attachments referred to herein.

BORROWER _____
Heidi Delone

BORROWER _____

SELLER _____
Homer Leavitt

SELLER _____

HUD-1 (3-86) RESPA, HB 4305.2

FIGURE 13-2   HUD Settlement Statement

L. SETTLEMENT CHARGES		
700. Total Sales/Brokers Commissions Based on Price $ 123,000.00 @ 6.0000 % = 7,380.00	PAID FROM	PAID FROM
Division of Commission (line 700) as follows:	BORROWER'S	SELLER'S
701. $ 3,690.00 to List-Rite Realty	FUNDS AT	FUNDS AT
702. $ 3,690.00 to Quick Sale Realty	SETTLEMENT	SETTLEMENT
703. Commission Paid at Settlement		7,380.00
704.		
800. ITEMS PAYABLE IN CONNECTION WITH LOAN		
801. Loan Origination Fee 1.0000 % to Acme National Bank	900.00	
802. Loan Discount % to		
803. Appraisal Fee to Acme National Bank	100.00	
804. Credit Report to Acme National Bank	55.00	
805. Flood Certification Fee to		
806. Title Exam Fee to		
807. Underwriting Fee to		
808.		
809.		
810.		
811.		
900. ITEMS REQUIRED BY LENDER TO BE PAID IN ADVANCE		
901. Interest from 09-15-96 to 10-01-96 @$ 18.493150/day(16 days 7.5000%)	295.89	
902. MIP TotIns. for LifeOfLoan for 360 months to US Department of HUD		
903. Hazard Insurance Premium for 1 years to Your Insurance Co. 240.00 [POC]		
904. to		
905.		
1000. RESERVES DEPOSITED WITH LENDER		
1001. Hazard Insurance 3.000 months @ $ 20.00 per month	60.00	
1002. Mortgage Insurance months @ $ per month		
1003. Village Taxes months @ $ per month		
1004. County taxes 10.999 months @ $ 66.67 per month	733.33	
1005. School Taxes 3.000 months @ $ 83.33 per month	250.03	
1006. months @ $ per month		
1007. months @ $ per month		
1008. Aggregate Adjustment	-413.36	
1100. TITLE CHARGES		
1101. Settlement or Closing Fee to Honen & Wood, P.C.	400.00	
1102. Abstract or Title Search to		
1103. Title Examination to		
1104. Title Insurance Binder to		
1105. Document Preparation to		
1106. Notary Fees to		
1107. Attorney's Fees to		
(includes above item numbers: 1101,1103,1105)		
1108. Title Insurance to Safety Title Insurance Company	525.00	
(includes above item numbers:)		
1109. Lender's Coverage $ 90,000.00		
1110. Owner's Coverage $		
1111. Buyer's Attorney to Law Office	400.00	
1112. Seller's Attorney to Law Firm		500.00
1113.		
1200. GOVERNMENT RECORDING AND TRANSFER CHARGES		
1201. Recording Fees: Deed $ 19.00 ;Mortgage $ 37.00 ;Releases $ 13.50	56.00	13.50
1202. City/County Tax/Stamps: Deed $;Mortgage $		
1203. State Tax/Stamps: Deed $ 492.00 ;Mortgage $ 650.00	650.00	492.00
1204. Equalization & Assessment to Any County Clerk	25.00	
1205. Gains Tax Affidavit to Any County Clerk		5.00
1300. ADDITIONAL SETTLEMENT CHARGES		
1301. Survey to		
1302. Pest Inspection to Dead Bug Company		120.00
1303.		
1304.		
1305.		
1400. TOTAL SETTLEMENT CHARGES (Enter On Lines 103, Section J and 502, Section K)	4,036.89	8,510.50

By signing page 1 of this statement, the signatories acknowledge receipt of a completed copy of page 2 of this 2 page statement.

(4/DELONE)
Certified to be a true copy

Honen & Wood, P.C.
Settlement Agent

FIGURE 13-2   Continued

given specific instructions of what to do at the closing, either by the terms of an irrevocable escrow agreement or in the earnest money contract itself. The use of irrevocable escrow agreements helps ensure the escrow agent's impartiality.

The relation-back doctrine applies to escrow closings. Under it, the seller is divested of title when he deposits his deed in escrow, but the buyer does not receive title until the deed is delivered to him. This permits transactions to be closed in a timely fashion in the situation when the seller dies after he deposits his deed in escrow but before the closing occurs.

An escrow agent generally has the legal duty to use due care, honesty, and integrity in closing a real property transaction. His basic liability is to bear the expense of restoring the status quo that would have existed if he had not made an error.

To avoid errors, brokers and lawyers often make checklists of documents and monies that should be distributed to their clients at closing. The checklist for the seller might include cash, and if seller-financing is involved, a mortgage or deed of trust, and a promissory note. The buyer's checklist might contain a deed, any warranties requested, an owner's title insurance policy, a bill of sale if personal property is being transferred, estoppel certificates, and a receipt for the purchase price paid.

When income-producing property is involved, the buyer might also receive estoppel letters from tenants; estoppel certificates from the previous landlord; assignment of service contracts, of warranties on mechanical equipment, of rents and deposits, of escrow funds in the seller's mortgage account, and of insurance policies; a letter from the seller to the tenants indicating the new ownership; a letter to the building manager indicating the change in ownership; certified rental rolls; copies of all leases; employment contracts; and any assignments of trade names.

Furthermore, if the closing checklist is for a condominium, the buyer might also receive copies of the master deed or condominium declaration, copies of the bylaws of the condominium homeowners' association, and copies of any builders' warranties.

Escrow officers, buyers and sellers, real estate agents, and attorneys all have specific roles at the closing. The escrow officer's role is to distribute all documents and monies as required by the escrow agreement or earnest money contract. If he represents a title company, he may also serve as agent of the title guarantor. When present, the buyer and seller generally are there to represent their own interests. They may also be represented by real estate agents and/or attorneys. The real estate agent's role at closing is that of chief negotiator and arbiter between the parties. The personal nature of the real estate transaction makes this a highly important role. An attorney protects his client's legal rights at the closing, and he is there to make sure his client receives everything that is due him.

The federally enacted Real Estate Settlement Procedures Act (RESPA) requires certain disclosures of closing costs prior to closing so that the parties will not be surprised by the magnitude of costs at the closing. RESPA is administered by the Department of Housing and Urban Development (HUD), principally through the promulgation of Regulation X. This regulation applies to all federally related loans; to any nonstate agency lender who loans more than $1 million annually; to loans guaranteed, insured, or assisted by the federal government; to loans made in connection with HUD programs; and to loans ultimately intended to be sold to FNMA, GNMA, or FHLMC. Regulation X primarily applies to residential loans.

Several kinds of loans are specifically exempt from RESPA. These include loans to finance the purchase of 25 or more acres; home equity line of credit transactions; the assumption of an existing loan if no lender approval is required; temporary financing such as construction loans; transactions involving only modification of existing obligations; bridge loans; and secondary market transactions.

In addition to the disclosure requirements for lenders, RESPA requires escrow agents to use a standard closing statement (except when the borrower pays no closing costs). It contains an itemization of closing costs.

RESPA prevents sellers from forcing purchasers to buy title insurance from a particular title company. It also prevents lenders from collecting escrow funds for insurance and taxes in excess of what is actually needed. It also sets out required escrow accounting procedures.

DISCUSSION QUESTIONS

1. Is it absolutely essential for the buyer, seller, real estate agent, buyer's attorney, or seller's attorney to be present at the real estate closing (settlement)?

2. Where are real estate closings (settlements) usually held in your area?

3. Why is the relation-back doctrine important to escrow closings (settlements)?

4. Who ultimately bears the cost of complying with RESPA requirements?

14

Real Estate Liens

A real estate lien is a security interest in a person's real estate, to ensure that some financial obligation will be discharged. A person who holds a lien against a specific tract of real estate is generally referred to as a *secured creditor,* and he may force the sale of his debtor's real estate to satisfy the debt.

The liens discussed in this chapter are limited to those that attach directly to real estate. Recall that some liens that do not attach directly to real estate, including chattel mortgages and other liens arising under the Uniform Commercial Code, were discussed in Chapter 4.

Real estate liens generally are categorized according to the source from which they are derived. In this chapter we discuss equitable liens (implemented upon principles of equity), statutory liens (implemented by statute), constitutional liens (implemented by the state constitutions), and contractual liens (liens created by contracts).

EQUITABLE LIENS

The principal requirement of an equitable lien is that the prospective lien holder must show an intention to charge the property with a debt. As its name suggests, an equitable lien is one that is recognized and enforced by the courts under equitable principles of fairness and good conscience. As with most other equitable principles, an equitable lien is founded on an express or implied contract pertaining to some specific real property, and will not be applied when the aggrieved party has an adequate remedy at law. Since an equitable lien is not usually recorded, it will not prevail against the claim of a subsequent purchaser or creditor who is not aware of its existence.

Equitable liens normally fall into two categories, a vendor's lien and a tenant's lien. In those states in which it is recognized, a *vendor's lien* is implied every time the real property is transferred by deed and the purchase money is not paid in full, *Estate of Somers* v. *Clearwater Power Co.*, 684 P.2d 1006 (Idaho 1984). A deed with a vendor's lien generally is interpreted as an executory contract, coupled with a power of rescission (right to rescind the contract) in the event of default. The rescission must be judicially imposed, and it applies to no other type of indebtedness except the purchase price of real estate.

Many transactions involve mortgage liens or deed of trust liens, mechanics' and materialmen's liens, and other express liens that can be recorded and are effective against subsequent bona fide purchasers and creditors, whereas, as already noted, a vendor's lien is not recorded and is not good against subsequent purchasers or creditors. For this reason a vendor's lien normally is relied on only as a "last resort" when a purchaser defaults. In upholding and enforcing this lien, courts generally determine that the purchaser holds title in trust for the seller until the purchase price is paid.

The second type of equitable lien is a *tenant's lien*. It may arise when the tenant constructs an improvement on the real property that increases the value of that property to the extent that the landlord would be unjustly enriched if the tenant was not adequately reimbursed. This improvement is made with the landlord's knowledge, and the tenant fully expects to be paid for it. Although it is advisable for the landlord and tenant to work out a compensation agreement prior to construction, a tenant's lien does provide a judicial remedy when the landlord refuses to reimburse the tenant for the cost of the improvements.

STATUTORY LIENS

Most states have basically two types of statutory liens affecting real property: judgment liens, and mechanics' and materialmen's liens.

Judgment Lien

A judgment lien is created by obtaining a state or federal court final judgment against a debtor, irrespective of whether it was obtained by default, by confession, or for a deficiency. The judgment usually does not become final until the period has elapsed for appealing a court decision. This period may vary among states, but typically is 30 days.

Once the judgment is final, the creditor must have the court's clerk "abstract" the judgment. The creditor may then record the abstract in the real property records in the appropriate public office in the county in which the land is located. This recording process is called *filing an abstract of judgment*. This is the essential step in creating the judgment lien.

Once the lien has been filed in the public records, it is said to be "perfected." The abstract of judgment may be filed in as many counties as the judgment creditor desires. It usually creates an independent lien in each county where it is recorded. Most states give full faith and credit to a court judgment decided elsewhere. So if the judgment debtor moves out of state, the abstract of judgment could also be filed and be effective in other states.

State laws provide for judgments to remain effective (collectible) for a specific period of time ranging from 3 to 20 years. Within this time period, the creditor must levy execution to force the sale of the property, or he may lose his right under the judgment. Most states, however, provide that judgments may be extended for the same length of time as the original effective period, if the judgment creditor follows the proper procedure for securing such time extensions. As in the case of any other lien, a judgment lien can be released if the creditor is satisfied (paid), or if the debtor files bankruptcy or otherwise loses his property.

Judgment liens generally follow the previously discussed "barber shop rule," and are given priority over all subsequent liens and interests in the real property (except for federal, state, and other tax liens as provided by law). Moreover, it is important to note that a judgment lien is a *general* lien (a lien that attaches to all property owned by the debtor in the county in which the lien was recorded). General liens attach to subsequent land acquisitions by the debtor. This is particularly beneficial to creditors when debtors inherit real estate.

Abstracts of judgments might not attach to homesteads or to marital or other exempt property. Likewise, the proceeds of the sale of such exempt property often remain exempt from forced sale for some fixed time period following such sale. If the proceeds are reinvested in exempt property, this property may also be exempt from forced sale pursuant to a judgment lien. Irrespective of these debtor family protection exemptions, once a judgment lien has been attached to real estate, most title companies will not guarantee title until the lien has been satisfied. For this reason, a judgment lien is often given more credence than is technically provided for by law.

Mechanics' and Materialmen's Liens

Mechanics' and materialmen's liens (also called either *mechanics' liens* or *M and M liens*) exist to protect the mechanic or materialman in the event of nonpayment of funds due him for supplying labor or materials for improving real property. Every state has a statute for creating mechanics' and materialmen's liens, and specific requirements must be met to perfect and enforce these liens. Two states, Texas and California, also provide constitutional protection for their mechanics' liens. The statutes in most other states vary widely in content and procedure, and it is difficult to find a common thread running among them. The Commissioners of Uniform State Laws attempted to create a Uniform Mechanics' Lien Act many years ago, but the statutory differences were so great and so ingrained in the various state laws that they gave up their attempt.

The difficulty in resolving the conflict among states is compounded because there are at least four people whose rights must be considered in a typical M and M lien situation: (1) the *original contractor,* who has a direct contractual relationship with the owner; (2) the *subcontractors* and *materialmen* (often called *derivative claimants*), who have a direct contractual relationship with the original contractor and in turn derive their rights to create an M and M lien through his contract with the property owner; (3) the *mortgagee,* who loaned money for the construction of the improvements, or who may have an underlying first lien mortgage on the property; and (4) the *owner,* who is seldom well versed in the law of M and M liens and contractors' rights.

Creation. Anyone who has supplied material or has furnished services or labor to real estate can file an M and M lien against the property. Claimants may perfect the lien by filing a contract prior to beginning work in some states (e.g., New Jersey), but most states do not permit M and M liens to be perfected until after the services have been performed and/or materials incorporated into the real property. In most cases, the lien does not extend to chattels/personal property delivered to the site, unless it was clearly intended that they should be incorporated into the real estate or that they should become a fixture under local law.

State requirements vary for filing notice of an M and M lien, depending on whether the claimant was the original contractor, subcontractor, or materialman. In most states, the effective date of the lien is the date that the contract to perform the services was signed, or the date that construction was begun, or when the lienor delivered his labor and material to the job. A few states postpone the lien's effective date to the time when it is formally filed in the county records. The effective lien date is often of critical importance when lien holders are competing for limited funds.

Effect. Aside from protecting the M and M lien claimant, publicly filing the lien gives all subsequent creditors and purchasers constructive notice of it. In this way, an M and M lien holder obtains priority over subsequent parties.

Rights under M and M liens may conflict with rights of other lien holders. Each state has developed rules to resolve these conflicts, with the most significant conflict often being between the mechanics and materialmen and the mortgagee. Generally, if the mortgagee files his mortgage prior to the M and M lien, the mortgage lien is given priority. However, there are exceptions, especially in the case of construction mortgages. If the contractor's work was begun prior to the mortgage lien being recorded, or if the material can be removed from the building without material injury to the structure, the M and M lien may receive priority.

Other conflicts may arise between the owner and subcontractors, between whom there is no direct contractual relationship. An owner may pay his contractor, but the contractor may fail to pay the subcontractor. If so, the subcontractor may be able to obtain an M and M lien against the property.

A property owner on whose property improvements are being made should take special precautions to protect himself and prevent M and M liens from arising. A purchaser of property on which improvements have recently been made should do likewise. These precautions might include:

- Dealing only with contractors who are adequately bonded.
- Contractually prohibiting subcontracting.
- Making direct payments to laborers and material suppliers to make sure that they are paid.
- Making checks jointly payable to both contractors and the subcontractors, laborers, or materialmen.
- Generally being alert and asking questions to make sure that the contractor pays or has paid everyone whom he hires or from whom he obtains construction materials.

Purchasers may also insist on copies of receipts from all laborers and materials supplied, and a copy of the seller's warranty that both have been paid.

On first impression, one might conclude that laborers and materialmen would be well protected by the many statutory provisions. However, this is not necessarily the case in all states. In some states, the perfection of an M and M lien is time-consuming, and the lien can be created only if the statutory method is strictly followed. Furthermore, debt collection may be difficult because of thinly capitalized property owners, and collection time may be substantial when a forced judicial sale is necessary. In most states, an M and M lien carries with it the right to be paid reasonable attorney's fees if it is necessary to hire an attorney in order to collect the debt.

CONSTITUTIONAL LIENS

In some states, certain liens may arise because of specific provisions in the state constitutions. These provisions may include M and M liens and liens for rent due to landlords. Although these liens arise automatically by law, they may also be recorded so as to ensure protection against subsequent creditors and lenders. Filing a constitutional lien essentially converts it into a statutory lien.

The important point to remember about constitutional liens is that they exist regardless of whether statutory filing deadlines are met.

CONTRACTUAL LIENS

Contractual liens arise when two parties contractually agree to create the lien as security for some type of obligation. A common example of a contractual lien is a real estate mortgage, which offers security for money to be loaned.

Leases are also a common source of contractual liens. Under them a tenant may offer his furniture and personalty in the leased premises as security for his rental payments. A lease may also provide for statutory landlords' liens and owners' of building liens.

REDEMPTIONS AFTER FORCED SALE

The forced sale of real estate may be the end result of creditors enforcing their rights under several different types of liens. In some states and under some liens, the debtor may have the right to redeem his property and retrieve title by reimbursing the buyer and paying all expenses incurred in connection with the forced sale. In other states, the right of redemption may be quite limited or nonexistent.

SUMMARY

A real estate lien is a legal claim that can be enforced against real estate. It represents a secured debt which, if not paid voluntarily, can be collected through a specific procedure leading to the forced sale of real estate.

Real estate liens are classified according to their source. They include equitable liens, statutory liens, constitutional liens, and contractual liens.

Equitable liens are those that arise judicially under principles of fairness and good conscience. As with any other equitable remedy, they are available only when the aggrieved party has no adequate legal remedy at hand. The major requirement for an equitable lien is that the prospective lien holder show an intent to charge a property with a debt.

There are two types of equitable liens: the vendor's lien and the tenant's lien. In those states in which it exists, a vendor's lien arises any time real estate is sold and the seller is not paid in full. A tenant's lien may arise when, with the landlord's knowledge, a tenant adds a permanent improvement to real property, one that would unjustly benefit the landlord if the tenant was not reimbursed. It is best not to rely on the prospect of a tenant's lien; rather, there should be an agreement for reimbursement executed in advance of construction.

Statutory liens are those arising because of some specific state law. Most states have at least two types of statutory liens: judgment liens, and mechanics' and materialmen's liens.

A judgment lien is based on a final court judgment for money damages issued in a lawsuit against a debtor. It involves filing an abstract of judgment in the appropriate county records. This causes a lien to attach to all nonexempt real property owned by the judgment debtor in that county.

Mechanics' and materialmen's liens (often called M and M liens) arise for the protection of parties who furnish labor or materials for improvements to real property. Those seeking the protection of this lien generally must follow a well-established and detailed procedure in order to establish their security interest. This is particularly true of subcontractors and other derivative claimants.

Property owners and purchasers should take certain precautions to avoid M and M liens, or else they may find themselves in the position of paying for labor or materials a second time. For the property owner, these precautions include insisting that contractors and subcontractors be bonded, denying contractors the right to subcontract, and/or making checks jointly payable to both contractor and subcontractor or material suppliers. The buyer may seek protection by obtaining copies of receipts from laborers and material suppliers, and by insisting on warranties from the seller that there are no outstanding M and M liens.

Constitutional liens refer to those that are created by state constitutional provisions. These liens vary from state to state, but often include M and M liens and certain landlord liens for rent due. They automatically arise by law, and public filing often converts them into statutory liens. Importantly, they exist even when statutory filing deadlines have not been met.

Contractual liens are those expressly created by contract. Some common examples of contractual liens include mortgages and liens created under leases. The latter often includes a tenant's personal property located on the leased property.

Property owners may have the right to redeem property from the foreclosure sale purchaser, depending on both the state and the type of lien involved.

DISCUSSION QUESTIONS

1. Define equitable liens, statutory liens, constitutional liens, and contractual liens.

2. Who may use an M and M lien to collect a debt due?

3. Under a tenant's lien, why doesn't the improvement added by the tenant become a fixture which becomes the landlord's property without any necessity of reimbursing the tenant?

4. Explain the abstract of judgment process.

15

Landlord and Tenant Relationships

In Chapter 2, freehold estates were defined as those lasting for an indefinite period of time. Ordinary residential and commercial real property leases may last for a specified period of time, and are common examples of leasehold estates. The person contracting away the right of occupancy, possession, and/or use is generally called the *landlord*, or *lessor*. The *tenant*, or *lessee*, is the party who has gained the right of occupancy, possession, and/or use for some specific lease period. A leasehold estate is also referred to as a *tenancy*. The person who holds tenancy rights has more than just the mere use of the premises; he also has the occupancy and possession rights superior to those of anyone else.

During the lease period, the lessor's rights are usually limited, and in some cases, certain of these rights may be inferior to the lessee's rights. Under certain circumstances, lessors may have no rights to possession during the lease period, and may even find it difficult to evict a non-rent-paying lessee in a timely fashion. In addition, recent years have seen much new legislation passed that is consumer- or lessee-oriented. Specific statutory provisions now exist in some states and have become very important factors in determining the precise rights held by both lessors and lessees.

In this chapter we investigate the types of tenancies generally available, the legal requirements for leases, the types of leases, the rights to assign or sublease, the legal remedies to evict lessees failing to make lease payments, and the lessees' rights against the lessors.

There are four basic types of tenancies or leasehold estates: (1) estates for years, (2) estates from period to period, (3) estates at will, and (4) estates at sufferance.

TYPES OF TENANCIES

Estates for Years　　An estate for years (tenancy for years) is characterized primarily as a tenancy with a definite termination date. It may be written or oral, although in most states the statute of frauds specifically provides that a lease for real estate for a term of more than one year is not enforceable unless it is in writing and signed by the person to be charged (sued). Typical examples of estates for years include long-term office leases, ground leases, and residential leases. There is no requirement that the term of an estate for years be of any specified length. It can be for a period of time less than a year, as long as there is a definite termination date. The manner and notice required to terminate an estate for years are generally set out in the lease agreement.

Estates from Period to Period　　An estate from period to period (tenancy from period to period) normally includes estates from month to month and/or estates from year to year, depending on the rent-paying period. Of the two, estates from month to month are much more common. In most cases they are created by oral leases, provided there is no written agreement to the contrary. In most states, tenancies from month to month must have either one month's or 30 days' written notice in order for either party to terminate the lease. In many jurisdictions, leasehold estates can only be terminated on a rent-paying date, and the day on which notice is given is not counted as part of the required time period. Thus, in some cases it may take up to one day less than two full months to terminate a tenancy from month to month. This illustrates the importance of delivering written notice of termination in a timely fashion.

Estates at Will　　An estate at will is an estate that is terminable at the will of either the lessor or the lessee. It is a lease of indefinite duration. It differs from a freehold estate (discussed in Chapter 2), because the lease may be terminated at any time with no particular period of notice required. An example of an estate at will is when the party takes possession of the premises without reaching any agreement on the terms of his lease. An employee who is provided with living quarters as part of his employment has been designated as "enjoying" an estate at will, *Sauce* v. *Monroe*, 39 So.2d 174.

Estates at Sufferance　　An *estate at sufferance (tenancy at sufferance)* is the estate that exists when a person lawfully began possession of real property but wrongfully continued possession after the termination of his right of possession. A common example of an estate at sufferance is when the lessee has entered into the possession under an effective lease and wrongfully remains in possession after his failure to pay rent. Another example is when a vendor sells his property and then fails to vacate the premises on the date he contractually agreed to deliver possession to the purchaser, *ICM Mortgage Corp.* v. *Jacob,* 902 S.W.2d 527 (Tex.—El Paso, 1995).

Typically under an estate at sufferance there are no rights and obligations existing between the parties. The lessor has no duty of reasonable care toward the lessee, and the lessee has no obligation to pay rent or give notice of termination. To prohibit this situation from arising, most leases and rental agreements provide that, upon unlawfully holding over, the lessee will remain subject to the same terms and conditions under the estate of sufferance as would have existed under an estate from month to month. This provision creates a tenancy from period to period, and specifies definite obligations between the parties.

LEASE AGREEMENTS IN GENERAL

Leases are contracts involving the transfer of possession of real property. In most states, the statute of frauds requires leases for terms longer than one year to be in writing in order to be enforceable. As with other contracts, leases are strictly interpreted and construed. Most leases, especially the more sophisticated varieties used for office space and retail (shopping center) space, have become so detailed that it is necessary to secure the services of a lawyer to adequately protect each party. Some of the more important rules of lease interpretation follow.

LEASE REQUIREMENTS

The legal requirements for leases are generally quite similar to those of other real estate contracts. Specifically, the lease must:

1. Be in writing and be signed by the party to be charged.
2. Contain a specific, identifiable lessor and lessee (the parties to the lease).
3. Show the intent of the lessor to grant the lessee the right to enter and possess the designated premises for a fixed consideration.
4. Give an adequate description of the leasehold premises.
5. Delineate a specific time period of occupancy.
6. Be delivered and accepted.

The first five items are self-explanatory. The sixth item, delivery and acceptance, is normally implied when the lessee takes possession of the premises. His possession generally binds him just as effectively as an express spoken or written acceptance.

Importantly, if the lessor sells the property, the lessee still holds his estate in land as against the new owner. His lease is not terminated by the sale unless the lease expressly so provides, *Carteret Properties* v. *Variety Donuts, Inc.,* 228 A.2d 674 (N.J. 1967), *New Freedom Corp.* v. *Brown,* 272 A.2d 401 (Md. 1971), and *Cohen* v. *Thomas & Son Transfer Line, Inc.* 586 P.2d 39 (Colo. 1978).

The lessee may further wish to protect his interest against bona fide purchasers by recording the lease or by some memorandum thereof. If so, the lease or memorandum will also need to be acknowledged.

TYPES OF LEASES

There are four types of leases, depending on the manner in which the rent is paid:

1. A lease for a fixed term (gross lease).
2. A percentage lease.
3. A net lease.
4. A ground lease.

It is important to note that any one of these types of leases is going to have its own character, depending on the type of premises it is intended to transfer. For instance, the terms of a gross lease vary widely, depending on whether the premises are a single-family residence, office space, or an apartment. No one standard lease form is applicable to all situations.

Gross Lease

A gross lease most often exists for a fixed period of time and requires rental payments of a fixed sum of money. The lessor is usually obligated to pay property taxes, insurance premiums, special assessments, and any needed repairs. In recent years, the fixed rental provisions have been made subject to some rental adjustment for operation costs and utility escalation, so that increased expenses can be passed on by the lessor. However, for the most part, the gross lease is considered to be one of a fixed term and fixed rental amount. This type of lease is commonly used when leasing office space and apartments.

Net Lease

A net lease is generally one in which, in addition to rent, the lessee pays all of the expenses of operation, and the lessor's only obligation is to make the mortgage payment. Although the term "net lease" has no true legal significance, the term *net lease* is standard jargon in the real estate business to describe certain types of leases, as follows. In a *net lease*, the lessee pays real estate taxes and special assessments in addition to his rent. In a *net-net lease,* in addition to the foregoing, the lessee pays insurance premiums, for both hazard and liability insurance. In a *net-net-net lease* (often called a *triple net lease),* the lessee also pays for repairs and maintenance of the property.

The net lease is often used by the passive investor-lessor who has a solvent, creditworthy lessee. For example, many retail fast-food establishments prefer to use triple net leases so that they have complete control over the maintenance and attractiveness of the premises, as well as over certain operating costs. The investor-lessor is normally guaranteed a fixed rate of return after his mortgage payment has been made. This lease plan also guarantees a fixed rental rate for the lessee. In some situations, the lessee will pay his lease payments directly to the lender, and the lender then sends a "difference" check to the investor-lessor after the mortgage payments and other costs have been deducted. This assures the lender of timely payments and in any of these situations, lending decisions are based on the quality of the lessee rather than on the financial statement of the investor-lessor.

Percentage Lease

A percentage lease is most often used for leasing retail premises, including shopping centers, shopping malls, and strip centers. It may be employed any time a lessee's business income is dependent upon sales volume purchased by the shopping public.

The percentage lease normally provides for the lessee to pay a relatively low base rent—often at least enough for the lessor to be able to meet his mortgage payment with perhaps a small amount of profit. Then, in addition to the base rent, the lessee also must make lease payments that are contingent upon a percentage of the gross sales that he makes. This percentage may vary from 2 to 11% or more, depending on the lessee's size and kind of business. Large, major lessees normally pay a much lower percentage of their sales as rent, because their volume of business is much higher and because they are often a "draw" for smaller lessees located nearby in other space owned by the same lessor. The percentage rentals may be paid monthly (after preliminary accounting for gross income), quarterly, or annually. Because of the volatile nature of utilities and other costs in recent years, most lessors prefer that the percentage rentals be paid monthly so that they may meet their financial obligations without depending on other sources of income.

The percentage lease provides many advantages to both the lessor and the lessee. The lessee gets a lower rate for his rental and has to pay an increased rent only if, in fact, his volume of business justifies it. There is also an implied obligation to continue use and occupancy, particularly if the tenant is a "draw" tenant, *Walgreen Arizona Drug* v. *Plaza Center Corp.*, 647 P.2d 643 (1982). The lessor, on the other hand, is not only assured of having his mortgage payments paid, but he stands to make higher profits if the lessee makes higher profits. Therefore, it is to the advantage of the lessor to maintain his shopping center in such a manner as to make it attractive and accessible to all potential shoppers. There is an incentive for both the lessor and the lessee to make their respective businesses as successful as possible. As a general rule, the percentage lease never creates a partnership agreement between the lessor and the lessee.

Ground Lease   A *ground lease* is quite similar to a gross lease in that it involves a simple lease payment to the lessor. However, the ground lease differs from a gross lease in that a ground lease involves a rather complicated method of mortgaging the leasehold estate so that the lessee can borrow money for the construction of improvements. In order to give lenders an incentive to make this type of loan, a ground lease normally allows for *subordination* of the leasehold premises, making the underlying lease rent collection rights inferior to the first lien construction mortgage. Because of its long-term nature, a ground lease often has liberal provisions permitting assignment and subletting. This type of lease is often one of the basic tools used in the sale and lease-back mortgaging technique discussed in Chapter 10.

ASSIGNMENTS AND   Under common law, the lessee had the right to transfer his interest
SUBLEASES   in the leased property. However, because the quality of the lessee may affect both ease of rent collection and the condition of the property at the end of the lease period, in more recent years, several states have passed laws prohibiting lease assignment or subletting without the lessor's consent. A few states provide that the lessor's consent must not be unreasonably withheld, *Cohen* v. *Ratinoff*, 147 Cal. App. 3d 321 (Cal. 1983).

In the *sublease* situation, there is still a direct contractual relationship (privity of contract) between the lessor and the lessee.

There is also a privity of contract between the lessee (sublessor) and the sublessee. There is no privity of contract between the sublessee and the original lessor. This absence of a direct contractual relationship makes the lessee (sublessor) still primarily liable on payments to be made to the original lessor.

In the *assignment* situation, all rights, title, and interest of the original lessee (assignor) are assigned to the assignee, who then has a direct privity of contract with the original lessor. This direct contractual relationship causes the assignee to be liable to the lessor for all lessee obligations contained in the lease.

Since assignments and subleases are distinctly different legal concepts (see Figure 15-1), to avoid potential misunderstandings it is essential that legal documents transferring the lessee's interest be carefully drafted. If it is not clear which—assignment or sublease—was intended, most courts tend to interpret the instrument as a sublease if there is any reversionary interest retained by the original lessee, *Walgreen Arizona Drug* v. *Plaza Center Corp., supra.* This interpretation keeps the lessee (sublessor) primarily liable for rent payments, and prevents the lessor from getting "stuck" with a sublessee who cannot meet the rent schedule set out in the lease and/or who will not leave the leased premises in good condition at the expiration of the lease.

A lease can have as many special provisions as the mind can imagine. The scope of these lease provisions has become so large in recent years that one finds typical office leases or retail leases

SPECIAL LEASE PROVISIONS

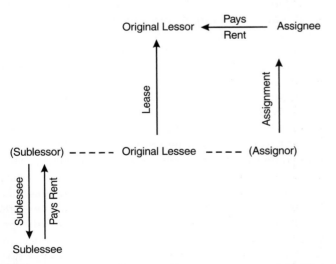

FIGURE 15-1 Illustration of Assignments and Subleases

bound in book form, rather than stapled together as a short-form document. Because of the variety of applicable special provisions in any given situation, we will not discuss any of these special provisions in detail. There are extensive treatises on lease law that would be of greater benefit to the more advanced student than any further discussion that could be given here.

Some recent case decisions, however, have a bearing on certain lease provisions which deserve discussion. For instance, if the lease contains an option to purchase, it has been held that, when the option to purchase has been exercised, the relationship of landlord and tenant ceases and that of a vendor and purchaser begins. No rent is then payable as the purchase and sale agreement becomes controlling. The tenant then has the right to enforce specific performance of his purchase contract, *Pitman v. Sanditen*, 626 S.W.2d 496 (Tex. 1981). There has also been considerable litigation over provisions for noncompetition clauses in leases. This type of clause typically prohibits a lessor from leasing to tenants in competition with each other. This allows a tenant to fully develop his own market share in the shopping center and provides for a more complementary tenant mix, which operates in the best interest of both the landlord and the tenant. There has been some concern that such clauses violate federal and state antitrust laws as a restraint of trade. The general theory in some states is that the noncompetition clause is legal if reasonably exercised. Another item of conflict that has frequently arisen is whether or not an agreed late charge in a lease agreement constitutes "interest" under state statutes. It is generally held that such a late charge is not a charge for the forbearance of money as defined by statute, and therefore is not a loan transaction that falls within the jurisdiction of usury laws.

REMEDIES FOR DEFAULT
Lessor's Remedies

The lessor's remedies against a defaulting lessee typically include ejectment or eviction of the tenant, physical repossession of the leased premises, and suit for recovery of damages caused by the lessee's breach of the lease contract. Other remedies which may be set out in the lease include taking physical repossession of the leased premises without first instituting judicial action, accelerating the due date for all rent for the balance of the term, seizing the lessee's personal property, and enforcing specific performance of the lease. These last types of remedies, however, are unavailable in most states because of specific state laws, court interpretations making these remedies violations of constitutional due process, and/or impracticality. Specific performance, for instance, may be impractical and difficult to enforce against a lessee who is no longer on the premises and/or has no money with which to pay his obligations. Similarly, the power to accelerate the due date of all rent for the balance of the term has often been treated as unjust enrichment for the lessor and as a penalty for the lessee rather than bona fide liquidated damages, *Friedman* v. *Colonial Oil Company*, 18 N.W.2d 196 and *Pierce* v. *Kennedy*, 169 S.W.2d 1115.

A lessor's remedies against a defaulting lessee are further limited by recent consumer-oriented landlord and tenant statutes that have been passed in most states. The simplest, safest, and most often used remedy for a lessor is the judicial action of *eviction* (also called *ejectment* and/or *forcible entry* and *detainer*), which provides for a fairly quick method of determining whether the lessor or lessee has the right of possession to the premises. Technically, an eviction action is proper for (1) any unlawful entry on to real property, or (2) any willful holding over by the lessee after his rights of possession have terminated, usually caused by failure to pay rent. The notice provisions for eviction are relatively short, but must be complied with in order that the lessee's rights will not be terminated without due process of law and a trial on the merits. Therefore, even with a short notice period being required for eviction and with early scheduling of hearing dates, a lessee with competent legal counsel may often forestall the eviction proceedings for two or three months before final adjudication of the right to possession can be determined. Delays in reaching a final judgment may result from improper service of process, postponements because of the temporary unavailability of parties or witnesses, time extensions to permit busy legal counsel to adequately prepare for the trial, and appeals from adverse judgments.

Another judicial remedy available to a lessor against the lessee is a lawsuit for damages caused by the lessee's breach of the lease agreement. The lessor's difficulty in pursuing this particular remedy is twofold: first, the damages are normally in excess of the jurisdictional amount that can be recovered in the court trying the possession issues (e.g., eviction actions may be tried in a small claims court while damage actions typically are filed in the basic trial court), and second, if the lessee refuses to pay his rent, the lessor may find it extremely difficult to force him to do so. The time and expense of establishing the damage claim, attaching assets, and forcing their sale may cause some lessors to decide that they will be better off financially to absorb the loss and not pursue their claim against the lessee. This is often the case, because a lessor ordinarily is not entitled to recover attorney's fees incurred in pursuing the damage claim unless the lease agreement specifically provides for the lessee to pay them.

Lessee's Remedies   In contrast to the diminishing number of lessors' remedies, the judicial remedies available to a lessee against a lessor have been substantially expanding. In recent years, local and/or state landlord and tenant statutes have typically been oriented more to lessees than lessors, and in some instances deceptive trade practices acts have favored lessees by permitting recovery of treble damages, punitive damages, plus the recovery of attorney's fees, *Geiger* v. *Wallace*, 664 P.2d 846 (Kan. 1983). In addition to the remedies specifically provided for by statute, the lessee typically has the right to sue the lessor for (1) damages for breach of the lease, (2) retaliatory eviction, (3) rent abatement, (4) rent application, and (5) rent withholding.

A cause of the action for *damages* is normally more effective against the lessor than against the lessee, because the lessor always has one or more assets that are attachable and subject to levy by execution. Therefore a lessee normally has a source from which he can recover if he sues for damages.

Rent abatement has recently been interpreted to be available for a wide range of situations, including partial destruction of the premises and depriving the lessee of the use of premises because of a lessor making repairs. Hawaii, Louisiana, Maine, and Wisconsin now provide rent abatement as a specific remedy in circumstances such as these.

Rent application generally provides that in the event of (1) a default by the lessor or (2) the lessor's failure to make certain required repairs, the lessee may make such repairs and deduct their cost from his rent. A number of states have passed statutes authorizing rent application under these circumstances, including New York, California, Montana, North Dakota, Massachusetts, Hawaii, and Washington.

Rent withholding, on the other hand, is usually an alternative to rent application. Rent withholding is normally not an advisable remedy *unless* statutorily or judicially provided for, because a lessee's refusal to pay rent may cause an automatic default under the terms of the lease agreement. In some jurisdictions default for withholding of rent may be avoided if the lessee pays his rent into an escrow account until the disputed repairs have been made, or until other obligations of the lessor have been satisfied.

Retaliatory eviction has been a remedy developed principally by the courts in most jurisdictions, although some states have enacted legislation providing lessees with this defense. The retaliatory eviction rules are designed to give the lessee the right to complain about conditions of his leased premises without fear of reprisal from the lessor. Retaliatory eviction guarantees the lessees' constitutional rights of free speech, *Edwards* v. *Habib*, 397 F.2d 687, cert.

denied, 393 U.S. 1016, and clearly prevents intimidation of the lessee by the lessor, *E. & E. Newman, Inc.* v. *Hallock,* 281 A.2d 544.

Warranty of Habitability

Historically, the doctrine of *caveat emptor* was the accepted rule in rental apartments. However, in recent years this doctrine has come under close legal scrutiny, and many states have adopted a *warranty of habitability* for leases of residential property. The warranty of habitability basically means that a landlord should provide a certain minimum level of "livability" in order to be entitled to collect rent. The definition of "habitability" varies widely from state to state, depending on each state's reasons for enforcing the warranty of habitability. Some courts have held that it is an enforcement of the housing code, *Javins* v. *First National Realty Corp.*, 428 F.2d 1071; others rely on consumer protection statutes, *Lemle* v. *Breeden*, 462 P.2d 470 and *Kamarath* v. *Bennett*, 568 S.W.2d 658. Some states have also recognized the implied warranty of habitability as an obligation because of the contractual nature of the lease agreement, *Boston Housing Authority* v. *Hemmingway*, 293 N.E.2d 831. Those states that have clearly recognized the implied warranty and habitability to date are New Jersey, New York, Hawaii, California, District of Columbia, Massachusetts, Washington, Minnesota, and Texas. When the lessor breaches his warranty of habitability, he becomes liable for one or more of the following tenant actions: damages, rescission, reformation, or specific performance.

The implied warranty of habitability, however, has been construed to reach leases of commercial real estate properties although the warranty is of <u>suitability</u> rather than habitability. Only Texas has enforced this so far, but the theory may be finding more favor with the courts, *Stevan* v. *Brown*, 458 A.2d 466 (Md. 1983). *Neuro-Development Associates of Houston* v. *Corporate Pines Realty Corp.*, 908 S.W.2d 26 (Tex. App.—Houston [1st Dist.] 1995). In many states that have not adopted the implied warranty of habitability, residential leases may be interpreted to include this same duty of ordinary care not to damage the lessee. For instance when a lessor retains control of a portion of the leased premises, some state laws charge the landlord with the duty of ordinary care in maintaining that portion so as not to damage the lessee, *Franklin Drug Stores, Inc.* v. *Gur-Sil Corp.*, 152 S.E.2d 77 (N.C. 1977) and *Kline* v. *7500 Massachusetts Avenue Apartment Corp.*, 439 F.2d 477, 141 U.S. App. D.C. 370, 43 A.L.R. 3rd 311. Often this means the lessee takes the full risk as to whether the premises are fit for the uses for which he intends to use them.

SUMMARY   One of the most common real estate transactions is the simple lease. In it, the landowner (usually called the *landlord* or *lessor*) transfers the occupancy, possession, and/or use rights to the tenant (also called the *lessee)* in exchange for some specified rental payment.

Leasehold estates are often called *tenancies* or *estates,* and consist of four principal types: estates for years, estates from period to period, estates at will, and estates at sufferance.

In most states the statute of frauds requires leases greater than one year in length to be in writing in order to be enforceable. For this reason most leases classified as estates for years will be in writing. Importantly, the method of giving notice and the time period required to terminate an estate for years are usually specified in the written lease agreement. Despite their name, estates for years may last for any definite and ascertainable period of time (ranging from a few weeks to several years).

Most oral leases create an estate from period to period. Such estates may be either from year to year or from month to month, depending on when rent is earned and payable. Most are the month-to-month variety. Since most estates from month to month are created orally, it becomes important to determine how they are terminated. Either one month's or 30 days' written notice is generally required to do so, and either the landlord or the tenant can terminate by giving proper notice. Many states permit the lease to be terminated only on a rent-paying date, and the day on which notice is given is not generally counted as part of the required notice period. Thus, the time period required for termination can extend upward to two full months, depending on when notice is given.

An estate at will is a leasehold estate of indefinite duration that can be terminated by either party. An example of an estate at will is when an employee lives on the premises as a condition of his employment.

An estate at sufferance occurs when a person lawfully comes into possession but unlawfully continues possession beyond the date on which his lease rights terminate. In essence, an estate at sufferance is equivalent to having no estate at all. However, in many jurisdictions the tenant continues to have the same rights and responsibilities as originally existed during the effective term of his lease.

There are several general rules of interpretations for leases, rules that exist in many states. Basically these rules hold true unless the lease agreement contains contrary provisions. For instance, generally a landlord makes no warranties to repair the premises or even to make the premises habitable. Rather the tenant is essentially in a "caveat emptor" position in these two respects.

Other general interpretations include that the landlord does have the legal duty to use ordinary care to maintain the leased property so as not to damage the lessee. Also, no warranties or representations will generally be implied; so the parties should be careful to include such items as their lease agreement.

In addition, the parties should be sure to meet all requirements for a lease. Depending on the state and the lease period, a lease should include the following requirements:

1. It must be in writing and be signed by the party against whom enforcement is sought.

2. The landlord and tenant must be specifically identified.

3. It must include a showing of intent for the tenant to take possession of the premises, for a specified consideration.

4. It must contain an adequate description of the subject property.

5. It must contain a statement of how long the lease shall last.

6. The lease must be delivered and accepted.

If the landlord sells the leased property, the lessee's rights are generally unaffected. The tenant may protect himself against the loss of his rights to a bona fide purchaser by recording his lease.

There are at least four different types of leases. These include a gross lease, net lease, percentage lease, and ground lease. This classification is based on the manner of calculating the rental payment, and two or more different types may sometimes be incorporated in the same lease.

A gross lease is one calling for a fixed rental rate, and is usually for a fixed time period.

Under a net lease, the tenant typically pays property taxes and special assessments in addition to rent. With a net-net lease, the tenant also pays his own hazard and liability insurance premiums. A net-net-net (or triple net) lease calls for the tenant to also pay for real property repairs and maintenance.

A percentage lease is quite common in retail merchandising, and generally calls for a basic lease fee plus some percentage of gross sales. The percentage rate often varies from 2 to 11% or more, depending on both the quality of the tenant and his business volume.

A ground lease is similar to a gross lease in that it involves a fixed rental payment. In addition, it contains a rather complex method of mortgaging the leasehold estate, with the mortgage funds being used to construct improvements on the leased property. Any prior mortgages are generally subordinated to the construction mortgage.

Under any type of lease, a tenant may be able to transfer his rights to a third party. This may occur by either an assignment or a sublease. When a lease is assigned, the assignee assumes all rights and obligations held by the tenant. Thus, the assignee has direct legal responsibilities to the landlord. When the tenant subleases to a sublessee, he continues to have direct legal responsibilities to make rent payments to the landlord. The sublessee has no such obligations, because he is not in privity of contract with the landlord. In order to protect landlords from being saddled with a poor quality tenant, the law in some states forbids tenants from assigning or subleasing. Thus, if these rights are desired in those states, the lease agreement must specifically so provide.

In all states, a legal procedure exists for evicting tenants who violate their lease agreement by failing to pay rent or in some other way. Other remedies available to a lessor against a defaulting lessee include physical repossession, a lawsuit for damages, rent acceleration, seizing the lessee's personal property, and specific performance of the lease agreement. Remedies and rights available to a lessee against a defaulting lessor include a lawsuit for damages, retaliatory eviction, rent abatement, rent application, and rent withholding.

DISCUSSION
QUESTIONS

1. Explain the difference between an estate for years and an estate from year to year.

2. Explain the difference between a sublease and an assignment of a lease.

3. List the major remedies which a lessor may have against a lessee who breaches their lease agreement.

16

Condominiums and Cooperatives

Condominiums have been one of the most interesting phenomena that the housing industry has seen for a number of years. Particularly in more urban areas, the condominium has become one of the cheapest and most efficient methods of home ownership. They have also provided prestigious, high-security residences for the wealthy. Cooperatives, although not as common, have equally as good an attraction, but people have been a little more hesitant to accept cooperative ownership. It is probably safe to say that the full effect of condominium and cooperative ownership has not yet been felt and may not be felt for some time to come. Only a small amount of the country has been urbanized to the point that condominiums and cooperatives could become an acceptable means of home ownership.

There is no common-law derivative of the concepts of condominium or cooperative in the United States. The creation of these two forms of housing has been one of statute and purely legal theory. As a result, this type of housing has been called *housing built on a statutory foundation.* A more current term reflecting both of these forms of ownership has been *shared facilities housing.*

CONDOMINIUMS

It is perhaps easier, for purposes of our explanation, to think of condominiums as ownership of single apartment units. If one can visualize the more typical garden-type apartment project, along with the individual ownership of each of those apartments, one begins to understand the true concept behind condominium ownership. Condominiums are generally cheaper to build than single-family houses or townhouses (for example, there are no major firewall requirements in most cities), and they (the condominiums) constitute a very high utilization of land. Also, more units can be built, and built faster, than comparable single-family residences. However, each unit has its own individual mortgage, as in other single-family residences. The condominium units may be either built new or converted to condominiums from existing apartment projects.

Statutory Definitions   Since condominiums are housing built on a statutory foundation, the specific statutory language existing in each state determines their creation, transfer, use rights, and legal relations. The Uniform Condominium Act has been approved by the National Conference of Commissioners on Uniform State Laws and is illustrative of the trend of the law in various states. It defines a *condominium* as:

> real estate, portions of which are designated for separate ownership and the remainder of which is designated for common ownership solely by the owners of those portions. Real estate is not a condominium unless the undivided interests in the common elements are vested in the unit owners [Sec. 1-103 (7)].

Condominium projects may include much more than residential units. For example, rooms, offices, or parking spaces in parking garages could be converted to condominiums (i.e., could be "condominiumized"). Moreover, the design of the physical structure itself has no bearing on whether a project is legally classified as a condominium. It can be a high-rise building, townhouse, garden-type apartment project, or a four-plex unit, as long as the statutory criteria are met. The Uniform Condominium Act permits any of these condominium projects to be divided into units, sold, and held in fee simple ownership.

Certain common areas serving condominium projects are owned by the condominium owners as tenants in common. Statutorily, these *general common elements* include "all portions of a condominium other than the units." More specifically, they include the following.

1. The land on which the building stands.
2. The foundations, load-bearing walls and columns, roofs, halls, lobbies, stairways, and entrances and exits.
3. The basements, flat roofs, yard, and gardens.

4. Premises for the lodging of janitorial or other persons in charge of the building.

5. The compartments for installation of central services such as power, light, gas, cold and hot water, refrigeration, central air conditioning and central heating, reservoirs, water tanks and pumps, swimming pools, and the like.

6. The elevators and shafts, garbage incinerators, and, in general, all devices or installations existing for common use.

7. All other elements of the building desirable or necessary to the existence, upkeep, and safety of the condominium regime [Uniform Condominium Act, Sec. 1-103 (4)].

Limited common elements, on the other hand, are common elements "allocated ... for the use of one or more but fewer than all of the units." Examples might include special corridors, stairways and elevators, and sanitary services common to the living units on a particular floor.

Unit means a portion of the condominium designated for separate ownership [Sec. 1-103 (22)].

Ownership Rights

Once the concept of apartment (unit) ownership is understood, one needs to recall the more fundamental theory of "estates in land" to grasp the full meaning of what this ownership means. To begin with, the condominium owner gets three separate, indivisible, and distinct types of ownership:

1. Fee simple to a portion of the common elements, which must be shared in common with the others.

2. Fee simple title to the condominium unit (compartment).

3. An exclusive easement for air space, which that unit may occupy from time to time.

Each of these types of ownership will be discussed separately.

Tenancy in Common. The fee simple ownership of a portion of the common elements is an undivided interest in the unit owner's proportionate share of the common elements. *Common elements* can generally be described as all of the real property existing outside of the individual's unit that technically belongs to all of the homeowners in undivided interests as tenants in common (it cannot be partitioned). The interests in the common elements must remain undivided and cannot be used such that they encroach upon the rights of the other owners. The concept of encroaching upon the rights of the others is probably one of the more important concepts for understanding shared facilities housing. The unit owner's portion of the common elements may be determined in two ways. First, it may be determined by the amount of square footage the owner occupies with respect to the entire condominium project, such as:

$$\text{Unit} \quad = \quad 1{,}500 \text{ square feet}$$
$$\text{Project} \quad = \quad 150{,}000 \text{ square feet}$$

$$\frac{1{,}500}{150{,}000} \quad = \quad .01 \times 100 = 1\% \text{ (proportionate ownership of the common elements)}$$

The owner of the 1,500-square-foot unit would thus own an undivided 1% of the common elements, shared in common with the other unit owners.

Second, the owner's proportionate share of the common elements may be determined by the unit versus the number of units in the project. For instance, if there are 300 units in the project and the unit owner owns one of the 300 units, his proportionate share of the common elements would be:

$$\frac{1}{300} \quad = \quad .00333 \times 100 = .333\% \text{ (proportionate share of the common elements)}$$

Fee Simple to Unit. The fee simple title to the unit refers only to the interior of the unit that the owner occupies. This is sometimes referred to as the *air space* contained *inside* the apartment unit itself. More common theories of ownership indicate that the owner owns from *paint to paint* and from *ceiling to carpet,* including the *non*load-bearing walls. Load-bearing walls are not included because it is understood that a load-bearing wall is probably critical to the unit ownership of another apartment owner, and demolition or removal of a load-bearing wall may affect the other owner's rights significantly.

Easement. The third type of ownership is an easement to the air space that the unit may occupy from time to time. This concept of easement for air space is particularly functional in high-rise structures. It is understood that air space for the unit may shift due to a variety of factors, and this may affect the owner's use. Rather than worrying about older, more difficult concepts of metes and bounds descriptions and rights of parties in the property of others, it is simpler to consider the air space that the unit may occupy from time to time as an easement for reasonable enjoyment and use, as long as it does not affect the rights of other unit owners. This gives the unit owner particular rights to permit access through his unit to part of the common elements that may be contained therein, whether it be a roof, foundation, certain plumbing fixtures, or other common element items that the other owners may have a right to.

All three of these ownership rights must be conveyed together and cannot be conveyed separately under any circumstances. An example of a deed used to convey a condominium unit is shown in Figure 16-1.

Creating a Condominium Project

The creation of a condominium project is similar to the process of creating an ordinary subdivision. In most states, the county land records office holder is required to keep a separate book for condominium records. In it shall be recorded all master deeds, master leases, or condominium declarations. Just as a subdivison developer draws a survey and records the subdivision plat, the condominium developer files a master deed, master lease, or condominium declaration to create the condominium regime. The instrument creating the condominium regime must contain the legal description of the land, including the location of each building and/or proposed building. Furthermore, each building generally must be denoted by some specific identification, such as a letter (e.g., *A*, *B*, *C*, etc.). It is also essential to include a general description and number assigned to each living unit, setting out the square footage, location, and other data necessary for its proper identification. The information is depicted on a plat of each floor of each building, showing the letter of the building, the number of the floor, and the number of each apartment. Furthermore, the instrument creating the condominium regime must contain a general description of each garage, carport, or any other area subject to exclusive individual ownership and control. It also must describe the general and limited common elements, and the fractional or percentage ownership interest that each unit bears to the entire condominium regime. The condominium-creating instrument may also include other provisions desired by the developer and needed for a particular project.

Control and Maintenance

Most of the detailed information concerning maintenance and control of the condominium is contained in the condominium bylaws. They are administered by the unit owners' association or council of

GENERAL WARRANTY DEED
(Cash)

THE STATE OF TEXAS   §
                            §   KNOW ALL MEN BY THESE PRESENTS:
COUNTY OF HARRIS   §

THAT THE UNDERSIGNED, I.M. Seller and wife, Happy Seller, hereinafter referred to as "Grantor", whether one or more, for and in consideration of the sum of TEN DOLLARS ($10.00) cash, and other good and valuable consideration in hand paid by the Grantee, herein named, the receipt and sufficiency of which is hereby fully acknowledged and confessed, has GRANTED, SOLD and CONVEYED, and by these presents does hereby GRANT, SELL and CONVEY unto N. Debted and wife, May B. Debted, herein referred to as "Grantee", whether one or more, the real property described as follows, to-wit:

> The following described apartment unit and an undivided interest in the Common Elements, located in and being part of The Barclay Condominium Residences, a Condominium regime in Harris County, Texas, according to the Declaration and the Survey Plats, Exhibits and By-Laws attached thereto, recorded in Volume 50 Page 12, Volume 50 Page 115, Volume 57 Page 38, Volume 64 Page 132, and Volume 157 Page 51, and Film Code Nos. 162129, 163092, 165029, 168050 and 169040 all of the Condominium Records of Harris County, Texas, to-wit:
>
> (a)   Unit 1061 in Building "Z"
>
> (b)   an undivided .930 percent interest in and to the General Common Elements of said Condominium project.

FIGURE 16-1 Warranty Deed to a Condominium Apartment Unit

(c)   together with use of the following Limited Common Elements:

(1)   Parking Space No. 5

(2)   Parking Space No. 7

This conveyance, however, is made and accepted subject to any and all validly existing encumbrances, conditions and restrictions, relating to the hereinabove described property as now reflected by the records of the County Clerk of Harris County, Texas.

TO HAVE AND TO HOLD the above described premises, together with all and singular the rights and appurtenances thereto in anywise belonging unto the said Grantee, Grantee's heirs, executors, administrators, successors and/or assigns forever; and Grantor does hereby bind Grantor, Grantor's heirs, executors, administrators, successors and/or assigns to WARRANT AND FOREVER DEFEND all and singular the said premises unto the said

FIGURE 16-1   Continued

Grantee, Grantee's heirs, executors, administrators, successors and/or assigns, against every person whomsoever claiming or to claim the same or any part thereof.

Current ad valorem taxes on said property having been prorated, the payment thereof is assumed by Grantee.

EXECUTED this 29th day of February, 1997.

_____
I.M. SELLER

_____
HAPPY SELLER

Grantee's Address:

_____

_____

THE STATE OF TEXAS   §
                                §
COUNTY OF HARRIS   §

The foregoing instrument was acknowledged before me on the 29th day of February, 1997, by I.M. Seller and Happy Seller.

_____
NOTARY PUBLIC, STATE OF TEXAS

FIGURE 16-1   Continued

co-owners, who may amend the bylaws [Uniform Condominium Act, Sec. 3-102].

Control and maintenance of the common area are generally the responsibility of the *executive board*. This board is a group of individuals designated by the bylaws to act on behalf of the unit owners' association. In essence the unit owners' association constitutes a homeowners' association and is usually organized as a corporation. As a practical matter, the condominium project developer may maintain control of the executive board for a significant period of time, because his ownership of unsold living units gives him considerable power in the election process. Maintenance of the common elements is a primary and extremely important function of the executive board. Whether it chooses to appoint its own administrator (or board of administration) or to hire an outside management firm, the day-to-day maintenance of the common elements is determined by this board.

All unit owners are usually obligated to make pro rata contributions toward maintenance and expenses for the repair of general and/or limited common elements. This is normally accomplished by monthly payments into a "maintenance fund" as provided by the bylaws. Generally, owners cannot avoid contributing toward such expenses by waiving or otherwise claiming no use of the common elements. This firmly supports the concept of shared facilities housing, and creates a high degree of interdependence among the unit owners in the condominium project. Furthermore, the bylaws generally ensure the board's maintenance and repair authority by prohibiting individual unit owners from maintaining, changing, or altering any of the general or limited common elements without executive board approval.

It is not uncommon for maintenance fund contributions to increase significantly over time. An additional area of potential concern and controversy is where one of the common elements (for instance, the roof) is in need of repair, but it only affects one (or a few) of the unit owners (for example, the person who lives on the top floor!). It may be difficult to convince the majority of the unit owners or the executive board to make repairs when such repairs benefit only a few of the unit owners.

Specific Condominium Problem Areas

A condominium ownership does, in fact, provide many of the benefits of home ownership along with the benefits of apartment ownership, which basically make the project free from the worries that accompany the ownership of a single-family residence. However, the drawbacks to condominium ownership need to be discussed in greater detail.

Casualty Insurance. A recurring problem of condominium ownership is casualty insurance. Normally, the council of co-owners maintains a casualty insurance policy in the event of fire, accident, or other hazard that may destroy the project or any individual unit. Therefore, there is a practical problem of whether or not the individual unit owner should also carry insurance in the event the policy owned by the council of co-owners lapses or is inadequate to fully protect the homeowner. This results in a duplication of insurance to assure proper coverage for the same unit.

Taxation. Taxation provides another area of controversy in condominium ownership. The condominium owner will pay the *ad valorem* taxes for his individual unit, and the council of co-owners will pay the taxes on the common area facilities out of the maintenance fund. However, a critical problem arises about the monthly contributions from the homeowners to this maintenance fund. The homeowners' association must normally report this income for the maintenance fund (along with the other contributions for insurance, maintenance, etc.) each month as a taxable income, since this income is subject to taxation like any other income for an organization that falls under the jurisdiction of the Internal Revenue Service. Therefore, there is a double taxation achieved, once when income is taxed going to the individual co-owner and again when it is contributed to the maintenance fund.

This problem has been solved to some extent, however, by the Internal Revenue Code, which provides that a condominium management association may elect to be treated as a tax-exempt organization. If such an election is made, the association is not taxed on fees, membership dues, and assessments from the members of the association who own residential units in the particular condominium or subdivision [I.R.C. Section 528(c)I(A)]. The association's taxable income is only that equal to the excess of the gross income over actual operating costs, less any deductions and exempt income. To qualify for the exempt tax qualification, substantially all of the units must be used as residences. There are additional requirements, too, in that the association must have at least 60% of the association's gross income solely from dues, fees, and assessments, and at least 90% must be expended to acquire, construct, manage, maintain, care for, or improve association property [I.R.C. Section 528(c)I(B)]. Although these provisions still leave many unanswered questions, at least some steps have been made toward eliminating a difficult problem.

Tort Liability. Tort liability is another area that has come under controversy in recent years. Take, for instance, the fact situation in which a young neurosurgeon breaks his hands on a negligently maintained exercise machine owned by the homeowners' association. There is a good chance that the homeowners' association may have an insurance policy that would provide for certain coverage in that case. However, if the limit on that insurance policy is too low, one may wonder where the doctor will pursue additional causes of action once he has surpassed the limits of the insurance policy maintained by the homeowners' association. There is at least some authority that the doctor may be able to take his cause of action against the homeowners individually, as the unit owners are proportionally liable for claims arising in the common areas, *Dutcher* v. *Owens*, 647 S.W.2d 948 (Tex. 1983) and *White* v. *Cox*, 17 Cal. App. 3d 824 (1973).

Timesharing. The objective of timesharing has been to provide the consumer with the exclusive right to use and occupy a structure during a particular time of year. The arrangement can be of two types: (1) a fee ownership for the requisite ownership period, or (2) a "right to use" timeshare. Most people consider the fee ownership timeshare as real property, as any leasehold or other type of interest would be. The "right to use" type, however may not be real estate, depending on the various state laws. This type of timeshare is characterized as nothing more than a license allowing the owner to reserve his unit for a time period during his reservation season. No title is conveyed, and no definite time period is assigned to the purchaser. It is little more than an available hotel room. Since it is not real estate, it is presumed that the salespeople selling the timeshare interests do not have to have real estate licenses.

COOPERATIVE HOUSING

Cooperative ownership is another method of apartment ownership or shared facilities housing. It is very similar to condominium ownership, but with a few major, distinct differences. The co-ownership and interdependence of the individual owners have many of the same drawbacks of any multifamily housing project. However, there are distinct differences in methods of control and type of unit ownership as used by cooperatives in comparison to condominiums.

Creation

A cooperative can take one of three forms: (1) tenancy in common, (2) the trust form, or (3) the corporate form.

The *tenancy in common* form is fairly widespread in California and basically consists of the tenancy in common estates that were discussed in Chapter 3. In this form, the homeowner owns his share of the cooperative project in undivided proportionate shares, along with a lease, or certificate of occupancy, for a particular unit. Rights and liabilities of tenancy in common generally apply, and to some extent, this form does not create the problems of interdependence as much as do the other two forms of ownership.

The *trust* form of ownership is an ownership in severalty by a trust (a single entity), which executes a single blanket mortgage for the entire cooperative housing regime. The basis for the creation of this form of cooperative ownership is the trust instrument under which the trust derives its ownership and control. In the trust form of ownership, there is a single mortgage and management function, operated solely through the trust.

The *corporate* form of ownership, also an ownership in severalty, is similar to the corporate ownership of the homeowners' association in a condominium. The basis for this type of ownership arises out of the charter and bylaws of the corporation as created according to state law. Similar to the trust form of ownership, the corporation executes the mortgage on behalf of all the owners and maintains the actual control and ownership of the building through the life of the cooperative.

Ownership and Control   The ownership and control under a tenancy in common cooperative is based on each owner's proportionate share of ownership in the cooperative regime. The owners normally elect a homeowners' association, which is primarily responsible for the maintenance and operation of the premises. The trust and corporate forms of ownership (both involving ownership in severalty) also have one blanket mortgage which is secured by the entire cooperative as a unit. This type of cooperative ownership usually relies on the lenders' being willing to take the proportional liability of each of the owners as satisfactory security for the blanket mortgage that has been issued to cover the entire cooperative housing unit.

The trust (or board of trustees) or corporation holds legal title to the property. The co-owners get a lease, or certificate of occupancy, under which they have the exclusive right to occupy their proportionate share of the property. To simplify this, you might want to think of a larger apartment project as an example. A corporation or trust would hold legal title to the project, and each of the occupants of the apartments, being a shareholder of the corporation (or beneficial owner of the trust), has the exclusive right of occupancy of his individual unit. This type of ownership normally involves obligations in the bylaws (or trust instruments) that require each owner to pay his fractional percentage of the mortgage each and every month, as well as his fractional percentage of the utilities, insurance, costs, and maintenance.

The certificate of occupancy (or lease) is regarded as personal property, not real estate. As in condominium ownership, there are fairly detailed and finite rules and regulations under the trust instrument or bylaws which each and every unit owner must comply with, so that he will not have a detrimental effect on the other unit owners. Normally, upon termination of the certificate of occupancy, or the lease, the unit owner must surrender possession of the unit (by sale or otherwise) to the corporation or trust, who, in turn, may resell that interest to another subsequent occupant. The charter and bylaws (or trust instrument) usually contain provisions whereby the corporation or trust has the right of first refusal to buy the certificate of occupancy and proportionate interest when the unit owner decides to terminate his residency. Since there is a great amount of interdependence because of the proportionate payments of mortgages, maintenance fees, and payments (much more so than in condominium ownership), it is critical that there be a strictly enforced agreement between the co-owners, carefully setting forth what all the rights and obligations are in order to ensure adequate functioning and maintenance of the cooperative housing development.

Advantages

Cooperative housing developments have had particularly good application in retirement and resort areas. Because of the lower construction costs of cooperative housing, similar to those of condominiums, cooperatives are substantially cheaper to build than are other forms of single or multifamily residential housing; thus the cost of these units is likewise much cheaper. In the retirement situation, you can understand why a person, in his old age, may decide to retire to a senior citizens' cooperative housing development (normally restricted to people 65 years of age or over), buying a 1,200 to 1,500 square foot unit for the price of $12,000 to $20,000 (perhaps his life savings). His future contributions, then, would be used only to pay utilities and maintenance fund costs for the rest of his life. He would get all the benefits of living in an apartment, but with all the attributes of home ownership. He would have no mortgage payments to pay (assuming his unit was paid for), and any future conveyance of his cooperative unit would be subject only to the right of first refusal of the homeowners' association, corporation, or trust. Thus, he would be much more comfortable living on a fixed retirement income. He also would probably have a higher quality of housing than he would have if he tried to buy a single-family residence or townhouse, or even a condominium unit, at the same price.

Disadvantages   The disadvantages of cooperative housing stand out primarily because of the extreme interdependence involved in this type of housing. For instance, if each unit owner has the obligation to pay his proportionate share of the mortgage payment, what would happen if several unit owners could not make their payments for one month? The obvious answer is that the remaining unit owners must come up with the rest of the money in order to assure that the mortgage payment is paid. The same is true of insurance, taxes, and maintenance costs. In the condominium ownership situation, a mortgage company can foreclose on one unit. The cooperative form of ownership, however, does not allow for this type of independence, except possibly in the tenancy in common type of cooperative ownership.

Thus, *financing* is the first major disadvantage of cooperative ownership. For example, a loan can be made only to the corporation or trust, and not to any of the unit owners independently. This disadvantage also exists in all services, utilities, and other obligations that may be undertaken by the cooperative housing association. There is, of course, the usual problem of trying to ascertain the appraised value of the property for loan purposes because of the interdependence and multiownership facets of cooperative housing.

The second major difficulty and complication arising out of cooperative ownership is that of *securities*. Since this form of ownership is evidenced by a certificate of occupancy, or "shares" of ownership, one may think that it would automatically be affected by the securities laws. This was a very heavily litigated area for some time. In 1975, the Supreme Court of the United States, in a landmark decision involving cooperative housing, *United Housing Foundation v. Foreman,* 412 U.S. 837 (1975), indicated that the housing aspect of a transaction that involved the purchase of stock in the co-op corporation was not making an *investment,* as that term is used in securities law, even though it was possible for the cooperative owners to sell their "shares" at a later time and even for a profit. Since the housing units themselves were used as primary residences by the occupants, the purchaser is seeking a place to live, regardless of how the cooperative was financed or sold. The shares of stock in this case were completely tied to the proprietary leases, a fact that negates some of the attributes of ownership and investment that most stock shares exhibit. The court also emphasized that the voting rights under the ownership in a cooperative

Summary

333

unit were not one vote per share of stock, but rather, one vote per homeowner.

So at least in very closely identified situations, the shares of ownership in a cooperative will not automatically be considered securities. However, this does not indicate that all cooperatives are not securities. As in condominium ownership, there can always be a situation involving the marketing, selling, and retransfer of the interest in the cooperative housing that would make securities an extremely troublesome situation if handled improperly.

Tort liability for corporate or trust form cooperatives is not nearly the problem that it is under condominium ownership, because the owners are, of course, insulated through the corporate veil or the trust form of ownership. Anyone who has a claim against the cooperative housing unit would have to sue the trust or corporation, and the homeowners would understandably be sufficiently insulated from liabilities so that they would not be personally liable. The same is true of most contractual liabilities.

It is assumed that the tort or contractual liability of a tenancy in common cooperative is the same as that of tenancy in common generally, rendering the owner liable only for his proportionate share, although the owners' personal liability may be unlimited.

In summary, it can easily be seen that both condominiums and cooperatives are heavily dependent on the shared facilities housing concept and that the mutual interdependence of both types of ownership may create problems. However, we are going to have to learn to live with these problems, because single-family housing is becoming more and more expensive in various parts of the country. In dealing with a purchaser or seller of a condominium or cooperative unit, the wise and astute attorney, and the real estate agent, must understand the various complications that are involved through securities, tort liability, organization of the ownership entity, and various aspects of interdependent living, all of which may make a substantial difference (especially to the purchasing client). Almost any of these facts and criteria could be a material consideration for a reasonable and prudent purchaser who is interested in purchasing a unit. It is therefore important that the real estate agent be familiar with this type of housing, particularly if he chooses to concentrate his marketing efforts in this area.

SUMMARY

Shared housing facilities involve individual ownership of units contained in a multiunit housing project. Conceptually, they might be thought of as ownership of individual apartments in an apartment building. They are a particularly attractive housing alternative to those who desire some of the advantages of home ownership without being responsible for home maintenance and lawn work.

Legal rules for ownership of shared housing facilities have come about by statutory authorization. Shared housing facilities may be organized and sold under either the condominium or cooperative form of ownership.

The simplest view of condominiums is that they constitute direct sole ownership of single-apartment units or other housing units with common elements. Condominiums might include residential units, rooms, offices, and even parking spaces in parking garages. Any physical structure (high-rise, townhouse, garden-type apartment, etc.) can be a condominium project, as long as the statutory criteria are met.

One can do virtually anything with a condominium unit that can be done with a single-family residence. It may be bought, sold, mortgaged, or leased.

Each condominium unit is individually owned. At the same time, all "common elements" are co-owned by the condominium owners, generally as tenants in common. Common elements may include the land on which the project is located, foundation, load-bearing walls, hallways, roofs, stairways, elevators, entrances and exits, yards, and other elements necessary to the use or existence of the total project.

In some cases, limited common elements exist and are also owned as tenants in common. Limited common elements are those shared and beneficially used by some but not all of the condominium owners.

In addition to fee simple ownership of the condominium unit and tenancy in common ownership of the common elements, the condominium owner also holds an exclusive easement for the air space that the unit occupies. As a general rule, all of these ownership interests must be conveyed together and cannot be conveyed separately.

Condominium projects are created in a manner similar to that followed for an ordinary subdivision. In most states, a separate condominium record book is kept in the local county land records office. All master deeds, master leases, and condominium declarations are recorded there. The filing of one of these instruments generally is essential to the creation of a condominium regime.

The condominium declaration is similar to a subdivision plat and generally includes the legal description of the land; the location of existing and proposed buildings; the description, location, and square footage of each condominium unit; the common elements; and other important items.

Most of the detailed maintenance and control rules and regulations are set out in the condominium bylaws. These rules and regulations are generally administered through an executive board elected by the members of the unit owners' association.

All condominium owners generally make pro rata contributions to cover maintenance and similar expenses, and such contributions must be made even when the owner is not using the condominium unit or any of its common elements. With respect to maintenance, a major area of difficulty often revolves around convincing the executive board to make repairs for something that affects only one or only a few of the unit owners.

There are other potential problems associated with condominium ownership. These may include the adequacy of casualty insurance, liability for property taxes assessed against the common elements, and the possibility of maintenance and other contributions being taxable income to the unit owners' association. The latter can be more easily avoided if provisions of the 1976 Tax Reform Act are complied with.

Another major area of concern for prospective condominium owners is tort liability. For some owners, and particularly for condominium project developers, the fact that condominiums may be classified as securities (rather than real estate) for SEC purposes may lead to expensive and time-consuming registration and full disclosure requirements. The securities classification problem is particularly acute for time-sharing, interval ownership, and resort condominiums.

Cooperative ownership is another type of ownership for shared facilities housing. It may consist of any of three different forms: tenancy in common, trust, or corporation.

Under the tenancy in common type, each co-owner holds an undivided interest in the entire project. He also holds a lease or certificate of occupancy for a particular "apartment" unit. It is the only form of cooperative ownership involving direct ownership; so its co-owners generally have less interdependence on each other than is true for the trust and corporate forms.

With the trust form of cooperative ownership, the trust owns all property and executes a blanket mortgage covering it. A trustee oversees the management and maintenance functions. The beneficiaries of the trust are its owner/residential occupants.

The corporate form of cooperative ownership is similar to the trust form in that it also constitutes ownership in severalty. The corporation generally executes a mortgage covering the entire project, and each shareholder holds a lease or certificate of occupancy to his residential unit.

The control of cooperatives may vary, depending on whether the ownership is held directly or indirectly by the shared housing occupants. Greater liability for mortgage debt, tort, and contractual obligation exists under the direct ownership of a tenancy in common. Even though occupancy rights may be specified in a lease or certificate of occupancy, each owner/occupant is generally obligated to pay his proportionate share of the mortgage, maintenance, and other project expenses.

Because the financial position of one corporate shareholder/trust beneficiary may be affected by the ability of fellow residents to meet their financial obligations, the trust and corporation cooperative forms of ownership generally reserve the right of first refusal when one occupant desires to sell out. The relatively high degree of interdependence among cooperative owners generally requires carefully detailed agreements to fully protect the interests of all parties.

DISCUSSION QUESTIONS	1. Why is it that shared facilities housing may be popular in vacation resort areas?

1. Why is it that shared facilities housing may be popular in vacation resort areas?

2. In large urban centers, are condominiums more likely to be located near downtown areas or in suburban areas? Why?

3. Which form of shared facilities housing—condominiums or cooperatives—is more popular in your area? Why?

4. With respect to tort liability for injuries to visitors, contrast the differences between being the owner of a condominium unit and being the owner of a detached, single-family residence.

17

Regulation of Real Estate

In any form of government, the government must have certain priorities with respect to the land contained within its jurisdiction, which has higher priority than any other individual or entity.

In the United States, the government has four chief methods for controlling land use or ownership:

1. Eminent domain procedures.
2. Taxation.
3. Escheat.
4. Police power.

The fundamentals of eminent domain and escheat were discussed in Chapter 8. Taxation is discussed in Chapter 18. The scope of this chapter is to dwell on the fourth governmental power, which is government regulation pursuant to the police power.

It is by the use of *police power* that the government regulates and enforces laws and regulations that pertain to land-use control. This is a relatively inexpensive process because there is no "taking" of property (as in eminent domain), and therefore no requirement for just compensation.

There has been such a voluminous amount of land-use control legislation passed at the federal level that it cannot all be discussed within the scope of this chapter, or even within this text. Therefore, in discussing federal land-use control, we will attempt only to highlight some of the more important legislative efforts, just so the reader can keep his sanity. Beyond the federal land-use controls, we will discuss controls at the state and county levels, as well as those at the municipal and local levels.

FEDERAL LAND-USE CONTROL

In an attempt to categorize federal land-use control as succinctly as possible, we will discuss each federal agency under which land use is controlled. The agencies to be covered are the Securities and Exchange Commission, the Department of Housing and Urban Development, the Federal Trade Commission, and the Environmental Protection Agency. From a land-use control aspect, it should be remembered that every time a new restrictive regulatory law is passed, some developers and investors will stop investing in the type of project being regulated, forcing their funds into other areas, and ultimately changing certain land-use patterns.

Securities and Exchange Commission

The sale of investment interests in real estate is subject to SEC registration and disclosure requirements if such interests meet the definition of a *security*. Registration with SEC may require as long as six months or more and may cost hundreds of thousands of dollars. Both the time and expense involved will increase holding costs and the price at which real estate must be sold in order to make a profit. Such costs are often passed on to the ultimate purchaser of real estate. In this way, SEC requirements affect land-use patterns because they affect the economics of real estate investment and development projects.

Although the basic purpose of SEC registration requirements is to protect investors (e.g., in real estate), some believe such requirements have lessened competition within the industry. Their reasoning is quite simple: Small projects are not required to meet SEC requirements. Middle-size projects (firms) are subject to SEC registration requirements, but often choose not to become involved in a project because they cannot afford the time and expense of registration. This leaves only the small and the very large firms to compete on projects, and the former cannot compete effectively with the latter.

Regulatory Pattern. SEC attempts to protect investors in four different ways, as follows:

1. By requiring *full disclosure* (to prospective investors) of all facts logically relevant to the financial performance of the investment.
2. By requiring syndicators (persons who put group real estate investments together) to take steps to determine whether each specific investor is financially able to handle the risks involved.
3. By setting up substantive standards and procedures, and

requiring syndicators to follow such procedures to restrict abuse.

4. By regulating middlemen (underwriters, officers, directors, real estate salespersons, etc.) via due diligence requirements to ensure investors are not misled.

Security Defined.   A security is a passive type of investment in which a return is expected from the activities of third parties. It may include profit-sharing agreements or investment contracts.

Most group investments in real estate will be classified as securities for SEC purposes. (They may also be subject to "blue sky" law requirements at the state level.)

Exemptions.   There are two major exemptions from SEC registration. The *private offering* exemption guidelines set out in SEC *Rule 146* set 35 as the maximum number of investors if registration is to be avoided. These guidelines also include rules regarding investor access to information, the suitability (financial risk-bearing capacity) of prospective investors, and prohibitions against public solicitation of investors.

This exemption has not been as widely relied upon since 1974, because it does not specify when the SEC will "integrate" two or more investment "offerings" and treat them as one for registration purposes. Without these integration rules, it would be possible to avoid registration requirements, for example, by dividing one 60-investor syndication into two 30-investor syndications. Basically, the SEC (and state "blue-sky" agencies) will integrate two or more syndications into one when justified by the economic realities (e.g., common acquisition dates and legal instruments, common financing instruments, etc.).

The second major SEC registration exemption currently is more popular, because it specifies that syndications will not be integrated so long as at least six months time elapses between their creation. For this reason, it leads to greater certainty of legal compliance. This exemption is called the *intrastate offering* exemption, guidelines for which are set out in SEC *Rule 147.* Under these guidelines, SEC registration is not required if the real estate syndication investment opportunity is only offered to residents of a single state. The real estate must be located in, and the syndicator a resident of, the same state as the investors.

It should be emphasized that registration exemptions are not always clear. For this and other reasons, it is a sound policy always to observe all disclosure regulations, buyer qualifications, general substantive offering procedures, and middlemen activity regulations. This practice will be helpful both in protecting investors and in minimizing a syndicator's potential financial liability.

The Department of Housing and Urban Development

The Department of Housing and Urban Development (HUD) has made great strides in controlling and regulating real estate. The agencies under HUD control to be discussed include the Federal Housing and Veterans Administrations, the Federal National Mortgage Association, the Government National Mortgage Association, the Office of Interstate Land Sales Registration, and the Federal Insurance Administration.

Federal Housing and Veterans Administrations. Neither the Federal Housing Administration (FHA) nor the Veterans Administration (VA) makes direct real estate loans except under limited and special circumstances. However, they both have a significant impact on real estate activity, particularly in the single-family residential market. Both the FHA and VA provide lower interest rates and closing costs than those generally available under conventional financing.

The FHA insures loans for qualified borrowers, but only on properties meeting its standards. It may insure several different kinds of loans, including loans on detached, single-family residences, condominiums, multifamily residential units, nursing homes, low- and moderate-income homes qualifying for certain governmental housing programs, urban renewal housing, urban rehabilitation housing, and public and experimental housing.

The VA is primarily involved in loans for detached single-family residences. It is not an insurer, but rather guarantees loans to eligible veterans of the armed services.

When these agencies guarantee or insure loans, lenders may make some loans that they otherwise would not have made. To this extent, funds may become more available or less costly to borrowers. In either event, the economic effect is to encourage purchases of properties on which the FHA or VA will insure or guarantee loans.

Federal National Mortgage Association. In 1935 the Reconstruction Finance Corporation Mortgage Company (RFCMC) was created as an emergency measure. Its principal goal was to provide liquidity for federally insured real estate mortgage loans. Its major impact was to develop a secondary real estate mortgage market.

The RFCMC was succeeded by the Federal National Mortgage Company, more popularly known as *Fannie Mae*. Originally part of

HUD, Fannie Mae's principal function was to buy and sell FHA-insured and VA-guaranteed residential mortgages. Since 1970 it has also dealt in conventional real estate mortgages.

In 1968 Fannie Mae changed its status to a private corporation, and it is now owned by private stockholders. These stockholders are required to purchase Fannie Mae stock when they sell mortgages to Fannie Mae. However, even as a private corporation, Fannie Mae remains subject to HUD regulation.

Fannie Mae stimulates the secondary mortgage market during tight money periods by increasing its purchases of mortgages. It operates on a bid basis. That is, it tells how much money it has available to spend, and then accepts the lowest bid. Fannie Mae money is continually circulated. As mortgages it holds are paid off, these funds become a new supply of money available to housing lenders.

Government National Mortgage Association. Until 1968, Fannie Mae also handled several special-assistance management and financial functions. In 1968 these functions were taken over by a new entity, the Government National Mortgage Association. Popularly known as *Ginnie Mae,* this agency also purchases mortgages executed by persons with low income. These are low-yield mortgages. They are purchased by Ginnie Mae at par and are then sold to Fannie Mae at the current market interest rate. Thus, it is not intended that Ginnie Mae profit on these mortgages, and in fact it ordinarily suffers losses on these transactions.

These low-income mortgages are referred to as *tandem* mortgages, because Ginnie Mae and Fannie Mae work "in tandem" on them.

Office of Interstate Land Sales Registration. The Office of Interstate Land Sales Registration (OILSR) is part of the federal Department of Housing and Urban Development (HUD). OILSR has the basic responsibility of enforcing the Interstate Land Sales Full Disclosure Act. As suggested by its title, this act is designed to protect land purchasers who may buy land in another state (1) without seeing it, or (2) without knowing or learning about major problems associated with the property. In short, it is an attempt to make it less likely that prospective purchasers will be misled in their investment decisions.

The law prohibits developers or their agents from selling subdivision lots *unless* the following two requirements are met.

1. A statement of record has been filed with OILSR.

2. Each purchaser or lessee is furnished with a property report 48 hours before he signs a contract to buy or rent.

These requirements affect large numbers of projects because they apply if the United States mails or any means of transportation and/or interstate commerce are employed to sell or lease unimproved lots in a subdivision.

Both time and money are required to meet filing requirements and to prepare and distribute the property reports. This makes project development more expensive. For developers to make a profit and stay in business, in the long run at least part of these increased costs must be passed on to the lot purchasers. Thus, the group being protected pays for part, if not all, of their protection in the form of higher lot prices.

Important Rules.   In addition to requiring the OILSR registration and property report, the law prohibits the use of fraud and/or misrepresentation in selling, leasing, or attempting to sell or lease unimproved lots. Moreover, a purchaser or lessee can void his contract if he was not provided a property report before he signed his contract. If the report was provided less than 48 hours before signing, the purchaser/lessee can revoke his contract without liability within three business days after the date of signing.

Fines of up to $5,000 and imprisonment of up to five years are possible for willful violations of the law.

Exemptions.   There are two different kinds of exemptions available to developers seeking to avoid the law. One is "self-determining"; the other requires determination by the government.

The non-self-determining exemption requires developers to obtain a formal determination of eligibility from OILSR. This basically means that they must detail their development marketing plans to OILSR administrators, who in turn will issue an "exemption order" if they determine sufficient safeguards exist to protect prospective purchasers. Importantly, this order must be obtained *before* the developer can offer to sell or lease his lots.

Eligibility for "self-determining" exemptions may be determined by the developer himself. An exemption exists if any of the following requirements are met.

1. The project involves 50 or fewer lots, provided such lots are not part of a larger, common promotional plan.

2. All lots are five acres or larger in size.

3. A residential, commercial, or industrial building is already on the lot, or if the lot *seller* is contractually obligated to build such a structure on it within two years.

4. All lots are sold or leased to a person (e.g., builder) who will resell or lease them.

5. Each lot will sell for less than $100, *including* closing costs, and purchasers are not required to buy two or more lots.

6. The lots are sold or leased under a court order.

7. The project involves evidence of indebtedness secured by a real estate mortgage or deed of trust.

8. The project involves a sale of securities issued by a real estate investment trust.

9. The project involves the sale or lease of cemetery lots.

10. The project involves the sale or lease of lots by any government or government agency.

11. The project involves the lease of lots for a period of less than five years, provided the lessee is not obligated to renew his lease.

12. The project involves the sale or lease of lots zoned for industrial or commercial development, if the purchaser/lessee is engaged in commercial or industrial business.

13. The project involves an incidental sale of fewer than 50 lots when such lots are 5% or less of the developer's platted lots of record, and the remainder of his lots are exempt because of buildings on them or a contractual obligation to place buildings on them.

Property Report. The property report is the legal mechanism used to achieve full disclosure under the law. It in no way implies that OILSR or HUD has reviewed the project and approved it on its merits.

This report basically outlines what the buyer may expect with respect to necessities and amenities for the development. For example, if the property report states that the development will contain an 18-hole golf course, the golf course must in fact be provided. Failure to build or provide promised necessities and amenities may cause the developer to (1) amend his property report, and (2) more importantly, offer refunds to purchasers.

In addition to listing amenities, there are a number of specific questions for which the property report must provide answers. Basically these include contractual and other rights that may affect the financial position and/or legal rights of purchasers and lessees.

Federal Insurance Administration. The *Federal Insurance Administration* was created to provide insurance for loss of properties as defined in standard insurance contracts. It has been particularly influential in providing for federal flood insurance under the *National Flood Insurance Act.* This act, along with the *Flood Disaster Control Act of 1973,* was designed to provide previously unavailable flood insurance to property owners in flood-prone areas. As almost all real estate agents know, the government's designation of flood-prone areas has taken a rather broad sweep along the Texas gulf coast and certain other areas near rivers, reservoirs, and even minor tributaries. The Flood Disaster Control Act basically makes it unlawful for any lending institution with funds underwritten or guaranteed by the federal government (which includes basically all lending institutions) to make loans on improvements in flood-prone areas unless the borrowers have flood insurance. There has been considerable controversy over how the *flood-prone areas* were designated by the U.S. Army Corps of Engineers, and a large amount of litigation has developed since the act was first passed.

One of the major concerns in the area of flood insurance has been the cost of obtaining the flood insurance. It was originally available at a relatively low cost. However, after major flooding in certain areas, the rates go up significantly; this is a cost that the homeowner must bear. If the rates do go up, the homeowner has no choice but to continue to purchase the flood insurance (regardless of the cost) to satisfy the requirements that have been imposed by the lender. It is arguable that this requirement for flood insurance makes a significant difference in the purchase price of a home built in a flood-prone area, since the purchaser may have undetermined future expenses.

New Communities Act. The New Communities Act (NCA) of 1968 was enacted to encourage private developers to initiate new community development projects. Under NCA, the secretary of HUD may guarantee loans to private developers for these projects, and such guarantees may range up to (1) 80% of the secretary's estimates of the project's completed value, or (2) the sum of 75% of his estimate of land value prior to development plus 90% of his estimate of the cost of development. The guaranteed limit on a single project is $50 million.

NCA also covers other areas related to new community development projects. It includes supplementary grants for water, schools, sewers, urban transit, and the like.

Urban Growth and New Community Development Act. In 1970, the Urban Growth and New Community Development Act (UGNCD) was passed to provide financial assistance to private developers and local public bodies. Its purpose was to promote orderly growth and development of both new and existing communities. The UGNCD created the New Community Development Corporation to handle loans and guarantees made pursuant to the law.

The Federal Trade Commission

The Federal Trade Commission has recently come into the limelight because it has strongly expanded its scope from financial areas to those of consumer protection and consumer credit. The rules and regulations of the Federal Trade Commission are implemented and enforced by the Federal Reserve Board. Some of the primary functions of this board are to oversee the implementation and enforcement of such legislation as the Federal Truth-in-Lending Act, the Equal Credit Opportunity Act, the Fair Credit Reporting Act, and the Home Mortgage Disclosure Act.

The *Truth-in-Lending Act* was originally passed to require lenders to make certain meaningful disclosure as to interest rates and costs of obtaining loans. The *Equal Credit Opportunity Act (ECOA)* went into effect in 1975 to prohibit discrimination in any aspect of a credit transaction on the basis of sex or marital status. In 1976, amendments were added to the ECOA to prohibit discrimination on the basis of race, color, religion, national origin, age, and other arbitrary requirements. The *Fair Credit Reporting Act* has its most significant application to credit bureaus. Prior to the passage of this act, it was possible to have a "bad" credit rating, and the person who had the bad credit rating could not find out the source of that information, even if it was untrue. The Fair Credit Reporting Act has opened up the vaults of credit bureaus so that consumers can determine their credit ratings and if necessary, correct any mistakes. The *Home Mortgage Disclosure Act* was passed in 1975 to force lenders to disclose in what areas of a town or metropolitan region they were making loans. This is to prevent "redlining" (making loans only to specified areas of town) and to encourage lenders to make loans in all areas of a town.

The most significant aspect of the FTC may be its attempt to *regulate* real estate brokerage through antitrust statutes as discussed in Chapter 5, *Real Estate Brokerage and Management*.

The Environmental Protection Agency

In a continuing effort to make our environment more habitable, the *Environmental Protection Agency (EPA)* has passed voluminous laws and regulations to control the use of real property if such use is considered to be a direct source or an indirect source of environmental pollution. The EPA has made an effort to control virtually every area of air, water, and industrial pollution, and many of its regulations have resulted in extreme controversy. The EPA administers the *Clean Air Act*, which was designed to maintain a national air quality standard, whether the source of pollution was from a stationary, mobile, or indirect source of pollution. The EPA also passed land-use regulations under the *Federal Water Pollution Control Act*, which provides for area-wide planning. The EPA has not had very much success at the courthouse, however, and many of its attempts at regulating land-use control through these laws have been substantially altered or struck down altogether. The Clean Air Act and its indirect source rule have been somewhat more successful in controlling the construction of certain sources of pollution, such as shopping centers, office buildings, and so forth. These examples constitute indirect sources of pollution due to the number of cars that the structures attract, thereby creating a large amount of exhaust and carbon monoxide pollution.

New areas of land-use regulation are emerging in which the EPA is taking a very strong position. These include hazardous waste disposal, asbestos regulation, and regulation of ongoing waste facilities.

The *Comprehensive Environmental Response, Compensation, and Liability Act of 1980 (CERCLA)*, which was amended by the *Superfund Amendments and Reauthorization Act of 1986 (SARA)*, defines "hazardous substance," which is a very broad and potentially changing definition. This statute puts liability for cleanup of the site on: (1) the owner and operator of the facility, (2) the person who operates the facility, and (3) the person who arranges for disposal or the transportation of materials to that facility.

Both EPA and the Occupational Safety and Health Administration (OSHA) now exercise certain regulations by promoting standards for asbestos insulation. This, in many instances, has resulted in significant changes in values of real estate when a potential purchaser realizes that the cost of complying with EPA and OSHA regulations can run into the millions of dollars for asbestos removal or encapsulation.

The *Resource Conservation and Recovery Act of 1976 (RCRA)*, which was amended by the *Hazardous Solid Waste Amendments of 1984 (HSWA)*, applies to the control of ongoing waste facilities. This statute creates significant liability for the property owner, without regard to fault, if an ongoing waste facility presents an imminent and substantial endangerment to health or environment. *United States* v. *Price*, 11 Envtl. L. Rep. 21047 (D.N.J.—1981).

The *Clean Water Act* authorizes the Corps of Engineers to issue permits for the discharge of dredged or filled material and also prohibits discharges of pollutants into navigable waters. The courts have further determined that the Clean Water Act was intended to apply to the full extent of Congress' power to "regulate among the several states." The Corps of Engineers and the Environmental Protection Agency have therefore defined "wetlands" by regulation, which is determined by the hydrology, soils, and vegetation in the field they are evaluating. Wetlands, then, come under specific federal jurisdiction of regulation of real estate development in that area. This has dramatic impact on properties along the Texas gulf coast. Almost any development now requires a Corps permit and the EPA can veto a Corps decision to grant a permit, if necessary. It goes without saying that obtaining permits in a wetlands area is a time-consuming process because it involves two federal agencies (see 33 *U.S.C.A.* §1251.

The *Federal Endangered Species Act* (16 *U.S.C.A.* §1531) creates a federal list of species which must be protected. The species include subspecies of fish or wildlife or plants as well as any distinct populations of a vertebrate species. The statute provides that the critical habitats may also be designated and prohibits a developer from "taking" property which would include harassing animals and disturbing their environment so that the animals won't want to live there. In many cases this requires a biological opinion.

One can also see how, by using the threat of public harm, the EPA can exercise broad jurisdiction over many other areas, establishing regulations for areas of environmental control for which, in many cases, acceptable standards have not yet been established.

The *Residential Lead-Based Paint Hazard Reduction Act of 1992* is a comprehensive statute applying to housing that is owned, subsidized, or the subject of mortgage guarantees by the federal government. It requires HUD to issue regulations for the disclosure of lead-based paint hazards in any target housing (housing constructed prior to 1978, except housing for the elderly or persons with disabilities, unless any child under six resides or is expected to reside in such housing, or any zero bedroom dwelling). The regulations must require that every contract for the purchase and sale of any interest in target housing shall contain a *Lead Warning Statement* and a statement signed by the purchaser that he has read the Lead Warning Statement and understands its contents, has received a lead hazard pamphlet, and has had a ten-day opportunity (unless the parties mutually agree upon a different period of time) before becoming obligated under the contract of purchase to conduct a risk assessment or inspection for the presence of lead-based paint hazards. The regulations are discussed in greater detail in Chapter 6.

Historic Preservation The *National Historic Preservation Act* (16 U.S.C.A., § 470) requires consultation between federal agencies and the Advisory Council on Historic Preservation before development can occur on certain sites. The consultation can be a lengthy process, and must be completed prior to the approval of any action by a federal agency. In some cases it is necessary to have an archaeologist do a survey of the property, even if it is raw land. Once there has been a determination that the site is eligible for the National Register of Historic Places, the developer must determine whether development will affect the site, and define the area of potential effect. Texas also has similar protection under the Texas Antiquities Code, V.T.C.A., Nat. Res. Code, § 191.

Fair Housing Act One of the more important pieces of federal legislation affecting real estate is the Fair Housing Act (FHA) of 1968. It prohibits housing discrimination on the basis of race, color, religion, sex, national origin, physical handicap, or familial status. It covers both refusals to sell and refusals to rent when any of these discriminatory factors is the reason behind such refusals. The FHA also makes it unlawful to discriminate on the basis of terms or conditions of real estate sales or rentals, and prohibits false representation about the property's availability. Discriminatory advertising is also prohibited.

Furthermore, FHA makes it illegal for one to induce or attempt to induce sales or rentals by representation about entry into the neighborhood of any of the previously listed factors of race, color, religion, etc. Finally, discrimination by lenders is also prohibited.

The FHA law contains a number of exemptions, including:

1. Sales or rentals of single-family residences by owners if the owner:
   a. Has three or fewer single-family houses.
   b. Personally makes the sale without employing a real estate agent or publicly advertising (including posting and mailing) the property.
   c. Was not residing in the house at the time of sale, or if he was not the most recent resident of the house. This exemption is only available once within a two-year period.
2. Rentals of housing quarters intended for four or fewer families if the owner personally resides in one of the living units.
3. Noncommercial sales or rentals by religious organizations and private clubs, unless their membership has restrictions based on race, color, or country of national origin.

4. Most sales and rentals of commercial property, although some exceptions are contained in the FHA regulations.

Coastal Zone Management

Because of the rate of change in and potential conflicts among different land uses in the coastal zone, this area has been singled out for special legislation. To explain further, land-use conflicts are most likely to occur in heavily populated areas, and it has been estimated that approximately one-half of our population resides within 100 miles of either our coastline or the Great Lakes. Thus, the Coastal Zone Management (CZM) Act has a potentially significant impact [P.L. 92-583, 92nd Congress, 2nd Sess., 1972].

The CZM federal legislation has provided federal funds to coastal states to use in planning, developing, and implementing regulations affecting land use in coastal areas. Each state has designated an administrative agency to oversee this task.

Regulations developed pursuant to CZM directives may encourage, inhibit, or eliminate real estate development in certain areas, which in turn will have differential effects on surrounding land values. As an illustration of potential impact, because of the importance of certain coastal wetland areas in providing food supplies for saltwater fish, in some instances real estate development might be prohibited. If so, the market values of these tracts are not likely to be as great as other tracts that are both physically and legally available for development.

CZM may also raise the "taking" issue. That is, since the owners of coastal wetlands may suffer substantial wealth losses when CZM regulations are implemented, does this constitute a "taking" of their property which should be compensated? (The "taking" issue will be discussed later in this chapter.)

Magnuson-Moss Warranty Act

The Magnuson-Moss Warranty Act (MMW) provides that consumer-product warranties must meet certain minimum standards [P.L. 93-637, 93rd Cong., 2nd Sess., 1974]. *Consumer products* include tangible personal property distributed in commerce and used for personal family or household purposes. This definition does not cover items that are an integral part of a structure (e.g., wiring, plumbing, building materials, etc.). However, MMW covers some consumer products that may be classified as fixtures under state law.

Real estate builders/developers are subject to MMW provisions. They have three alternative methods of compliance. First, they may make no warranties on either the structure or the consumer products, but simply assign all manufacturer warranties on consumer products (e.g., air conditioners, appliances) to the purchaser. This exempts them from MMW coverage, because the law only applies to warrantors making written warranties. However, the builders/developers must either display the manufacturers' warranties or must make them available prior to the sale as prescribed by MMW regulations.

Second, the builders/developers may make warranties about structures, but not about consumer products. They must carefully follow the procedures set out in the MMW regulations, which basically require listing those consumer products covered by warranties complying with MMW, and putting any warranties against structural defects in a separate document.

Third, the builders/developers may make both structural and consumer product warranties as required by MMW.

Many states have additional laws protecting real estate purchasers from defective structures and fixtures or other unsound consumer products. State coverage may be either broader or narrower than the rules set out for MMW.

Net Effect of Federal Regulation

One can easily see that in land-use control, the federal government has been fairly significantly involved in a number of different areas. Through the Securities and Exchange Commission, it controls the methods by which we can offer parcels or real estate for sale, or present investment prospectuses and real estate promotional schemes. The federal government also regulates the sale of units of real estate through the Office of Interstate Land Sales Registration, the quality of housing and the availability of loans through the Federal Housing Administration, closing disclosure requirements through the Real Estate Settlement and Procedures Act, and availability of certain funds to primary lenders through Fannie Mae, Ginnie Mae, and Freddie Mac. The federal government also protects the consumer from himself by requiring flood insurance for homes in government-designated flood-prone areas. Through the Federal Trade Commission, the federal government requires that certain disclosures to be made to the consumer as provided by the federal Truth-in-Lending Act. It also requires disclosures under the Fair Credit Reporting Act, and it provides for additional disclosures to be made through the Home Mortgage Disclosure Act by the requirements imposed on lenders. The Environmental Protection Agency also helps in controlling land use by its regulations on construction through the Clean Air Act and the Federal Water Pollution Control Act. These acts significantly affect where factories and industry can be located, and major traffic patterns may be substantially altered if the federal government feels that these may hurt our pollution standards. Most of these regulations require extensive fees to be paid by the people regulated, and ultimately by the consumer, since these costs are passed on in the price of consumer products.

Some of the governmental functions have been outstanding in contributing to the overall welfare of the American public. However, this is not always the case. The most disturbing area of federal land-use control is the extended implementation of the acts as passed by Congress. Each of the foregoing federal agencies passes its own regulations in an attempt to clarify its positions, and sometimes an agency expands upon the authority given to it under the original statutes. It must be emphasized that although these regulations are not passed by Congress, they have the force of law until they are challenged in the federal courts. Challenging any federal regulation is an expensive, time-consuming, and high-risk process on the part of any private land developer. Not only does he run the risk of losing the case, but risks incurring the wrath of that federal government agency he chooses to challenge. In addition, there is no control whatsoever on these federal government agencies as they pass these regulations. They are not subject to any system of checks and balances, and there is no authority to discipline them if there is any type of injustice or selective (unfair) enforcement involved, other than through the federal courts. If there is a basic injustice in any of the federal land-use controls, it is that there are no watchdogs over the federal government, whereas the federal agencies are acting as watchdogs over the private landowner and developer.

An interesting anomaly to the land-use control pattern of the federal government has been the proposal of a National Land-Use Planning Act. This article of legislation provides incentives for national land-use control (often referred to as *national zoning*). This legislation has been introduced into both houses of Congress for several years and has not been passed to date. Oddly enough, one of the major lobbying efforts in attempting to stop passage of the act has expressed that "we do not want the federal government to control our land use."

State law is the source of a multitude of land-use regulations. In some instances, state legislatures have passed enabling legislation authorizing city, county, and regional governmental units to become involved in specific land-use regulatory activities. Four principal types are: building codes, subdivision regulations, zoning, and special districts. Each will be briefly discussed.

STATE AND LOCAL LAND-USE REGULATIONS

Building Codes   Cities carry significant impact in being able to regulate land-use control through indirect sources, that is, sources that do not directly affect the use of property. One of these methods is the *building code*. This code regulates the minimum standards of construction for building within the city. The municipality has additional power through the control of *utility extensions* and capacities for those utilities as they are extended. For instance, if the city constructs a utility system in a particular subdivision that has just enough capacity for single-family homes, this literally denies the use for any multifamily homes or higher density use for that property. *Maintenance and construction of city streets* also have a particular impact on where and what direction the city will expand and how fast. *Subdivisions' regulations* are controlled through the city planning department, through which all land plans and subdivision plats must be submitted for approval, so that the city can check the proposed development versus the capacity of existing utilities and traffic control problems. Thus, major city concerns can be monitored to be sure that the new development would not be one that creates a difficulty for the city's existing facilities. The city is additionally given certain powers under the new federal statutes to enforce provisions of federal legislation such as the Clean Air Act and the Clean Water Act.

Zoning   Zoning is perhaps the most well-known and controversial government tool to control land use. It seeks to avoid mixing incompatible land uses, such as a slaughterhouse located in the middle of a residential subdivision.

Zoning ordinances are promulgated as a part of a long-range land-use plan. They delineate separate areas for residential, commercial, industrial, agricultural, recreational, and other uses. In doing so, they essentially "freeze" land in sub-markets for specific uses by making it difficult for land to be employed in higher-valued uses. In this way, zoning arguably lessens economic speculation in land. However, critics argue that economic speculation may be replaced by political speculation, at least in cases in which zoning changes have been obtained through political influence.

Concepts and Procedure.   Zoning goes hand in hand with comprehensive planning. Therefore, a comprehensive plan is the legal prerequisite to the adoption of zoning ordinances. Later, as new or changed ordinances are proposed, public hearings again exist as a safeguard against zoning decisions not in the public interest.

Once a zoning code (aggregation of all ordinances) has been adopted, all new structures and land uses must conform with it.

However, almost all states permit prior nonconforming uses to continue. Substantial financial losses could result if all previous uses were required to conform to the comprehensive plan, and arguably this would be unfair to owners of specific businesses and property who made their purchases when such uses were freely permissible. In some cases, prior nonconforming uses are permitted to continue for an indefinite time period. In other states, their continuance may only extend for such time period as reasonably required to recoup their initial investment.

When landowners seek to secure permission to make different uses of their land than what has been provided for under the zoning code, care must be taken to follow the precise legal procedure called for by state law and by the zoning code itself. Failure to do so ordinarily precludes judicial review of unfavorable decisions.

A typical procedure is to first appear before the zoning commission at a public hearing. Changes recommended there may then be taken before the city council or other public body. Appeals from decisions there generally go to a board of adjustment, and then to the courts. Note, however, that the specific procedures and names of the various groups involved may vary substantially among states.

Special exceptions to the zoning code are sometimes requested and granted. These exceptions are uses that do not conform to the zoning code, but that may be permitted under detailed and tightly controlled circumstances. If such use should become or prove to be objectionable in an area, it will be terminated.

A *variance* from the zoning code may be permitted when a strict application would work a hardship on a particular landowner. For example, if the topography is such that building setback requirements can be met only at extremely high price, a variance might be granted.

Special Districts

A multitude of special districts affecting land use are authorized in various states. These are often designed to encourage certain kinds of uses, such as the development of single-family residential subdivisions. Often, but not always, located outside of municipalities, these special districts may include municipal utility districts (MUDs), water districts, sewer districts, drainage districts, irrigation districts, and the like.

Zoning Issues

A number of issues continually recur in the zoning process that bear some additional discussion. Those to be considered will be the "taking" issue, spot zoning, contract zoning, nonconforming use, exclusionary land use controls, and nuisance law.

The "Taking" Issue.   There has long been an argument that zoning a property for a particular use is, in fact, *taking* that property from the owner who can no longer determine its highest and best use and perhaps cannot even build for a profit. An example of this would be a piece of prime commercial frontage property, which, for various reasons, is rezoned for residential use. In this situation, the owner, expecting to sell the property for a commercial use, feels that his right to build on the property profitably has been taken from him. The courts have, however, consistently held that this is a legal regulation of land use and *not* taking. One Texas case has even held that the required dedication of park land by the developer is not taking, *City of College Station* v. *Turtle Rock Corp.,* 680 S.W.2d 802 (Tex. 1984). Therefore, there is no requirement for just compensation, and the city is not liable for any just compensation, as it would be in an eminent domain proceeding, unless the city exercised its rights of police power arbitrarily, *City of Austin* v. *Teague,* 566 S.W. 2d 400 (Tex. Civ. App.—Waco, 1977) and *Agins et ux* v. *City of Tiburon,* 100 S.Ct. 2138 (1980). In the event a city "takes" a property by eminent domain, it is not bound by its own zoning ordinance, *City of Lubbock* v. *Austin,* 628 S.W.2d 49 (Tex. 1982).

It should be pointed out that recent trends in the taking issue seem to be more supportive of landowner's rights. In two significant cases, the United States Supreme Court has held that a temporary regulation which prohibits the use of a landowner's property can constitute a taking and be compensable, *First English Evangelical Lutheran Church* v. *County of Los Angeles,* 107 S. Ct. 2378 (1987). The same taking issue was also upheld in a land-use regulation issue, when the Court held that refusing to issue a building permit was held to constitute a taking, *Nollan* v. *California Coastal Commission,* 107 S. Ct. 3141 (1987). Similarly, when a property has been zoned so that it no longer has an economic use, it is a taking, *Lucas* v. *South Carolina Coastal Council,* 112 S. Ct. 2886 (1992).

A condemnation decision came from the United States Supreme Court in *Lucas* v. *South Carolina Coastal Council, supra.* There has always been a gray line between the right of the government to regulate real estate versus the right of the private property owner to have property condemned if the regulation denies the use of the property. Regulations do not require compensation to the property owner. Condemnation does require compensation to the property owner. This is commonly referred to as the "taking" issue, that is, whether or not the government's interference in land ownership results in a taking and therefore needs to be compensated. In *Lucas,* the legislature of South Carolina enacted a Beach Management Act which barred erecting of permanent habitable structures along certain areas of the beach. In effect, it denied all economically viable use of the property. The Supreme Court held that this constituted a taking under the 5th and 14th Amendments of the U.S. Constitution and required payment of just compensation. In an extremely well-written opinion the U.S. Supreme Court reinforced some basic private property values that are worthy of note. The Court noted that there is a "bundle of rights" acquired when private owners take title to the property. A complete extinguishment of the property's value entitled the owner to compensation regardless of whether the legislature had acted to further legitimate police power objectives in passing the new state law. Referring to a 1922 U.S. Supreme Court case, the Court noted that if "the uses of private property were subject to unbridled, uncompensated qualification under the police power, the natural tendency of human nature [would be] to extend the qualification more and more until at last private property disappeared." At this point it is now virtually impossible to determine what effect this will have on the Texas Open Beaches Act. The Supreme Court refused to review Texas' Open Beaches Act in 1987.

In *Dolan v. City of Tigard,* 114 S. Ct. 2309 (1994), the landowner petitioned for judicial review of a decision of the Oregon Land Use Board of Appeals which affirmed conditions placed by the city on development of commercial property. Dolan's application to expand her commercial store and pave her parking lot received conditional approval provided that Dolan: (1) provide for a public greenway along Fanno Creek to minimize flooding; and (2) provide for a pedestrian/bicycle pathway intended to relieve traffic congestion. The Court held that the city's dedication requirements for a "public greenway" constituted an uncompensated taking of property. The Court noted that while it had the sufficient nexus with legitimate public purpose, the requirement of the city that the landowner dedicate a portion of her property in the flood plain as public greenway did not show a reasonable relationship necessary to satisfy the requirements of the Fifth Amendment of the U.S. Constitution (prohibiting taking without just compensation).

The "nexus" doctrine, cited in *Nollan v. California Coastal Commission,* 483 U.S. 825, 837 (1987), is a test between the legitimate state interests and the permit condition. Provided that the essential nexus exists, the new standard provided in *Dolan* states that the court must decide whether the degree of exaction demanded by the permit condition bears the required relationship to the projected impact of the proposed development. This was termed by the Court to be the "rough proportionality connection." The city must make some sort of individualized determination that the required dedication is related both in nature and extent to the proposed development's impact. The Court noted that the city never stated why a public greenway, as opposed to a private one, was required in the interest of flood control.

Spot Zoning. Spot zoning has been described as the process of singling out a small parcel of land for a use classification that is different and inconsistent with that of the surrounding zoned areas. Zoning of this type is normally to the benefit of the lot owner but to the detriment of the surrounding area. An example of this would be to allow a townhouse zoning use in the middle of a single-family residential area (by permitting one of the owners to sell his lot off to a townhouse developer who may build four or five townhouses on that property). This use would not fit into the overall land use of the neighborhood or of that section of the city, and it creates a spot zoning issue. Spot zoning is illegal and prohibited in Texas, *Burke* v. *City of Texarkana*, 500 S.W.2d 242 (Tex. Civ. App.—Texarkana, 1973).

Contract Zoning. Contract zoning is an agreement by a governing body to enact a change in land-use classification in exchange for certain concessions to be granted by the developer or applicant. It is "zoning by agreement," which does not fit into the criteria of providing for the health, safety, and welfare of the citizens. This has been held to be invalid as an improper "bargaining away" of the city's police power, *Marta* v. *Sullivan*, 248 A.2d 608 (Del. 1968). This should be distinguished, however, from *conditional zoning,* wherein the zoning authority unilaterally requires a property owner to subject his land to certain restrictions without a prior commitment to rezone. When the conditions of conditional zoning are not inconsistent with the underlying goals of zoning generally and are in conformance with the comprehensive plan of the city, conditional zoning provides for flexibility so that a city cannot be bound by traditionally more restrictive zoning regulations. This has recently been used to support the theory of planned unit development zoning. This is when a large tract may be zoned for flexible uses subject to proper plan submittals from the owner of the property. As long as the flexible conditions are imposed on the property itself and not on the developer, the conditional zoning is legal, *Teer* v. *Duddlesten*, 664 S.W.2d 702 (Tex. 1984) and *City of Pharr* v. *Tippitt*, 616 S.W.2d 173 (Tex. 1981).

Nonconforming Use. Nonconforming use relates to a zoning change or a new zoning designation. The nonconforming use is maintaining the previous use of an area, a use that does not properly fit into the new zoning classification. For instance, suppose a particular area of town was zoned R1-residential and, at the time of the zoning change, there were two commercial uses in that zoning district. The two commercial uses would be allowed to remain, but they could not be materially changed or altered (or even improved) if they did not comply with the new existing zoning classification. The owner is allowed to repair the existing improvement, but cannot materially alter it. The theory is that, if the area has been properly planned and a new zoning designation has been given, the nonconforming uses are supposed to eventually cease to function, and the new classification designated by the plan would be the only existing classification. There have been successful efforts at putting a limit to the use of the nonconforming structure by designating a certain number of years by which that nonconforming use must cease to exist.

Exclusionary Land-Use Control.   There has been considerable litigation in recent years over what rights the city has to zone properties to exclude certain uses. This practice is referred to as *exclusionary zoning*. If zoning, for instance, is used to limit construction to homes on two-acre lots, and the city contains no apartments, no middle-income housing, or no low-income housing, that city may be determined to be using an exclusionary zoning technique, which would be illegal. Basically, the court would say that the city is excluding certain people from living in the town, which would be a violation of an individual's right to travel interstate, as provided for by the U.S. Constitution, *N.A.A.C.P. v. Button*, 371 U.S. 415 and *Southern Burlington County N.A.A.C.P. v. Township of Mount Laurel*, 336 A.2d 713 (Supreme Ct.—N. J., 1975). Two recent cases, however, reaffirm the city's ability to use wide discretion in zoning its areas, as long as it has a permissible, constitutional objective for its land use regulation, *Construction Industry Association of Sonoma County v. City of Petaluma*, 375 F. Supp. 574 (1975) and *Village of Belle Terre v. Boraas*, 416 U.S. 1 (1974).

Nuisance Law.   Nuisance law is of common law origin, and is quite similar in all states. It provides that no one shall unreasonably interfere with an individual's enjoyment of his property. Such unreasonable interference legally constitutes a nuisance.

Conduct that could constitute a nuisance includes (but is not limited to) air, water, solid waste, and noise pollution. For example, if a slaughterhouse was located and operated in or near a residential area, offensive odors, noises, and the like emanating from it could constitute a nuisance.

Technically, a nuisance exists whenever a jury finds an unreasonable interference with a landowner's enjoyment, and different decisions are possible with different juries. Since the existence of a nuisance is primarily a factual rather than a legal question, it typically is determined by a jury rather than a judge.

In a very real sense the nuisance law "regulates" the uses of land that may legally occur. Since the threat of being sued by private landowners effectively inhibits certain uses, the nuisance law may be considered to be private regulation of pollution.

Landowners may seek either an injunction against or damages from a nuisance law offender. The injunctive action involves a balancing of the parties' interests. In the preceding example, it means protection of the investment of one party and maximizing his profit versus the right of the other parties to be free from offensive living conditions that may decrease their property values and even be a health hazard.

If the rights of a large number are being unreasonably affected, it is more likely that an offensive land use will be judicially stopped. Stated simply, when the respective interests of the parties are weighed, *public* interests (the large number affected) are likely to outweigh *private* interests (the polluter). At the same time, the benefit to the community of continuing the offending business (i.e., jobs for citizens) may make continuance desirable. The trend in these cases is to deny the request for an injunction, but to require the offender to modify his land-use practices so that they are less offensive to nearby residents.

Affected landowners may also seek money damages from persons responsible for unreasonably offensive land uses. Damages may be sought to place affected parties in the same financial position they would have occupied if the nuisance had not existed and, in severe cases, multiplied in order to deter the offender and others in similar positions from creating this kind of land-use condition in the future.

Clearly, nuisances can negatively affect nearby land values. At the same time, business profits may be capitalized into land values on which a nuisance-causing activity is located. Thus, an injunction terminating or modifying such land use may negatively affect the value of that land. Hence, both the creation and the termination of nuisances can affect land-use patterns and can cause a redistribution of wealth among landowners.

PRIVATE LAND-USE REGULATIONS

Not all land-use regulations come from public sources. Two principal types arise privately. One comes from the nuisance law, the other from deed restrictions.

Deed restrictions are the primary private source of land-use regulation. They are generally created in one of two ways: (1) by incorporation in subdivision plats (as part of a developer's overall plan for maintaining the quality and environment), or (2) as a reservation in a deed transferring adjacent property (to maintain existing quality and environmental conditions). Since deed restrictions are normally recorded, all subsequent purchasers and creditors have constructive notice of them, *Hawthorne* v. *Realty Syndication, Inc.,* 268 S.E.2d 494 (N.C. 1980).

Deed Restrictions

Deed restrictions are a contractual agreement between private parties. As such, they may be more comprehensive than public land-use regulations, because deed restrictions need not relate to the health, safety, and welfare of the citizenry. Common deed restrictions include quality requirements for roof shingles, minimum square footages, building materials, and the like. Almost anything can be regulated by deed restrictions, so long as it does not violate the United States Constitution (e.g., racial discrimination), see *Shelly* v. *Kramer*, 334 U.S. 1.

Since deed restrictions are a private contract, only a party benefitting from them (i.e., the grantor or another subdivision property owner) may initiate court action to enjoin violation or seek enforcement of deed restrictions.

On occasion there are two or more possible interpretations of deed restrictions. If so, the court will generally interpret in favor of the less restrictive use, *Sylvan Glens Homeowners' Association* v. *McFadden*, 302 N.W.2d 615 (Mich. 1981). However, these restrictions will still be strictly enforced, *Stephenson* v. *Perlitz*, 524 S.W. 2d 516.

Deed restrictions may exist perpetually, *Moore* v. *Smith*, 443 S.W. 2d 552, but are usually limited by their own terms to a specific number of years.

The procedure for changing deed restrictions is typically set out in the restrictions themselves. If no procedure is provided, a 100% vote of persons affected may be required to change them, *Norwood* v. *Davis*, 345 S.W. 2d 944.

Public land-use regulations may be achieved under four main governmental powers: eminent domain, taxation, escheat, and police power.

SUMMARY

Many regulations affecting real estate emanate from the federal government. Some group real estate investments meet the legal definition of a security, and may be subject to expensive and time-consuming Securities and Exchange Commission registration and disclosure requirements.

The Office of Interstate Land Sales Registration (OILSR) covers many sales of unimproved lots, and requires prospective purchasers to be provided with property reports.

The Federal Trade Commission has enforcement powers in the areas of unfair competition and deceptive trade practices. It is also involved in monitoring several federal laws, including Truth-in-Lending, Equal Credit Opportunity, Fair Credit Reporting, and Home Mortgage Disclosure acts.

Coastal Zone Management rules exist in coastal states and affect land uses near the coast.

Flood-plain zoning and insurance rules now exist with the purpose of minimizing future financial losses from flooding.

Several federal agencies indirectly encourage real estate activity through their activity with real estate mortgages. These include the Federal Housing Administration, Veterans Administration, Federal National Mortgage Association, and Government National Mortgage Association.

Public land-use regulation at the state and/or local level may come from three or more distinct sources. These include building codes, zoning, and special districts.

The major source of private land-use regulations is deed restrictions. Private enforcement of rights under the nuisance law also inhibits unreasonably offensive land uses.

DISCUSSION
QUESTIONS

1. Who has the legal authority to enforce deed restrictions?
2. How does the nuisance law affect decisions on how land should be used?

18

Taxes Associated with Real Estate

Real estate owners are subject to two distinctly different taxes: (1) Real property taxes are assessed against real estate, and their magnitude is directly related to the real estate values; (2) income taxes are assessed on income earned from real estate.

Both property and income taxes will be discussed in this chapter.

PROPERTY TAXES

Depending on the state, *ad valorem* real property taxes may be assessed and collected by the state, county, municipality, school district, or other special taxing district. The term *ad valorem* means "according to value."

Laws may require real property to be assessed on the basis of fair market value, or perhaps on some fraction of fair market value. In either event, so long as the assessing officer treats all property equally, the taxes collected will be the same. The key to any "fair" property tax system is equality of treatment by assessors.

For any desired level of public service, a specific number of tax dollars is required. Once an assessed value has been assigned to all property within a jurisdiction, a tax rate is computed that will generate the needed funding. The important point is that once the needed amount of revenue has been determined, if all property has been treated equally, the same total amount of revenue can be collected with low assessed values and higher tax rates as with high assessed values and lower tax rates.

There is one important consideration, however, that causes property owners to prefer low assessed values and correspondingly high tax rates. Many states have established statutory tax rate limits that cannot be exceeded without approval of a majority vote in a bond election. This periodically subjects decisions about levels of public service to voter scrutiny.

On the other hand, public employees responsible for establishing budgets generally prefer high assessed values and lower tax rates. This practice creates greater certainty in the budgeting process, and generally provides greater flexibility in determining the levels of public service that will be provided.

Why Have Real Property Taxes?

Property owners have often asked why real property should be singled out for taxation. Several answers have been given.

First, one principle of taxation is that the largest tax burdens should be carried by those with the greatest ability to pay. This has generally been ascribed to real estate owners, although clearly their wealth may vary substantially, depending in part on whether they owe a large mortgage or own their property free and clear.

Second, real property is difficult to conceal from the tax assessor. Devious taxpayers may move or conceal personal property, but real property remains out in the open. Thus, one justification for taxing real property lies in the convenience of assessment and ease of collection. Clearly, this may appear unfair and inequitable under some circumstances, such as when a real estate owner has the same wealth as a renter owning three boats and a motor home. Therefore, in the interest of fairness, many states have attempted to tax personal property.

Finally, there is a long history of taxing real property. Real estate owners expect it and simply consider it a cost of ownership and/or doing business. In the minds of some, this alone is a sufficient justification to tax real property.

Property Tax Procedure

Although slight variations may exist among states, there generally are nine distinct steps in assessing and collecting real property taxes:

- *Step one:* Each taxing authority must prepare an annual *budget* outlining its specific and total needs.
- *Step two:* Next, an *appropriation* may occur, which formally enacts into law the spending scheme outlined in the budget.
- *Step three:* The *levy* refers to the formal imposition of taxes by the taxing unit. It must set out and follow the technical procedures required by law. Any variance from procedural technicalities may permit tax avoidance or collection delays by astute taxpayers.

- *Step four:* Each tract of real estate must be assigned a value for tax purposes, known as the *assessment*. This function is handled by a public official, usually called the *assessor*. In some jurisdictions, the land may be assessed separately from any buildings located on it. Again, uniform treatment of all taxpayers is essential for the equitable administration of property taxes. At the same time, careful attention must be paid to exempting and/or preferentially assessing specific properties as required by law. For example, preferential assessment laws or ordinances may exist to encourage manufacturers to settle in a particular area, or to assist farmers in remaining in farming at their present location.

- *Step five:* To avoid unfair results and the possibility of erroneous judgments by assessors, procedures exist to assure that all property owners may have their *assessed values reviewed*. Often this is by appeal to a body known as the *board of equalization*. Appeals to higher boards or the courts may also be authorized. At any rate, the existence of a review procedure helps assure uniformity of treatment among all taxpayers.

  For example, suppose a homeowner discovers a major structural defect in his home (e.g., a cracked foundation). If the assessor was unaware of this defect, his assessed value may have been somewhat higher than justified because homes with structural defects may be substantially discounted in the marketplace.

- *Step six:* In larger jurisdictions with two or more taxing districts, the next step is the *equalization* of assessed values among such districts. This process is generally handled by the board of equalization, and exists to assure fair and equitable treatment for taxpayers from different taxing districts.

- *Step seven:* The *computation* of the tax is determined by multiplying the assessed valuation by the tax rate. Once the tax is determined and entered in the appropriate records, the actual tax collection process may proceed.

- *Step eight:* The vast majority of property owners *voluntarily pay* their taxes by the deadline, which usually is December 31. If they fail to do so, state laws generally provide for unpaid and overdue taxes to become a lien against the land. Prospective real estate purchasers may rely on public records indicating that all property taxes have been paid. However, this is not necessarily true for tax receipts issued but not a matter of public record.

• *Step nine:* Overdue taxes may be *involuntarily collected* via legislatively established proceedings. Liens for unpaid taxes take precedence over real estate mortgage and UCC liens. The collection procedure generally involves public advertisement and/or personal notification to the owner, followed by a public tax sale. The property owners often have the right to "redeem" (repurchase) their property by reimbursing tax sale purchasers in the amount of their expenditures. In some states the tax sale purchaser immediately receives title; in others, he obtains a certificate entitling him to a deed when the owner's redemption period expires. The purchaser usually takes title subject to any existing defects, and tax sales may be set aside if the proper sale procedure has not been followed. In modern times, it is relatively rare for a tax sale purchaser to obtain and ultimately retain title unless the sale price was at or near the fair market value.

The involuntary sale procedure (Step nine) does not apply to some property owners in the military service. Rather, the Soldiers and Sailors Civil Relief Act calls for judicial permission for forced sales when the owner's ability to pay his property taxes has been materially affected by his military service. This act applies only if the taxpayer (or his dependents) was an owner/occupant of a residence, or a professional, business, or agricultural property at the time he entered the military service. Interest charged on delinquent taxes cannot exceed 6% annually, and, where sales are permitted, the redemption period is extended until six months following his separation from the military.

Special Assessments

A great deal of property tax is collected through special assessments. Special assessments are taxes collected from only some of the property owners in a particular jurisdiction, and the taxes are then used to benefit the specific area from which the taxes were collected. Examples might be special assessments collected to finance a drainage project, curbs and guttering, a local library, additional fire protection, or other public services or improvements.

Most special assessments are approved after a public hearing or in an election by the property owners affected. In some cases, this does not involve a formal vote on the project, but rather a vote on whether to become members in a district created for a specific purpose.

In 1986, Congress passed a tax law known as the *Internal Revenue Code of 1986*, or, alternatively, as the *Tax Reform Act of 1986*. It was a sweeping change of income taxation, attempting to eliminate some inequities in the existing tax structure and to encourage simplification. The new statute did simplify income taxation to some extent, but the transition rules (because of the existing tax laws prior to 1987) created a difficult evolution into the new finalization of this tax simplification. For our purposes, this necessitates the discussion of the previous tax law, with emphasis on the 1987 changes. The new definition of "income" will be discussed first, then the special tax treatments for real estate will be discussed.

FEDERAL INCOME TAXATION

Prior to 1987, all income was categorized as "income" and there were certain tax-sheltered advantages to ownership of real estate. These "tax shelters" allowed real estate investors to offset their income by taking deductions for certain non-cash "losses" attributable to real estate. This gave many people the perception that tax laws favored the wealthy (who are often perceived as the primary investors in real estate) and resulted in Congress' 1986 attempt to limit these "abuses." Unfortunately, the new tax laws applied to small investors as well, and the long-term impact of these changes is yet to be determined.

Income

The new tax law separates income into three categories: (1) active income, (2) passive income, and (3) portfolio income. *Active income* follows our traditional theories of income from a primary source of employment. This includes salaries and income or loss from the conduct of a trade or business in which the taxpayer materially participates. A taxpayer is deemed to be materially participating only if the taxpayer is involved in the operations of the activity on a regular, continuous, and substantial basis. It is necessary to look at the particular business activity and determine which functions are typically concerned with operations. If it is determined that the taxpayer is materially participating in those functions, the income derived would be deemed active income.

Passive activity is defined as any activity that involves the conduct of any trade or business in which the taxpayer does not materially participate. One of the most important defined "passive" activities is rental activity for income-producing property. Rental activity is generally deemed to be passive without regard to the level of participation by the taxpayer. There are two exceptions, however. The first is for an individual taxpayer who actively participates in real estate rental activities. In this case, passive losses can be offset against active income, so long as the passive activity loss and the deduction equivalent of that passive activity loss do not exceed $25,000 per year. The $25,000 offset is not available to corporations, estates, or trusts regardless of their level of participation. In no event, however, is a taxpayer deemed to be actively participating in real estate rental activities when his ownership interest is less than 10 percent during the applicable year.

The second exception focuses on real estate brokers, salespersons, and other real estate professionals. These eligible taxpayers can deduct unlimited real estate activity losses from active income and portfolio income. Individuals are eligible if: (1) more than half of all personal services they perform during the year are for real property trades or businesses in which they "materially participate," and (2) they perform more than 750 hours of service per year in those real estate activities.

Portfolio income is income that is not active income or passive income. Interest, dividends, annuities, or royalties not derived from the ordinary course of business, or a gain or loss from the disposition of property producing interest, and dividends or annuities that are held for investment are some examples of portfolio income. Expenses directly allocable to the property producing this interest, dividends, annuities, or royalties can be applied against the portfolio income.

The most significant change under the Tax Reform Act of 1986 is that the passive and portfolio losses cannot offset active income, which virtually destroys the tax shelter nature of real estate investment. The special tax benefits for real estate, to the extent they still exist, are discussed in the subsequent portions of this chapter. It must be kept in perspective, however, that the effect of the special tax treatment of real estate is somewhat tempered by the limited ability of any taxpayer to offset the losses generated against his active income.

As previously stated, the tax laws provide some areas of special treatment for real estate. Since the subject of federal income taxation involves volumes of treatises at the professional level, only the fundamentals of taxation most significant to real estate will be discussed here. These are:

1. Depreciation;
2. Accelerated Cost Recovery System;
3. Capital gains tax treatment;
4. Tax-deferred exchanges;
5. Installment sales;
6. At-risk rules; and
7. Homeownership benefits.

Depreciation is generally defined as an allowance for loss of value. The federal government, through the Internal Revenue Service, recognizes the intrinsic loss of value of improvements (land may not be depreciated) and allows the taxpayer to provide for this loss of value by allowing these decreases in value to be deducted from gross income before the income is taxed. This, in effect, reduces the amount of taxes the taxpayer will pay, even though he has made no actual or "out-of-pocket" expenditures. Depreciation is often used synonymously with the term "tax shelter" because it is a deduction from gross income even though: (1) no payment is made; (2) no actual loss is suffered; and (3) depreciation is allowed in excess of the owner's equity invested. Since land cannot be depreciated, an allocation of the purchase price must be made between the improvements and land purchased. The most common allocation method used is the ratio of fair market value of the component (land or improvements) to the total value.

Depreciation

There are now three systems involved in the computation of depreciation: (1) MACRS, which is the *Modified Accelerated Cost Recovery System* for property placed in service after 1986; (2) ACRS, the *Accelerated Cost Recovery System*, for property placed in service after 1980 but before 1987; or (3) the straight-line method based on the useful life of the property as established by federal law.

There are specific rules for determining which depreciation method a taxpayer can use and, in the final analysis, neither the IRS nor the courts will allow an individual to claim more depreciation than he is entitled to. Additionally, depreciation is limited to commercial (industrial and office space) and investment (residential rental) property. One's primary residence cannot be depreciated. Each taxpayer should consult his tax counsel and accountant to determine if depreciation is applicable and, if it is, which of the depreciation methods is more advantageous for his particular needs.

The Internal Revenue Code of 1986, however, made extensive efforts to eliminate investments in tax shelters. Depreciation can no longer be deducted against "active income" if it is a "passive loss" from an activity in which the taxpayer does not materially participate. Virtually all rental activities are treated as passive activities. However, if the taxpayer "actively participates," individuals can offset up to $25,000 of nonpassive income with losses from real estate rental activities. Even this benefit, however, is reduced if the taxpayer's income for any given year exceeds $100,000.

Straight-Line Method. The *straight-line method of depreciation* is the one type of depreciation that can always be used. The first step in determining the amount of straight-line depreciation is to establish the correct useful life of the asset. In computing the straight-line rate, one takes the basis (cost or value of the improvement) less any salvage value and divides the remainder by the number of years of economic life the taxpayer intends to use for that improvement. For instance, if a dishwasher costs $200, has a five-year life, and has no salvage value, the taxpayer is allowed 20 percent each year ($40) as a depreciation deduction from gross income. If a two-year life is used for the dishwasher, 50 percent each year ($100) can be deducted.

Accelerated Cost Recovery System

In 1981, Congress passed the Economic Recovery Tax Act. The act eliminated the use of depreciation for property placed in service after December 31, 1980, by enacting another form of tax recovery for capital costs called the *Accelerated Cost Recovery System.* Low-income housing is permitted to be depreciated under the 200 percent declining-balance method, while other 15-year real estate may use the 175 percent declining-balance method with a switch to the straight-line method at the optimum time.

While it eliminates the flexibility that the taxpayer had under the old depreciation system, this system has some benefits for the taxpayer. The new ACRS clearly and simply sets out how much can be deducted in each year, and there is very little room for error or negotiation in determining the proper deduction for the taxpayer in any given year. The ACRS eliminates the need for useful life determination on property, as all depreciable real property is written off over the applicable 15-year period.

The only variable for 15-year property is when the property is put into use. The following chart shows how the deductions are calculated under the ACRS system.

It is important to note that with the ACRS, there is no salvage value, allowing the taxpayer to write off the entire cost of the investment. In addition, there are no distinctions between new and used property. All real property qualifying as 15-year utility property has the same deductions (see Table 18-1). Buildings placed into service (basically, property which has begun construction) after March 15, 1984, have an accelerated recovery period of 18 years. If the property was placed in service after May 8, 1985, and before January 1, 1987, the accelerated recovery period is 19 years.

For assets placed in service after 1986, the Tax Reform Act of 1986 provides for a *Modified Accelerated Cost Recovery System (MACRS)* that applies to all tangible property placed in service after December 31, 1986. Whereas the MACRS establishes new depreciation guidelines for certain assets, real estate is limited to two classes:

TABLE 18-1

15-Year Utility Property

Ownership/ Year 1–15	Placed in Service after December 31, 1980
1	5%
2	10%
3	9%
4	8%
5	7%
6	7%
7	6%
8	6%
9	6%
10	6%
11	6%
12	6%
13	6%
14	6%
15	6%
	100%

1. Nonresidential real property. This class includes any real property that is not residential rental property and is depreciated over 31.5 years. If the property is placed in service after May 12, 1993, the minimum write-off period is increased to 39 years.

2. Residential rental property. This class includes any real property that is a rental building or structure (including mobile homes) for which 80 percent or more of the gross rental income for the tax year is rental income from dwelling units. If any part of the building or structure is occupied by the taxpayer, the gross rental income includes the fair rental value of the part the taxpayer occupies. This property is depreciated over 27.5 years.

Recapture. One negative aspect of an accelerated depreciation method is that it may convert long-term capital gain to ordinary income when the asset is sold for a gain. This procedure is called the *recapture* of the excess depreciation. When depreciation is computed using an accelerated method, the excess amount of that depreciation over a hypothetical straight-line amount must be reported as ordinary income upon disposition of the property. It may come as quite a shock for someone using accelerated depreciation to discover that when he sells the asset, a large amount of his profit may be taxed as ordinary income because it was allocated to excess depreciation. The amount of recapture depends on the type of asset disposed of, either personal or real property, and the amount of gain realized on the disposition. As previously stated, only excess depreciation must be recaptured on the disposition of real property, but all depreciation claimed must be recaptured on the sale of personal property. Recapture on both types of property is limited to the lesser of the recapture amount or the gain.

The rules for depreciating real estate have eliminated the possibility of recapture upon the disposition of most real property placed in service after 1986. Since residential rental and nonresidential real property placed into service after 1986 are limited to straight-line depreciation, regardless of the depreciation system used, recapture is unlikely to occur.

Capital Gains Tax Treatment

Capital gains tax treatment refers to the special tax rate paid on profits from the sale of capital assets. A *capital asset* is generally defined as property which is *not* stock in trade (inventory), property used in trade or business of a kind subject to depreciation, and notes and accounts receivable acquired in the course of a trade or business.

There are two types of *capital gains:* long-term and short-term capital gain. Long-term capital gain is gain on the sale of a capital asset held for more than one year. A short-term capital gain is gain on the sale of a capital asset held for less than one year.

The Internal Revenue Code of 1986 repealed the capital gains deduction for individuals. Long-term capital gains were taxed at the same rate as ordinary income. This was amended again in 1990. The Internal Revenue Code now specifically limits the maximum tax rate for long-term capital gains to 28 percent. Short-term capital gains are taxed at the taxpayer's normal income rate.

The tax to be paid is applied to the *profit* made, which is calculated as the *sales price* less the *adjusted basis* (discussed next) the taxpayer has in the property. A confusing part of computing capital gains is determining the basis (the original cost or value) of the asset at the time of its acquisition.

Basis is generally considered to be of two types: *original basis,* which is the original cost of the asset, and *adjusted basis,* which is the original basis plus the cost of capital improvements less any allowances for depreciation. Graphically, adjusted basis may be shown as follows:

Original Basis + Capital Improvement − Depreciation
= Adjusted Basis or,

$$OB + CI - D = AB$$

As an example of how capital gains may be calculated, suppose that Mr. Garrison acquires a building at a cost of $100,000, which is his *original basis*. After holding the property for one year, he sells it for $200,000. The amount to be taxed would be calculated by deducting the basis ($100,000) from the sales price ($200,000), which determines how much of the income ($100,000, or his profit) is to be taxed at capital gains rates.

If the building has been depreciated, the *adjusted basis* must be used. For example, Mr. Garrison purchases the property for $100,000. During the course of his ownership he adds capital improvements in the amount of $25,000 and depreciates the asset over a 20-year life, yielding a straight-line depreciation allowance of 5 percent of $100,000, or $5,000. His adjusted basis, therefore, would be his original basis, $100,000, plus capital improvement of $25,000, minus depreciation, which in this case is $5,000. Using the formula $AB = OB + CI - D$, this would give him a taxable income of only $80,000, since the adjusted basis is subtracted from his sales price of $200,000.

Tax-Deferred Exchanges

Tax-deferred exchanges are often referred to as *tax-free exchanges*. However, nothing could be further from the truth, as the tax will ultimately be paid. The tax-deferred exchange procedure allows only for deferment of taxes. The theory behind tax-free exchanges is that the exchange of property of value for other "like-kind" (same type) property of the same value or higher value should not result in taxable income to the exchanging parties, with certain exceptions. If the trade is for property of higher value and a gain is realized, the gain is not taxed (recognized) until the taxpayer chooses to sell the property at a later date. The exchange involves two title transfers, the original property from seller one to seller two, and the exchange property from seller two to seller one.

As an example, assume that Mr. Martin buys some apartments for $50,000. He has a contract to sell them for $100,000; however, instead of effecting a sale and taking a $50,000 profit and paying tax on the profit, he trades for like-kind property, owned by the purchaser, which is worth $100,000. There is no taxable gain to Mr. Martin on that particular transaction. If Mr. Martin trades for property worth $150,000 and sells later for $200,000, he would have to pay tax on the gain only upon the sale of the second piece of property. In determining the amount of gain on the sale, Mr. Martin's original basis in the first project (which may have been quite low) would carry over to the newly acquired property. He would subtract it from the new sales price. Therefore, he would pay tax on a much larger amount of money, but the advantage would be that he could defer this gain until he is ready to sell the second piece of property, or he trades it again for a more expensive piece of property to be sold at some subsequent date.

In this manner, Mr. Martin may continue to "trade up" to other pieces of more expensive property, realizing that on the sale of the final piece of property he will have a very large tax liability. However, one would assume that he will wait to sell the property when his overall personal income tax rates would be lower.

The tax deferral is only applicable to property that is held for productive use in a trade or business or for an investment that is exchanged solely for property of like kind which is held for the same purposes. There are three basic statutory requirements: (1) both the property transferred and the property received must be held by the taxpayer for productive use in a trade or business or for investment (it cannot be your primary principal residence); (2) the property transferred in the exchange and the property received must be like-kind; and (3) there must be an exchange of one property for another. The term *productive use or investment* is liberally interpreted to include a wide range of properties. The term *like-kind* refers basically to the nature of the property as realty and not to its grade or quality. Virtually any type of real estate and any interest in real estate can qualify as like-kind property. Although the statute does not specifically require a written exchange agreement, it is always advisable. In addition, the exchange must be reasonably simultaneous. The exchange property must be identified within 45 days of the transfer of the original property, and the exchange must be actually transferred within 180 days of the original transfer, *I.R.C., §1031.*

Installment Sales   One of the simplest major tax advantages of owning real estate is the *installment sale* benefit. It applies to all types of real estate, including residential property. Recent legislative changes have eliminated a number of previous requirements. Now there must be at least two payments, the first being in the year of sale. The remainder of the income is taxed as it is received over the future years. This allows the taxpayer to sell his property and report the gain over a period of years. Assume that the taxpayer sells property yielding a $100,000 total profit, and will receive equal payments over a ten-year period. Under the installment sale provisions, instead of paying tax on $100,000 profit in one year (which may be taxed at a very high rate), the taxpayer is allowed to spread this profit over 10 years at $10,000 each year (which would probably be taxed at a much lower rate, depending on the taxpayer's tax bracket).

The Tax Reform Act of 1986 made significant changes in the installment sale rules. The bigger change, however, appears to be in the *Revenue Act of 1987*. The statute apparently divides the classes of sellers under the installment sale method into two basic categories, casual sellers and dealer sellers. Casual sellers are presumed to be private investors and individuals who are not *dealers* in real property. "Dealers" have generally been characterized as real estate developers and brokers engaged in buying and selling of real estate in the normal course of business.

For the casual seller of real property, the new law repeals the complex *proportional disallowance* rule which was enacted under the Tax Reform Act of 1986. Dealer property, however, faces significantly different rules. The new 1987 law repeals the installment sale method altogether, forcing taxpayers who are dealers to recognize their income and pay tax on dealer sales even though the payments on the installment sale receivables may stretch out for years.

After January 1, 1988, installment sales will not be recognized for dealer property.

For nondealer property, the installment method rules revert back to the same rules that were in effect before the proportional disallowance rule of the Tax Reform Act of 1986 was enacted.

At-Risk Rules

The Internal Revenue Code of 1986 provided special *at-risk limitations* on losses from income-producing activities with respect to property placed in service after 1986. Under the at-risk rules, the taxpayer's deductible losses from an activity for any taxable year are limited to the amount that the taxpayer has at risk in that particular activity. The initial amount at risk is generally considered to be the sum of the following items: cash contributions, the adjusted basis of the property contributed, and amounts borrowed for use in the activity for which the taxpayer has personal liability.

One major exception to the at-risk rules as they apply to real estate is that the taxpayers are not subject to these rules to the extent they use arm's-length, third-party, commercial financing secured solely by the real property. This exception applies only if there is a third-party lender and that third-party lender is not related to the taxpayer, the seller of the property or someone "related" to the seller, or a person who is paid a fee with respect to the taxpayer's investment in the property.

Homeownership Benefits   The Internal Revenue Code retains excellent tax benefits to homeowners. Home mortgage interest, with certain qualifications, and property taxes continue to be deductible. Homeowners still do not need to recognize the gain on the sale of a personal residence when "buying up" into another residence. In addition, the $125,000 exclusion of gain on a personal residence by taxpayers age 55 and over is retained.

Deductibility of Interest.   Generally, some home mortgage interest payments for acquisition indebtedness and home equity indebtedness continue to be deductible from your gross income. Under the Internal Revenue Code, this interest deduction is limited to the first and second residences. The aggregate amount of acquisition indebtedness may not exceed $1,000,000 (or $500,000 for a married individual who files a separate return). The aggregate amount of home equity indebtedness may not exceed $100,000 (or $50,000 for a married individual who files a separate return). Acquisition indebtedness cannot be increased by refinancing. The total mortgage loans cannot exceed the lesser of: (1) the fair market value of the residence, or (2) the purchase price of the residence.

The overall impact of these interest deductions (particularly in light of the nondeductibility of other interest payments under the new Internal Revenue Code) has created a tremendous market for loans secured by residential real estate to buy other items. For instance, if you bought a car, the interest payments on the car loan are not deductible. If, however, you use your home as security for the loan, the interest payments would generally be deductible. Therefore, a second mortgage on your house to finance a car creates a deductible interest payment. The difficulty of this in Texas is the Texas homestead law, which makes all equity loans on homes unenforceable. This is, therefore, another good example of federal law versus state law. The federal law allows the deductibility of the interest for income tax purposes, but the state law does not allow the lien to be enforceable because of Texas homestead law purposes. At this point, Texas lenders are simply wrestling with the potential problems of making these loans in Texas.

The Trade Up Exemption.   Another excellent homeownership benefit is the ability to "trade up" from an old residence to a new residence and not recognize the profit or gain on the sale of the old residence. For instance, if a person paid $100,000 for his home in

1976 and sold it for $150,000 in 1983, he would not have to pay income tax on the profit on that sale, provided he falls within the guidelines on the sale of his principal residence.

Generally stated, the Internal Revenue Code requires that it must be the taxpayer's primary principal residence. If this property is sold by the taxpayer and, within a period beginning two years before the date of such sale and ending two years after such date, the new residence is purchased and used by the taxpayer as his principal residence, the gain from the sale of his first residence is recognized only to the extent that the taxpayer's adjusted sales price of the old residence exceeds the taxpayer's cost of purchasing the new residence.

For purposes of the Internal Revenue Code the "adjusted sales price" means the amount realized on the sale of the property, reduced by the expenses for work performed on the old residence in order to assist in its sale, provided that those expenses are for work performed during the 90-day period prior to the sale and are paid on or before the 30th day after the date of the sale of the old residence and these expenses are not allowable as deductions in computing taxable income. This allows the adjusted sales price to be somewhat less than the gross sales price of the taxpayer's previous residence. The general rule is that the taxpayer can then buy a house equal to this adjusted sales price or greater than the adjusted sales price and not have to pay any tax on the gain (increase in value) on his previous house, so long as he acquires his new house within two years before or after the sale of the previous house. Another peculiarity of this statute, however, is that it now apparently requires a taxpayer to sell his previous principal residence within two years before or after he acquires his new principal residence. This can create a difficult situation for retiring homeowners who buy a new home, but yet cannot sell their old home within the required two-year disposition period, *I.R.C., §1034.*

Over-55 Exemption. The federal government has also seen fit to provide a special tax benefit to help older homeowners. A taxpayer who has attained the age of 55 or over may sell his principal residence, where he has lived for three of the last five years, tax-free if the gain realized on the sale is $125,000 or less, *I.R.C., §121.* If the gain realized on the sale of the house is in excess of $125,000, it is only partially tax-free. The amount that is tax-free is $125,000 and the amount of the realized gain in excess of $125,000 is taxable. For instance, if Ben A. Youngster, age 65, sells his personal residence realizing a gain of $150,000, the taxable amount would be computed as follows:

$$\$150,000 - 125,000 = \$25,000$$

Therefore, instead of paying taxes on a $150,000 gain, the taxpayer gets $125,000 tax-free and only $25,000 is to be taxed, resulting in a substantial tax saving. This exclusion may be used only once, however, so if one has a client who is a taxpayer at age 54, he may want to advise him to wait until he is 55 before he sells so that he can take advantage of the tax-free *over-55 exemption.* The agent may use this very simple mathematical calculation to explain what advantage it may have for his client. However, the concerned agent will probably refer the entire matter to the homeowner's accountant to investigate the matter in greater detail.

As one might see, there are a number of different tax ramifications in any single transaction. To be sure, the foregoing was only a very cursory explanation. Each of the individual tax benefits of real estate ownership is very lengthy and involved, and should be left to people who are trained in the business. However, it is an astute real estate agent who has at least a good working knowledge of tax benefits, so that he may advise his client as to the initial ramifications that a transaction *might* have. One has only to read the Internal Revenue Code, or one provision thereof, to get an inkling of how complicated the tax laws, rules, regulations, bulletins, and tax court decisions can be. To compound the problems and responsibilities of the real estate licensee, one only has to remember the duty of care to which all American citizens are held. Ignorance of the law is no excuse!

SUMMARY   The primary concerns in real estate taxation are ad valorem taxes and special tax benefits under federal income taxation.

Ad valorem taxation is assessed on real property in proportion to its value which shall be ascertained as provided for by law. The formula for determining the tax payment is:

$$\text{Assessed Value} \times \text{Tax Rate} = \text{Tax Payment}$$

The assessed value is determined by the assessor and collector of taxes who determines an assessed value, which is equal to the fair market value. The tax collector assesses the real estate according to the budget requirements for the taxing jurisdiction. The tax rate is set by the taxing authority in accordance to statutory formula.

In the event ad valorem taxes are delinquent, there is a penalty and procedure for judicial foreclosure against the property. In the event a foreclosure occurs, there is a two-year right of redemption during which the property owner can redeem his property after payment of taxes, fees, and penalties.

The advantages of federal income taxation are primarily attributable to depreciation, tax-free exchanges, and installment sales. Depreciation is an allowance for loss of value and can be calculated several different ways. Tax-deferred exchanges are means by which an owner may exchange property and defer the payment of taxes until the sale of the second piece of property. The installment sale benefit applies to any seller who sells his property, receiving at least two installment payments, the first being paid to the seller in the year of the sale.

Table of Cases